DATE DUE

DEMCO 38-296

Securities Markets in the 1980s

Volume 1

The New Regime, 1979–1984

Securities
Markets
in the 1980s *Volume 1*

The New Regime, 1979–1984

BARRIE A. WIGMORE

New York   Oxford   •   Oxford University Press   1997

Oxford University Press

Oxford   New York
Athens   Auckland   Bangkok   Bogota   Bombay   Buenos Aires
Calcutta   Cape Town   Dar es Salaam   Delhi   Florence   Hong Kong
Istanbul   Karachi   Kuala Lumpur   Madras   Madrid   Melbourne
Mexico City   Nairobi   Paris   Singapore   Taipei   Tokyo   Toronto   Warsaw

and associated companies in
Berlin   Ibadan

Copyright © 1997 by Oxford University Press, Inc.

Published by Oxford University Press, Inc.
198 Madison Avenue, New York, New York 10016

Oxford is a registered trademark of Oxford University Press

Library of Congress Cataloging-in-Publication Data
Wigmore, Barrie A.
     Securities markets in the 1980s : the new regime, 1979–1984 / by Barrie A. Wigmore.
          p.   cm.
     Includes bibliographical references and index.
     ISBN 0-19-510632-6
     1. Securities—United States.   2. Capital market—United States.   I. Title.
HG4910.W426   1997
332.63'2—dc20   96-30659

9 8 7 6 5 4 3 2 1

Printed in the United States of America
on acid-free paper

This book is dedicated to John C. Whitehead
with grateful thanks for his guidance,
friendship, and example over many years

Preface

This book is about the transition from erratic policies and crisis-riddled securities markets in the 1970s to steady economic growth and attractive securities markets in the 1980s. The transition reflected conscious policy changes by the Federal Reserve and the Reagan administration, but also fortuitous changes, such as the decline in oil prices and the strong dollar. This theme is very much of a piece with contemporary economic theory of rational expectations under changing policy regimes, but I did not go looking for it; it forced itself on me. I began simply with the idea of chronicling the history of an interesting period in the securities markets.

The story parts with rational expectations notions, however, in that many markets reflected the new regime slowly, and in no case were the changes painless. The transition was punishing, and major sectors of American industry were permanently disrupted.

There is already an oversimplified image of securities markets in the 1980s that misses this transition. Investment lore, the media, and even presidential politics paint the decade as one of record stock returns, huge bond profits, and rampant mergers fueled by declining inflation, steady growth, lower taxes, and free markets in which financial buccaneers created some of the largest fortunes since the 1920s. This image reflects the last half of the 1980s rather than the first half of the decade, which began with financial markets in despair over accelerating oil prices, inflation, and a declining dollar that had produced almost ten years of persistently poor returns in the stock and bond markets. It took almost two years for the markets and the economy to evolve into the steady growth that characterized the rest of the decade.

The second volume of this work will examine how the policies that produced such a favorable transition from 1979 to 1984 created a mixed result from 1985 to 1989, when securities markets provided some of the best returns of the century and new companies and industries came strongly to the fore, but were accompanied by a merger frenzy, the stock market runup and crash in 1987, the junk bond collapse in 1989, crises in the banking and savings & loan systems, corruption of varying degrees, and excessive leverage among business, consumers, and governments.

The interpretations of the securities markets offered here are my own. They reflect thirty years as a practitioner in the stock, bond, and merger markets. I benefited greatly from extensive discussions with many colleagues at Goldman, Sachs & Co., as well as from their willingness to provide me with extensive data. My colleagues in the Goldman Sachs library were unstinting in providing me with data, books, articles, and media searches.

Peter Temin exceeded the bounds of professional courtesy and friendship in offering me advice, insight, and encouragement over many years. He read the entire manuscript with great care, various parts several times. His detailed suggestions and criticism were of immense help. I am very grateful to him.

Robert Shiller, Eugene White, Edward Altman, Louis Lowenstein, and two anonymous referees also reviewed the manuscript and provided helpful suggestions. Jeffrey Miller of Miller, Tabak, Hirsch & Co. read the entire manuscript with academic intensity and provided many practical suggestions.

Various organizations were extremely considerate in providing me with data or access to their files and libraries, including Jones, Lynch & Ryan, the publisher of the Institutional Brokers Estimate System, Standard & Poor's, Moody's Investors Service, Veronis, Suhler & Associates Inc., Manfredi & Associates Inc., Value Line, and Compustat.

My wife, Deedee, has been an unfailing supporter of this and my other writing efforts, despite the time they have taken from our personal activities. I wish I showed my appreciation every day.

Contents

Securities Markets in the 1980s

Volume 1

The New Regime, 1979–1984

1

Introduction

The decade of the 1980s was one of the most favorable in the twentieth century for securities markets. The stock market had an average annual total return of 17.5%, as Standard & Poor's Composite Stock Price Index (the S&P 500) rose from 108 to 353. This was the second best decadal return since 1929—only bettered by the 19.3% return of the 1950s when the world was recovering from the Depression and World War II. Long-term government bonds had the best annual returns since 1929 (12.6%) as ten-year treasury rates declined from 10.4% to 7.8%. Real returns were equally impressive. Table 1.1 outlines the average annual decadal returns since 1929 for both of these sectors on a nominal and real basis. If the reader reviews this for a moment it will be clear just how impressive the decade's returns were. No other decade, excluding the 1950s, had stock market returns that were within 50% of the 1980s on a real basis, and the 1930s were the only other decade that came close to the real returns in the bond market. A new market for junk bonds was also born in the 1980s. It combined with oil riches and greatly relaxed antitrust rules to fuel a fivefold increase in merger and acquisition activity from $43.5 billion to $221 billion. Both the stock and bond results and the merger boom were a radical about-face from the 1970s, when common stocks had an average annual return of only 5.9% and government bonds of only 5.5% (both were negative in real terms) and when merger activity was quiescent.[1]

The 1970s were plagued by repeated crises over oil prices, inflation, and the dollar. In the last half of the 1970s, the Carter administration's ef-

Table 1.1. Average Annual Decadal Returns

Years	S&P 500		Long-term Treasuries	
	Nominal	*Real*	*Nominal*	*Real*
1929–1939	0.001	0.021	0.049	0.069
1939–1949	0.092	0.038	1.032	−0.022
1949–1959	0.194	0.172	−0.001	−0.023
1959–1969	0.078	0.053	0.014	−0.011
1969–1979	0.059	−0.015	0.055	−0.019
1979–1989	0.175	0.124	0.126	0.075

Source: Ibbotson Associates, *Stocks Bonds Bills and Inflation*, Chicago, Ill.: 1992.

forts to deal with these problems were erratic and unsuccessful. There were financial crises in 1978, October 1979, early 1980, and yet another crisis was building in late 1980 as President Carter left office. The administration's emphasis on wage and price controls and energy regulation, and the Federal Reserve's weak application of monetary policy prior to October 1979 and its erratic application in 1980, rendered the prospect for steady economic growth poor and the securities markets subject to constant outside shocks.

The election of President Reagan introduced a new regime in more ways than one. There was a dramatic reduction in personal income taxes and a tripling of the federal deficit as a share of gross national product (GNP) from 2% to 6%. There was a shift to free-market policies that did away with wage and price controls and intervention in the energy markets. And there were 180-degree changes in the trends of the dollar, oil, other commodities prices, and inflation generally, and a complete revision of antitrust policies. Most important, monetary policy under the aegis of Paul Volcker, strongly supported by President Reagan, was firmly established as the tool for suppressing inflation.

There are various theoretical ways of describing the difference between the 1970s and the 1980s. Economists, such as Thomas J. Sargent and Robert E. Lucas,[2] have theorized about changes in regimes or rational expectations. Thomas Kuhn has developed the concept of a new paradigm. Financial professionals think in terms of new valuation parameters, new trends, or a change in fundamentals. The common investor would simply resort to the well-worn phrase, "this time it's different."

I prefer to bow to economists and to use Sargent's concept of a change in regimes for what changed the economy and markets in the early 1980s—not in the narrow sense that Sargent thought fiscal discipline was necessary to lower inflation, but as a descriptive device for new policies that produced a radical change in inflation and markets. I think of the old regime as characterized by accelerating inflation, which the federal authorities tried to deal with through bureaucratic controls on wages, prices, and energy production while the Federal Reserve fluctuated half-heartedly between fighting inflation and trying to maintain economic growth. The result was repeated crises that disrupted the securities markets. The new regime embodied a concerted attack on inflation through stringent monetary policy, lower taxes, and dedication to free markets that facilitated a strong dollar, declining oil prices, and a merger boom. The authorities were also managerially adept at handling financial crises, which resulted in a long period of uninterrupted economic growth and high financial returns.

I do not intend to argue, however, that the change in regimes involved a swift and painless transition to superior economic and financial results simply through changing expectations. On the contrary, the transition was initially as punishing for securities markets as prior years had been, principally because monetary policy was such an important vehicle. Stock prices dropped almost 25% as interest rates rose to record levels. Many observers thought that the international financial system might collapse because of the pressure on less-developed countries. The automotive, electric utility, and farm industries suffered serious credit crises that were only resolved by governmental actions. It was not until 1982, when the Federal Reserve dramatically lowered interest rates, that the securities markets began to emerge from a long nightmare of weak performance stretching back to 1973. Even in recovery, however, the stress of the transition in regimes bore heavily on the oil, metals, commodities, and heavy equipment manufacturing industries that underperformed the S&P 500 and suffered a 52% decline in credit ratios, as we shall see in chapters 4 and 8. These and the auto and electric industries accounted for 53% of the public, nonfinancial corporate debt issues in the fifteen years 1970 to 1984.

Nor do I intend to argue that the transition was smooth. The administration's acceptance of a tripling in the deficit from 2% to 6% of GNP appeared to run totally counter to controlling inflation, which created a constant battle over whether taxes should be raised following the 1981 reductions. Likewise, the Federal Reserve only appeared staunchly directed against inflation in retrospect. Its abrupt easing of monetary policy in the middle of 1980 severely hurt its credibility at the time and its degree of restraint fluctuated under political and economic pressures during 1981.

The decline in inflation—the most important indicator of the change in regimes—was almost the only thing that was smooth. As measured by the consumer price index (CPI), it declined from 13.3% in 1979 to approximately 4% between 1982 and 1984, as the United States finally broke its sixteen-year trend of escalating inflation. As the reader can see in figure 1.1, inflation had been rising steadily from 1% in 1964 to a monthly peak

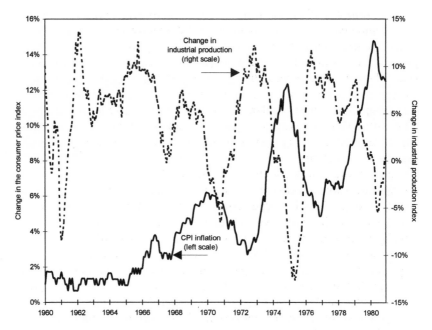

Figure 1.1 Inflation and changes in industrial production. Sources: Bureau of Labor Statistics and Federal Reserve.

of almost 15% in early 1980, ratcheting up in the peaks and troughs of each business cycle. The disjunction occurred sharply in the fourth quarter of 1981 (not shown), after which hitherto predictable relationships between inflation and money supply, unemployment, and interest rates were disrupted, as inflation declined steadily and remained low in the recovery of 1983–1984. At that point, the new expectations were the basis for a period of uninterrupted GNP growth that stretched from the fourth quarter of 1982 through the third quarter of 1990—the longest period on record, and a sharp contrast to the stop-and-go experience of the 1970s.

Other aspects of the new regime were unanticipated. The 55% rise in the value of the dollar between 1980 and 1985 outlined in figure 1.2 was a vital part of the new regime but a considerable surprise after a decade of weakness. Most economic opinion treats this strength as a function of real U.S. interest rates and the budget deficit, but the dollar's rise was neither anticipated nor well understood by either the Federal Reserve or the Reagan administration, nor was it predicted by contemporary economic theory. Oil prices, outlined in figure 1.3, began to decline in 1981 after rising horrendously in 1979 and 1980, providing vital assistance in the battle against inflation. At the time it looked like good luck, but in retrospect, it appears the natural outcome of economic forces.

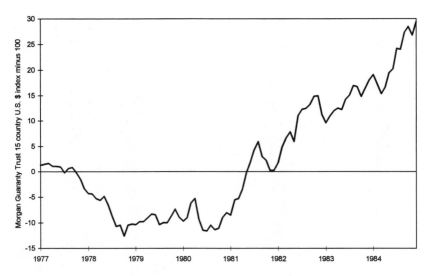

Figure 1.2 The U.S. dollar. Source: Morgan Guaranty Trust.

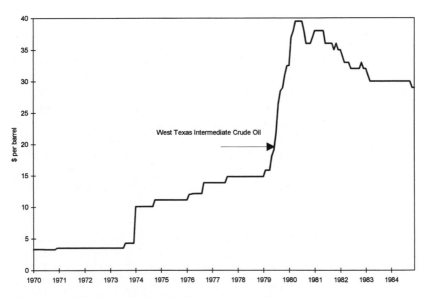

Figure 1.3 Oil prices. Source: Goldman, Sachs & Co.

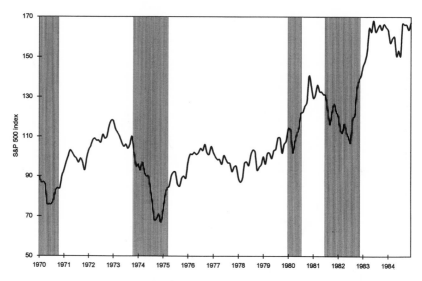

Figure 1.4 The S&P 500. Shaded areas indicate recessions. Source: Standard & Poor's Corp.

Initially, the effects of the new regime on the stock and bond markets looked like a worse version of the 1970s. The slowness with which stock market recovery proceeded at the beginning of the new regime can be seen in figure 1.4, which outlines the month-end S&P 500 from 1970 to 1984. It lost almost 25% between mid-1981 and mid-1982 so that it was still below its 1972 peak in mid-1982. It was not until the last half of 1982 that the stock market soared, providing a 35% return in six months and beginning a rise that by 1984 produced a highly satisfactory average annual total return of 14.8% (9.7% real) for the first half of the decade, compared to 5.9% (minus 1.5% real) between 1969 and 1979. However, this return was well below the average annual return from 1984 to 1989 of 20.4% (16.7% real).

The bond market suffered horrendously at first and was the locus for many of the negative effects of the new regime. Rates for ten-year treasuries rose steadily from 7.2% to 12.8% between 1977 and early 1980, as the reader can see in figure 1.5, but, after a brief decline in mid-1980, they rose again to 15.3% in mid-1981. Total returns on long-term treasuries, outlined in figure 1.6, were negative from late 1979 through September 1981. Again, as with stocks, it was not until the last half of 1982 that the bond market surged, vividly portrayed in figure 1.6, producing total returns of 32% in six months. These gains, and the subsequent lesser ones, were large enough that the average annual return on long-term treasuries between 1979 and 1984 was 9.8% (4.7% real), compared

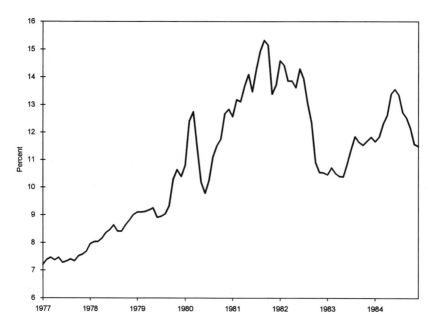

Figure 1.5 Ten-year U.S. treasury rates. Source: Federal Reserve.

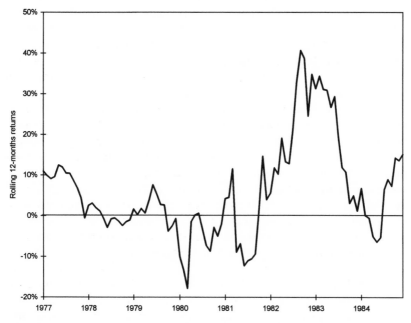

Figure 1.6 Total returns on long-term treasuries (rolling twelve months). Source: Ibbotson Associates.

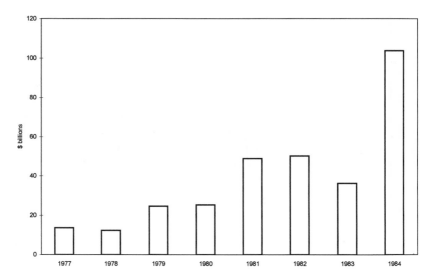

Figure 1.7 Merger and acquisition volume (top 100 deals). Sources: *Mergerstat Review* and author.

to 5.5% between 1969 and 1979 (minus 1.9% real). As with stocks, bond returns from 1979 to 1984 were substantially below the returns from 1984 to 1989 of 15.5% (11.8% real). On the corporate side, the oil-related, metals, commodities, and equipment manufacturing industries suffered severely reduced credit ratios, the credit crises in the auto and electric utility industries were only resolved by considerable government intervention, and the farm crisis was still brewing.

The only market that grew steadily throughout the transition in regimes was the merger market, which more than tripled from $30 to $110 billion, as can be seen in figure 1.7. This growth occurred under the impetus of changing antitrust policies, various oil industry factors, and unprecedented easy credit terms from the leading banks and the junk bond market. The administration formally published new "merger guidelines" in 1982, but in practice it began changing the antitrust rules immediately and loosened them further after 1982 with numerous case-by-case decisions. The change in attitude was particularly important to oil industry acquisitions, which were one-third of the total.

There are good reasons for focusing on 1979–1984 separately from the second half of the 1980s. This was the period in which the change in regimes took place. It encompassed all of the trend changes in fiscal and monetary policy, the dollar, oil and other commodities prices, and inflation. Most of these factors, other than oil prices and the dollar, showed modest volatility during the balance of the decade. A corresponding shift

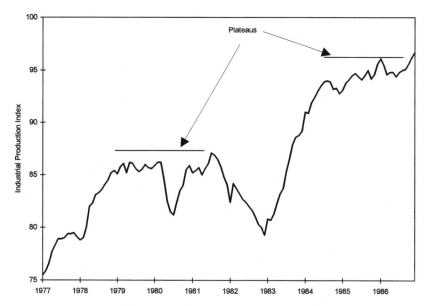

Figure 1.8 Industrial Production Index. Source: Federal Reserve.

in the attractiveness of the stock and bond markets from the discouragement of the 1970s occurred in this period, and it encompassed a highly distinctive period of record real interest rates. On a microeconomic level, most of the distress that developed in the oil-related, commodities, and equipment manufacturing industries was apparent within this period, as were the structural changes in the securities markets that became important in the last half of the decade, such as the growth in junk bonds, mortgage-backed securities, derivatives, and merger activity. For my purposes it also makes sense to break the decade in 1984 because of the sharp increase in private debt relative to GNP that began in 1985, introducing a controversial new consideration of excessive leverage into the factors affecting the economy and securities markets in the last half of the decade.

The period 1979–1984 can easily be construed as a complete business cycle from peak to trough to full recovery. As can be seen in figure 1.8, industrial production plateaued from 1979 to 1981, reached a low point in late 1982, recovered from 1983 to 1984, and then plateaued again during 1985–1986. This makes peak-to-peak comparisons between 1979 and 1984 valid, even though we know in retrospect that economic growth resumed in mid-1986.

This volume is a "historical analysis"—as Joseph A. Schumpeter called it—of the ramifications in the securities markets of the transition in regimes brought about by the Reagan administration and the Federal Reserve. My emphasis is on the disequilibriating shocks to the markets rather than their equilibrium tendencies. At the time, the ability to anticipate the eleven external shocks to the markets between 1979–1984 from fiscal and monetary policy, oil prices, and the dollar was the key to investment success. And while the pattern of these external shocks may not be susceptible to modeling, investors can still learn from studying them.

In many respects, my interpretations of events are traditionally Keynesian. The decline in inflation is best explained by high interest rates, three years without industrial growth, the foreign trade competition resulting from a strong dollar, declining oil prices, a declining long-term commodities price cycle, and a decline in the wage increases for unionized labor, although we need to add a large element of rational expectations to explain the huge drop in inflation in the last quarter of 1981. Traditional Keynesian fiscal stimuli and the decline in nominal interest rates (not in real rates) best explain the economic recovery. My emphasis on the reversal of fortunes in the oil, agriculture, commodities, and heavy machinery industries also reflects a Keynesian bias, as does the attention I give to the effect of changing credit attitudes among banks and junk bond investors in stimulating the growth of the merger market.

I agree with Keynes's characterization of the stock market as a game concerned with what the next person will pay. I attach little importance to dividends in determining stock prices. Stock prices are too volatile relative to dividends, as Robert Shiller has shown. I attach a great deal of emphasis to what Fischer Black called "the magic in earnings." The relevant earnings are expected earnings, however, which almost never correspond to actual earnings (except when it has become trivial near the end of the year), and expected earnings are very much a matter of changing psychology.

I frequently emphasize institutional behavior rather than theory. The institutional behavior of the Federal Reserve, rather than economic theory, best explains the course of interest rates in this period. Short-term rates were determined by the Federal Reserve, and long-term rates responded principally to the Federal Reserve's actions in the short-term market and to the first Reagan budget, rather than to the traditional economic forces of savings, investment, inflation, money supply, or international currency flows. The long-term bond market is as much a game as the stock market, and because Paul Volcker's monetary policy and the first Reagan budget were such powerful forces, they dominated it. The peculiarities of the oil industry make it important time and again. Deposit deregulation in 1982 led to loan and investment practices by banks and savings and loans that were vital to the merger market.

Most academic analyses of the stock, bond, and merger markets give less emphasis to the interactions among them than do professionals. The

Wall Street Journal, Barron's, and Wall Street strategists habitually link changes in stock prices to changes in interest rates. I do this in a two-factor model of stock prices based on interest rates and analysts' earnings projections. I also go to some length to show the link between changing credit standards in the bank loan and junk bond markets and the surge in merger activity in the 1980s.

The structure of this volume, following a general review in chapter 2 of the change in regimes produced by new monetary and fiscal policies, is to first review each of the major securities markets—stocks, bonds, and mergers—outlining each market's performance, the macroeconomic impact on it, and the factors peculiar to it, especially legislation and regulation. Following the stock and corporate bond chapters, I then examine specific industries for the losers and winners entailed by the change in regimes. The problems of the losing industries translated into severely underperforming stock prices and sharp reductions in ratios measuring corporate credit quality. The decline in credit quality was due to inadequate operating income—not voluntarily increased leverage, which became the issue in the last half of the decade—thereby confirming the public concern at the time about deindustrialization.

Each chapter also examines changes in the structure of securities markets. The most dramatic change was in the merger market, where I will trace the transition from relatively modest merger activity in the oil industry to a boom in which no corporation, no matter how large, was invulnerable to attack by corporate raiders benefiting from unprecedented high leverage and new antitrust attitudes. By 1984, oil industry mergers presaged the general merger boom in the last half of the decade.

I will also focus on numerous other important changes in the structure of securities markets. The derivatives markets of futures, options, and stripped treasuries burgeoned well beyond investors' simple needs of hedging themselves. The mortgage-backed securities market changed from a backwater into one of the largest markets due to the problems of the savings and loan industry and the Federal National Mortgage Association (FNMA). Corporate raiders provided a peculiarly American feature to the merger market and made huge opportunistic profits.

Finally, each chapter explores the extent of speculative activities in the various markets in order to provide insight into the excesses that developed in the last half of the decade. There was an unusual amount of speculative activity in the U.S. treasury market; the high volatility and complexity of the derivatives markets naturally attracted speculators; the junk bond market underwent a transition from rational origins to merger financing with unsustainable credit ratios; and the banks in 1982 aggressively entered highly leveraged, unfriendly merger transactions and leveraged buyouts with a new appetite for risk.

To some extent speculation merges indistinguishably with optimism. The development of this optimism in the stock market after Ronald Reagan's election was evident in earnings forecasts by securities analysts that consistently exceeded reality by 20–40%. My two-factor model for stock price changes based on earnings and interest rates also indicates that optimism temporarily raised stock prices 10–20% in late 1980, 1983, and 1984. These overreactions corresponded to periods of high consumer confidence and surges in common stock new-issues.

The final chapter pulls together conclusions about the impact of the new regime on the stock, bond, and merger markets, and their interrelationships. This final chapter also evaluates how well various theories explained events in the securities markets and the economy.

2

The Change in Regimes
Fiscal and Monetary Policies and the Economy

The changes in fiscal and monetary policies, the dollar, oil prices, and regulatory policies that accompanied the first Reagan administration constituted a dramatic change in regimes that broke the back of an extended sixteen-year inflation cycle and reestablished the attractiveness of securities markets. Ronald Reagan took office opposed to the wage and price controls, regulatory bent, and energy policies of the Carter administration, and espoused strong ideological commitment to free markets, lower taxes, economic growth, and the intention to lead the free world fight against communism—themes particularly attractive to international owners of capital.

Monetary policy was an equally important part of the new regime. Paul Volcker and the Federal Reserve are well recognized for their prolonged effort to reduce inflationary expectations, but it is worth a historical reminder that the Federal Reserve's aggressive easing in mid-1980 left its reputation in tatters, and that its effort only achieved constancy after Reagan was elected and personally gave it strong support. Less well recognized is the vital institutional role of the Federal Reserve in maintaining the stability of the international and domestic banking systems from 1982 to 1984, when the growth in both the economy and the securities markets could easily have been derailed by financial crises reminiscent of the 1930s.

Fiscal and monetary policy combined unintentionally to produce a 55% rise in the dollar between 1980 and February 1985 that was an important part of the change in regimes. Linked to this strong dollar, but also somewhat fortuitously, oil and other commodities prices began an extended decline in 1981 that lasted for the rest of the decade and was fundamental to the decline in inflation.

The change in regimes took place over several years and involved contradictory crosscurrents, particularly the budget and trade deficits. The Reagan tax cuts of 1981 led to a federal deficit equal to 6% of GNP and a trade deficit of $112 billion (3% of GNP) by the end of 1984 that so unnerved many investors, as well as the Federal Reserve, that it was not until after the economic recovery of 1983–1984 that these centers of traditional financial opinion were prepared to concede that the twin deficits would not necessarily stimulate inflation. It was also several years before the economy and securities markets benefited from the change in regimes, and here, too, there were numerous contradictory crosscurrents, particularly the depression in the oil, metals, commodities, and trade-sensitive equipment manufacturing industries and the extreme fragility of the banking system.

The initial effects of these conscious policies, unintended effects, and fortuitous oil and other commodities price declines were a stinging recession in which industrial production showed no growth for thirty-six months and unemployment reached postwar records, a dramatic decline in inflation from 12% to 4%, and punishing securities markets until the Federal Reserve eased monetary policy in the last half of 1982 under the twin imperatives of economic growth and preserving the financial system. At that time, the tax cuts also began to take effect and the economy was able to grow strongly without inflation. By 1984 it was clear that expectations about inflation, wage rate growth, oil prices, the dollar, real interest rates, and profits growth had changed in important ways. Consumer confidence was also rising strongly. Whether one attributes the changes to the Reagan administration, the Federal Reserve, or the luck of a long-cycle commodities price decline is unimportant. From the point of view of the securities markets, they were all working together in the same direction.

It will be helpful to our later consideration of individual securities markets to first review this change in regimes. While practicing economists may have the changes well in mind, the general reader may not, and both types of reader will be interested in the relationships between policy changes and the securities markets. A detailed historical review also helps to point out where events signaled changing trends and thereby accelerated market reactions—a matter of particular interest to investors.

My review of the changes in the merger market—another important aspect of the change in regimes—will be deferred until chapter 9.

The Carter Administration's Fiscal and Monetary Policies

Jimmy Carter's presidency began optimistically in the aftermath of Watergate and was initially buoyed by recovery from the severe recession of 1973-74. His economic strategy was the happy combination of tax cuts and economic growth. However, by the fall of 1978 this strategy was disrupted by rising inflation and a weak dollar. U.S. inflation rose from 5.8% in 1976 to 9.0% in 1978, and the merchandise trade deficit slipped from $8 billion to $31 billion, which was a record at the time. Currency markets reacted by pushing the dollar down 11% in 1978 measured against the United States' fifteen largest trading partners,[1] but 22% against the yen and 26% against the Swiss franc. Europe reacted angrily to the trade deficit and weak dollar. European economic growth in the mid-1970s had been hobbled by the first oil crisis in 1973 when oil prices rose from $3 per barrel to $12, and by the resulting high interest rates as governments tried to control inflation—"Eurosclerosis" the *Economist* called it. Now, Europeans saw America as enjoying its growth at Europe's expense by exporting its inflation to them.

In the last half of 1978, domestic reactions against rising inflation and international pressures from a weak dollar won out, and President Carter resolved to stem inflation and defend the dollar. "Voluntary" wage and price controls were set, the 1979 budget moderated federal spending growth and reduced the federal deficit, despite a slight reduction in personal income taxes, and the Federal Reserve discount rate was raised progressively from 6.5% to 9.5%. Concerted efforts were made to support the dollar, including $6.4 billion of treasury foreign currency borrowing ("Carter bonds"), International Monetary Fund (IMF) drawings, and swap arrangements with foreign central banks.[2]

The Carter administration's efforts to control inflation were doomed during 1979, however, by the second oil crisis. The Iranian revolution in 1979 drastically cut Iranian oil exports and disrupted international oil marketing. Oil prices rose from $14.85 to $19 a barrel and a gasoline shortage developed because of a combination of federal rationing efforts, disrupted wholesale markets, and crowd psychology. Angry drivers, some with guns, lined up at gas stations all around the country in what Daniel Yergin has called "The Great Panic." On the first weekend of the summer of 1979, over 50% of America's gas stations were closed, leaving drivers stranded.[3] Mid-1979 inflation accelerated to 12%, and the dollar declined 4.5% in six weeks, despite more than $4.5 billion in Federal Reserve and Treasury dollar purchases.[4]

Jimmy Carter, his administration in disarray, retired to Camp David in July, as oil prices rose to $22, for a week of interviews with experts and brainstorming with his advisers. He returned to make his "national malaise" speech and to announce a major cabinet shuffle. Michael Blumenthal was fired as secretary of the Treasury and was replaced by the Textron industrialist G. William Miller, who had been chairman of the Federal Reserve Board. Paul Volcker, president of the Federal Reserve Bank of New York, was nominated to replace Miller.

Thus was introduced one of the major policymakers of the 1980s. The fifty-one-year old son of the city manager of Teaneck, N.J., Volcker was Phi Beta Kappa at Princeton, did graduate work at Harvard and the London School of Economics, got his first job at the Federal Reserve Bank of New York, served in the Treasury in both Democratic and Republican administrations, and worked as an economist at Chase Manhattan Bank. In 1971, as deputy under-secretary of the Treasury for monetary affairs, he managed the U.S. withdrawal from a policy of fixed exchange rates. As early as 1965, Henry H. Fowler, President Johnson's secretary of the Treasury, had recommended Volcker for the chairmanship of the Federal Reserve Board,[5] and he was appointed president of the Federal Reserve Bank of New York in 1975. His experience was sophisticated, extensive, and pragmatic.

This intensely private man—6' 7" tall and frequently veiled by a wreath of blue cigar smoke, who cared for his invalid wife and was totally absent from New York and Washington social circles—ushered in the most volatile period in modern monetary policy. Although he was adept with the press and Congress, became an icon of antiinflation policy, and presided over a dramatic decline in inflation and a resurgence in financial asset values, Volcker was also the guiding figure in nine major shifts in monetary policy in the space of five years that left considerable wreckage around them and permanently altered the structure of many financial markets.

Volcker's appointment in July 1979 was swiftly followed by an increase in OPEC oil prices to $26.50 in August, a jump in the CPI inflation rate from 12% to 13% (even higher excluding food and energy), and a further decline in the dollar. He was quick to raise interest rates in response, moving the discount rate from 9.5% to 11% by September 18, after almost nine months in which the Federal Reserve Board had disapproved district bank requests for increases.[6] Almost two years previously, at the American Economic Association annual meeting in December 1977, Volcker presented a paper in which he argued for tighter control over the money supply—what he termed "practical monetarism." Now, after less than a month in office, he told reporters that "monetary discipline" was necessary to curb inflation.[7]

At his first meeting as chairman on September 18, as oil prices rose to over $28 a barrel and the dollar dropped a further 2%, Volcker raised the issue of a stronger Federal Reserve focus on money supply. The issue had been building up for some time. A potent body of academic opinion, led by Milton Friedman, ascribed inflation to money supply growth, and

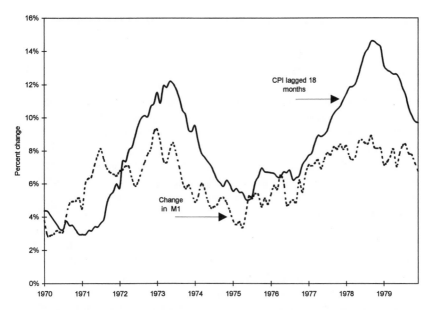

Figure 2.1 Inflation and changes in money supply. Sources: Federal Reserve and Bureau of Labor Statistics.

many nonacademic observers focused on growth in money supply (M1) as the cause of inflation. The relationship between the two, outlined for 1970–1979 in figure 2.1, appeared to be obvious. The St. Louis Federal Reserve staff had accepted this theory for some time and had done extensive practical work on the subject. The staff of the board of governors had come around to this view by 1979. Germany, in particular, appeared to be a practical example of where focus on money supply had been able to dampen the inflationary impact of rising oil prices. Broader opinion swung strongly toward the monetarists' views in mid-1979 when M1 grew 17.2% in April, 15.7% in June, and 12.2% in July, and inflationary psychology became pronounced.

Volcker's suggestion provoked a spirited debate, but consensus within the Federal Open Market Committee (FOMC) was for only a modest increase in interest rates. The financial markets considered the Fed's actions ineffectual, and, as oil prices continued to rise, inflationary psychology accelerated. The Commodity Research Bureau (CRB) index of twenty-seven commodities futures rose 12% between mid-August and October 3. Gold prices rose from an average of $302 in August to $357 in September, and gold futures at one point hit $409. Silver prices rose 50% in one month to almost $14 an ounce, and copper prices rose 5.7%.[8] Europeans—particularly the Germans—at the International Monetary Fund (IMF) meeting in late September in Belgrade were adamant that further Federal Reserve actions were necessary. Volcker briefed the European bankers and accompanying Carter administration officials on his proposal to shift Federal Reserve policy to a focus on money supply rather than interest rates. The Carter officials expressed opposition to the idea, but Volcker was nonetheless determined to pursue the change.[9] He flew home to attend a secret Saturday Federal Reserve meeting, where he got unanimous agreement for the change in monetary policy.

That afternoon, October 6th, 1979, he announced the changes. What first caught attention was an increase in the discount rate from 11% to 12% and an 8% marginal reserve requirement on large banks' managed liabilities (mostly increases in large deposits, repurchase agreements, and federal funds purchases). More importantly, however, Volcker announced that the Federal Reserve henceforth would seek "to restrain expansion of reserve aggregates" rather than focus on interest rates. In case observers missed the point, he made clear the change in policy a few days later in a speech to the American Bankers Association,[10] and a special meeting was held at the Federal Reserve Bank of New York with primary treasury dealers on Tuesday, October 9 to explain the changes in procedures that were envisaged.[11] They were told what the minutes of the FOMC meeting explicitly recognized—"that the shift to an operating approach that placed primary emphasis on the volume of reserves would result in both a prompt increase and greater fluctuations in the federal funds rate."[12] Behind such innocuous language lay a shift in monetary policy that gave it the leading role in both the Carter and Reagan administrations' anti-inflation efforts and an impact on the economy beyond any previous conscious intent. This emphasis produced unprecedented volatility in fixed income markets, as nine major moves in monetary policy occurred between 1979 and 1984. It led to three years of the highest interest rates in modern U.S. history, three and a half years without any growth in industrial production, the highest unemployment rates since the Depression, and a dramatic decline in inflation.

The initial reactions of the stock and bond markets to the new policy were tumultuous. Ten-year treasury rates surged from 9.3% to 10.6% in just two months and the S&P 500 plunged 7%. However, the stock market more than recovered its losses by January.

The Carter administration's own efforts to deal with the developing economic crisis were focused on energy policy. Energy legislation was stalled in Congress, partly due to the nuclear accident in March 1979 at General Public Utilities' nuclear power plant at Three Mile Island, but the 1979 oil crisis provided the stimulus for an energy bill emphasizing regulation and government intervention. Under the bill, domestic oil and gas prices were to remain under controls that gradually lapsed by 1985; intrastate natural gas was brought under federal price controls; energy taxes were imposed on gas-guzzling cars; electric utilities and industrial plants were pushed to convert from oil to coal; and homeowners were given tax credits for insulating. The oil and gas industry was given tax incentives for exploration and development; purchases for the Strategic Petroleum Reserve were authorized; cooperative international measures were established to deal with future oil embargoes; a fee was threatened on oil imports if they exceeded 8.2 million barrels per day; and a standby gasoline rationing plan was established.[13]

Neither the switch in monetary policy nor this first step toward a national energy policy had appreciable effects on the rapidly escalating inflationary trend. Both were too little, too late. Inflationary expectations were rising so fast that real interest rates were still insignificant, and the new energy policy was aimed at oil prices only half of the $30 level prevailing by the end of October.

As 1979 turned into 1980, the economy continued to expand, stimulated by inflationary expectations that overwhelmed the otherwise depressive effects on the economy of higher oil prices, a slight fiscal drag, and higher interest rates. At the same time, turmoil in the Middle East raised international uncertainties. The Shiites successfully took over in Iran and invaded the U.S. embassy in November, taking its occupants hostage. The Soviet Union installed Babrah Kumal as the puppet leader of Afghanistan in December and dispatched thirty thousand troops there. Between Afghanistan and the anti-Americanism of Iran, it appeared as if the perennial fear of a major Soviet military presence in the Middle East might come to pass.

Under the twin stimuli of inflation and international unrest, gold prices skyrocketed. COMEX gold futures hit a high of $960 in January 1980, versus under $400 just three months previously. Silver futures exceeded $50 an ounce versus an average cash price of $16.55 in November. Rumors circulated that the Hunt brothers in Dallas were cornering the silver market.[14]

Federal Reserve Board governor Henry Wallich called the gold market a "sideshow," but it caught the general atmosphere of inflationary panic. Oil prices rose even further to $37 a barrel in February 1980. The Commodity Research Bureau's futures index of twenty-seven commodities rose 5.7% between the beginning of January and mid-February. Copper futures hit a high of $1.48 a pound in February versus an average November cash price of $0.98. The consumer price index rose at an annual rate of 18% in January and February, and consumers began a surge of inflation-induced buying, boosting retail sales 43% in January. Auto sales jumped from a rate of 9.4 million units in October to 11.9 million units in January—in the dead of winter. Wage settlements escalated to over 10%.[15] Henry Kaufman, Salomon Brothers' respected economist, despaired that "the path to sustainable economic growth seems lost to us," and called for controls on credit, foreign exchange, wages, and prices.

Rumors of credit and price controls were widespread, stimulating the price increases mentioned above, as well as a 24% rate of growth in business loan demand between December and February, a time when it normally declined seasonally.[16]

On March 14, 1980, only eight months before the presidential elections, the Carter administration responded to the developing hysteria with a new anti-inflation program. Most of the government's emphasis was on further direction and regulation of the energy markets. Congress had just approved a $20 billion Synthetic Fuels Corp. New proposals included a gasoline tax of 14 cents a gallon and an oil and gasoline import fee equal to 10 cents a gallon at the pump; decontrol of domestic oil prices; a windfall profits tax on higher oil prices; efficiency standards for autos, buildings, and equipment; inducements for mass transit; tax incentives for new energy technologies; increased coal and nuclear electric generation capacity; and an Energy Mobilization Board to speed up construction of electric utility generating plants.[17] The administration also revised the budget it had submitted only two months earlier, proposing further cuts of $13–14 billion, doubling the staff of the Wage and Price Council, and a 15% withholding tax on interest and dividends. All of these proposals had to go through the legislative process.

The administration's proposals were accompanied by drastic changes in monetary policy that faced no Congressional delay. A 3% surcharge was added to the discount rate, which was already at 13%; loans for speculation or acquisitions were restricted; and various reserve requirements were added for increases in banks' managed liabilities and the assets of money market funds. Partly as a political statement, and over the opposition of Paul Volcker, a 15% down payment was required from applicants for new consumer loans and loan growth at banks and finance companies was limited to 6–9%.[18]

These were untried monetary policies, particularly the restrictions on down payments for new consumer loans, and they had unpredictable consequences. The economy took a nose dive, and it was suddenly transparently obvious that monetary policy was a powerful tool that acted directly on the "real" economy when pursued aggressively enough. The Fed had excluded new loans for autos and housing from the new down payment restrictions because the credit controls "were not intended to bite hard," according to Paul Volcker;[19] however, consumer reactions proved to be substantial and rapid. The Consumer Confidence Index—already terribly low, as can be seen in figure 2.2—plunged from 66.9 to 56.5 in one month, and by May was down to 51.7, its lowest point between 1977 and 1984. Real consumer credit, outlined in figure 2.3, was liquidated at a 19% annual rate between March and July. Auto sales—pummeled by both high gas prices and high interest rates—endured their worst slump in decades as they dropped from a 9.75 million rate in the fourth quarter of

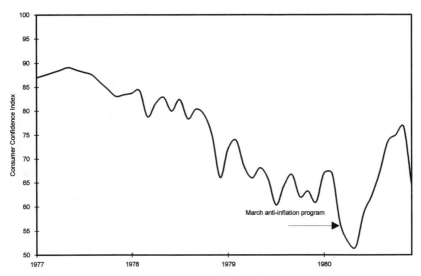

Figure 2.2 Consumer Confidence Index. Source: University of Michigan.

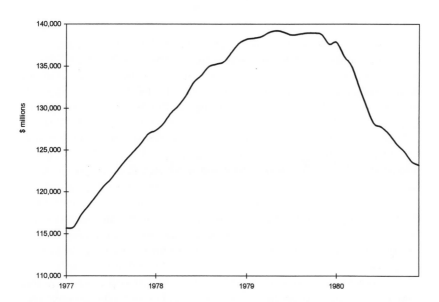

Figure 2.3 Real consumer credit. Source: Federal Reserve.

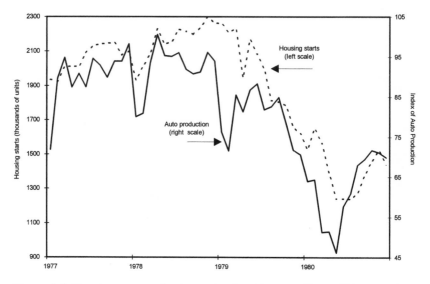

Figure 2.4 Housing starts and auto production. Sources: Census Bureau and Federal Reserve.

1979 to 7.75 million. Chrysler Corp., which had been staggering for years, was almost knocked into bankruptcy and approached the Carter administration at the end of July for a U.S. guarantee on $1.0 billion in new debt to keep it solvent. Residential housing starts fell by a third, from a 1.5 million rate to 1.0 million (both auto sales and housing starts are outlined in figure 2.4). In the broader economy, second-quarter 1980 GNP declined at a 10.0% annualized rate, the sharpest drop since World War II. This result was telegraphed earlier by the index of the National Association of Purchasing Managers, which fell from 51.1 in February to 29.2 in May, and by the leading indicators index, which dropped from 101.5 in February to 93.6 in June. The Federal Reserve's index of industrial production dropped from 152.6 to 140.4, as capacity utilization declined from 85% in March to 79% in July. Real plant and equipment spending dropped for three quarters in a row. Unemployment rose quickly from 6.3% to 8.0%.

The powerful impact of the March anti-inflation program on consumers was indicated by the concentrated decline in credit-sensitive consumer durables. The 10% second-quarter decline in GNP was only 1.5% excluding autos and housing. The shock to consumer borrowing can be seen in figure 2.5, which indexes the year-to-year changes in real consumer credit and real disposable personal income. As the reader can see, the relationship between the two variables was usually strong, but consumer credit plunged relatively in 1980.

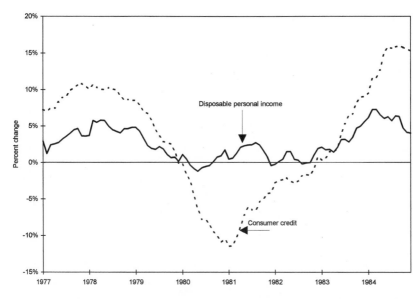

Figure 2.5 Changes in real consumer credit and real disposable personal income. Sources: Bureau of Economic Analysis and Federal Reserve.

The monetary shock abruptly reversed the intense inflation speculation of January and February. Gold futures, which had been as high as $960 an ounce in January, dropped to $469 on March 18th and closed April at $543. Silver prices, which had been over $50 an ounce in the futures market in January, dropped to under $10 when the Hunt brothers were caught under-margined at Prudential-Bache Securities and defaulted on a silver futures contract with Englehard Minerals for 19 million ounces worth $665 million. As a cheap play on gold, the Hunts had bought 170 million ounces of silver at prices up to $35 per ounce, and borrowed $1.8 billion in the process. Now they were caught in the largest personal bankruptcy in U.S. history. The change in other futures prices was reflected in a 13.5% decline in the Commodities Research Bureau's futures index in just four weeks.

Inflation as measured by the Consumer Price Index immediately declined to under 12% for March through May from the 16.4% average for December through February, and then to only 1.5% in June. Inflation as measured by the Producer Price Index (PPI) came down steadily from over 17% in January and February to 5.6% in May.

The stock and bond markets had been declining sharply for three weeks in anticipation of the administration's program, as virtually all of the details were discussed in advance in the press and with Congress. The stock market declined 16% from mid-February to mid-March, and

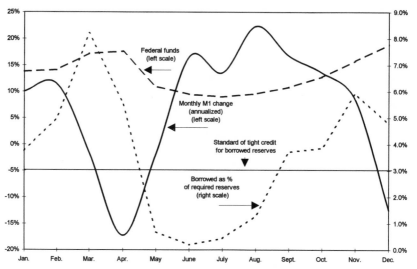

Figure 2.6 Measures of credit conditions in 1980. Borrowed reserves are adjusted. Source: Federal Reserve.

ten-year treasury rates rose from 10.8% to 12.4%. After the anti-inflation program was announced, federal funds rates briefly soared to 25% versus 14.1% in February, and ten-year treasury rates initially rose slightly to 12.8%; however, as it became evident that monetary policy was dramatically cooling both the economy and inflationary expectations, ten-year treasury rates began to decline. The yield on ten-year treasury bonds went from 40 basis points under treasury bills (i.e., already inverted) to 610 basis points under between February and April. The S&P 500 initially dropped 10% from 113 to 102, but it too reversed direction quickly, and rose steadily for the rest of the year.

Neither the administration nor the Federal Reserve anticipated such a quick reaction to the March anti-inflation program, but it was certainly convenient with the election so near. The Federal Reserve abruptly eased credit between May and July. The credit controls were dismantled and the discount rate reduced by six points to 10%. As can be seen in figure 2.6, federal funds dropped from 17% in March to 9.0% in July, banks' borrowed reserves dropped from 8.2% of required reserves to only 0.4%, and monthly M1 growth surged to over 15%. The yield on ten-year treasury bonds dropped from 13% to 10%, and the yield curve from three-month treasury bills to ten-year U.S. treasuries was positive by 279 basis points after being negative by 610 basis points in April. The S&P 500 rose 15%, from 106 at the end of April to 122 at the end of July.

The economy surged back, and the consumer confidence index rose from 51.7 in May to 76.7 by November. The Index of Leading Indica-

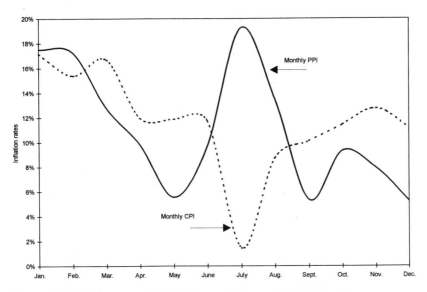

Figure 2.7 Inflation rates in 1980. Source: Bureau of Labor Statistics.

tors rose from 93.6 in May to 104.1 in November, and the National Association of Purchasing Managers' index rose from a low of 29.2 in May to 56.0 in November. The Federal Reserve's industrial production index rose from 140.4 to 148.5 as industrial capacity utilization recovered from 79% in July to 82.5% in December.[20] But inflation also began to escalate again. Oil prices rose to $40, and drought in the Midwest drove corn prices from approximately $2.50 to $3.50 a bushel, and cotton from 65 cents to 80 cents. The Commodity Research Bureau's Futures Price Index rose from 260 in April to 330 in September—a 53% annual rate of increase! The Consumer Price Index grew at a 12.0% rate from September through December.

In fact, inflation had never really declined to the same extent as the economy or interest rates in response to the March anti-inflation program. As can be seen in figure 2.7, which shows 1980's monthly CPI and PPI inflation rates, the reduction in CPI growth was all concentrated in its drop to 1.5% in July, and by then PPI growth was already back up to 19%. CPI growth was back up to 8.7% in July. Nor was inflation just due to oil and food prices. The CPI, excluding food and energy, was actually growing faster than the general CPI, and growth in unit labor costs never dipped below 10%.[21] Union wage settlements averaged 9% in 1980 versus 7% in 1979, and rose further to 9.7% in 1981.[22]

The sharp turnaround in monetary policy did much to undermine faith in the Federal Reserve's efforts to control inflation. Political motivations appeared to be the Fed's chief weakness in preventing the buildup of inflation under chairmen Burns and Miller, and now Paul Volcker appeared too involved in politics. He had been intensely involved with the Carter administration in preparing the March anti-inflation plan. His involvement went far beyond simply monetary policy, including White House strategy sessions and discussions with Congress in which political considerations were frank and immediate,[23] all of which made the Fed look overtly political when it cut the discount rate by six percentage points, reduced banks' borrowed reserves back to the low levels of 1977, and dismantled the consumer credit controls in just two and a half months. M1 was allowed to grow 14.6% in the third quarter, and M2 grew 16.0%. Lacking confidence in the Fed's political motives, the dollar sank 6%, back to its December 1979 level, and gold futures rose almost 50% to $748.[24]

The Federal Reserve could not be inactive in the face of rapidly rising inflation and this money supply expansion right in front of the election, however, without appearing a total tool of the administration. The Federal Reserve raised the discount rate from 10% to 11% in September, which was the extent of its public action. Its unpublicized variables indicated greater credit restraint, as can be seen by referring back to figure 2.6. Federal funds rose from 9.0% in July to 12.8% in October, and banks' borrowed reserves rose from 0.4% of required reserves to 3.9% in the same period. But the Federal Reserve felt compelled to wait until after the November elections to make an all-out attack on inflation. It raised borrowed reserves to 5.9% in November, federal funds to 19% in December, and actually reduced M1 by 12.5% in December.

However, the Fed's reticence had little effect on the elections. Ronald Reagan got 51% of the vote, versus only 41% for Jimmy Carter and 7% for John Anderson, and the polls consistently showed Reagan in the lead.[25]

The Reagan Administration's Fiscal Policy

Ronald Reagan scooped Jimmy Carter on taxes early in the election. Cutting taxes was part of both parties' political dialogue throughout the 1970s because inflation continually pushed taxpayers with the same real income into higher tax brackets; but Carter set aside this option in his 1980 budget in the interest of reducing both the budget deficit and inflationary pressures. He was still wrestling with this righteous course in the midst of the election campaign when Reagan announced his commitment to a 30% cut in personal taxes and accelerated depreciation write-offs for business equipment. The contrast remained when President Carter left office. His "lame-duck" budget recommended deferring personal tax cuts and imposing a gasoline tax.

The Reagan administration came into office, however, in no mood to accede to the Carter administration's recommendations. Reagan won in a landslide, cutting into Democratic strength in key industrial states, with Catholics and Jews, with labor, and in the South. The Republicans gained twelve Senate seats and control of the Senate for the first time since 1952. Prominent liberal Democrats such as senators George McGovern (S.D.), Birch Bayh (Ind.), and Frank Church (Id.), and congressmen John Brademas (Ind.), and Al Ullman (Ore.) were defeated, and the Republicans won four new governorships in Arkansas, Missouri, North Dakota, and Washington. The administration was determined to not only reduce income taxes but to reverse the Carter administration's regulatory proclivity. Addressing the country's economic problems in his inaugural address, President Reagan declared that government was the problem—not the solution. At his first press conference he disbanded the Council on Wage and Price Stability, which had been a keystone of the Carter administration's anti-inflation policies, and promised to eliminate the Department of Education and the Department of Energy. He also announced that the Office of Management and Budget (OMB) would henceforth weight the cost-benefit tradeoffs of all proposed regulations. Vice President Bush was assigned to lead a new presidential task force on regulatory relief. The last vestiges of oil price controls and allocations to small refiners were removed before the end of January, including all emergency rationing plans.

Initially, fiscal policy fell under the sway of the new director of the Office of Management and Budget. David Stockman was a thirty-four-year-old, two-term Michigan congressman who espoused the nostrums of supply-side economics. In his own words, he was drafting a "comprehensive, multi-element plan that can basically shock and shift the economy to a different path in terms of output growth, performance of the financial markets, and the inflation trend." He implausibly projected economic growth of 4–5% for the next four years, and was backed up by administration economists Craig Roberts and Lawrence Kudlow and by Arthur Laffer, supply-side theory's most prominent media personality. Al Ullman, as chairman of the House Ways and Means Committee, would have given short shrift to this rhetoric, but he was defeated in the Reagan sweep and was replaced by Dan Rostenkowski. Rostenkowski was a relatively conservative south-side Chicago Pole who was pro-business, amenable to the Reagan tax cut proposals, personally close to Vice President George Bush, and anxious to put his stamp on the pending tax bill. Rostenkowski and Stockman cooperated on the Economic Recovery Tax Act of 1981, which passed with strong Democratic support in August.

The act cut tax rates for individuals in three stages (5% on October 1, 1981; 10% on July 1, 1982; and 10% on July 1, 1983), the top rate on "unearned income" was reduced from 70% to 50%, the capital gains tax rate was cut from 28% to 20%, estate taxes were eliminated for all but the very wealthy, and IRA benefits were expanded so that they amounted to hundreds of thousands of dollars annually for the very highly paid.

For business, the act provided accelerated equipment depreciation over three, five, or ten years, depending on the nature of the equipment, and over fifteen years for buildings and utility plant. If companies could not use this much depreciation they were empowered to "sell" it and their investment tax credits in the form of tax benefit transfers to investors who could use them. The act also reduced the windfall profits tax on oil, and provided a tax credit for 25% of research and development outlays.

The revenue losses from these tax cuts were partially offset by $140 billion of expenditure cuts over four years, in which Democrats joined with equal gusto, as the House committees sometimes approved greater cuts than the administration had requested. Over two hundred programs were either killed or had their revenues reduced, including synfuels, urban development, CETA grants, medicaid, education aid, extended unemployment benefits, food stamps, and highways. But enthusiasm only went so far. When the administration tried for sharp reductions in social security benefits, both the elderly and the Democrats attacked, and the administration backed off, leaving a huge gap between revenue and expenditure reductions.

The impact of this budget on the federal deficit was expected to be huge. Early in the budget process there was considerable supply-side economics rhetoric about income growth making up for the loss in revenues from lower tax rates, but by midyear this had been discarded even by the theory's adherents within the administration.[26] Stockman simply ignored the revenue losses, and in an act in which cynicism competed for outrageousness with amateurism, had the Office of Management and Budget issue projections of future deficits of $45 billion in fiscal 1982, $23 billion in 1983, balance in 1984, and a small surplus in 1985, based on highly fanciful assumptions about the resulting economic growth.[27] By contrast, fellow conservatives at the American Enterprise Institute projected deficits of $100–150 billion in 1982, $150–200 billion in 1983, $200–250 billion in 1984, and $225–275 billion in 1985.[28] Financial market economists had similar projections. Salomon Brothers' Henry Kaufman labeled the budget "exceedingly expansionary" and predicted a conflict between an expanding deficit and restrictive monetary policy.[29] Al Wojnilower, First Boston's economist, and consulting economists such as Alan Greenspan, Allan Sinai, and Michael Evans, were vociferous in criticizing the expected deficits.

The bond market had accepted this result from the beginning, as ten-year treasury rates rose steadily from 12.6% in January to 15.3% in September. Much of this time federal funds rates were declining, which indicated the independence of this move from monetary policy. The S&P 500 was flat at approximately 130 from January through July.

Interspersed with the unsettling effect of the budget was the administration's very strong stand in the Public Air Traffic Controllers (PATCO) strike, which Paul Volcker called "the most important single action of the administration in helping the anti-inflation fight."[30] PATCO was one of the few unions that supported Reagan in the election, and the Department of Transportation tried to avert a strike by agreeing at the last minute to a multitude of concessions. However, there had been years of declining goodwill between the air controllers and the Federal Aviation Administration (FAA) due to overwork, strain, and weak management. The union membership, too, had overinflated expectations; they were looking for a four-day week and a pay package that would raise the top controllers' pay to over $100,000 with overtime. In late July, 95% of the PATCO membership voted to strike.

They had not reckoned on the Reagan administration's hardline response. A strike was illegal for federal employees, and the air controllers' demands were a threat to the Reagan administration's cost-cutting efforts in wage negotiations with other federal employees, especially the Post Office. The strike had been anticipated by the FAA for months and its strategy was well prepared. The administration warned that it would not tolerate a strike, that strikers would be replaced with no amnesty afterward, and that it would seek court penalties against the union. Registered mail notices went out to individual controllers telling them they would be fired unless they could prove they were not strike participants. The FAA went to court and got leaders of the five locals jailed and daily fines assessed. Over 40% of the controllers stayed at work and the military filled in for the balance. The FAA received over nine thousand applications for air controllers' jobs and immediately began training classes.

Important support came from Canada's Conservative government under Prime Minister Brian Mulroney, which sought fines or jail terms for any Canadian air traffic controllers joining the protest; otherwise, U.S.-European traffic would have been severely disrupted. The pilots' union declared that air safety actually improved. AFL-CIO chief Lane Kirkland also refused support for sympathy strikes. The public was strongly supportive of the administration, despite the disruption of travel and transportation.

The strikers never had a chance. PATCO was bankrupted, their leaders convicted, and the strikers lost their jobs. President Reagan, by contrast, established himself as intolerant of lawbreakers, firm against inflationary wage settlements, and little prone to compromise. Whether this was President Reagan's most important act to control inflation is debatable, but in Paul Volcker's mind it was a symbol of the administration's support for his own difficult task.

No such firmness prevailed on fiscal matters. As the personal and business tax cuts of 1981 took effect, the deficit rose to $128 billion in fiscal 1982 and $195 billion in fiscal 1983,[31] producing a seesaw competition within the administration and among its supporters for tax increases and expenditure cuts. In early 1982, Senators Dole (R-Kan.) and Domenici (R-N.M.), and Congressman Gramm (D-Tex.) put forth a plan to cut Social Security benefits by $40 billion. This, however, was scuttled by a Democratic attack led by Senator Robert Byrd (D-W.Va.). President Reagan gained the political high ground by countering with demand for a balanced budget amendment to the Constitution, which Paul Volcker quickly supported as well. In August 1982, Congress passed a package of increases in minor taxes to provide $98 billion of revenues over three years and $30 billion of spending cuts. The corporate tax benefit transfers of 1981 were virtually eliminated, the aggressive depreciation allowances of 1981 were scaled back, and a minimum corporate tax of 20% was introduced.

President Reagan was prepared to go even further. As oil prices came under pressure, in a televised speech in November 1982 he floated an outline for a 5 cents per gallon gasoline tax, which he endorsed soon afterward when it received the support of Speaker Tip O'Neill (D-Mass.) and Senate Leader Howard Baker (R-Tenn.). Legislation was introduced and passed the House by December, but ran into a Republican filibuster in the Senate by Senators Humphrey (R-N.H.), Helms (R-N.C.), East (R-N.C.), and Nickles (R-Okla.). The necessary votes could not be achieved to stop the filibuster, and the bill was shelved. Senator Dole termed the effort a "miscalculation."

Expectations were high in 1983 for a reduction in the deficit. The Reagan budget for fiscal 1984, submitted in January 1983, dropped the tendentious supply-side projections of previous budgets, projected a $180 billion deficit, and volunteered to negotiate with the Democrats on tax increases and expenditure cuts. Many, including Paul Volcker, believed that the decline in oil prices presented a "compelling" case for some form of energy tax to offset the deficit. The costs of agricultural programs, due to a rising dollar and declining grain prices, also became so extreme that they presented another area for bipartisan expenditure cuts. Direct farm subsidy programs cost nearly $20 billion in fiscal 1983 — five times what they had in 1981. The Payment-in-Kind program was expected to add $10 billion to this, and the OMB estimated that all forms of farm subsidy were up to $54 billion.

Major bipartisan changes in social security taxation were achieved in 1983 along the lines of recommendations by a commission headed by Alan Greenspan. Increases in Social Security taxes legislated in 1977 under the Carter administration were accelerated from 1990 into the 1980s. Rates for the self-employed were doubled, new federal civil servants and employees of nonprofit institutions were required to join the Social Security program, and Social Security payments to higher income individuals were made partially taxable. The total effect of these reforms at their peak amounted to $55 billion annually—almost 1% of the GNP.[32]

Further tax increases were hamstrung, however, by a major division of opinion within the administration. On the one hand, a number of cabinet officers pressed for tax increases, and Martin Feldstein claimed that a $200 billion deficit was certain unless changes were made. In line with this, Senator Dole (R-Kan.) and Congressman Rostenkowski (D-Ill.) worked out bipartisan plans for a $150 billion package of new taxes and Social Security cuts. On the other hand, President Reagan was attracted to the Bradley-Gephardt theme of tax simplification. Senator Bill Bradley (D-N.J.) and Congressman Dick Gephardt (D-Mo.) had advanced the proposal in May 1982 that the top personal tax rate could be reduced to 30% without reducing revenues if all forms of deductions were eliminated. In January 1983, President Reagan had announced that he was considering massive tax simplification along these lines, just before disclosing the new budget and making his State of the Union speech.

By the end of 1983, fiscal policy was in complete disarray. President Reagan vowed to veto the Dole-Rostenkowski deficit reduction plan because it contained new taxes, and both Dole and Rostenkowski publicly chastised the president for resisting tax increases. Larry Speakes, the president's chief spokesman, and Treasury Secretary Donald Regan publicly contradicted Council of Economic Advisors Chairman Martin Feldstein's assertion that there was a structural deficit of $200 billion, and consciously slighted him by mispronouncing his name.[33] The president called for a bipartisan Congressional panel to work with the administration in 1984 to produce a $100 billion cut in expenditures to halve the deficit, but any such hope in a presidential election year was forlorn. All of the emphasis for control of the economy and inflation fell on the Federal Reserve, which reversed direction and began tightening credit again.

Tax proposals in the administration's January 1984 budget submission were a charade. President Reagan's State of the Union message called for a study of tax reform to be delivered to him after the November elections, although the administration itself had given the matter no study at all. It was greeted with laughter. Martin Feldstein got a provision in the budget for a "contingency tax plan" to raise taxes if the deficit exceeded 2.5% of GNP, but the provision had no administration support. The Federal Reserve responded by raising federal funds rates from approximately 9.5% to 11.5% between February and August. Senator Dole led a persistent effort that resulted in a "myriad of tax changes" that at their peak would raise $31 billion annually, but nothing more could be expected in an election year.[34]

In November 1984, after the election, the Treasury ultimately pro-

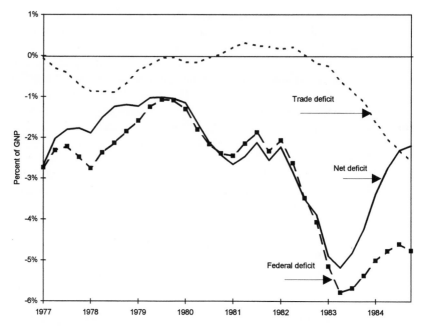

Figure 2.8 Trade and budget deficits as a percentage of GNP. Source: Bureau of Economic Analysis.

duced a plan for tax reform that proposed three personal income tax brackets of 15%, 25%, and 35%, versus a present top rate of 50%. They also proposed eliminating deductions for state and local taxes, most charitable contributions, and second home mortgage interest, and taxation of fringe benefits provided by employers, particularly health insurance. Capital gains would be taxed at these same rates, but gains and tax brackets were to be indexed for inflation. The plan proposed to drop corporate rates from 46% to 33%, allow deductions for half of dividends paid, eliminate the investment tax credit and entertainment expenses, and reduce depreciation. The net effect was an 8.5% reduction in personal taxes at the expense of a 37% increase in corporate taxes. Presidential aides reflected that "it looks like a system designed by a lot of academics." Congressional and media reception was lukewarm, at best. No one could have predicted that the proposal would evolve into the historic Tax Act of 1986.[35]

It can be seen from this brief history that the Reagan administration's fiscal policy was the most difficult aspect of the change in regimes for which the administration was striving. The administration did not have some subtle theoretical plan that the Federal Reserve would keep money tight to extinguish inflation while deficit spending was used to revive the economy. Nor was the resulting mix of forces expected. The fiscal stimulus to the economy rose from approximately 2% of GNP during 1979–1981 to almost 6% in mid-1983, pulling the country out of recession, but the trade deficit also grew rapidly, countering this stimulus, as can be seen in figure 2.8. The current account balance on goods and services moved from a modest surplus in the first half of 1982 to a deficit equal to 1% of GNP by the end of 1983 and 2.5% by the end of 1984. The net stimulus from these mutually offsetting deficits, outlined by the heavy line in figure 2.8, dropped from a 5% peak in 1983 to only 2% at the end of 1984—the same as prevailed in 1981 before the tax cuts took effect.

The resulting policy mix had a highly unsettling effect on the Federal Reserve and on financial traditionalists. Both were surprised by the strong dollar that ensued, and both persistently predicted that the twin budget and trade deficits would result in a weaker dollar and higher inflation. Their pressures on the government to reduce the deficit produced the prolonged debate cited above over the need to raise taxes. As a result, the tax situation became highly unstable, perhaps offsetting to some degree the expected effects of the deficit. Eugene Steuerle, who was a tax specialist in the Treasury department during this period, summed up the focus on taxes in the introduction to his own book, *The Tax Decade*, as follows:

> Between 1981 and 1990, the United States witnessed more frequent and detailed changes in federal tax law than ever before in its history. Barely had one new act passed Congress than another was being debated. A dramatic cut in income taxes in 1981 was followed by large tax increases in 1982, 1983, and 1984—both to reduce the deficit and to deal with the long-term solvency of the Social Security program. By mid-1984, analysis and debate on major tax reform was underway, culminating in the Tax Reform Act of 1986—the most comprehensive reform of U.S. tax laws ever undertaken.[36]

Monetary Policy 1980–1984

Paul Volcker made a mistake in easing credit so dramatically in mid-1980, but he was not going to repeat it. As both the economy and inflation rates picked up in the last half of 1980, the Federal Reserve began raising the discount rate, first by 1% to 11% on September 25, and then in two jumps after the election to 16%, including a 3% surcharge. The federal funds rate averaged 12.8% in October, 15.9% in November, and 18.9% in December. Borrowed bank reserves jumped from insignificance in August to 5.9% of required reserves in November.[37] Such aggressive monetary tightening, as one administration lost its influence but before the new one took office, appeared highly opportunistic politically, but the

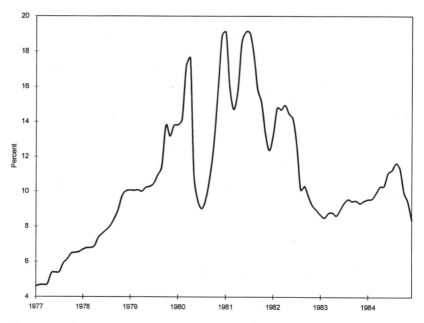

Figure 2.9 Federal funds rates. Source: Federal Reserve.

Federal Reserve expected strong support from the new Reagan administration. Fighting inflation was good politics, and control of the money supply to control inflation was the accepted dogma with Donald Regan, the new Treasury secretary, with Beryl Sprinkel, the new under-secretary of the Treasury for monetary affairs, and with the president himself. At the beginning of the new administration, tight monetary policy appeared likely to be linked with restrictions on the growth in government spending to slow down inflation, but as fiscal policy evolved and the deficit grew, monetary policy became the point of emphasis for inflation control by all of the parties.

The Federal Reserve maintained relatively tight credit conditions through 1981 and the first half of 1982. This was reflected in federal funds rates, outlined in figure 2.9, which were over 14% for twenty months from November 1980 to June 1982, and over 19% twice in 1981. Tight credit was also reflected in banks' borrowed reserves as a percentage of their required reserves, which are outlined in figure 2.10. Total borrowings from the Federal Reserve banks, which were insignificant in the easy credit environment of the summer of 1980, rose to 5.9% of required reserves in November 1980. Borrowed reserves showed sporadic signs of tightening and easing thereafter; but in general banks' borrowed reserves were above 3% (an unambiguous measure of tight credit) through April 1982.[38]

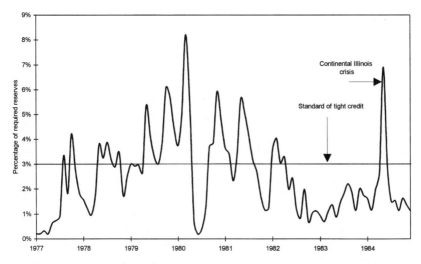

Figure 2.10 Borrowed reserves (adjusted for extended borrowings). Source: Federal Reserve.

The Federal Reserve's discount rate, which is a more formal indicator of monetary policy, stayed similarly high. The Board of Governors refused requests by various district banks in the spring of 1981 to reduce the discount rate on the basis that "such action might give an unintended signal of an easing in the general course of monetary policy."[39] In early May 1981, the Federal Reserve raised the effective discount rate to 18% by increasing the nominal rate 1% to 14% and the surcharge from 3% to 4%.

In the fall of 1981, Congress began to discuss credit controls, a windfall profits tax on high interest rates, reorganization of the Federal Reserve System, and wage and price controls as alternatives to monetary policy. Treasury Secretary Regan pressed publicly for faster money supply growth and lower interest rates because M1 growth had dropped down to 1.0% from May through October.[40] Europeans, too, pressed the Federal Reserve to lower interest rates on the grounds that the strong U.S. dollar (the strongest in six years) exported inflation to their countries.

The Federal Reserve was not immune to these pressures. The effective discount rate was lowered in four steps from 18% to 12% between September and December 1981, as the nominal rate was reduced from 14% to 12% and the 4% surcharge eliminated. The federal funds rate dropped from 15.9% in September to 12.4% in December, and treasury bill yields dropped from 14.7% to 10.9%. Banks' borrowed reserves dropped from a peak of 5.6% of required reserves in May to 1.2%. For political purposes, the Federal Reserve claimed that the reductions in the discount rate were following interest rate declines in the money market and did not reflect a change in policy.[41]

This accomodation ended, and the political critics were stilled, when there was a surge in M1 to 13% annualized growth from November 1981 through January 1982, even though inflation continued to decline to below 4%. Indeed, this jump in M1 growth led both President Reagan and Treasury Secretary Regan to chastise the Federal Reserve for overly fast monetary growth.[42] The Federal Reserve moved to tighten credit again by reducing its U.S. treasury portfolio by $5.5 billion in January and February 1982.[43] Banks' borrowed reserves surged back up to 4.0% of required reserves in February, and the federal funds rate jumped from 12.4% in December to 14.8% in February. Paul Volcker was very aggressive in telling the Congressional Joint Economic Committee in January 1982 that the present course of tax and spending policies would create wider deficits and "a critical problem" even as President Reagan stated in his State of the Union speech that his program "shouldn't be tampered with."[44]

The Federal Reserve began to ease credit noticeably in mid-1982. Banks' borrowed reserves dropped first, in May, from 3.3% of required reserves to 2.0%. Federal funds rates began to decline in June. Public notice of the change to lower interest rates came in July, when the Federal Reserve began a series of seven .5% reductions in the discount rate, which brought it down to 8.5% by December. Ten-year treasury rates dropped from 13.9% in April to 10.5% at the end of the year, and the S&P 500 rose 31% between July and December.

The Fed's move to lower interest rates reflected its reaction to the depressed state of the economy, crises in the financial system, and irate politicians. Economists debate whether the Federal Reserve had needlessly prolonged the recession by this time, and what caused the Federal Reserve to persist for so long. They generally blame the delay on the Federal Reserve's desire to establish its credibility as an inflation-fighter after having mistakenly pumped up demand in mid-1980, and on a certain amount of poor information and miscalculation, especially the impression that the economy was already recovering.[45] These judgments can be easily affected by the knowledge in hindsight that inflation in the last half of 1982 averaged less than 1%, and that industrial production continued to decline through December. But we have to offset against this hindsight the fact that, from the Federal Reserve's point of view at the time, rolling twelve months' inflation was still 7% and the annualized monthly rates in April and May were 11.4% and 13.8%—much too high for the Federal Reserve to declare victory. Figure 2.11 indicates the high inflation pattern that the Federal Reserve had to deal with as it began to lower federal funds rates and banks' reserve borrowings, as well as how little lag it showed in reacting as inflation came down.

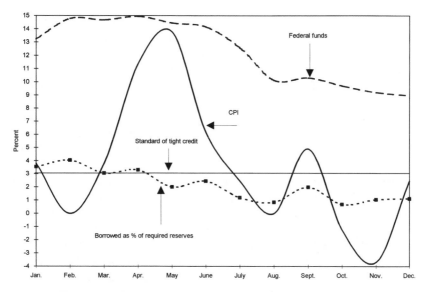

Figure 2.11 1982—federal funds, inflation, and borrowed reserves. Sources: Federal Reserve and Bureau of Labor Statistics.

The Federal Reserve itself emphasized its focus on the general economy, as has Paul Volcker in public comments since then.[46] However, subsequent testimony from Federal Reserve insiders is subject to both hindsight modification and political motives. There is no question that the recession had been unusually long and deep by mid-1982. Industrial production had not risen since 1979 (see figure 1.8 in chapter 1), the interest-sensitive and commodities sectors of the economy were in deep recession, the oil and gas industry was contracting, blue-collar unemployment was over 16%, and bankruptcies were rising sharply. However, staff projections at the May, June, and August FOMC meetings were for the economy to "expand moderately over the balance of 1982," and committee members agreed. This partly reflected the fact that the fiscal stimulus would approach 6% of GNP after the last two stages of the 1981 tax cuts took effect.[47] That this stimulus was slow in coming only became obvious toward the end of 1982, when the economy was still showing few signs of recovery except in housing starts.

The political pressures to ease credit were quite clear. Congress passed the Tax Equality and Fiscal Responsibility Act of 1982 in August, reversing many of the corporate tax benefits given out in 1981, and thereby taking at least a modest step toward the fiscal responsibility that the Federal Reserve regularly preached. Midterm congressional elections were pending in November, and the sentiment in Congress and most of the administration was uniformly in favor of lower interest rates. Senator

Byrd had introduced a bill to take more political control over the Federal Reserve and force lower interest rates, and Treasury Secretary Don Regan had begun a publicly announced review of what the administration's powers over the Federal Reserve should be. James Baker, then White House chief of staff, had also suddenly veered into opposition to Federal Reserve policy. These were balls that, once set rolling, could be difficult to control.[48]

These pressures notwithstanding, the critical factor in the timing of the Federal Reserve's shift to much lower interest rates appears to have been the sudden crisis in the banking system caused by credit problems among the less-developed countries, particularly Mexico, and in the oil industry. These problems were great enough to threaten the integrity of the financial system for the first time since 1933. They also brought the financial community around to a different focus than inflation. It was only after the Federal Reserve was well on its way to lowering interest rates in the second half of 1982 that inflation rates dropped to under 1% and that it became evident that the economy was not already recovering, giving the new policy the hindsight justification of good economics.

The importance of the banking crisis to the Fed's timing in easing interest rates generally validates the views of neo-Keynesians who emphasize that the Fed's ultimate concern is the safety of the financial system rather than inflation. The timing was also of critical importance to investors. From both points of view we are justified in giving considerable attention to this crisis, to which I will now turn.*

The financial problems of the less-developed countries' (LDCs) first surfaced in 1980, when Brazil appeared likely to default on approximately $90 billion of international debt.[49] But Brazil's problems could be ascribed at least in part to high oil prices and its lack of indigenous oil supplies. When the possibility of Poland defaulting on its $2.4 billion of international debt arose in 1981 it could be ascribed to international geopolitics. But when Mexico could not meet its obligations on $85 billion of international debt in August 1982, the international financial system appeared fundamentally at risk. Mexico had oil, even if its price was falling somewhat. Mexico's problems were too much debt, low commodities prices, weak export markets, and high interest rates—common problems throughout South America.

Mexico's problems were so closely intertwined with the timing in which the Federal Reserve eased credit that it is difficult to avoid ascrib-

---

*The savings and loan crisis was also raging at this time, but I will deal with it in chapter 7 in the context of the mortgage securities market. The savings and loan crisis never challenged the safety of the system as the banking industry's problems did.

ing the change in policy to this crisis. The Federal Reserve was acutely aware of the Mexican crisis before it blossomed in August. There had been a run on the peso in February, Volcker and other officials met monthly with Mexican finance officials, the Federal Reserve engaged in several months of window-dressing Mexico's reserve figures, and in July the Federal Reserve lent the Mexican government $700 million under intercountry swap procedures as both sides tried unsuccessfully to wait out the markets until the new president of Mexico took office.[50] Finally, flight capital became so great that Mexico's credit collapsed. The Federal Reserve organized a temporary international bailout package in an atmosphere of great crisis during August 1982. Negotiations among the IMF, the commercial banks, and the Mexican government finally bore fruit in renegotiated bank loans in early 1983. But Argentina, Brazil, Venezuela, Peru, Chile, Colombia, Ecuador, and the Philippines—any number of countries—had the same problems as Mexico and required similar protracted negotiations. The implications for the money center banks were profound, since the ten largest U.S. banks had $50 billion in loans to these countries—double the banks' equity at the end of 1982. For the broader population of banks, 150 had LDC loans averaging 165% of capital.[51] The *Wall Street Journal* carried November 1982 headlines featuring fear of a "world banking bust." Alan Greenspan, a past chairman of the president's Council of Economic Advisors and future chairman of the Federal Reserve Board, said, "As we read the numbers, the chances of a dangerous breakdown are the greatest in a half century."[52] To Paul Volcker, the international financial strains posed a threat "essentially without precedent in the postwar world."[53] Secretary of State Shultz spoke of an international "debt bomb."[54] In response, the IMF was brought into debt negotiations with the less-developed countries as a nonpolitical supervisor, and the IMF emergency fund was expanded from $7.1 billion to $19 billion in January 1983. But the LDC default problem surged on. New countries joined the default list in 1983—Nigeria, Venezuela, Colombia—and the original fixit packages began to come unglued. The LDC borrowers remained chronic credit problems throughout the 1980s.

The crisis with the LDC borrowers coincided with a surge in domestic loan problems due to the decline in oil prices, rising real estate defaults, serious farm credit problems, and near bankruptcies among trade-sensitive companies such as Chrysler and International Harvester. Nonperforming loans of the top ten banks rose 51% in 1981 to $7.1 billion and 68% in 1982 to $11.9 billion, as can be seen in table 2.1. The true trend was even worse than this, as very few LDC loans were classified as nonperforming at this stage.

These combined domestic and international problems genuinely threatened the stability of the money center banks, and therefore the whole financial system. Table 2.2 indicates for each of the ten largest money

Table 2.1. Money Center Banks' Nonperforming Loans ($ Millions)

Institution	1979	1980	1981	1982	1983	1984
Bank of America	304	396	1,223	2,404	3,314	3,507
Bankers Trust	318	318	400	444	558	708
Chase Manhattan	869	900	1,400	1,900	2,200	2,000
Chemical	398	324	524	737	876	1,196
Citicorp	1,095	800	1,000	1,700	2,100	2,400
Continental Illinois	446	444	653	1,900	1,900	1,900[1]
First Chicago	904	831	564	847	854	758
Manufacturers Hanover	360	351	624	786	831	1,700
J. P. Morgan	134	111	377	518	628	948
Security Pacific	194	216	333	676	865	1,123
Totals	5,022	4,691	7,098	11,912	14,126	16,240
% Increase		−7%	51%	68%	19%	15%

[1]Uses 1983 value because the FDIC took over nonperforming loans in 1984.

center banks as of 12/31/82 their combined nonperforming domestic assets[55] and loans to LDC countries with serious financial problems* as a percentage of total equity plus reserves for losses. For the top ten banks, these combined nonperforming assets and loans to troubled LDCs averaged 189% of total equity and reserves, and at Manufacturers Hanover Trust and Bank of America were over 250%. This is not to suggest that the banks would lose 100% on these loans, but clearly the banks' creditworthiness and liquidity were threatened.

I do not want to overstate these loan problems. The operations of most of the money center banks were not seriously disequilibriated as early as 1982. Their stocks at the end of 1982 were still level with the end of 1981, which was only 15% under performance versus the S&P 500. However, several major banks had stumbled seriously already, and the fear among regulators was that confidence in the system could be destroyed rather easily if precautions were not taken quickly.

As early as 1981, Bank of America had problems with escalating real estate and agricultural loans. Its net income dropped from $646 million in 1980 to $447 million in 1981 as nonperforming loans jumped from $396 million to $1.2 billion. Nonperforming loans jumped further to $2.4 billion in 1982, or $3.1 billion if all loans past-due ninety days were in-

*Principally Mexico, Brazil, Argentina, Venezuela, Colombia, Peru, Ecuador, and the Philippines. Total troubled LDC loans were clearly larger, but individual loans were not disclosed in bank financial statements when less than .75% of total loans. Virtually no East European loan problems were disclosed in 1982 even though Poland, Rumania, Hungary, and Yugoslavia were in serious financial trouble.

Table 2.2. Money Center Banks' Nonperforming Loan Exposure—December 31, 1982 ($ Millions)

Institution	Equity	Reserves	Domestic Nonperf'g Assets	LDC Loans[1]	Domestic Non-performing + LDC as a % of Equity + Reserves
Bank of America	4,300	670	2,500	10,100	254%
Bankers Trust	1,400	232	295	2,400	165%
Chase Manhattan	3,300	558	700	6,100	176%
Chemical	1,900	318	624	4,300	222%
Citicorp	4,800	771	551	10,100	191%
Continental Illinois	1,700	381	1,706	2,500	202%
First Chicago	1,500	203	550	1,800	138%
Manufacturers Hanover	2,500	371	556	7,200	270%
J. P. Morgan	2,700	346	350	4,200	149%
Security Pacific	1,500	298	487	1,800	127%

Sources: Annual reports of institutions.

[1]Loans to identified countries, principally Mexico, Brazil, Argentia, Venezuela, Peru, Colombia, and the Philippines.

cluded. While nonperforming loans rose sixfold in two years, the bank's annual provision for loan losses only doubled. Had the annual provision kept pace with nonperformance, huge losses would have resulted.

Crocker National Bank in San Francisco, which was not in the top ten but was still one of the nation's more prominent banks, had similar problems beginning in 1981. Nonperforming loans rose from $165 million in 1979 to $434 million in 1981—half in real estate—and net income was halved. If loan loss provisions had kept pace with nonperforming loans, the bank would have reported a loss. England's Midland Bank bought a minority position in 1981 and was invited to inject further equity in January 1982, only to have nonperforming loans rise further to $771 million. The bank also had an unusually large position in LDC loans for its size. LDC loans and domestic nonperforming assets at the end of 1982 were 233% of total equity plus reserves.

Problems also came to light at Continental Illinois Bank & Trust in mid-1982, as its nonperforming loans tripled from $643 million to $1.9 billion due to problems with oil industry borrowers. Continental Illinois was recognized as one of the five best managed companies in the U.S. in 1978 by *Dun's Review* and was a leader in lending to the oil and gas industry. Continental's loan losses in oil and gas were historically only half that of its other commercial and industrial loans, but it became much too concentrated in energy lending. Its energy portfolio doubled in 1980 and rose a further 50% in 1981. Its oil and gas portfolio accounted for two-thirds of its loan losses in the next two years when oil prices declined.[56]

Continental Illinois' greatest problem was with the loans it bought from Penn Square Bank in Oklahoma City, which was closed by the FDIC in July 1982. Headquartered in a local shopping center and with total assets of only $30 million in 1977, Penn Square Bank went on a rampage of speculative oil and gas lending after Billy Paul "Beep" Jennings, an unindicted coconspirator in the Four Seasons Nursing Home scandal, became chairman in 1980.[57] By March 1982, its assets had grown to $437 million; it had attracted brokered deposits of over $100 million from over 170 credit unions, savings and loans, and small banks; and it had resold over $2 billion in energy loans to some of the top banks in America. Executive Vice President Bill Patterson, who led the charge, partied hard, drank beer from his boot, and even wore a Mickey Mouse beanie or duck decoy hat on business calls to attract attention. His loan targets were the roughest, most promotional elements of the oil and gas industry, particularly drilling fund managers who secured their loans with letters of credit from their investors. Director Carl W. Swan got loans to affiliates of this sort amounting to $342 million—far over the legal limit for the bank. Patterson himself got a $3 million line of credit and borrowed under it even before the board of directors approved it. Documentation was scanty and sloppy, the liens on some collateral went unperfected, and illegal insider lending was significant. In 1980 and 1981 when regulators visited to review the bank's loans, it warehoused a number of them with friendly banks.

When Penn Square's problems began to show up in the second quarter of 1982 and it experienced a liquidity crisis, the FDIC was unable to find a merger partner for it on any terms. On July 6, 1982 the Comptroller of the Currency closed the bank. Attention then shifted to the banks that had purchased $2 billion in energy loans from Penn Square. At the top of the list was Continental Illinois Bank & Trust. In a fateful slip of its internal controls, it bought almost $1 billion of oil and gas loans from Penn Square Bank in less than 18 months between January 1981 and June 1982; by 1984 its losses on these loans would exceed $550 million.

Two other scandalous oil industry bankruptcies in which Continental Illinois was the lead bank—Nucorp Energy and Good Hope Refinery—surfaced almost simultaneously with the Penn Square closing. Nucorp Energy filed for bankruptcy in July 1982 owing $300 million to banks, with Continental Illinois at the top of the list for $173 million. Nucorp was an oil field supply company created out of a small real estate company that made fifteen acquisitions between 1980 and 1981 and saw its stock grow 2,100% in two years. In 1981, when the oil business began to slow down sharply, Nucorp's CEO, Richard C. Burns, made a huge gamble that it would recover quickly, and made forward commitments to purchase oil pipe for over $600 million in anticipation of shortages. When the shortages didn't come and orders from customers failed to appear,

Burns began "pre-billing" orders—which is to say, faking them. Nucorp's cash needs spiraled upward, as the fake orders produced receivables but no cash, until it was forced into bankruptcy.

Good Hope Refinery filed for bankruptcy on $1.4 billion of debts in September 1982. Again Continental Illinois was at the top of the list, this time for $165 million. Good Hope Refinery had one of the largest refineries in the U.S. and 350,000 acres of gas holdings, primarily in West Texas, but it was run with lawless abandon by Jack Stanley, a forty-three-year-old high school dropout. He had no formal budgets, no systems, and a phony list of directors. The company had already been in bankruptcy from 1975 to 1980, when it ran roughshod over its creditors, doubling the refinery's assets while holding its creditors at bay. Now Good Hope Refinery had piled up a huge list of 1,800 creditors again.

Continental Illinois also had loan problems outside the oil industry. It lent aggressively to less-developed countries so that by the end of 1982 its loans to troubled LDC borrowers totaled $2.5 billion. Its nonperforming real estate loans totaled $385 million by the end of 1982. Its combined domestic nonperforming assets and troubled LDC loans at the end of 1982 were 202% of its equity and reserves—the fourth highest of the money center banks.

Continental Illinois reported 1982 net income of $77 million versus $254 million in 1981, and the Comptroller of the Currency placed it under a "formal agreement" that gave the Comptroller extensive management control over the bank. Continental Illinois struggled thereafter. It had persistent problems attracting large depositors, on which it depended inordinately, and increasingly relied on foreigners and the federal funds market. Its net interest margin on earning assets never recovered, while most of the money center banks' margins expanded in succeeding years, helping to overcome their mounting loan loss provisions. Lee Iacocca, making a speech to the Chicago Economics Club in early 1983, prompted Continental Illinois' CEO, Roger Anderson, to leave the dais by quipping, "If I had known how easy it was to get a loan from Continental Illinois, I would never have gone to the government."[58] Anderson couldn't take the joke, because it wasn't a joke. Continental Illinois was in trouble.

The oil loans that began to plague Continental Illinois in 1982 were also a problem for a number of other banks. The FDIC had to arrange mergers in 1982 to save the Abilene National Bank ($310 million in deposits) and Oklahoma National Bank and Trust ($134 million in deposits)—two normally conservative banks with extensive oil industry loans. The Texas banks had an alarming 236% increase in nonperforming loans in 1982 at the top eight banks. Most of these banks still reported increased profits, but only because their allowances for loan losses failed to rise in line with nonperforming loans. Federal regulators commenced a special review of the ten largest Southwest energy lenders.

It became apparent how far the problems with oil loans had spread when Seattle-First National Bank, better known as Seafirst, began to have serious troubles related to the loans it had bought from Penn Square. Seafirst had enjoyed a dramatic twenty-year growth into the top twenty U.S. banks under the leadership of William M. Jenkins, but by the middle of 1982 Seafirst had bought over $400 million in oil loans from Penn Square and energy loans were up from zero in 1979 to $1.25 billion versus $10 billion in total assets. Many of the credit review procedures on these oil loans were defective. Some files contained no more than names, addresses, and credit authorizations. Some of the loan approvals seemed vague because they had not gone through proper channels, but the upper management squelched complainers. Just three weeks before Penn Square was closed down, Seafirst was still buying loans from it.

Chairman Jenkins admitted that the relationship with Penn Square made Seafirst "look dumb," but it was worse than that. The bank had been frightfully mismanaged and was going broke. Too much of its assets were in energy loans and too many of these were going bad. Seafirst had a 1982 loss of $90 million after making provisions for $288 million in loan losses—almost $170 million on Penn Square loans. Nonperforming loans rose to $800 million versus capital of only $458 million. That was too much for depositors, and they quickly began a run on the bank. What became common emergency responses followed: Jenkins and the rest of the "growth" crew were fired or retired, Arthur Andersen & Co. was retained to do an independent review of the bank's assets, the dividend was cut from $1.44 per share to 48 cents, the headquarters building was sold for over $120 million, and the Federal Reserve pushed a group of fourteen banks led by Bankers Trust in New York to provide a "safety net" loan of $1.5 billion to replace fleeing deposits.

By April 1983, Seafirst was past saving. It had a first quarter loss of $133 million, and Arthur Andersen & Co. indicated that a further write-off of up to $85 million was called for. The new chairman, Richard P. Cooley, went to Washington to brief federal regulators on the bank's problems, and Salomon Brothers was hired to seek out an acquirer that would give some value to Seafirst's 40% share of the deposit market in Washington state because it had little, if any, net worth. Bank of America struck a deal to buy the bank for $125 million in cash plus $117.5 million in "contingent" preferred stock. The preferred stock was structured so that its eventual value depended on the results of the now $900 million classified loan portfolio. If losses on classified loans exceeded $50 million over the next five years, the value of the preferred stock would be reduced dollar for dollar to a minimum of $9.4 million. Its final value in 1988 was $16.8 million.

Given the scale of the problems in the less-developed countries and among some money center banks, it is almost petty to bring up the problems of a few marginal dealers in the treasury market as part of the stimulus to the Federal Reserve to lower interest rates. Nonetheless, the default of Drysdale Securities on $2 billion of repurchase market borrowings on May 17, 1982, just the day before an FOMC meeting that marked the beginning of credit easing, was bound to affect the psychology of FOMC members. The Federal Reserve was directly responsible for overseeing the treasury market, and there was a brief crisis that challenged the infrastructure of the treasury market when Chase Manhattan Bank refused to honor its repurchase market obligations related to Drysdale, as we shall see in chapter 6. Drysdale was followed by another $2 billion default at Lombard Wall Government Securities in August, and the Federal Reserve was well aware of related problems in Charles Atkins' mini-empire, which included New York Hanseatic Corp.—a recognized treasury dealer.

Thus, there was a powerful confluence of pressures on the Federal Reserve to lower interest rates in mid-1982—the extended economic recession, pressures from the administration and Congress, the problems of the less-developed countries, and the deterioration in the soundness of the nation's financial system. The only opposing pressure was from convinced monetarists. When M1 grew at an annualized average rate of 16% between August and November 1982 they became alarmed, but the Federal Reserve simply announced in October that it was reversing the historic shift in focus on money supply that it had adopted in October 1979 and would place "much less than usual weight" on it.[59] When M2 grew 33.3% in January 1983 and 23% in February because of banks' new money market deposit accounts, the Federal Reserve simply rebased its estimates of acceptable M2 growth to exclude the explosion in January and February, and directed its principal attention to "total debt of domestic non-financial sectors" rather than to money supply. The Federal Reserve was determined to lower interest rates.

The decline in interest rates ended in 1983 once it became clear that the economy was recovering. Not a single change in the discount rate occurred in 1983. The board turned down fourteen requests by district Federal Reserve banks to reduce their rates and three requests to increase them during 1983.[60] In May through August, the Federal Reserve began to tighten credit slightly in response to the rapid economic recovery then underway and the expansion of consumer credit for new homes and autos. A rapid rise in the CRB futures price index, outlined in figure 2.12, from 246 in June to 279 in August (80% annualized) appeared to confirm that inflation was heating up again. The federal funds rate rose from 8.6% in May to 9.6% in August. Banks' borrowed reserves rose from 0.7% in February 1983 to 2.2% in August, and stayed near there through the rest of the year.

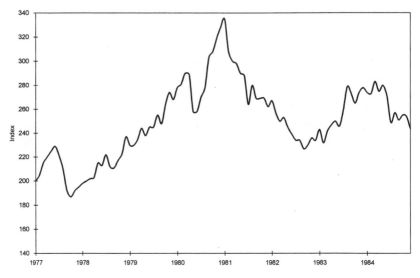

Figure 2.12 The CRB Futures Price Index. Source: Commodities Research Bureau.

At the beginning of 1984, the Federal Reserve expected inflation to increase to between 4.5% and 5%, and perhaps more if the dollar weakened significantly. The Federal Reserve clearly expected the twin federal budget and foreign trade deficits to produce greater pressures in this direction, and so the minutes of FOMC meetings early in the year indicated a general preference for tighter credit and higher rates.[61] By mid-1984 the recovery was the strongest since the Korean War. Industrial production was up 18.5% from December 1982. Credit demands were exceptionally heavy from government, business, and consumers as total nonfinancial sector debt increased 13.4%. Real consumer credit, in particular, was growing at over 15%, outstripping disposable income by almost ten percentage points, as can be seen by referring back to figure 2.5. Faced with this strength, the Federal Reserve moved federal funds rates up from 9% at the beginning of 1984 to over 11% by April.

These credit-tightening steps confirmed the Federal Reserve's will to contain inflation despite the risks of aborting economic recovery and incurring political disfavor, and established that the earlier decline in inflation was not simply a cyclical phenomenon. William Greider has outlined extensively the opinion conflicts within the Federal Reserve with respect to the wisdom of these two credit tightening steps in 1983 and 1984 and the contrary political pressures from Congress and from some officials within the Reagan administration as they looked ahead to the 1984 elections, but the bottom line is that the Federal Reserve tightened.[62]

In retrospect, the impact on the financial markets and the economy was quite clear. The S&P 500 was effectively stalled around 165 from May 1983 through the end of 1984, and ten-year treasury rates rose from 10.5% to 13.5%. Industrial production flattened out from mid-1984 through mid-1986. Inflation (CPI) dropped from approximately 4.5% to 3.5%, and growth in the producer price index dropped from 2.5% to under 1%. Thus, expectations in many respects worked quickly in the direction of the Federal Reserve's intentions.

Milton Friedman predicted at the time that there would be a sharp recession and rapid growth in inflation, neither of which occurred. This period was disastrous for money supply theorists, and an institutional victory for the Federal Reserve.

All thought of further credit tightening was set aside in midyear, however, when a number of financial collapses, led by that of Continental Illinois Bank & Trust, revealed how fragile the banking system was. Neo-Keynesians could rightfully say again that the Federal Reserve's ultimate loyalty was to the stability of the financial system.

Continental Illinois had never recovered from the problems that became evident in 1982 at the time of Penn Square Bank's collapse. It lost commercial and industrial loans during the expansion of 1983–1984, its net interest margin as a percentage of earning assets did not grow in 1982–1983 as interest rates declined and other banks' margins rose, and it was shunned by large domestic depositors, which forced it into sourcing approximately 50% of its deposits from abroad. Profits in 1983 were only 40% of 1981 at a time when other money center banks were setting records. The weakness that had been creeping up on the bank is vividly portrayed by figure 2.13, which compares Continental Illinois's stock price with an unweighted average of the other money center banks from 1979 to 1984. In 1982 its stock price had dropped from 120% of the other nine money center banks to approximately 60%, and then in five months in 1984 it declined to under 20%.

Concerns about the seriousness of the bank's condition escalated from the turn of the year through April 1984. President John Perkins resigned in December 1983. Chairman Roger Anderson was forced to take early retirement in February 1984, and the bank arranged to sell its credit card operation in order to bolster reported profits for the first quarter of 1984. First quarter profits, reported in April, revealed an increase in non-performing loans from $1.9 billion to $2.3 billion and an operating loss when adjusted for the profit on the sale of the credit card unit. What is more, Charter Oil, to which Continental Illinois was a major lender, declared bankruptcy following the end of the quarter. Continental Illinois' stock dropped from $21.75 at the end of 1983 to $13.75 by the end of April 1984. Rumors that the bank might declare bankruptcy swirled in early May, European and Japanese depositors withdrew several billion dollars, the bank borrowed almost $4 billion from the Chicago Federal

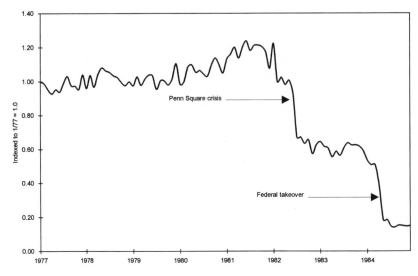

Figure 2.13 Continental Illinois stock price relative to nine money center banks. Source: *Wall Street Journal.*

Reserve on May 11, and its stock dropped further to $12. Continental Illinois put together a private safety net on May 14 of almost $5 billion in credit from sixteen banks led by Morgan Guaranty Trust Company, but deposit outflows continued unabated as the bank's overnight borrowing ballooned to $8 billion.

The stage had been reached at which the nation's ninth largest bank would fail unless the government stepped in to save it. On May 17 the FDIC announced a temporary stopgap of $2 billion in new capital for Continental Illinois, plus a commitment to protect all of the bank's depositors, irrespective of whether they exceeded the $100,000 FDIC deposit limit, as well as creditors of the holding company. This was a crucial commitment, as insured depositors had only $3 billion at stake versus $30 billion uninsured, and the bankruptcy of the holding company would have created enormous credibility problems for the other money center banks.*

---

*Federal Deposit Insurance Corporation, 1984 Annual Report, Washington, DC: Federal Deposit Insurance Corporation, 1985, p. 4. The rescue of the holding company was very controversial. The holding company's rescue stemmed from many factors besides fear of the ripple effect on other bank holding companies, including uncertainty whether the bank was still solvent and only had a funding problem, the ability of holding company bondholders to fight or thwart closing the bank and reopening it under federal control if it was not insolvent, and the local political consequences for branch banking and New York banks'

The FDIC took full control of the bank, eliminated dividends, and in the ensuing two months tried to find a merger partner for the bank. By mid-July, however, it was apparent that no private resolution of the bank's problems was possible. The extent of its nonperforming loans was too uncertain, and its daily funding shortfall had risen to $14 billion.

A permanent solution was devised by the FDIC, Federal Reserve, and Comptroller of the Currency, with the advice of Morgan Stanley, in late July. The FDIC took over $3.5 billion of Continental Illinois' borrowings at the Federal Reserve in exchange for $5.1 billion of the bank's problem loans. Continental Illinois charged off $990 million in bad loans, resulting in a second quarter loss of $1.16 billion and book common equity of under $700 million. The FDIC also injected $1.0 billion of capital into the bank via the holding company in return for 80% of the bank's equity, and potentially 100%, depending on the writeoff experience with the $5.1 billion of problem loans.[63] John Swearingen, former chairman of Amoco, was installed as chairman and CEO of the holding company. William Ogden, former vice-chairman and chief financial officer of Chase Manhattan, was installed as chairman and CEO of the bank. Treasury Secretary Donald Regan blasted the plan as "unauthorized and unlegislated expansion of federal guarantees in contravention of executive branch policy," but he was ignored.[64] The bank's stock dropped to $4¾, but shareholders nonetheless approved the plan in September. It was their only choice. In the fourth quarter of 1984 the bank returned to modest profitability, earning $36 million.

In the heat of this crisis the S&P 500 dropped 6%, and ten-year treasury rates rose from 12.5% to 13.5%, but these losses were more than reversed in the easier credit conditions that ensued.

Continental Illinois was not a self-contained problem, which of course was the fear of the federal authorities. Skepticism about the health of other money center banks spread quickly, threatening a broader run on the banks. Manufacturers Hanover Trust and Bank of America were particularly affected because of their large LDC loans. Their stocks indicated the market's measure of their problems. Manufacturers' stock fell

---

share of the Chicago commercial loan market. This was also the first time that the federal authorities had dealt with an insolvent bank of this size, so policies were not well developed. When the major Texas banks subsequently failed, the holding companies were not rescued.

The impact on the securities issued by Continental Illinois Holding was obviously significant. Its preferred stock fell from $45½ at the end of April to $14⅞ at the end of June, but recovered to $38 by October. It had two note issues due in 1989. One dropped from $50 to a low of $37 and recovered to $52. The other dropped from $100 to a low of $85 and recovered to $97.

40% versus 6% for the S&P 500 in the first six months of 1984, and Bank of America's stock fell 35%. Stocks of the seven other money center banks fell 21%.

A number of lesser, but important financial disasters coincided with the collapse of Continental Illinois, increasing the general concern about the fragility of the financial system. A run began on Financial Corporation of America's savings and loan subsidiary, American Savings & Loan Association, in midyear, partly in reaction to the collapse of Continental Illinois. Financial Corporation of America (FCA) had expanded pell-mell under the flamboyant leadership of Charles Knapp, a forty-nine-year-old former investment banker. Armed with new powers under the Garn-St. Germain Bill, Knapp tried all of the financial angles simultaneously, funded by brokered large-denomination CDs. He acquired Mark Taper's First Charter Financial Corp., which raised FCA's assets from $10 to $20 billion. He aggressively pushed risky real estate construction and development loans, made fixed-rate mortgage loans, leveraged the bank in the mortgage securities market, bought junk bonds, and even tried to greenmail American Express. The profits in all this activity were obliterated when short-term rates began to rise again in 1983–1984, and, under pressure from the Securities and Exchange Commission, FCA was obliged to restate its second quarter 1984 earnings from a profit of $31 million to a loss of $107 million. Its stock plunged from $15 in April to a low of $4 in August, and a run on the bank began. It lost almost $7 billion of deposits in the third quarter. The bank sought help in August from the Federal Home Loan Bank (FHLB) system and the Federal Savings and Loan Insurance Corporation (FSLIC), the price of which was that Charles Knapp was forced out. Following the Continental Illinois pattern, federal authorities guaranteed all of the savings and loan's deposits and provided $4 billion in aid, $3.3 billion of it through the FHLB of San Francisco. Had they not guaranteed all depositors, the resulting turmoil would have been imponderable. Orange County alone had $155 million on deposit at the time, and up to $400 million at its peak.

At this point Crocker National Bank's loan problems also came to a head. The bank lost $121 million in the first quarter of 1984 due to non-performing real estate, oil, and agriculture loans, and continued to deteriorate during the rest of 1984. In October, Midland Bank received approval to raise its stock ownership from 57% to 100% and put its massive international capital behind the bank. Crocker lost $324 million for the year.

First National Bank of Chicago, Continental Illinois' neighbor, which had been gradually recovering from a loan debacle at the end of the 1970s, was forced to report a loss of $70 million in the third quarter of 1984 as a result of a Comptroller of the Currency review that raised the level of its nonperforming loans.

Table 2.3. The Eight Largest Texas Banks

	1980	1981	1982	1983	1984
Totals					
Nonperf'g loans ($B)	0.2	0.5	1.5	2.3	2.9
Real Estate loans ($B)	8.2	10.3	13.8	19.9	25.5
Growth Rates					
Nonperf'g loans	—	89%	236%	46%	27%
Real Estate loans	—	26%	34%	44%	28%
Nonperf'g + real est loans + past due over 90 days as % common + reserves	222%	234%	285%	346%	395%

Source: Data from annual reports of eight largest Texas banks.

Banking conditions also continued to deteriorate in the Southwest. The FDIC declared 1st Midland Bank of Texas insolvent in October 1983, after losses for eight months totaled $121 million and the bank could not muster further collateral for borrowings from the Federal Reserve. It was already borrowing $535 million. 1st Midland's $1.4 billion of assets ranked it second only to the insolvency of Franklin National Bank in 1974. First Oklahoma Bancorp, the largest holding company in Oklahoma, was also in distress. It had a third quarter loss of $58 million, eliminated its dividend, and was struggling to maintain deposits.

The largest Texas banks were also becoming a problem. Interfirst reported a loss of $194 million in the third quarter of 1983 as its loan loss provisions skyrocketed to $430 million. It experienced a short-lived run on deposits. At the end of 1984 the combined nonperforming loans of the eight largest Texas banks were more than ten times 1980 levels, as can be seen in table 2.3. However, the true picture was even worse than this. The banks' nonperforming loans reflected only minor real estate defaults, but Texas real estate was coming under great pressure because of its dependence on the oil and gas industry. The office vacancy rate in Houston, for example, was 28%. The Texas banks had increased their real estate loan exposure by over 200% between 1980 and 1984, as is also outlined in table 2.3, in order to sustain their income growth as oil lending opportunities declined. As a result, the combined value of nonperforming loans, loans more than ninety days past due, and real estate loans rose from 222% of equity plus reserves in 1980 to 395% in 1984 (table 2.3). If real estate, which was very sensitive to interest rates, slipped into the nonperforming loan category, these banks would be in very serious trouble.

Financial strains were also spreading outside the banking industry. Baldwin-United Corp., a Cincinnati-based insurance company, couldn't meet its short-term debts in March 1983, and went into bankruptcy in

September 1983. Baldwin-United had sold pianos and organs for almost 100 years, but had also started selling single premium deferred annuities through securities brokers in 1979 and by 1981 had annual premiums of $1.5 billion. This enormous cash flow stimulated an acquisition spree in which the company bought S&H Green Stamps for $356 million and Mortgage Guaranty Insurance Corp. (MGIC) for $1.2 billion. The company overpaid for MGIC and suddenly found itself seriously over-extended when state insurance commissions in Arkansas and Indiana obstructed the company's intention to pay off the short-term debt for the acquisition with MGIC's own financial assets. Insurance sales immediately plummeted, customers began redeeming policies, MGIC's guarantee business dropped, and state regulators began restricting asset movements to protect policyholders.

Baldwin-United's problems led to scrutiny of its principal competitor selling single premium deferred annuities, the Charter Company, which had sold over $4 billion of annuities. Investors became concerned about the company's accounting, its investment of insurance premiums in its own oil refining and other businesses, its high leverage, and its lavish management style. Sales in 1983 dropped to $850 million from $1.7 billion in 1982, and the company was overwhelmed by redemption requests by the time it filed for bankruptcy in mid-1984.

There were also severe credit problems in the farm economy due to low grain prices, high interest rates, and excessive debts, as I will review in chapter 8. These problems were reflected in rural bank defaults throughout the early 1980s. Problems in the Farm Credit System were just around the corner, and would get prominent publicity in mid-1985. However, the full story of the collapse of the Farm Credit System will be covered in volume 2.

In the succeeding chapters on the stock and bond markets we will find that results in those markets were closely related to monetary policy and economic recovery, and that there was a persistent layer of optimism, despite the fact that many of the most astute financial minds believed the U.S. was facing a financial crisis of historic proportions that threatened to produce a depression similar to the 1930s.

George Soros, the famed speculator, was a good example. He completely dropped out of the markets at the time because of his distress over the course of international events. He later concluded that, "If it had not been for the successful intervention of the monetary authorities, the international debt crisis would have led to a collapse of the banking system."[65] To Soros and his like, the recoveries in the securities markets and economy reflected a triumph of institutional expertise, leadership, and statesmanship that was unrelated to theory.

Money Supply and Federal Reserve Policy

It is worth focusing specifically on the Federal Reserve's responses to changes in money supply, since for almost three years between October 1979 and mid-1982 the Federal Reserve was prepared to raise or lower interest rates based on the behavior of money supply, irrespective of the current state of the economy or inflation. At least for a while, the focus on money supply was an important part of the new regime.

I have already noted the September and October 1979 debates on the Federal Reserve Open Market Committee once Paul Volcker became Chairman, and their ultimate resolution in favor of stricter control over the monetary aggregates irrespective of the effect on interest rates. The policy shift in October 1979 was followed by three months in which monthly M1 growth dropped to under 2%, as can be seen in figure 2.14, but monthly M1 growth climbed back to almost 11% in January and February 1980 when inflation psychology became extreme. M1 growth was stopped by the monetary policy component of President Carter's March 1980 anti-inflation program, particularly the new consumer credit controls. M1 declined 1.5% in March and a striking 17.3% in April. It was still declining slightly (1.9%) in May 1980 when the Federal Reserve abruptly reduced the federal funds rate from 17.6% to 11% and dismantled the consumer credit controls.

Money supply growth surged, however, as quickly as the Federal Re-

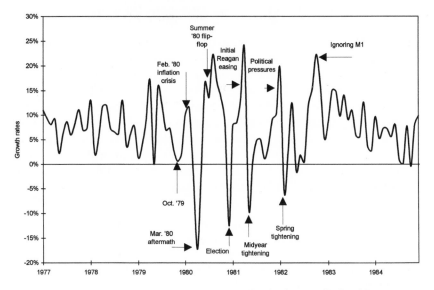

Figure 2.14 M1 monthly growth rates (annualized). Source: Federal Reserve.

serve relaxed its efforts to control it. M1 growth reached 22.3% in August and averaged 15.2% from June through November 1980, prompting the Federal Reserve to move the federal funds rate back up to 19% after the elections. M1 responded by declining 12.5% in December. Just as soon as the Federal Reserve reduced rates slightly in February and March 1981, however, M1 growth accelerated again to 13.3% in March and 23.5% in April. From June 1980 through April 1981 M1 growth had averaged 12.0%. This overall rate, and the sharp increases that occurred whenever the Federal Reserve eased credit, provoked considerable concern within the Federal Reserve, the administration, and financial markets, causing the Federal Reserve to raise federal funds rates to over 19% again in mid-1981, despite the weak economy. M1 thereupon dropped 9%, and from May through October 1981 grew at an average annual rate of only 1.0%, which appeared to validate Federal Reserve policy. However, when the Federal Reserve let federal funds drop below 13% at the end of 1981 under pressure from the administration, Congress, and our European trading partners, the monthly M1 growth rates rose sharply to 9.2% in November, 10.3% in December, and a shocking 19.5% in January 1982. This appeared to be persuasive evidence that monetary policy could not be relaxed, so the Fed raised the federal funds rate from 12.4% in December to 14.8% in February. M1 growth correspondingly entered another low growth phase averaging only 1.7% from February to July 1982. The Federal Reserve began to ease credit again in May 1982, and in July began a series of seven .5% cuts in the discount rate so that the federal funds rate fell below 9% by year end. Unfortunately from the point of view of a policy focus on money supply, M1 started to rise again with this easing, averaging over 15% growth from August through November 1982, even though monthly CPI growth rates averaged under 1% in the same period and the economy was in severe recession.*

M1 measures were very erratic and difficult for the Federal Reserve to use as a policy measure during 1980–1982 compared with prior years; these erratic changes are obvious in figure 2.14. The problem stands out equally starkly in terms of standard deviations for M1 and M2, which are outlined in figure 2.15. The standard deviation of M1 monthly growth rates rose from 4% in 1977 through early 1979, to over 9% from mid-1980 through the end of 1982, before dropping back down to 4% again in 1984. While M2 volatility in absolute terms was not as great as M1,

---

*In a recent review of monetary policy in this period, James E. Alt claimed, "The narrow money supply M1 grew exactly as hoped in 1981 and 1982." This was hardly the case. See James E. Alt, "Leaning Into the Wind or Ducking Out of the Storm?" U.S. Monetary Policy in the 1980s," in Alberto Alesina and Geoffrey Carliner (eds.), *Politics and Economics in the Eighties*, NBER Project Report, Chicago: Unviersity of Chicago Press, 1991, p. 46.

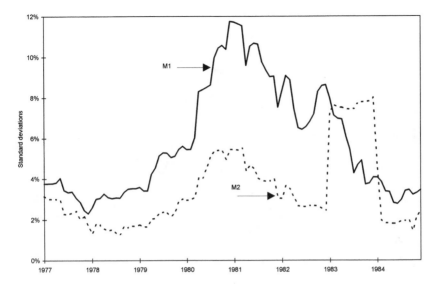

Figure 2.15 Standard deviations for M1 and M2 growth (rolling twelve months). Source: Federal Reserve.

the proportionate increase in volatility from 1981 to 1982 was even greater, from 1.5% to 5%, and even to 8% in 1983. This volatility was due to changes in banking regulations that allowed new types of interest-bearing checking accounts; dramatic variations in the economy; and the consumer credit controls of 1980. Academics and the Federal Reserve expressed this volatility as changes in the velocity of money use, which the Federal Reserve initially passed off as "atypical behavior," but more fundamentally the volatility changes challenged the whole concept of managing the money supply to control inflation.

The contrast in the last half of 1982 between rapid M1 growth, a very depressed economy, and inflation below 1% led to an important announcement on October 7, 1982 that the Federal Reserve was reducing its emphasis on money supply in favor of a broader view of factors affecting inflation and the economy—almost three years to the day since the historic October 6, 1979 announcement that the Federal Reserve's emphasis was shifting to money supply.[66]

The issue of money supply became even more complicated in 1983. The average monthly growth rate for M1 from August 1982 to July 1983 was 12.8%. The Federal Reserve had deemphasized M1 on the technical basis that new forms of deposit accounts were distorting it, but M2, which was not similarly distorted, grew at a 33.3% rate in January 1983 and 23.0% in February, while the inflation rate was only 1.2%. The Federal Reserve made a pragmatic decision that it would simply ignore this

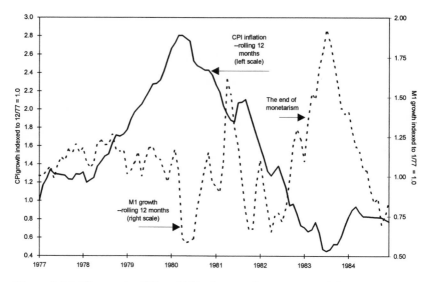

Figure 2.16 Changes in CPI and M1. Sources: Department of Commerce and Federal Reserve.

rapid growth and "rebase" its interpretation of an acceptable growth rate on that following March 1983.[67] Before 1983 was over, the Federal Reserve relegated control of the money supply to a minor policy role, emphasizing instead the "total debt of domestic nonfinancial sectors."[68] This completed the Federal Reserve's transition back to basing monetary policy on general economic and credit conditions—the same basis that had prevailed before October 1979. Such pragmatism proved highly successful as inflation averaged 3.8% in 1983 and 4% in 1984, despite a very strong economic recovery.

The lack of connection between money supply growth and inflation can be visualized in figure 2.16, which indexes the rolling twelve months' growth rates for CPI and M1. Paradoxically, the connection was already broken when money supply theory won over practitioners during the huge rise in inflation between 1978 and 1980. This increase in inflation actually corresponded with a decline in M1 growth rates. Then, as monetary policy won the battle against inflation from 1981 through mid-1982, M1 growth rates were virtually unchanged. The denouement for money supply theory occurred when M1 surged between mid-1982 and the end of 1983, in its most dramatic movement in the seven years covered by figure 2.16, but inflation only rose modestly.* It was not surprising that the

---

*The disjunction between money supply growth and inflation that prevailed after 1979 contrasted with a strong relationship between 1960 and 1978. The difference between the two periods is statistically modeled in James E. Alt, "Leaning

Federal Reserve gave up its emphasis on controlling money supply under these circumstances. As Friedman and Kuttner have shown, the strong correlation between growth in money supply and growth in nominal income in the period 1950–1979 disappeared entirely in the 1980s.[69]

The theory was already losing its appeal before this disjunction, however. There were too many money supply definitions to choose among— old M1, M1-A, M1-B, M2, and M3—and the emphases of the money supply advocates appeared too arbitrary. For example, there were two ways to define M1 to reflect the new forms of deposit accounts, and velocity under the two definitions moved in diametrically opposite directions from 1981 to 1984.[70] There were still scholars who continued to advocate control of the money supply, of course, based on both theory and econometrics, but their arguments appeared too ex post facto rather than predictive. Both the managers of the economy and securities market participants required plainer, rougher guidelines, as Paul Volcker often pointed out.

The Dollar

The foreign exchange value of the dollar appreciated 55% between October 1980 and February 1985[71] with many ramifications. It had a negative impact on the level of economic activity and on the stock prices and credit of many traditional heavy industries such as autos, steel, aluminum, mining, farm equipment, construction equipment, and machine tools. Even the high technology industries of office equipment and semiconductors were negatively affected. The strong dollar held down wage demands in the former industries, which had strong unions that were usually wage leaders, helping to break the cycle of wage demands chasing inflation. The strong dollar also reduced import prices, put a cap on competing domestic prices, and reduced the prices of commodities traded around the world in dollar terms. Farm commodity prices in particular were depressed, creating a crisis in the Farm Credit System in 1985 and for many midwestern banks. Export prices for the commodities on which most South American countries relied were similarly depressed, throwing them into default and threatening the stability of the largest U.S. banks.

I treat the strength of the dollar as an independent factor in the new regime because it was not a conscious object of either monetary or fiscal policy. The Federal Reserve tended to give little attention to the strength

---

Into the Wind or Ducking Out of the Storm?" in Alesina and Carliner, *Politics and Economics in the Eighties*, p. 51.

of the dollar, but such as it did was consistent with my approach. The Federal Open Market Committee's discussions throughout 1983 and 1984 reflected an expectation that the dollar would decline sharply because of the growing trade deficit, rather than correctly anticipating its rising path.[72]

The strength of the dollar under President Reagan was a dramatic change of trend from under President Carter, who was persistently forced into restrictive economic policies because of a weak dollar. In 1981 the dollar rose to its highest level in eleven years, due to high real interest rates, the election of a socialist (President Mitterand) in France, tensions between Poland and Russia, and flight money from South America, especially Mexico. As the dollar rose approximately 15% in 1982, European governments pressed for U.S. intervention in the foreign exchange markets to strengthen their currencies, and were promised it in European summit meetings in April 1983 as part of the bargaining over placing additional missiles in West Germany. The Federal Reserve, in cooperation with West Germany and Japan, began to intervene in the foreign exchange markets in July. The effort was half-hearted, however. Federal Reserve interventions in 1983 had a total value of only $333 million, and only $288 million in 1984. Actions by foreign authorities were larger, but still only totaled $2.25 billion in 1984.[73] Despite these official efforts, the dollar rose 6% to a new peak in 1983 and a further 10% in 1984. Dramatic government intervention by both the United States and its major trading partners did not occur until the Plaza Agreement of February 1985, by which time the dollar had risen a further 7.5% — 55% above the October 1980 level before President Reagan was elected — and the more activist James Baker had become secretary of the Treasury, trading places with Donald Regan. The Plaza Agreement will be dealt with in the next volume.

Prior administrations would probably have tried to restrain the rise in the dollar by having the Federal Reserve sell dollars. However, the Reagan administration, and particularly Treasury Secretary Don Regan, took pride in the strength of the dollar, considering it a measure of international approval for its policies. Intervention also ran against the administration's free markets credo. The administration decided in March 1981 as a matter of principle that it would not intervene in the foreign exchange markets. Federal Reserve intervention was absent until July 1983 and inconsequential until 1985.*

Federal Reserve Annual Report 1981, p. 26. There is no question that the Federal Reserve was not consciously managing the course of the dollar. There were no staff reports on the dollar cited in FOMC meetings during 1981–1984, and very little discussion of the dollar at FOMC meetings. Attention was focused almost totally on inflation, the state of the economy, money supply, and interest rates,

Don Regan believed that flight capital coming to the U.S. as a "safe haven" was important to the dollar's strength, along the lines of my argument that a change in regimes took place. Capital flight from the less-developed countries generally began in 1979 and was particularly strong during 1981 to 1984. It also came out of France after President Mitterand and the Socialists gained power in 1981 and nationalized the banks. President Reagan's strong anti-Communist ideology and support for free markets encouraged these flows into the U.S., but it is hard to measure their size, as private capital transfers are the most difficult to track statistically. Worldwide transfers may have amounted to as much as $200 billion between 1975 and 1985, including $50 billion from Mexico alone. Argentina and Venezuela were estimated to have lost over $25 billion each. But by no means did all of these funds go to the U.S., even indirectly.*

Unfortunately, even the data for foreign trade and legitimate international capital flows is rather unreliable, so that it is impossible to statistically determine flight capital flows into the United States. Even straightforward trade flows between partner countries show very large discrepancies as reported by the two partners,[74] and statistical discrepancies in flow of funds reports on international capital are almost as large as the largest individual sector flows. Much legitimate international activity is unreported, and a very large proportion prizes secrecy to avoid government restrictions and

---

with occasional significant attention paid to threats to the structure of the credit system. The dollar was not mentioned in one of the numerous dissents by governors to FOMC policy directives between 1979 and 1982. The effect of the strong dollar on domestic industry and export competititveness was first mentioned in policy discussions in meetings held June 30–July 1, 1982, but even in 1982 the Federal Reserve's foreign concerns were more with LDC debts than trade. The first time the strenth of the dollar entered strongly into policy discussions was at the May 24, 1983 meeting, in which a majority favored slightly tighter credit as the economy recovered but an unusually large group of five governors dissented. Their dissents particularly mentioned the impact of a stronger dollar on industrial competitiveness. A similar dissent occurred at the December 19–20 meetings. There were no such dissents in 1984, although the problems in various industries related to the strong dollar were regularly mentioned.

*These estimates reflect the World Bank's definition of capital flight as the total buildup of foreign assets by LDC nationals. This includes what might be considered normal international capital flows. Annual estimates are derived essentially by treating capital flight as the difference between inflows from direct investment and incremental international debt and the outflow for the trade deficit. See Robert Cumby and Richard Levich, "On the Definition and Magnitude of Recent Capital Flights," in Donald R. Lessard and John Williamson (eds.), *Capital Flight and Third World Debt*, Washington, D.C.: Institute for International Economics, 1987, pp. 27, 38–43.

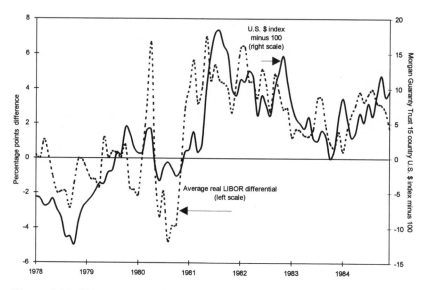

Figure 2.17 Changes in the U.S. dollar and real LIBOR differentials (U.S. vs. averages of Germany, Japan, and the U.K.). Sources: Federal Reserve, Deutsche Bundesbank, Bank of Japan, Bank of England, U.K. Central Statistical Office, Bureau of Labor Statistics, Morgan Guaranty Trust.

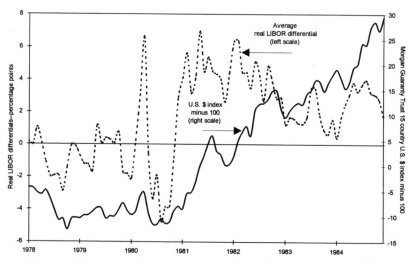

Figure 2.18 The U.S. dollar and real LIBOR differentials (U.S. vs. average for Germany, Japan, and the U.K.). Sources: Federal Reserve, Deutsche Bundesbank, Bank of Japan, Bank of England, U.K. Central Statistical Office, Bureau of Labor Statistics, Morgan Guaranty Trust.

crime enforcement. Switzerland, the largest source of international flows into financial instruments, does not reveal the countries receiving those flows.

Financial professionals gave much less emphasis to the effect of flight capital on the dollar. Both European authorities and the Federal Reserve attributed changes in the dollar to international interest rate differentials. Indeed, the Fed's model for exchange rates was based exclusively on interest rate differentials. The strong impact of real interest rate differentials on the dollar can be easily seen in figure 2.17. It tracks the percentage change in the dollar (Morgan Guaranty Trust Company's fifteen-country index) and the inflation-adjusted (CPI) differential between ninety-day London Inter-Bank Offered Rates (LIBOR) rates for the U.S. and the average for Germany, Japan, and the U.K.[75] Although the amplitudes of changes in the dollar were frequently much greater than in the real LIBOR differential, the two series moved in remarkably similar patterns for much of 1980–1983.

This argument must not be made too simplistic, however. Figure 2.18, which outlines the dollar itself (rather than changes in it) and the same real interest rate differential, indicates that the interest rate differential was not rising while the dollar strengthened. A large positive LIBOR differential was established in 1981 and the dollar continued to rise thereafter as long as the differential was maintained—sort of a super-charger effect—rather than finding a new equilibrium.*

Despite the large real interest rate differentials favoring the U.S., the Federal Open Market Committee minutes during 1981 to 1984 make clear that the Federal Reserve continually expected the dollar to decline because of the trade deficit, and was surprised at its continued strength. As can be seen in figure 2.19, the dollar's rise in 1982 to 1984 corresponded to a plunge in the current account deficit to over $110 billion, upsetting all conventional interpretations of the currency markets.

Academics jumped into the intellectual gap provided by the inability of traditional theories to explain the dollar's strength. Paul Krugman, Rudiger Dornbusch, Martin Feldstein, and Jeffrey Frankel emphasized the effects of capital flows on exchange rates, arguing that the huge U.S.

---

*There was a similar relationship between real ten-year U.S. treasury rates and long-term rates in Germany, Japan, and the U.K. Jeffrey A. Frankel, "Exchange Rate Policy" in Martin Feldstein (ed.), *American Economic Policy in the 1980s*, pp. 295–296, suggests that real long-term interest rate differentials continued to rise from 1981 to 1984 for a much larger group of trading partners. However, foreign exchange trading activity was heavily concentrated in the Deutsche mark, yen, and sterling, so that interest rate differentials with other countries were less important.

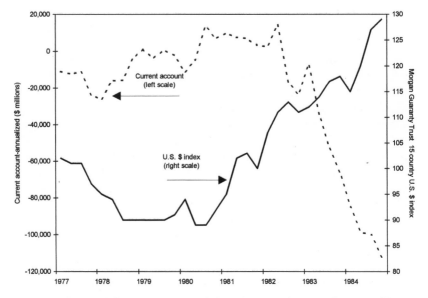

Figure 2.19 The dollar and the trade deficit. Sources: Morgan Guaranty Trust and Bureau of Economic Analysis.

budget deficit and the powerful economic expansion coupled with high real U.S. interest rates, pulled in capital from abroad, causing the dollar's strength, and that the trade deficit was simply the corollary of the budget deficit, creating dollars abroad to match foreign capital inflow. However, even the academics were at a loss to explain the dollar's continued rise in 1984–1985, and ended up ascribing it to a "speculative bubble." Their theory worked tolerably well for the United States, which appeared to have an almost inexhaustible supply of financial and property assets that foreigners wanted, and which was enjoying declining inflation, but the theory worked less well for other countries. A less-developed country running large fiscal and trade deficits was more likely to be troubled by inflation, flight capital, and plunging exchange rates, rather than by its currency strengthening. Other countries fell along the spectrum between the United States and the LDCs. It was understandable that many investors did not accept this theory when the United States became the world's largest debtor and the trade deficit proved intransigent despite reductions in the budget deficit.

Inflation

The ultimate indicator of the Reagan administration's change of regimes was its victory over inflation. It stood at 11% when President Reagan

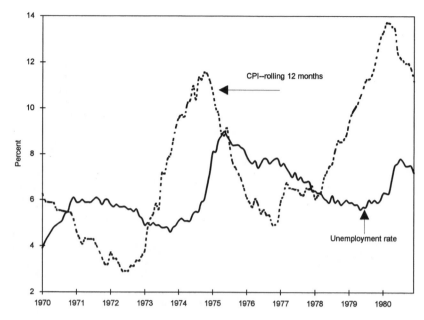

Figure 2.20 Inflation and unemployment rates. Source: Bureau of Labor Statistics.

took office amid a widespread feeling of economic crisis, and he kept a drumbeat focus on it for his first six months, saying that the country was "Heading towards economic disaster," "in the worst economic mess since the Great Depression," and "threatened with economic calamity of tremendous proportions." Inflation had been ratcheting up ever since 1964 as a result of the Great Society programs of the Johnson administration and miscalculations at the Federal Reserve of the tradeoff between inflation and economic growth. With each economic cycle the inflation peaks were higher and the troughs were deeper, as the reader can see in figure 2.20. Unemployment of 5% in 1973 was followed by inflation of almost 12% in 1974, and unemployment of 6% in 1979 was followed by inflation of almost 14% in 1980. Oil price shocks in 1973 and during 1979–1980 exacerbated the underlying trend and created such a fear of permanently reduced living standards that the Federal Reserve was constantly pressured to avoid damping economic activity.

The problem was much worse in the U.S. than in Germany, where anti-inflationary policies were strongly entrenched. As can be seen in figure 2.21, U.S. inflation was approximately one and a-half times that of Germany from 1974 to 1977, and rose to over three times Germany's inflation in 1978 and 1979. And U.S. inflation, although initially lower than Japan's throughout 1971 to 1977, ultimately rose to over three times higher

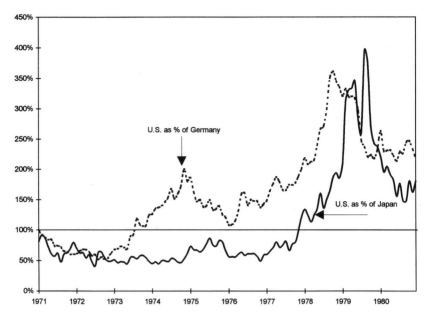

Figure 2.21 U.S. inflation rates relative to Germany and Japan. Sources: Bureau of Labor Statistics, Deutsche Bundesbank, Bank of Japan.

than Japan in 1979, as outlined in the same figure 2.21. Fears of hyperinflation were widespread.

Rolling twelve months inflation actually began to trend down in the second quarter of 1980 following President Carter's anti-inflation program, but the change was invisible to contemporaries amid wildly fluctuating monetary policy and the volatility that pervaded the economy, securities markets, and commodities prices. Indeed, monetary policy, which was a crucial element of the ultimate victory over inflation, almost came into disrepute when the Federal Reserve eased credit so aggressively in mid-1980.

The largest decline in inflation occurred in October 1981 when the annualized monthly rate dropped from 11.7% to 4%, as can be seen in figure 2.22. This followed on the heels of several concurrent events: the Federal Reserve's decision to tighten monetary policy further in midyear despite the weak economy, a sharp drop in industrial production, an 18% rise in the dollar, and a decline in oil prices to $35.00. After this sudden drop inflation averaged less than 4% for the next three years—a level much closer to that of Germany and Japan, as can be seen in figure 2.23. Great Britain underwent an even greater decline (not shown), thanks to its own change of regime under Margaret Thatcher.

There are various factors to which one can point as the cause of the

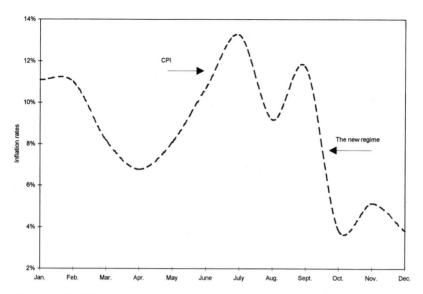

Figure 2.22 1981 monthly inflation. Source: Bureau of Labor Statistics.

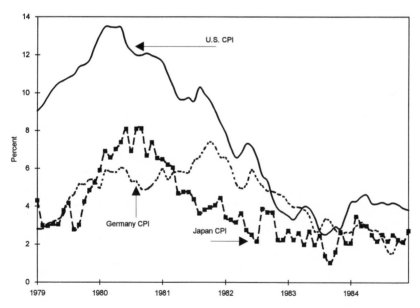

Figure 2.23 International inflation rates (rolling twelve months). Sources: Bureau of Labor Statistics, Deutsche Bundesbank, Bank of Japan.

decline in inflation during the recession years 1980–1982: they include three and a half years of stalled or declining industrial production, the strong dollar, declining money supply growth, declining oil prices (which I will review next), reduced capital spending (covered in chapter 9), and the weakness of manufacturing unions in collective bargaining situations. But the suddenness of the decline in late 1981 suggests a sharp change in expectations characteristic of a change in regimes. This is particularly borne out by the abrupt decline in union wage settlements from over 10% to almost 2% in the first quarter of 1982, as I will note below.

Inflation's failure to surge again during the economic recovery of 1983–1984 even more strongly suggests a change in expectations. As can be seen in figure 2.24, a surge in inflation followed the strong 5–10% advances in industrial production throughout 1976 to 1979, but inflation only rose modestly to 4% when industrial production growth surged again to well over 10% in 1983 and 1984.

There was a similar change in the relationship between inflation and unemployment, outlined in figure 2.25. When unemployment fell to approximately 5% in 1974, inflation surged to almost 12%. Then, with expectations ratcheting upward, inflation surged to almost 14% in 1979, although unemployment was still at 6%. However, as unemployment declined in 1984, inflation remained at the 4% level of the early 1970s instead of ratcheting up.

Nonetheless, financial traditionalists in 1983 saw little reason to assume the inflation cycle was permanently broken. Commodities prices began to rise strongly with the economy, as can be seen in figure 2.26. The twin budget and trade deficits also appeared likely to rekindle inflation, and money supply was surging. Only the strong dollar and declining oil prices were holding inflation down, the traditionalists argued, and they could be reversed at any moment.

This was a valid argument. There was undoubtedly a strong relationship between the powerful rise in the dollar and the reduction in inflation, as can be seen in figure 2.27. The surge in inflation in 1979 to 1980 lagged a very weak dollar, and the steep decline in inflation from late 1981 to 1983 lagged exceptionally strong increases in the dollar in 1981 and 1982. The rise in the dollar did much more than simply hold down prices in the trade-competitive industries. Prices of commodities that were traded on world-wide markets, particularly metals, paper, and grains, plunged to low levels that decimated these industries, as I will review in detail in chapters 4 and 8.* Reflecting these price pressures, the

---

*The behavior of industrial commodities prices in the 1980s is a worthy study in itself. Their depression was not due simply to the strong dollar, since the depression persisted when the dollar weakened after 1985. Other factors were overin-

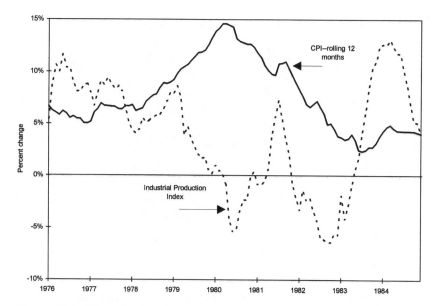

Figure 2.24 CPI and industrial production growth rates. Sources: Bureau of Labor Statistics and Federal Reserve.

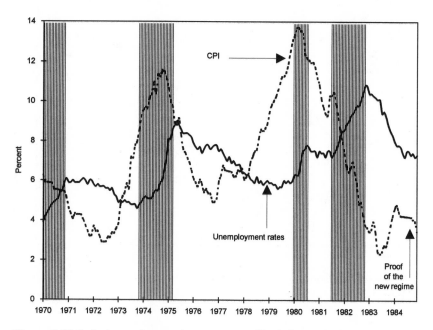

Figure 2.25 Inflation and unemployment rates. Shaded areas indicate recessions. Source: Bureau of Labor Statistics.

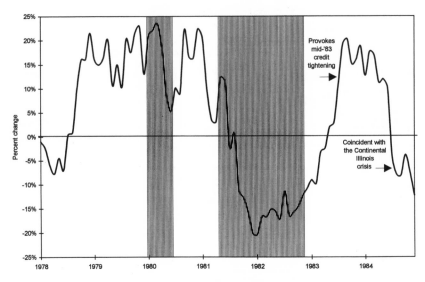

Figure 2.26 CRB Futures Price Index (percent change). Shaded areas indicate recessions. Source: Commodities Research Bureau.

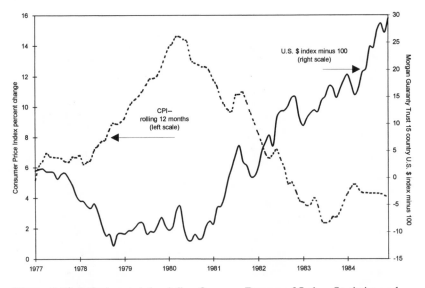

Figure 2.27 Inflation and the dollar. Sources: Bureau of Labor Statistics and Morgan Guaranty Trust.

Commodities Research Bureau's Futures Price Index dropped from a peak of almost 340 in November 1980 to below 230 in the summer of 1982, and after a brief rise in 1983 dropped again to 244 at the end of 1984.[76] The strong dollar also restrained wage settlements in the consumer and manufacturing durables industries—such as autos, electronics, white goods, farm equipment, earth-moving equipment, steel, and aluminum—where unions were historically the strongest and the pacesetters in terms of inflationary wage settlements. These unions went through their toughest times since the Depression.

The fall of oil prices in 1981 also took much of the steam out of inflationary psychology. The coincidence in the peaks in oil prices and inflation can be starkly seen in figure 2.28; as oil prices began to fall in 1981, inflation declined steadily.

However, this was not particularly related to U.S. policies. In early 1981, Saudi Arabia consciously began to overproduce at 10.3 million barrels per day in order to reduce oil prices to $32 a barrel for the sake of preserving long-term oil markets from other energy alternatives. Traditional demand and supply forces were also at work. Demand was reduced by high oil prices and recession throughout Europe and North America, while supply was increased by major production expansions in the North Sea and Mexico, the increased flow of Prudhoe Bay oil through the Trans Alaskan Pipeline System, and the huge stimulus of $40 a barrel to production from marginal reserves. Spot prices began to drop, and for the first time the international oil companies dropped contracts when OPEC producers would not cut prices. A major decline in oil prices began in the summer of 1981. Mexico cut its prices $4 per barrel in June. In August, OPEC production dropped to 20 million barrels per day—a thirteen-year low compared with 31 million barrels in 1979—and OPEC made a historic proposal to cut prices, although it seriously lagged the market. OPEC continued to cut production into mid-1982 when it dropped to 17.5 million barrels per day, and a great effort was made to maintain a $32 price. OPEC even provided financial aid to Nigeria and Ecuador to help them sustain lower production, and great pressure was put on the major international oil companies to keep up their purchases from OPEC. Iran, however, was a major flaw in the cartel, as it increased production and discounted prices to gain revenues to support its war with Iraq. In early 1983, OPEC reduced its oil price from $34 to $29 a barrel and finally adopted a quota system for all producers

---

vestment in these industries due to the inflation stimuli of the 1970s, excessive capital investment in the 1970s because of low real interest rates, "panic" pricing by bankrupt LDCs, and generally reduced investment rates in the 1980s. The extended length of this commodities price cycle is still not well explained.

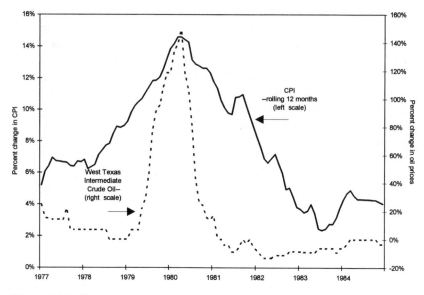

Figure 2.28 Changes in inflation and oil prices. Sources: Bureau of Labor Statistics and West Texas Intermediate Crude Oil.

out of fear of "a bottomless fall" in oil prices. Washington actually found itself "worried sick" about a "real break" in oil prices to $25 a barrel out of fear that the ensuing problems for the big borrowers among the oil producers—Mexico, Venezuela, Nigeria, Indonesia—would create an international financial collapse.[77]

To some degree it was the Reagan administration's good luck to be in power when the natural economic forces of conservation and increased supply were reducing oil prices, but at least the administration aggressively adopted free market policies that permitted these economic forces to work. It abolished the remaining controls on oil prices, ceased oil allocations to small refiners, wound up the $20 billion Synfuels Corporation, pressed the World Bank to end its energy promotion schemes, accelerated offshore oil leasing and production from the National Petroleum Reserve, and even briefly discussed privatizing the Tennessee Valley Authority and the various federal regional power agencies. It was also clear that nothing was likely to bring price controls back. The Council on Wage and Price Stability had been abolished, as had the Carter administration's standby emergency oil and gas rationing schemes.

The strength of the dollar and declining oil and other commodities prices could not by themselves explain the change in inflation's trend, however, especially when money supply and the federal deficit exerted contrary pressures. A change in expectations also took place that resulted

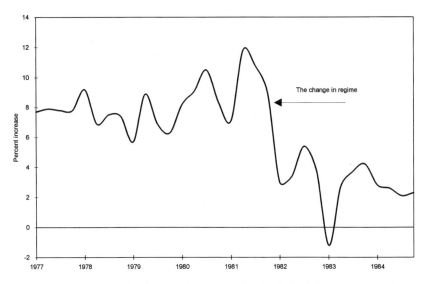

Figure 2.29 First-year wage settlements in collective bargaining (percent increase). Source: Bureau of Labor Statistics.

in greater price restraint, confounding the predictions of financial traditionalists. The suddenness with which inflation dropped from 11.7% in September 1981 (9.4% in the prior six months) to under 4% in the three succeeding months indicates a major change took place. Nothing shows this change better than first-year union wage gains in new contracts, which were one of the primary ratcheting mechanisms of inflation and were widely believed to be so institutionally inflexible that only gradual changes in inflation were possible. They dropped sharply from a peak of 11.8% in 1981 to only 3% in the first quarter of 1982, as can be seen in figure 2.29, only one quarter behind the sharp drop in the CPI. Wage gains were only 2.5% in 1984, their lowest rate of increase since 1967.[78] These lower first-year gains were not temporary concessions. As the reader can see in figure 2.30, historically, first-year gains were approximately two percentage points higher than the contract average, but from 1982 to 1984 first-year gains became indistinguishable from the contract average, except for briefly in the first quarter of 1983, when they were three percentage points lower. Nor was the decline in wage demands a matter of having caught up with inflation—quite the opposite. As the reader can see in figure 2.31, which shows the cumulative difference between union wage gains and inflation, wage gains enjoyed a premium over inflation of 2.3 percentage points in 1977, but were cumulatively over eight percentage points behind inflation by the end of 1981 and continued to lose ground through the end of 1984, when they were over twelve percentage points behind.

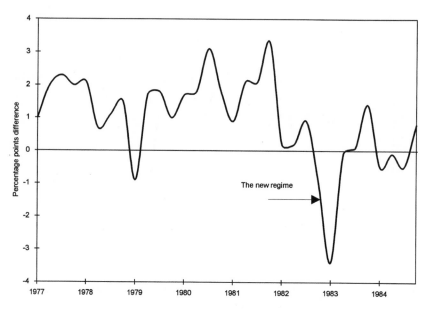

Figure 2.30 First-year wage increases minus the contract average increase (contracts covering 1,000 plus workers) (percentage points). Source: Bureau of Labor Statistics.

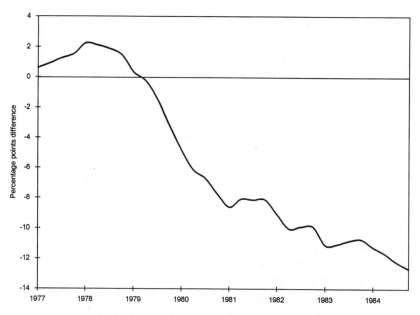

Figure 2.31 Cumulative first-year wage gains/losses vs. inflation (percentage points difference). Source: Bureau of Labor Statistics.

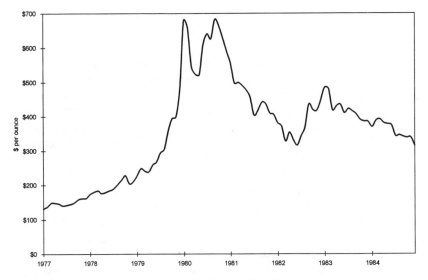

Figure 2.32 Gold prices (per ounce). Source: Dow Jones.

The change in psychology was also evident in the price of gold, a favorite financial indicator of inflation expectations, as illustrated in figure 2.32. It dropped from a peak in early 1980, when futures prices hit $960 per ounce, to below $400 in June 1981, and to only $317 in June 1982. It moved back up to $485 in January 1983, but soon resumed a downward trend until it dropped below $300 in February 1985. We can debate whether this was all inflationary psychology, or whether it also reflected that the Arab world got its fill of gold and came up the learning curve in employing its newfound oil wealth in interest-bearing instruments and productive businesses. Prices for D flawless one-carat diamonds, which had a similar allure to gold, but less so for Arabs, dropped from $65,000 in March 1980 to $10,000–14,000 in 1984. The Antwerp diamond trade experienced its "deepest depression since the 1930s."[79]

The Federal Reserve was universally given credit for achieving the decline in inflation expectations as the principal federal agent in that respect since there was no remaining vestige of the government apparatus of price controls set up under President Carter, and fiscal policy was given over to political and ideological purposes. The Federal Reserve's power to dramatically affect the economy and securities markets was undoubted after the recession of 1981 to 1982, as was its intention to continue to use this power at the first signs of rising inflation, as it had shown in both 1983 and 1984.

I attach considerable importance to various actions of the Reagan administration as well. Paul Volcker himself highlighted the administration's strong stand in 1981 against the wage demands of the Public Air Traffic Controllers Union as its single strongest action against inflation. The administration's wholesale replacement of the strikers was unprecedented in either government or industry, and began a trend that greatly undermined labor's power. The administration also showed unusually strong support for the Federal Reserve's efforts to control inflation, William Greider's tales of conflict in *Secrets of the Temple* notwithstanding. The administration called for tighter money in the fourth quarter of 1981 when money supply growth accelerated, even though the country was already in recession; President Reagan insisted that he would "not retreat one inch" in attacking inflation, and he campaigned in the 1982 off-year elections on the slogan "stay the course." The administration showed only modest resistance to the Federal Reserve's credit tightening in mid-1984, even when it was an election year; nor did the administration make any efforts to weaken the strong dollar or prop up oil prices.

The administration's free-market bias also reinforced the change in inflation expectations. The administration articulated strongly founded international free-trade principles. It did nothing to offset the effects of sharply declining prices in the oil, mining, and metals industries (steel was an exception), instead relaxing antitrust rules (as I will review in detail in chapter 9), which encouraged mergers that accelerated downsizing and other readjustments. It provided no succor to the ailing machinery and equipment industries, although it did complete the aid to Chrysler Corp. that was begun by the Carter administration, and it indirectly advanced almost $10 billion to the electric utility industry to facilitate construction of nuclear power plants (in part because it felt regulation was burdening them). It encouraged the evolution of the transportation industries to free markets begun under President Carter. Except for the stimulus provided by the budget deficit, the administration and the Federal Reserve presented powerful coherent pressures to reduce inflation expectations.

Summary

The Reagan administration, the Federal Reserve, declining oil prices, and the strong dollar combined in the early 1980s to reverse the crisis-ridden interventionist policies of the 1970s and the long trend of escalating inflation. The Carter administration had coped poorly with double-digit inflation, a second energy crisis, and a weak dollar by promoting wage and price controls, gasoline rationing, and extensive federal intervention in energy markets. Even when the Federal Reserve under Paul Volcker switched monetary policy to a focus on money supply and cut inflation to zero in mid-1980 by rationing consumer credit, the effect was diluted because it quickly reversed course under broad pressure to sustain employment and economic growth.

The Reagan administration, by contrast, had a strong free market orientation. It disbanded the Council on Wage and Price Stability, removed the remaining price controls on oil, halted small refiner entitlements, did away with all emergency energy rationing schemes, required cost-benefit analyses of all regulations, set up a commission to propose regulatory relief, and refused to intervene in the foreign exchange markets. It cut income taxes 25%, reduced the top rate on personal taxes from 70% to 50%, cut the capital gains rate from 28% to 20%, phased out the windfall profits tax on oil, and dramatically increased business depreciation allowances. It also set a new standard for union conflict by replacing PATCO strikers, ultimately bankrupting the union and jailing its leaders.

Monetary policy also acquired a new steadiness in attacking inflation under President Reagan. Even after thirty-six months without growth in industrial production he and most of his advisors strongly supported controlling money supply growth. Federal funds rates, banks' borrowed reserves, and the discount rate all indicated tight credit with only slight variations from the fall of 1980 into the middle of 1982. The Federal Reserve did not hesitate to tighten credit again in mid-1983 and early 1984 when the economy recovered.

The attack on inflation was aided by a 55% rise in the dollar and a decline in oil prices from $40 to $29 per barrel. These were partly fortuitous trends, but they were abetted by the administration's free-market policies.

The transition to a new regime was not without contradictions, nor was it immediate. The escalation of the budget deficit to 6% of GNP and the trade deficit to 3% profoundly upset financial traditionalists, incuding the Federal Reserve, and there was persistent wavering within the administration over whether to introduce new taxes. Many of the tax benefits handed out in 1981 were reversed in 1982, the administration flirted with a gas tax, and Social Security Tax increases equal to 1% of GNP were implemented in 1983.

There were two turning points that justified the new regime's strategy. The first occurred in October 1981 when inflation dropped from 11.7% to 4% and union wage increases dropped to only 2.5% in the next quarter. The second was in mid-1982 when the Federal Reserve dramatically eased credit, reducing federal funds rates from 15% to 9%, under the twin pressures of thirty-six months without growth in industial production and a faltering banking system. Lower interest rates and the fiscal stimulus of the 1981 tax reductions combined to produce the strongest economic recovery since the Korean War and the best stock and bond markets since 1972. Fortunately, the Federal Reserve abandoned its focus on money supply when it escalated rapidly as part of deposit deregulation, or the Fed would have been compelled to tighten credit immediately. Although many experts thought that the recovery would be aborted by problems in the banking system of 1930s proportions caused by loans to the less-developed countries, oil and gas companies, and on real estate, adept intervention by the Federal Reserve, the administration, and international financial authorities avoided disruption of the recovery and sustained the generally optimistic environment.

Looking back on the first half of the 1980s from the vantage point of mid-decade, the Reagan administration and the Federal Reserve had cause to congratulate themselves. The economy had experienced high growth rates for two years without resurrecting inflation, taxes had been reduced, the oil crisis had been surmounted, and the dollar was strong. The federal deficit and its side effect, the foreign trade deficit, were the principal remaining structural problems in the economy, but much as they worried financial traditionalists and the Federal Reserve, their effects accrued very slowly. As we shall see in the next chapter, the new regime reversed a decade of pessimism that had plagued the stock market and set it on a new course of high returns and record new-issue activity.

3

The New Regime Revives the Common Stock Market

The new regime outlined in chapter 2 dramatically changed the stock market. At the macroeconomic level, returns on the S&P 500 rose from an annual average of only 5.9% (−1.5% real) in the 1970s to 14.8% (9.7% real) between 1979 and 1984,[1] despite the fears kindled by the twin budget and trade deficits and crises in the banking system. Most of this improvement was not due to higher actual earnings, however, but rather to both a 20% rise in price-earnings ratios (adjusted for interest rates) and earnings projections by analysts that were steadily 30–40% above those realized. On a microeconomic level, there was a harsh sorting out of winners and losers according to how various industries were affected by declining inflation and oil prices, high interest rates, the strong dollar, the 1981–1982 recession, and the eventual expansion in consumer spending.

In this chapter I will consider the macroeconomics of the stock market, sorting out the causes of its recovery, particularly the fundamentals of earnings, interest rates, and taxes, and the psychological factors of confidence, optimism, or reduced risk premiums.

To do this I will use the analytical procedures of a market practitioner. My discussion will focus on what Fischer Black called "the magic in earnings" rather than on dividends. Stock prices are too volatile to be explained by dividends, as Robert Shiller has shown, and, as any practitioner knows, the analytical effort directed at earnings outweighs that directed at dividends by over one hundred to one. The relevant earnings are expected earnings, however, which almost never correspond to actual earnings and are strongly affected by changing levels of optimism. Most of the data in this chapter is presented in nominal rather than real terms, and changes in price-earnings ratios are treated as a function of both interest rates and optimism.

Chapters 4 and 5 will examine the microeconomics of the stocks that underperformed and overperformed the S&P 500.

The 1970s

The stock market was a highly unsatisfactory investment in the 1970s— so bad that *Business Week* ran a cover in August 1979 proclaiming "The Death of Equities." The S&P 500 only rose from 92 at the end of 1969 to 108 at the end of 1979, an average annual return of only 5.9% including dividends. Inflation reduced the real return to minus 1.5%. The only worse decade on a nominal basis was the 1930s, and in real terms it was the worst performance of the century. The reader may refer back to table 1.1 to revisit this data.

The decade began with considerable promise as the S&P 500 rose to a peak of almost 120 in 1972, following Richard Nixon's reelection, but it plunged to 64 in mid-1974 in the midst of the first oil crisis, severe recession, tight credit, and the turmoil of Watergate. The market recovered to approximately 105 in 1976 in conjunction with recoveries in both the economy and confidence once Watergate was resolved and Gerald Ford became president. The market varied only modestly from that level through the end of the decade, as rising inflation, a second energy crisis, rising interest rates, and foreign exchange crises continued to plague it.

A radical revaluation of stocks occurred in this decade of turmoil. Earnings per share for the S&P 500 actually grew from $5.78 in 1969 to $15.29 in 1979—a compound annual rate of 9.9%—and although three-year treasury rates rose from 8.1% to 10.7% that was not enough to cause the poor stock market returns that resulted. If the S&P 500 had followed a two-factor model based on the changes in 3 year treasury rates and realized earnings twelve months hence,[2] it would have been 86% higher than it was at the end of 1979, as can be seen in figure 3.1.

The underperformance of the S&P 500 versus this model reflected that the price-earnings ratio of the S&P 500, outlined in figure 3.2, underwent a decline from 16–18 times earnings, which prevailed throughout the 1960s, to 7 times earnings at the end of the 1970s. A rise in interest rates from 8.1% to 10.7% accounted for a decline in price-earnings ratios from 17.9 in December 1969 to 13.8 in December 1979, but the balance of the decline to 7.0 times earnings requires other explanations.

Many contemporaries blamed the decline on inflation. There are several ways to look at inflation's effects. The simplest is to adjust earnings growth rates for inflation, as outlined for the S&P 500 in figure 3.3. An-

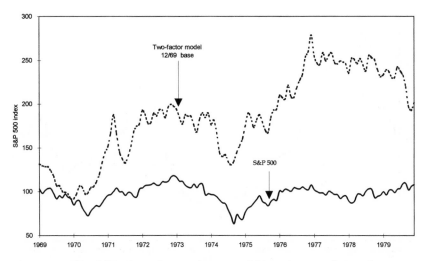

Figure 3.1 The S&P 500 and a two-factor model based on earnings twleve months forward and three-year treasury rates. Sources: Standard & Poor's Corp. and Federal Reserve.

Figure 3.2 Price-earnings ratios for the S&P 500 (based on actual earnings twelve months hence). Source: Standard & Poor's Corp.

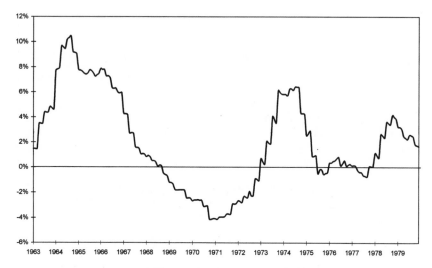

Figure 3.3 Average annual log growth rates for real S&P 500 earnings (based on rolling three-year periods deflated by CPI). Sources: Standard & Poor's Corp. and Bureau of Labor Statistics.

nual log earnings growth, deflated by CPI, over rolling thirty-six-month periods,[3] declined from 8% during 1964–1966 to an average below 2% in the 1970s, but this trend began in the late 1960s, five years before price-earnings ratios fell. Earnings growth actually showed some recovery in 1973–1974 and 1978–1979, but price-earnings ratios continued to decline.

A favorite comparison at the time was to adjust reported earnings downward by the the extent of inventory profits and underdepreciation versus replacement costs in the National Income and Products (NIPA) accounts. The S&P 500 still underperformed a two-factor model using these earnings[4] twelve months hence and three-year treasury rates by 25–30% throughout most of 1976–1978, as outlined in figure 3.4, although by early 1979 the model and the S&P 500 had converged. The model collapsed, however, when it was carried forward into the early 1980s, as in figure 3.5, when the S&P 500 appeared to ignore inflationary adjustments, overperforming the model by 50–100%.

It is not surprising that this model failed to account for the stock market's underperformance in the 1970s. Most public companies switched to last in-first out (LIFO) accounting during the 1970s, eliminating inflationary inventory profits, and a variety of tax changes had been made to compensate for economic underdepreciation, incuding investment tax credits, higher depreciation rates, and shorter depreciation lives. The NIPA corporate universe was also significantly different from the S&P 500 in terms of profitability, cash flow, and leverage. Its definition was also very different. It

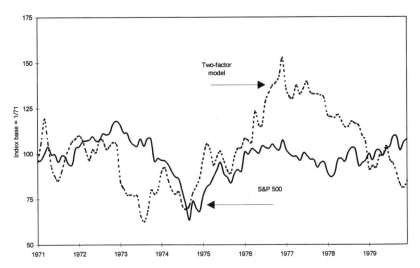

Figure 3.4 The S&P 500 and a two-factor model based on three-year treasury rates and earnings twelve months forward adjusted for inventory valuation and replacement cost depreciation. Sources: Standard & Poor's Corp. and *Survey of Current Business*.

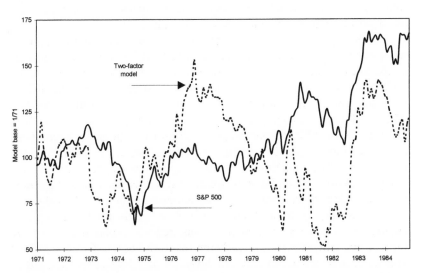

Figure 3.5 The S&P 500 and a two-factor model based on three-year treasury rates and earnings twelve months forward adjusted for inventory valuation and replacement cost depreciation. Sources: Standard & Poor's Corp. and *Survey of Current Business*.

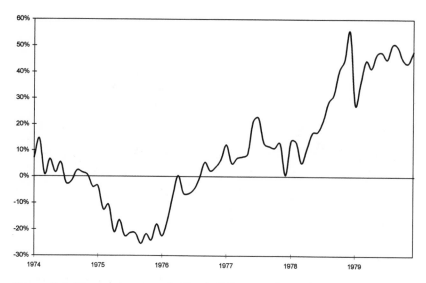

Figure 3.6 Changes in value of office building construction (rolling twelve months). Source: Census, Construction Expenditures release.

included cooperatives, government businesses, not-for-profits, and pension funds, and it made no adjustments for shares outstanding, capitalized interest, writeoffs, investment tax credits, or depletion.[5]

Another contemporary argument was that investors were moving capital away from the securities markets into "real" goods that were perceived as inflation hedges. The favored institutional investment in the late 1970s and early 1980s was commercial real estate, as it benefited from rents that rose with inflation, low real interest rates, and high leverage. The Frank Russell index of commercial real estate prices rose from 70 in 1977 to 100 in 1982 without relapse, in contrast to the sharp fluctuations and modest growth in the securities markets.[6] Greenwich Research estimated that 22% of one thousand large corporate pensions owned real estate outright in 1980 and that 40% expected to buy real estate in the next two years.[7] Insurance companies also stepped up their direct real estate investments. For example, Metropolitan Life bought the Pan Am building in New York for $400 million, and entered a $2.3 billion joint venture for real estate investment, while Aetna Insurance entered a $400 million joint venture with Marvin Davis to develop Fox Film's properties. Office building construction was increasing at 50% annually by 1979 under the stimulus of these institutional funds flows, as can be seen in figure 3.6.

Institutional purchases of equities dropped from 30–35% of their incremental financial assets to approximately 10% through most of 1974–1978.[8] What enthusiasm institutional investors could muster for stocks was concentrated on oil and gas and small companies. The annual total return for the latter averaged 11.5% from 1969–1979—almost double the 5.9% average for the S&P 500.[9]

For individuals, tangibles such as real estate, art, antiques, and jewelry were more popular than stocks in the 1970s and their returns were much higher.* Douglas Elliman's index of the selling price per room for Manhattan cooperative apartments rose from $11,050 in 1975 to $75,310 in 1981. Sotheby's Art Index rose from 100 in 1975 to 253 in 1980, and the price in Amsterdam of a one-carat D-flawless diamond rose from $1,200 in 1970 to $65,000.[10] The strongest competition to these investments on the securities side was tax shelters. Between 1975 and 1982, individuals' partnership losses for tax purposes rose from $7.6 billion to $28.3 billion, almost 60% of which was in oil and gas and real estate.[11]

Another contemporary argument for the poor performance of the S&P 500 from 1969 to 1979 was that stocks were overvalued in the 1960s. The S&P 500 at the end of 1969 had a price-earnings ratio 17.9 times earnings twelve months hence, and a number of important stocks were preposterously high. This was the beginning of the craze for the "Nifty Fifty"—fifty growth stocks that the investor was supposed to be able to buy and hold for life as their growth continuously outstripped the general market. Table 3.1 outlines fifty stocks that might be considered the "Nifty Fifty" and their peak price-earnings ratios in 1969,† which averaged 39.9! These stocks went through dramatic revaluations in the decade ahead. This revaluation can be seen in industry terms in table 3.2, which outlines the decline in price-earnings ratios for thirteen industries that had declines 50% larger than that of the S&P Industrials. The computers and drug industries were the largest ones affected, based on their respective weights in the S&P 500 of 7.54% and 3.99%.

However, it would be a mistake to place too much emphasis on these high price-earnings ratios. The peak 1969 price-earnings ratio for the S&P 500 of 18.4 times current earnings had held steady at that level, with only modest variation, every year since 1958. The decline in the price-earnings ratio of the S&P 500 to only 7 in 1979 was not merely a reaction to prior overvaluation.

The sorry performance of the stock market in the 1970s led to a new category of security analysts—financial strategists—who were popular interpreters of the many factors impinging on stock prices. They not only tried to interpret the anomalous behavior of stocks throughout the

---

*Real estate was the only category large enough to truly compete with the securities markets.
†The "Nifty Fifty" was not a defined term. These fifty stocks had the highest price-earnings ratios in Moody's Investors Services Inc., *Moody's Handbook of Common Stocks* 4th 1970 edition, New York: Moody's Investors Services Inc., 1970, excluding stocks with low returns on equity.

Table 3.1. Peak P-E Ratios for the Nifty Fifty (1969 High and 1969 EPS)

Polaroid	75.5
Baxter Laboratories	66.7
American Hospital Supply	60.8
Becton Dickinson	60.4
Avon Products	59.2
Johnson & Johnson	56.6
Hewlett-Packard	56.4
Xerox	55.6
International Flavors & Fragrances	55.5
Burroughs	50.3
Dow Jones	48.0
Texas Instruments	46.1
IBM	44.8
Nalco Chemical	43.7
Tampax Inc.	42.7
Bausch & Lomb	42.2
Walt Disney	41.5
Eli Lilly	41.5
Corning Glass	41.3
Coca-Cola	41.2
Merck	41.2
Holiday Inns	40.9
Honeywell	38.3
McDonald's	37.9
Minnesota Mining	37.0
Anheuser-Busch	36.5
ARA Services	35.9
Tandy Corp.	34.9
Revlon	34.1
Bristol-Myers	33.6
Eastman Kodak	33.5
Sterling Drug	32.1
Black & Decker	31.4
Chesebrough-Pond's	31.4
Warner-Lambert	31.1
Schlitz Brewing	31.0
Pfizer	31.0
Moore Corp.	31.0
Electrical & Musical Industries	30.6
Max Factor	30.3
Abbot Laboratories	30.2
American Home Products	29.6
Dun & Bradstreet	29.3
Squibb Beech-Nut	29.0
Emerson Electric	28.9
International Nickel	28.2
J. C. Penney	26.5
Alberto-Culver	26.4
Richardson-Merrell	26.2
Sears Roebuck	25.9
Average	39.9

Source: Moody's Handbook of Common Stocks, Fourth (1970) Edition.

Table 3.2. The Largest Declines in S&P Industry Price-Earnings Ratios[1]

Industry	1969 PE	1979 PE	Decline	% Wt in S&P 500 12/79
Industrials	17.5	7.1	10.4	—
Medical Products & Supplies	49.9	11.9	38.0	1.52%
Pollution Control	41.5	9.0	32.6	0.13%
Semiconductors[2]	42.2	10.3	31.9	0.96%
Cosmetics	40.2	10.8	29.4	0.75%
Computers	39.8	11.8	28.0	7.54%
Restaurants	34.9	8.9	26.0	0.47%
Instruments[2]	38.2	14.0	24.2	0.83%
Toys	28.7	5.9	22.8	0.03%
Soft Drinks	31.1	10.4	20.8	0.98%
Hotel-Motel	29.3	8.9	20.5	0.22%
Airlines	29.8	10.7	19.1	0.38%
Drugs	27.9	11.4	16.5	3.99%
Leisure Time	21.9	6.5	15.5	0.21%
				18.01%

Source: S&P Analyst's Handbook.

[1]Average of high + low prices divided by current-year earnings.
[2]No 1969 data—uses 1970.

decade. They equally had to explain how the S&P 500 could rise from 96 at the end of 1978 to approximately 108 at the end of 1979—an 18.2% total return with dividends reinvested—in the midst of a second oil crisis, record inflation, $700 gold prices, a flight from monetary to tangible assets, the Volcker-inspired shift by the Federal Reserve to a monetary policy focused on money supply, record interest rates, experimentation with credit controls, stalled industrial production, and the bailout of Chrysler Corp. The market breezed through a turbulent international scene as the Russians invaded Afghanistan, revolution occurred in Iran, the American embassy there was captured, and Congress was at a stalemate over Salt II.

It had, in fact, begun to appear as if the stock market had very low valuation parameters. The dividend yield on the S&P 500 was 5.2%, and earnings for the S&P 500 had grown at a compound annual rate of 9.9% for the last decade, which could lead to a total return on stocks of 15.1% —4.4 percentage points above the current three-year treasury yield. The market-to-book-value ratio for the S&P Industrials was below 1.1 times—only slightly above the low point in the economic and political crisis of 1974–1975, and otherwise the lowest in over twenty-five years. Strategists such as Leon Cooperman at Goldman Sachs and Barton Biggs at Morgan Stanley tried to balance these parameters against the oil crisis, inflation that was approaching 15%, a period of great volatility in monetary policy, weakness in the dollar, the distinct possibility of more stringent price controls, and the inertia of a decade of poor returns.

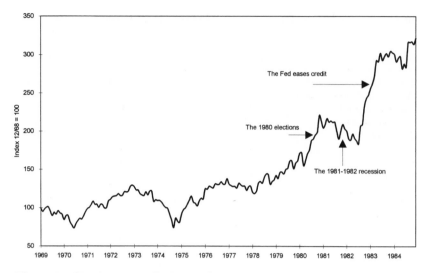

Figure 3.7 Total return index for the S&P 500 (dividends reinvested). Source: Ibbotson Associates.

The Course of the Stock Market from 1980 to 1984

The new regime's impact on the stock market occurred principally in three stages, as can be seen in figure 3.7, which is a total return index for the S&P 500 from January 1969 to December 1984. Most of the increase took place in the last half of 1980, during the presidential elections, and between July 1982 and April 1983, when the Federal Reserve dramatically reduced interest rates. In the recession of 1981–1982, the index declined from May 1981 through July 1982. On an annual basis, total returns for the S&P 500 were 32.4% in 1980, (4.9%) in 1981, 21.4% in 1982, 22.5% in 1983, and 6.3% in 1984.[12]

The rise in the S&P 500 from 114 to 140 during the second half of 1980 coincided with high expectations that Ronald Reagan would be elected president and would enact policies distinctly favorable to investors. Reagan scooped Carter during the election campaign by promising a 30% cut in personal income taxes and faster business depreciation—proposals that Carter had been considering, but had rejected because of their effects on the budget deficit. Reagan also promised higher defense budgets, import controls on autos and steel, and less regulation. The new optimism was reflected in new issues of common stock, which were a record $12.7 billion in 1980. Genentech made a permanent impression in stock market folklore on October 14, 1980 when it went public at $35 and immediately soared to $89! When Reagan was elected by a landslide in November and Republicans also gained control of the Senate for the first time since the 1952 elections, the stock market soared, providing a total November return of 10.2%, the third highest monthly return since 1945. Analysts' estimates of future earnings for the S&P 500 also soared, as we shall see below.

But even at this time, there were significant negative trends that argued against higher stock prices. Oil prices hit $40 a barrel at the end of 1980, and interest rates rose throughout the election campaign. They rose even more sharply after it, as the Federal Reserve received strong Reagan administration support for a restrictive monetary policy. Federal funds rose to almost 19% in December 1980, and two-year treasuries over 14%. There was a record New York Stock Exchange (NYSE) short interest of 76.4 million shares at the end of the year.

The smooth sailing in the stock market was short-lived. In the second phase of reaction to the new regime, there was a 24% decline in the S&P 500 throughout 1981 into the middle of 1982 that brought it back down to 107—the same level as at the ends of 1976 and 1979, and 9% below the end of 1972. This was a terrible period in the stock market, during which investors watched a seventeen-month slide in the index of industrial production from a peak of 87 in mid-1981 to 80 in late 1982. Earnings for the S&P 500 declined from $14.82 in 1980 to $12.64 in 1982. Investors became very discouraged. The compound total return on the S&P 500 had averaged only 5.7% annually since the end of 1969, compared to the 14% currently available on federal funds and ten-year treasuries—7% after inflation. New-issue volume was more than halved from a twelve-month peak of $17 billion in early 1981 to only $8 billion in mid-1982.

There was no coincident positive reaction in the stock market to the Reagan tax package of a 25% cut in individual tax rates over three years, a reduction in the maximum rate on "unearned" income from 50% to 70%, a cut in the capital gains tax rate from 28% to 20%, large Individual Retirement Account (IRA) benefits, the end of windfall profits taxes on oil, and faster business depreciation. Instead, as the budget debate wore on through the summer of 1981, the general reaction among Wall Street economists was that a hugely stimulative federal deficit and tight credit presaged a collision in the credit markets that would produce high interest rates and, ultimately, a weak economy and poor profits.

This forecast was borne out in the recession of 1981–1982, which occurred despite an increase in fiscal stimulus as the federal budget deficit rose from 2.4% of GNP in 1980 to 4.1% in 1982. Instead, consumer confidence reversed, dropping from a peak of 77 in November 1980 to 65 in mid-1982. Consumers' purchases of major durable goods, outlined in figure 3.8, took a second steep drop to levels even lower than in mid-1980 when President Carter's anti-inflation program was introduced. Housing starts dropped to an annual rate of 900,000 units compared to

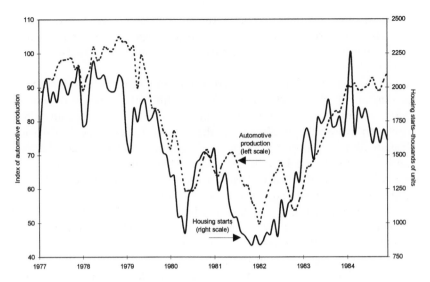

Figure 3.8 Year-to-year changes in housing starts and automotive production.
Sources: Census Bureau and Federal Reserve.

their peak of two million units in 1977–1978. Motor vehicle production dropped to half its 1978 level.

The financial system was also in a state of crisis by 1982, as we have seen in chapter 2. The largest commercial banks were severely weakened by the financial problems of the less-developed countries, of which Brazil and Mexico were the two most prominent; and, when oil prices dropped, financial problems spread throughout the domestic econmy as well, especially in the energy states of Texas, Louisiana, Oklahoma, and Colorado. High interest rates and real estate problems (especially in the oil states and California) wreaked havoc in the savings and loan industry.

The Reagan administration itself was at low ebb in 1982. Financial traditionalists were disillusioned by the spiraling federal budget deficit and its counterpart in the trade deficit. Various members of the cabinet appeared either inept or corrupt, and stories were legion about the president's own lack of sophistication and inattention to detail. The Democrats won back control of the Senate in the 1982 elections, and further progress on a "Reagan agenda" appeared stalled.

This low point for the Reagan administration, the economy, and the financial system marked the turning point in the stock market, and the beginning of the third phase of reaction to the new regime. The S&P 500 rose steadily from 107 in July 1982 to 168 in June 1983, producing a total return of 63%. This far outstripped the dozen other peak return periods between 1970 and 1990 when returns exceeded 30%, as can be

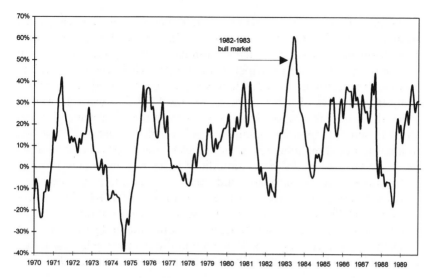

Figure 3.9 Changes in an index of total S&P 500 returns (rolling twelve months). Source: Ibbotson Associates.

seen in figure 3.9, which tracks rolling twelve-month changes in an index of S&P 500 total returns.

The stock market's rise initially coincided with the Federal Reserve's decision to reduce interest rates. Two-year treasury rates plummeted from 14.5% in June 1982 to 9.7% in December. The stock market continued to rise in the first half of 1983, even though two-year treasury rates were stalled around 9.5%, because the market received stimulus from economic recovery as the industrial production index rose from approximately 79 in December 1982 to 89 by the end of 1983. As can be seen in figure 3.8, housing starts increased from an annual rate of 1 million units during the summer of 1982 to 1.8 million units by the summer of 1983, and domestic auto production rose over 50%. As analysts in 1983 looked ahead to 1984 they estimated that earnings for the S&P 500 would be up 28%.

After mid-1983, stock market moves were limited. The S&P 500 stalled from mid-1983 through January 1984 as the Federal Reserve raised two-year treasury rates from 9.5% to 10.8% in response to the rapid economic recovery and a rise in CPI inflation from under 1% to almost 5%. When the Federal Reserve raised rates another notch in the second quarter of 1984, the stock market dropped 6% and growth in industrial production and business capital spending came to a halt. The stock market recovered these losses when the Federal Reserve reduced rates again in the last half of 1984.

The general environment at the end of 1984 left the stock market in an ambiguous position. Consumer confidence was high, having risen from 65 in mid-1982 to 94 at the end of 1983 to over 100 in September 1984. Consumer credit grew at 18% annualized through the second half of 1984, providing the principal thrust for the whole economy and an optimistic atmosphere for President Reagan's easy reelection. However, analysts' estimates of 1985 earnings for the S&P 500 were flat versus 1984; the economy was too dependent on consumer borrowing; the dollar had risen 43% since President Reagan's election, creating a Rust Belt in the traditional manufacturing industries of the Midwest and pushing prices down severely in the commodities industries, especially farming and mining; and the oil-related industries were in sharp decline as oil prices fell from $40 in early 1981 to $29 by the end of 1984. The administration and its supporters in Congress were also continually of two minds about raising taxes substantially to reduce the budget deficit. The stock market's uncertainty could be seen in the steep drop in new-issues of common stock from $38.3 billion in 1983 to $9.7 billion in 1984.

Traditional Measures of Stock Market Value

Opportunities for stock market profits in the '70s and early '80s were frequently telegraphed by the three traditional measures of stock market value—price-earnings ratios, market-to-book value ratios, and dividend yields—provided investors recognized that they were in a new investment environment from the 1960s. The signals always led to gains but didn't always telegraph the losses.

Returns on the S&P 500 and price-earnings ratios based on the latest twelve months' earnings are outlined in figure 3.10. Low price-earnings ratios of 7 or 8 in 1974, 1979, and 1982 signaled stock market returns of 40–60% in the following years of 1975, 1980, and 1983, but the 20% gain in the stock market in 1979 had no price-earnings signal as the ratio continued to decline into 1980, and the decline in the market in 1981–1982 did not have a prior signal as price-earnings ratios were only nine times earnings in 1980.

Market-to-book value ratios (outlined in figure 3.11), of approximately 110% in each of 1974, early 1980, and 1982 signaled stock market returns of 40–60% in 1975, 1980, and 1983, but the 20% gain in the stock market in 1979 had no market-to-book value signal since the ratio continued to decline into 1980, nor did the decline in the market in 1981–1982 have a prior signal of high market-to-book value ratios since they only reached 130% in 1980.[13]

High dividend yields on the S&P 500 provided excellent signals for all of the big rises in the stock market, as can be seen in figure 3.12.[14] High yields in 1970, 1974, 1978–1980, and 1981–1982 were followed by peri-

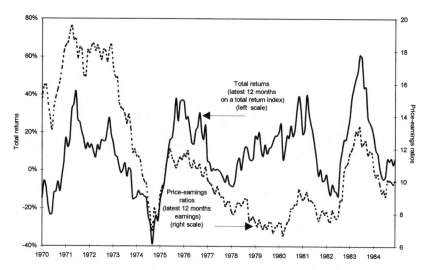

Figure 3.10 Returns and price-earnings ratios for the S&P 500. Sources: Ibbotson Associates and Standard & Poor's Corp.

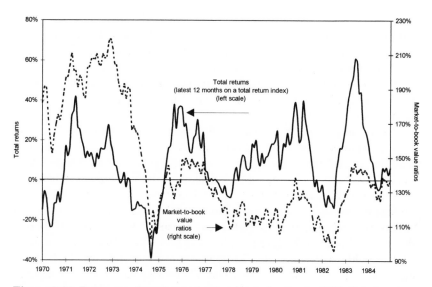

Figure 3.11 Returns and market-to-book value ratios for the S&P 500. Sources: Ibbotson Associates and Standard & Poor's Corp.

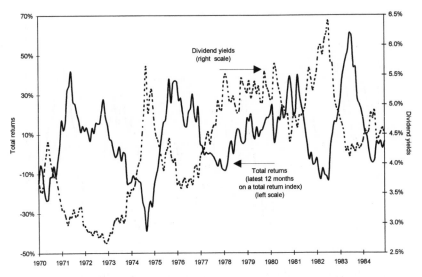

Figure 3.12 Returns and dividend yields for the S&P 500. Sources: Ibbotson Associates and Standard & Poor's Corp.

ods of 40% or greater returns in 1971, 1975, 1980, and 1982–1983; but it was difficult to discern "sell" signals based on dividend yields, as the low yields preceding declining markets rose from 2.5% in 1972 to 3.5% in 1976 and 4.5% in 1980. Any investor picking the 4.5% yield in 1983–1984 as a "sell" signal would have missed the subsequent run up in the market in 1986–1987.

One is tempted to argue that as interest rates rose one had to scale up what constituted a low yield. This approach has two problems, however. It requires an indicative low yield of approximately 6% in 1984, which would have been a false signal of a decline in the subsequent markets. It also results in no signals at all when dividend yields are expressed as a percentage of three-year treasuries, as in figure 3.13. In that figure, there is a confusing combination of low relative yields in 1970 and 1980–1981 that signalled subsequent high returns in 1971 and 1982–1983, but also high relative yields in 1974 and 1977 that were perversely followed by high returns in 1975–1976 and 1978–1979. There were also low relative yields in 1980 that were perversely followed by low returns in 1980–1982.

Fundamental Causes of Changes in the S&P 500 1979–1984

The impact of the new regime on stock prices can be divided into the effects of monetary policy, more optimistic earnings expectations, the

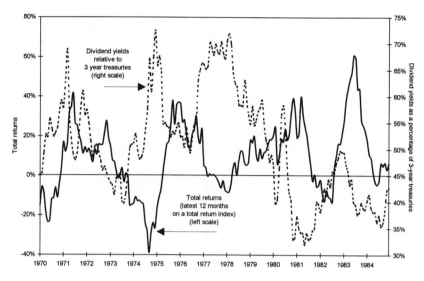

Figure 3.13 Returns and relative dividend yields. Sources: Ibbotson Associates and Standard & Poor's Corp.

1981 tax reductions, mergers and acquisitions, and generally increased optimism. My principal technique for sorting out these effects is a two-factor model based on analysts' estimates of future earnings and two-year treasury rates, but for the moment it will be helpful to look at the effects of these two factors separately. The effects of financial crises, the twin budget and trade deficits, declining oil prices, and the strong dollar were subsumed by these two factors at the macroeconomic level, although they had widely divergent impacts on individual industries at the microeconomic level, as we shall see in chapters 4 and 5.

Interest Rates

Although it is common lore that the stock market rises and falls with changes in interest rates, which are usually induced by Federal Reserve policies, there were many pronounced exceptions between January 1977 and December 1984, as can be seen in figure 3.14, which outlines the S&P 500 and inverted two-year treasury rates,[15] both indexed to 1/79 = 1.0. There were seven sustained stock market moves (up or down) in excess of 10% between 12/77 and 12/84, which are outlined by shaded areas and numbered consecutively, three of which (and arguably four) were contrary to the expected relationship with interest rates.

In the first major stock market move, which occurred between 6/77 and 2/78, the S&P 500 declined 13% while two-year treasury rates rose

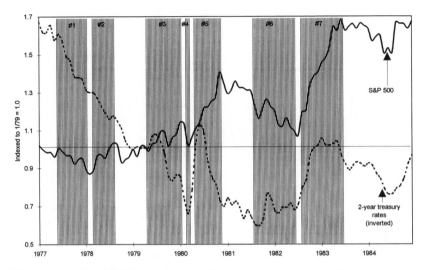

Figure 3.14 The S&P 500 and inverted two-year treasury rates (indexed to 1/79 = 1.0). Market moves greater than 10% are shaded and numbered. Sources: Standard & Poor's Corp. and Federal Reserve.

from 6.1% to 7.6%—the expected relationship. In the second major move, between 2/78 and 8/78, the S&P 500 rose from 87 to 103 while two-year treasury rates rose from 7.6% to 8.4%—contrary to the expected relationship.

In the third major move between 5/79 and 1/80, and before Paul Volcker had established that the Federal Reserve was going to be an active protagonist of inflation, the stock market rose again despite rising interest rates. There was a temporary decline in the stock market when the Federal Reserve announced its switch to a focus on money supply in October 1979, but over the broader period the S&P 500 rose from 99 to 114 while interest rates rose from 9.1% to 11.5%.

Federal Reserve actions that tightened credit were the crucial policy component in the Carter administration's March 1980 anti-inflation program which sharply depressed the stock market (the fourth major move).

In the spring of 1980, at the beginning of the fifth major move, the Federal Reserve ignited a stock market rally when it began to ease interest rates. However, when the Fed shifted to raising rates again in mid-1980 as inflation resumed, the stock market ignored the higher rates in anticipation of a Reagan victory. As two-year treasury rates rose from 9% in July to over 13.5% in November, the S&P 500 skyrocketed from 114 to 141. This, of course, was the crucial moment of transition between the old and new regimes.

Even in the recession of 1981–1982, which was almost exclusively induced by monetary policy, the stock market did not follow interest rates (the sixth major move). The S&P 500 did not begin to decline seriously until July 1981, by which time the rise in interest rates was complete. While the S&P 500 declined from 131 in 7/81 to 107 in 7/82, two-year treasury rates actually declined from 15.4% to 14.5%.

The Federal Reserve had a decisive influence, however, on the seventh, and most famous, major market move when the S&P 500 had a record postwar rise from 107 in July 1982 to 168 in June 1983. The Federal Reserve triggered the move when it reduced two-year treasury rates from 13.8% in July to 9.3% in January 1983; however, even in this case, the S&P 500 continued to rise from February through June 1983 because of the impetus of rising corporate earnings, despite the fact that interest rates had flattened out.

The impact of interest rates on stock prices is much more mixed than common lore suggests, because other factors frequently overwhelmed the influence of interest rates. The most fundamental of these factors was corporate earnings, to which I will now turn.

Earnings

The new regime had a powerful impact on investors' expectations of corporate earnings, not only raising them when President Reagan was elected, and keeping them high throughout the recession of 1981–1982, but also raising expectations well above earnings actually realized. It is possible to measure these expectations directly for the first time beginning in October 1978, using the Institutional Brokers Estimate System (IBES) published by Jones, Lynch & Ryan. IBES provides systematic monthly earnings estimates for the current year (Year 1) and the next year (Year 2) by several thousand analysts for each of the stocks in the S&P 500. Each estimate is available for approximately two years. Using the mean of all estimates for each company and the appropriate weighting for each company in the S&P 500 index, IBES provides monthly estimates of earnings for the S&P 500 in the current and next year. These are commonly known as "bottom up" estimates of S&P 500 earnings, in contrast to the estimates of fifteen to twenty equity strategists who provide their own estimates of S&P 500 earnings. The IBES bottom up data for 1979–1989 is provided in appendix 3.1.

Figure 3.15 shows the monthly mean IBES estimates for S&P 500 earnings for each year from 1980–1985 as they existed in the years indicated on the X axis. For example, estimates were quite stable throughout 1979 and 1980 for 1980 earnings of approximately $15, in contrast to estimates for 1982 earnings, which started at approximately $21 in early 1981 but slid steadily to approximately $13 by the end of 1982.

The tendency for analysts to initially overestimate earnings after Rea-

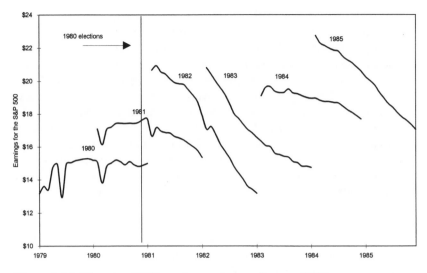

Figure 3.15 Changing IBES earnings estimates. Source: IBES.

gan's election is a striking feature of figure 3.15. Their initial estimates had to be persistently lowered as the reality of reported earnings intervened. The most striking cases were for 1982 and 1983, when initial earnings expectations were for $20.94 and $20.82 but which in reality turned out to be only $12.64 and $14.03. However, analysts' confidence that the new regime's policies would be translated into higher earnings was such that, just as as they were steadily forced to lower their estimates of the current year's earnings, they replaced them with a higher estimate for the next year, so that they continually had a high earnings forecast just ahead. Thus, as the original estimate for 1982 earnings of $20.94 slid to $12.64 it was replaced with a 1983 estimate of $20.82, and when actual 1983 earnings turned out to be only $14.03 they were replaced with a 1984 estimate of $20.00. This general tendency throughout 1981–1984 can be seen in figure 3.16, which shows the Year 2 IBES earnings estimate for the S&P 500 at all times. The 24% surge in estimates just following President Reagan's election stands out clearly and explains the dramatic rise in the stock market surrounding the elections. Even the impact of the 1981–1982 recession on earnings estimates is relatively muted. The jagged peaks in the graph occur because of discontinuity in the IBES data, as the estimates for Year 2 became available abruptly each January or February. The reader can reasonably assume that analysts were nonetheless using these estimates earlier and that the line in the chart should be smoother.

This optimism was very much a product of the new regime. Analysts in early 1979 projected S&P 500 earnings 25% and 12%, respectively,

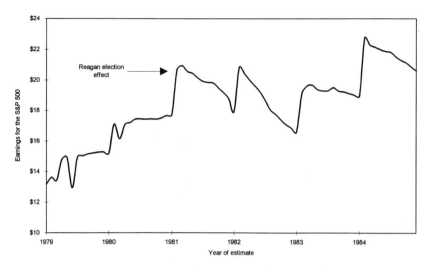

Figure 3.16 Year 2 IBES earnings estimates for the S&P 500. Source: IBES.

below the actual results for 1979–1980, but by early 1981 Year 2 projections were 36% above actual results. These overly optimistic estimates persisted through 1984, as can be seen in figure 3.17. As a result, it was optimism that powered much of the 55% rise in the S&P 500 Index from 108 to 167 between 1979 and 1984, as IBES Year 2 earnings estimates rose 35% while actual earnings only rose 12%.*

There is little to be gained, however, by looking separately at the impact of earnings estimates on stock prices. A balanced picture requires combining the effects of earnings and interest rates, to which I will now turn.

A Two-Factor Model of the S&P 500

When Year 2 IBES earnings estimates and two-year treasury rates are combined in a two-factor model for stock prices, as in Figure 3.18, it becomes quite clear that new valuation parameters—a new regime—prevailed from 1980 to 1984. In mid-1980 the S&P 500 switched from regularly underperforming what was indicated by changes in earnings and interest rates to frequently outperforming them. I cannot illustrate this for all of the 1970s because of lack of IBES data prior to October 1978, but we have already seen in figure 3.1 that the S&P 500 dramatically un-

---

*The difference between these estimates and actual earnings illustrates the pitfall in econometric models that relate stock prices to actual earnings some period of time later.

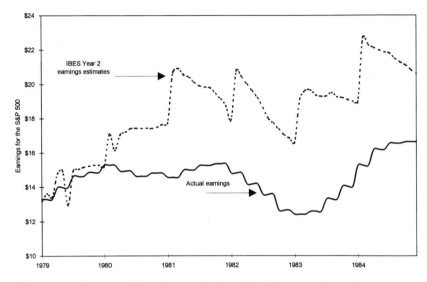

Figure 3.17 Year 2 IBES estimates for the S&P 500 vs. actual earnings.
Sources: IBES and Standard & Poor's Corp.

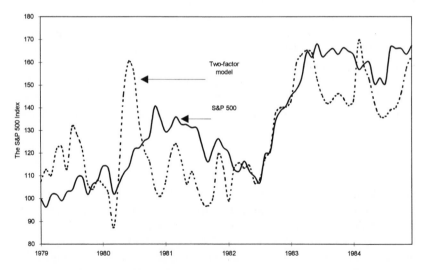

Figure 3.18 The S&P 500 vs. a two-factor model based on Year 2 IBES
earnings estimates and two-year treasury rates. Sources: Standard & Poor's
Corp., Federal Reserve, and IBES.

derperformed what was indicated by changes in actual earnings and interest rates in the 1970s.[16] The big change in valuation occurred when the S&P 500 rose from 114 to 141 between June and November 1980 despite rising interest rates. In 1981 the decline in the S&P 500 tracked the direction of the model quite closely, and the differences between the two were virtually eliminated in 1982, but in mid-1983 the S&P 500 outperformed the model again by staying flat at approximately 160 when the model indicated a substantial decline because the Federal Reserve began to raise interest rates. The divergence disappeared in early 1984, but the S&P 500 outperformed the model again when the Federal Reserve raised interest rates further in the first half of 1984.

It is important to emphasize that the model does not measure what the stock market "ought" to be, nor does it represent a model that we expect the stock market to fit. The dramatic difference between the S&P 500 and the model in the 1970s, outlined in figure 3.1, reflected clearly that something else had a major impact on stock prices. It is just as interesting when the stock market does not fit the model as when it does, because it helps us to isolate the extent to which other factors are affecting stock prices. This model is a benchmark to which I will frequently return. My implicit assumption is that changes in earnings expectations beyond the IBES data can be lumped in with other unmeasurable factors such as changes in risk premiums, propensity to buy stocks, and the degree of optimism or pessimism.

The change in valuation parameters from 1980 to 1984 reflected a rise in price-earnings ratios beyond the changes induced by interest rates, which can be illustrated by comparing the actual S&P 500 price-earnings ratio in any month with that indicated by the model, as outlined in figure 3.19 (see appendix 3.2, "A Note on the Two-Factor Model," for further details). There was erratic fluctuation in price-earnings ratios beyond that induced by interest rate changes in 1980 due to the extreme volatility of monetary policy, but we can, nonetheless, broadly assert that in 1980 there was a movement from price-earnings ratios 20% below those indicated by interest rates to ratios 20% higher. This was the equivalent of a 40% gain in the S&P 500. Half of the gain was lost in 1982, but it was partially recovered during much of 1983 and 1984. Periods in which price-earnings ratios were higher or lower than the model indicates can quite appropriately be considered periods of optimism or pessimism.

The Causes of Improved Price-Earnings Ratios Beyond Those Induced by Interest Rates

Merger and acquisition activity is a natural candidate to explain the periods of rising price-earnings ratios in figure 3.19. Merger and acquisition

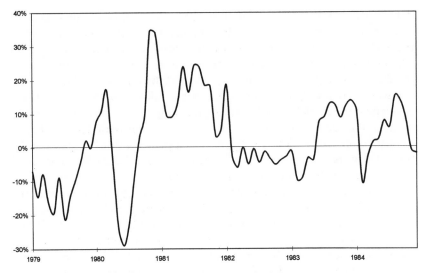

Figure 3.19 Changes in price-earnings ratios adjusted for changes in two-year treasury rates (12/79 base). Sources: IBES, Standard & Poor's Corp., and Federal Reserve.

activity doubled in 1981 and then doubled again in 1984,[17] and it was frequently cited by market professionals as raising the general level of stock prices. Acquiring firms paid average premiums 45% over prevailing stock prices between 1979 and 1984,[18] stimulating widespread anticipation of future acquisition candidates. Analysts began to analyze companies in terms of their susceptibility to takeover attempts and by calculating their "break-up values." A few activists, such as Boone Pickens and Carl Icahn, picked out companies that they thought were susceptible to takeover or worried about it, and bought minority positions, usually of 5–10%, in an attempt to push the companies into mergers. Other investors followed the more successful of these activists.

The impact of acquisitions on the S&P 500 cannot have been very great, however. The premiums paid for each of the companies that was acquired and removed from the index, outlined in table 3.3 for each year from 1980 to 1984, only amounted to increases in the index of between 0.2% and 2% annually. Cumulatively from 1/80 to 12/84, acquisition premiums raised the S&P 500 index by 7.15 points, or 6.6%. These 7.15 points amounted to 12.1% of the 59-point increase in the S&P 500 between 12/79 and 12/84.[19] This result should be adjusted down by the extent to which acquiring companies' stocks fell when they announced acquisitions, but this evidence is inconclusive.[20]

The effect for each acquired company on the S&P 500 was calculated as its acquisition premium times the company's weighting in the S&P

500 Index the month it was removed. Acquisition premiums were taken from W. T. Grimm's *Mergerstat Review* and alternatively from Goldman Sachs records, or as a last resort were calculated from SEC filings.

Another effect of the acquisition boom was an increase in the relative weight that investors gave to the sale value of assets, or "break-up values," in valuing stocks. If a company could sell its assets at higher multiples of cash flow than the stock market accorded them, there was a probability-adjusted reason to value its stock accordingly. This was particularly true in industries subject to a high degree of acquisition activity at prices based on projected cash flows, such as cable television, cellular telephone, and media properties, but it was also true of many companies that had underperforming assets or assets with ready markets, of which oil and gas properties were probably the best example. Similarly, whenever a major acquisition took place, stocks of other companies in the same industry invariably rose in sympathy as investors anticipated further acquisitions or management actions to improve stockholder values within the industry. In industries subject to frequent acquisitions, such as oil and gas, food, pipelines, media properties, and department stores, these anticipations were often correct. However, the probability adjustment to stock prices for perfect foresight into acquisitions should have been the same as the ex-post facto results outlined in table 3.3, so that the stock values for companies not taken over would revert to their previous levels. This reversion would depend on the "decay life" for the asset valuation emphasis. The decay life relates to both what other stock investors will pay for asset values and the actual rate of takeovers. For example, independent oil and gas companies' stock prices appear to have embodied very persistent asset valuation by investors because of the ready markets for oil and gas assets, as we shall see in chapter 4. Given the relatively modest market impact of actual acquisitions, the "decay life" effect of other anticipated acquisitions cannot have been very large.

A third effect of acquisitions on stock prices occurred to the extent that the threat of being acquired stimulated some companies to make various leverage, investment, cost-control, pricing, and asset disposition decisions favorable to stockholders. However, the direct effects of these decisions should have shown up in earnings projections, which have already been taken into account in my two-factor model. I will cover the indirect effects in the next volume, covering the years 1985–1989, when acquisition activity reached its peak and the decade can be considered as a whole.

Even though acquisition effects on the S&P 500 did not appear large, the cumulative effect of acquisition premiums artificially inflated the S&P 500 Index, since the premiums raised the index up to the point that the acquired company was removed from the index, but no adjustment was made when the replacement company lacking this premium was in-

Table 3.3. Annual Effects of Acquisition Premiums on the S&P 500

Year	Number of Acquisitions	Premium Effect	
		Percent	*Points*
1980	9	0.4%	0.45
1981	18	2.0%	2.51
1982	17	1.9%	1.02
1983	7	0.2%	0.40
1984	26	1.7%	2.77

Note: Each acquired company's weighting in the S&P 500 index was multiplied by the premium paid for it to obtain the impact on the index in terms of points.

Sources: Standard & Poor's Corp., *Mergerstat Review*, Goldman, Sachs & Co., and SEC filings.

cluded in the index. Therefore, to facilitate my attempts to explain differences between the S&P 500 and the two-factor model, I have reduced the S&P 500 each month, beginning in 1980, by the cumulative effect of acquisition premiums (the "adjusted S&P 500"). I will now turn to other explanations for why price-earnings ratios rose beyond what was indicated by interest rates.

The reader should be under no illusion that the improvement in price-earnings ratios was related to improved real earnings growth rates, despite the decline in inflation that occurred. Figure 3.20 indicates that real earnings growth rates for the S&P 500 did not match those of the last half of the 1970s until after the crash of 1987. The graph data represents annual averages over thirty-six-months to smooth out short-term effects, and log rates to provide comparable growth data from month to month. Lower real earnings growth rates may have reduced price-earnings ratios in the 1970s versus the 1960s, but no such logic was available to explain the higher ratios of the 1980s.

A possible explanation for the improvement in price-earnings ratios is the prospect of lower tax rates explicit in a Reagan victory.[21] The tax act of 1981 produced a substantial increase in after-tax returns on common stock investments, principally because of declines in the capital gains tax rate from 28% to 20% and in the maximum tax rate on dividends from 70% to 50%. These tax reductions increased individuals' after-tax returns in stocks by at least 20%.[22] Since individuals held approximately 50% of all common equities, we would expect such a radical change in personal taxes to be quickly capitalized in common stock prices. This tax-oriented explanation also fits with the stock market's anticipatory tendencies and explains why no positive change in price-earnings ratios occurred later in 1981, when the tax cuts were ultimately implemented. There was also a reduction in corporate income taxes, but this was reflected in corporate earnings and does not need to be accounted for separately from our model.

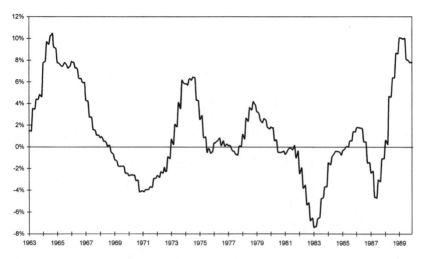

Figure 3.20 Average annual log growth rates for real S&P 500 earnings (based on rolling three-year periods deflated by CPI). Sources: Standard & Poor's Corp. and Bureau of Labor Statistics.

Tax reductions, however, only explain 20 of the 40 percentage points change in price-earnings ratios in late 1980. We are left with the need to explain a further 20% rise in 1980 and the 10% rises in 1983 and 1984. Stock market participants at the time had various explanations for what was moving stock prices. Insofar as these explanations included money supply, the budget deficit, the dollar, inflation, and oil prices, they were reflected in interest rates or earnings, however, and are therefore captured by my model. The principal remaining factor is investor optimism or confidence.

Two good measures of confidence substantiate its impact at these times. The Consumer Confidence Index rose from 51.7 in June 1980 to 77.2 in August 1981 and from 65.4 in August 1982 to 100.9 in September 1983, at the same time that price-earnings ratios temporarily rose beyond what was indicated by interest rates. Changes in the two, which coincided strongly throughout 1979–1984, are outlined in figure 3.21. New issues are another good measure of confidence. They rose to a record $14.5 billion in 1981, finally surpassing the $10.8 billion record set in 1972. New issues rose again in 1983 to a record-shattering $38.5 billion. The close relationship between these peaks and the rise in price-earnings ratios can be seen in figure 3.22.

It should be emphasized that price-earnings ratios rose beyond what was indicated by interest rates in 1983 and 1984 despite the obvious problems with the federal budget deficit, the trade deficit, the banking system, and high real interest rates. All indications are that these prob-

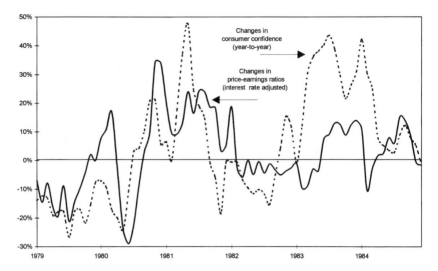

Figure 3.21 Changes in price-earnings ratios (net of interest rates) and consumer confidence. Sources: Standard & Poor's Corp., IBES, Federal Reserve, and the University of Michigan.

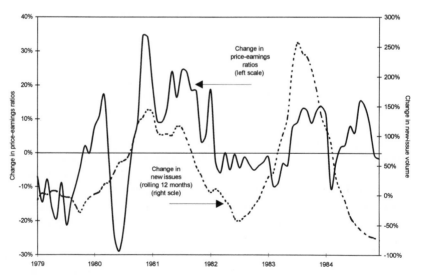

Figure 3.22 Changes in price-earnings ratios (net of interest rates) and new issues of common stock. Sources: Standard & Poor's Corp., IBES, Federal Reserve, and Securities Data.

lems simply did not matter to the stock market beyond their effects on earnings and interest rates, and that they could not damp down the generally optimistic attitudes of investors.

The changes in institutional funds flows into equities approximated the pattern of changes in price-earnings ratios beyond what was indicated by interest rates, as the share of institutional funds flowing into equities rose from 10.2% in 1978 to 21.6% in 1981 and 26.6% in 1983; however, emphasizing funds flows as a causal factor is problematic. Increased institutional flows were matched by declining household flows, and there is no reason to emphasize one over the other. Net institutional purchases were also too small relative to trading volume to be a major factor in stock prices, accounting for only 5.6% of NYSE volume during 1980–1984.[23]

The changes in funds flows are better considered as reflections of causal forces in stock market valuation than as causal factors themselves. The rare occasions when funds flows may be considered an independent technical factor in stock market valuation have occurred when a particular market sector has diverted abnormal proportions of funds into stocks, ignoring portfolio allocation factors. For example, private pension funds allocated 90% of their funds flows to stocks in 1968–1971, and there is some evidence of skewed institutional funds allocations leading up to the crash of 1987. More recently, household mutual fund purchases in 1993–1996 have influenced stock values. But even in these cases there is nothing about the flows themselves to indicate whether they reflected fundamental or other factors.

Summary

The early 1980s witnessed a dramatic recovery in the stock market after the punishment of the 1970s, when price-earnings ratios for the S&P 500 shrank from 17.9 to only 7.0 and the S&P 500 underperformed by 86% what was indicated by a two-factor model using changes in interest rates and earnings. The higher price-earnings ratios of the 1980s and the stock market's renewed responsiveness to changes in earnings and interest rates reflected the new regime brought about by the activist role of the Federal Reserve in fighting inflation, the policies of the Reagan administration, particularly its tax cuts, and the combined ability of the Federal Reserve and the administration to keep the crisis in the banking system between 1982 and 1984 from disrupting the economy and the securities markets.

The impact of the new regime was immediately obvious in the second half of 1980, when the Federal Reserve righted its policy course after a period of embarrassing volatility and the stock market began to anticipate a Reagan victory. Despite rising interest rates, the S&P 500 rose 23%. This was the equivalent of a 40% improvement in price-earnings ratios, adjusted for higher interest rates. Half of the rise in the stock market was due to the Reagan administration's promise of a cut in tax rates, but there was also a sharp upward shift in analysts' projections of future earnings. We are uniquely able, for the first time in stock market history, to directly measure earnings expectations after October 1978, thanks to the systematic publication of IBES earnings estimates. General optimism also received a boost, after a decade of decline, upon Reagan's election.

Despite the immediate positive impact on the stock market of Reagan's election—a good example of how quickly changing expectations were translated into stock prices—it was almost two years before the stock market began to generate consistently attractive returns. This occurred because, although the S&P 500 no longer underperformed my two-factor model of earnings and interest rates, interest rates were driven so high by the Federal Reserve that stock returns were negative into mid-1982. At that point, when the Federal Reserve reduced interest rates dramatically and revoked its emphasis on money supply in order to continue reducing rates, the stock market began a rise that raised the S&P 500 57% in the next eleven months, a post-war record. During 1982, this rise was due solely to declining interest rates, as IBES earnings estimates failed to change, but in 1983 earnings estimates began to rise and powered the stock market higher, even though interest rates had stopped falling.

This dramatic rise in the stock market occurred despite a developing crisis in the banking sector that unnerved many financial traditionalists, especially those with a sense of history who identified the problems of the 1930s with the collapse of the banking system. The first signs of crisis were in the large city banks that had lent aggressively to less-developed countries, especially Brazil and Mexico, that were unable to keep up debt service in a weak world economy with declining commodities prices and high real interest rates. The Federal Reserve and the administration did a masterful job of containing this problem, mostly through policies of delay and patchwork. As banking problems spread throughout the south and west due to the collapse of the oil and real estate industries, the Federal Reserve and the administration were forced to intervene aggressively to save Continental Illinois Bank & Trust in 1984, but lesser banks were allowed to flounder. To any traditionalist investor, these banking problems, combined with the twin federal budget and trade deficits, presented a very negative outlook for the securities markets and the economy; but it must be emphasized that the stock market paid them little heed, either because it trusted in the managerial skills of the authorities or because the traditionalist theoretical framework was simply wrong.

Accepted signals for pending stock market recovery—low price-earnings ratios, low market-to-book value ratios, and low absolute dividend

Table 3.4. Constituent Parts of the Increase in the S&P 500 12/79 to 12/84

	12/79	12/84	% Change
S&P 500	108	167	55%
M&A adjusted S&P 500	108	160	48%
2-factor model	108	163	51%
2 factor model based on actual earnings	108	119	10%
IBES Year 2 earnings estimates	15.29	20.61	35%
Actual earnings 12 months ahead	14.82	14.61	−1%
2 Year U.S. treasury rates	11.39	10.18	−11%

Sources: IBES, Standard & Poor's Corp., and Federal Reserve.

yields—gave good indications of the profit potential in the stock market in 1980 and 1982, and the S&P 500 at the end of 1984 was very close to what was indicated by my two-factor model, especially when adjusted for merger premiums; but such apparent dominance of rational factors must be tempered by appreciation of the psychological aspects involved. Earnings and interest rates had almost nothing to do with the S&P 500 in the 1970s, and stock prices only came into line with these fundamentals in the 1980s after a 40% rise in interest-adjusted price-earnings ratios in 1980–1981. Even thereafter, IBES next-year earnings estimates, which rose 31% from $15.29 in 1979 to $20.02 in 1984, greatly outstripped actual earnings, which were virtually flat at $14.82 in 1980 and only $14.61 in 1985. Over the five years, IBES estimates ranged from 25–40% above those actually realized. If the S&P 500 had followed actual year-ahead earnings and interest rates, it would have been only 119 at the end of 1984 instead of 167.[24]

We can parse the 55% increase in the S&P 500 from 108 to 167 between 12/79 and 12/84 into its constituent parts as I have done in table 3.4. A 7% increase was due to acquisitions. My two-factor model indicated an increase of 51%, of which only 10% could be ascribed to changes in interest rates and actual year-ahead earnings and the balance to higher earnings estimates than actually occurred. Tax cuts moved the S&P 500 approximately 25 points in late 1980—a 23% increase on the 12/79 base of 108—but this made up for the underperformance of the S&P 500 in the first half of 1980 rather than adding to the increase between 12/79 and 12/84.

The fundamental change in investors' psychology that was exhibited in the high IBES estimates was one of the new regime's most important contributions to the stock market. This optimism was also reflected in three periods between 1979 and 1984 when the S&P 500 rose beyond what was indicated by my model—in late 1980, in mid-1983, and in mid-1984. These periods evinced considerable optimism as indicated by the consumer confidence index and the volume of new common stock issues. One naturally wonders whether the sharp decline in inflation was responsible for the general improvement in psychology, but, if so, it was in itself psychological. There was no change in real earnings growth waiting over the horizon. Inflation-adjusted earnings growth throughout the 1980s was actually lower than in the 1970s and only began to exceed the 1970s after the crash of 1987. Nor should the reader assume that there was an indiscriminate air of optimism. As we shall see in the next chapter, what had been favorable trends in the 1970s turned sharply negative for many of the largest industries, particularly the oil, commodities, and equipment manufacturing industries, disrupting much of the American economy.

Appendix 3.1. IBES Bottom-up Earnings per Share Estimates for the S&P 500

Date of Estimate		Earnings Year 1979	1980	1981	1982	1983
1979	1	11.86	13.18			
	2	11.16	13.62			
	3	12.25	13.42			
	4	13.38	14.78			
	5	13.78	14.94			
	6	12.01	12.94			
	7	14.08	14.97			
	8	14.30	15.04			
	9	14.47	15.16			
	10	14.58	15.22			
	11	14.69	15.28			
	12	14.80	15.29			
1980	1					
	2		15.08	17.10		
	3		13.81	16.15		
	4		14.82	17.07		
	5		15.02	17.21		
	6		15.20	17.43		
	7		15.11	17.45		
	8		14.92	17.43		
	9		15.11	17.45		
	10		14.92	17.43		
	11		14.81	17.50		
	12		14.88	17.67		
1981	1		14.99	17.71		
	2			16.66	20.68	
	3			17.18	20.94	
	4			16.97	20.57	
	5			16.87	20.44	
	6			16.84	20.15	
	7			16.64	19.92	
	8			16.54	19.85	
	9			16.41	19.80	
	10			16.21	19.50	
	11			16.02	19.15	
	12			15.79	18.75	

Appendix 3.1. (*continued*)

Date of Estimate		Earnings Year					
		1982	1983	1984	1985	1986	1987
1982	1						
	2	17.08	20.82				
	3	17.24	20.43				
	4	16.77	20.01				
	5	16.18	19.62				
	6	15.77	19.21				
	7	15.32	18.64				
	8	14.79	18.02				
	9	14.40	17.74				
	10	14.03	17.39				
	11	13.62	17.07				
	12	13.43	16.86				
1983	1		16.59				
	2		16.34	19.11			
	3		16.08	19.63			
	4		16.01	19.67			
	5		15.62	19.38			
	6		15.54	19.30			
	7		15.43	19.31			
	8		15.37	19.52			
	9		15.11	19.28			
	10		15.04	19.23			
	11		14.82	19.11			
	12		14.82	19.01			
1984	1		14.75	18.95			
	2			18.96	22.74		
	3			18.83	22.30		
	4			18.75	22.15		
	5			18.75	21.99		
	6			18.69	21.87		
	7			18.67	21.81		
	8			18.47	21.50		
	9			18.26	21.28		
	10			18.10	21.12		
	11			17.9	21.36		
	12			17.69	20.61		
1985	1			17.39	20.26		
	2				20.03	21.89	
	3				19.76	21.98	
	4				19.33	21.73	
	5				18.97	21.36	
	6				18.63	21.26	
	7				18.39	21.04	
	8				18.08	20.91	
	9				17.82	20.74	
	10				17.62	20.59	
	11				17.36	20.36	
	12				17.06	20.21	
1986	1				16.99	20.13	
	2					19.78	22.40

(*continued*)

Appendix 3.1. (*continued*)

Date of Estimate		1986	1987	1988	1989	1990	1991
				Earnings Year			
	3	19.28	21.97				
	4	18.95	21.67				
	5	18.61	21.31				
	6	18.38	21.23				
	7	18.19	21.14				
	8	17.77	20.83				
	9	17.44	20.64				
	10	17.2	20.52				
	11	16.88	20.37				
	12	16.74	20.26				
1987	1		20.12				
	2		20.05	23.48			
	3		19.95	23.34			
	4		19.96	23.33			
	5		20.08	24.50			
	6		19.71	23.76			
	7		18.92	23.89			
	8		18.71	24.15			
	9		18.82	24.26			
	10		18.59	24.22			
	11		18.55	23.94			
	12		18.47	23.70			
1988	1		18.16	23.46			
	2			23.57	26.11		
	3			23.57	26.09		
	4			23.68	26.08		
	5			24.38	26.71		
	6			24.55	26.88		
	7			24.61	27.05		
	8			24.89	27.34		
	9			24.95	27.46		
	10			24.90	27.41		
	11			25.08	27.59		
	12			25.12	27.61		
1989	1			25.39	27.89		
	2				28.10	30.11	
	3				28.26	30.69	
	4				28.22	30.45	
	5				28.23	30.38	
	6				28.18	30.49	
	7						
	8				27.78	30.25	
	9				27.72	30.16	
	10				26.43	29.86	
	11				25.77	29.53	
	12				25.34	29.25	
1990	1				24.90	28.92	
	2					28.43	32.00
	3					28.06	31.98
	4					27.69	31.70
	5					27.36	31.58

Appendix 3.1. (*continued*)

| Date of Estimate | Earnings Year | | | | | |
	1986	1987	1988	1989	1990	1991
6					27.10	31.40
7					26.71	31.10
8					26.53	30.88
9					26.21	30.20
10					25.76	29.57
11					25.18	28.74
12					24.64	28.10

Appendix 3.2   A Note on the Two-Factor Model

The two-factor model resembles many multifactor macroeconomic stock market models in measuring changes in stock prices versus a chosen factor(s) from an arbitrary starting point. This approach avoids the problems of discounted cash flow models (whether dividends, earnings, or cash flow) that try to determine intrinsic present value. These models all require assumption of an arbitrary terminal value, and, except for when dividends are discounted, have a problem with discounting earnings or cash flow that is reinvested to produce future earnings.

My model differs from macroeconomic models that use lagged GNP, industrial production, or corporate profits as variables, in that it incorporates contemporary earnings expectations in the form of Year 2 IBES estimates for the S&P 500. Its other variable is two-year constant maturity treasury rates—a term that matches the Year 2 IBES forecasts used and which also minimizes the differences between the model and the actual S&P 500 (see below). Earnings and interest rates represent the two "fundamental" factors affecting stock prices that are emphasized by investors and the financial media. The reader can see in figure 3.23 that the model corresponded quite well with the actual S&P 500 throughout the decade with the notable exception of the market boom leading up to the crash of 1987.

The formula for the model is as follows:

$$SP_n = SP_{12/79} \times \frac{EPS_n}{EPS_{12/79}} \times \frac{I_{12/79}}{I_n}$$

where:

SP_n = predicted S&P 500 in period "n",

$SP_{12/79}$ = the closing S&P 500 price in December 1979,

EPS_n = the Year 2 IBES bottom-up earnings projection for the S&P 500 as of month "n",

$EPS_{12/79}$ = the Year 2 IBES bottom-up earnings projection for the S&P 500 as of December 1979,

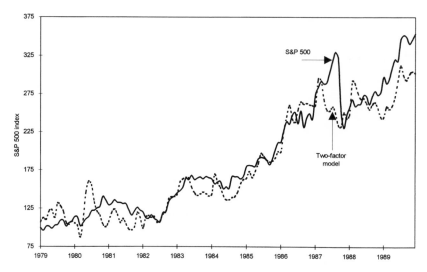

Figure 3.23 The S&P 500 and a two-factor model based on Year 2 IBES estimates and two-year treasury rates. Sources: Federal Reserve, Standard & Poor's Corp., and IBES.

$I_{12/79}$ = the two-year U.S. treasury constant maturity index as published by the Federal Reserve Bank of New York for December 1979,

I_n = the two-year U.S. treasury constant maturity index as published by the Federal Reserve Bank of New York for month "n".

The model is not sensitive to what base date is chosen.

Since the two-year U.S. treasury rate is in effect being used as the discount rate, the effect on the S&P 500 of changes in earnings and interest rates is the multiplicand of the changes in the two factors.

For example:

if SP_n is the present value of a projected constant cash flow PCF_n at interest rate I_n, $SP_n = \dfrac{PCF_n}{I_n}$,

and if SP_{n+1} is the present value of another projected constant cash flow at interest rate I_{n+1}, $SP_{n+1} = \dfrac{PCF_{n+1}}{I_{n+1}}$;

then $\dfrac{SP_n}{SP_{n+1}} = \dfrac{PCF_n}{PCF_{n+1}} \times \dfrac{I_{n+1}}{I_n}$

and $SP_{n+1} = SP_n \times \dfrac{I_n}{I_{n+1}} \times \dfrac{PCF_{n+1}}{PCF_n}$

Not knowing projected cash flows, our model uses the Year 2 IBES projections and in effect assumes a constant price-earnings ratio other than related to interest rate changes. Insofar as investors actually assumed changing long-term future earnings growth rates, I make no distinction between this and changing optimism.

At first it may appear as if this model commits the error of discounting future years' earnings when current years' earnings are reinvested to produce the future earnings. The only cash flow from stocks not subject to this problem is dividends, but that does not make dividends the determinant of stock prices. For market practitioners, price-earnings ratios are the mechanism that reflects the discounting of future factors, but price-earnings ratios reflect various factors, such as earnings growth, risk, merger market value, degree of optimism, and popularity. The predicted stock price in this model is independent of the absolute price-earnings ratio for the S&P 500 at any time, and simply suggests that changes in the price-earnings ratio will be proportionate to changes in interest rates. Therefore, the predicted stock price does not discount earnings.

The two-year treasury was used for the model because it coincides with the maximum Year 2 earnings projections in the IBES forecasts. It also showed the best fit to the actual S&P 500 over 1978–1990. The mean differences between the S&P 500 and the model using different U.S. treasury constant maturity indexes were as follows:[25]

	Mean:
3 months	−21.6%
2 year	−0.6%
3 year	6.3%
5 year	0.1%
7 year	11.4%
10 year	12.1%

Some comment is necessary on the IBES earnings estimates. S&P 500 earnings estimates are available monthly for the current year (Year 1) and the next year (Year 2) as measured by "bottom-up" earnings estimates of several thousand analysts following S&P 500 stocks, courtesy of Lynch Jones & Ryan. IBES earnings estimates began in 1975, but at first were expressed as percentage increases rather than as actual S&P earnings estimates, and in a subsequent variation were presented as actual estimates but unweighted by the size of the company to which they applied. IBES estimates fully consistent with S&P 500 earnings were first published in October 1978 and are included in appendix 3.1. I have tried without success to make the earlier data consistent with that after October 1978.

The model uses the estimate for Year 2 earnings to reflect changes in earnings estimates. This results in the projected period varying over the year. The projected period amounts to almost two years early in each year, when projections for the next year are first recorded; at the turn of each year the projected period is as short as eleven months, while analysts are awaiting earnings reports for the year just passed and most have not yet developed projections two years ahead. Projections for the second year ahead usually become numerous in the second quarter. This is unfortunate from the point of view of consistency, but it does reflect analysts' general practice. Using the Year 2 IBES estimate also results in discontinuous changes in earnings estimates when a new year is first recorded.

A constant twelve-month IBES earnings projection that only changes gradually can be constructed by weighting the Year 1 estimate by the months remaining in the current year and the Year 2 estimate by twelve minus the Year 2 weighting. I have used the Year 2 estimate, despite its fluctuating time period and discontinuous changes, rather than this weighted estimate, because the rolling twelve months estimates tend to be late in picking up the earnings effects of turning points in the business cycle. There were considerably higher mean monthly differences between the model using a constant twelve-month earnings projection and the actual S&P 500.

The two-factor model can be manipulated to display the change in price-earnings ratios that is unrelated to changes in interest rates, as was done in figure 3.19. This change is the difference between the actual price-earnings ratio (APE) in month "n" and the forecast price-earnings ratio (FPE) in the two-factor model in month "n", expressed as a percentage of the forecast price-earnings ratio. The formula for the actual price-earnings ratio is:

$$APE_n = \frac{S\&P500_n}{EPS_n}$$

where:

$S\&P500_n$ = the S&P 500 in month "n", and

EPS_n = the Year 2 IBES estimate for S&P 500 earnings in month "n". The formula for the price-earnings ratio forecasted by the model in month "n" is:

$$FPE = S\&P500_{12/79} \times \frac{EPS_n}{EPS_{12/79}} \times \frac{I_{12/79}}{I_n} \times \frac{1}{EPS_n}$$

$$= \frac{S\&P500_{12/79}}{EPS_{12/7}} \times \frac{I_{12/79}}{I_n}$$

where:

$S\&P500_{12/79}$ = the S&P 500 at the end of December 1979,

$EPS_{12/79}$ = the Year 2 IBES estimate for the S&P 500 in December 1979,

EPS_n = the Year 2 IBES estimate for the S&P 500 in month "n",

$I_{12/79}$ = the two-year treasury constant maturity index for December 1979,

I_n = the two-year treasury constant maturity index for month "n".
The formula for the interest rate-adjusted change in price-earnings ratios is:

$$\frac{APE - 1}{FPE}$$

4

The Underperforming Industries

The change in regimes that restored favorable returns in the securities markets, beat back inflation, and initiated sustained economic growth carried a fearful price in terms of the decline of a number of industries that had benefited from previous trends. They are the subject of this chapter, which deals with the industry stock groups that underperformed the 55% gain in the S&P 500 by twenty percentage points or more. Any popular image of a decade of easy stock gains and business profits is belied by the large proportion of the S&P 500 accounted for by underperforming stock groups—43% in 1979—and by the depth of their decline—an 88% decline in return on equity, 69% decline in net capital expenditures as a percentage of capitalization, and 16% decline in employment. These industries' protracted problems also contradict various academic theories that a favorable change in expectations or regimes can achieve rapid, painless transition to superior economic performance.

This chapter outlines pronounced industry factors in stock underperformance—a variable that receives little reference in academic studies of industrial decline in this period. The oil-related, metal and other commodities, heavy equipment, auto, and banking industries made up most of the underperforming industries. Both stock and financial results in these industries underwent a dramatic change in trend, since until 1981 they or their customers were beneficiaries of rising oil prices, commodities inflation, and a relatively weak dollar. Only the steel and chemical industries were in previous secular decline. The Council of Economic Advisors and numerous academics have focused on equipment manufacturers in this period and have argued that their problems were simply part of a long-term trend, particularly in the Midwest.[1] The stock market, however, reveals a serious decline over a much broader range of industries, and in most cases their declines were contrary to the trend that prevailed in the inflationary environment of the 1970s.

The driving forces behind the underperforming industries, were changing oil prices and the strength of the dollar. The initial rise in oil prices to $40 per barrel had a severe impact on the auto, chemical, and aluminum industries, where energy was a large cost element. Even when oil prices subsequently declined to $29 per barrel in 1984 the impact remained. But the obvious impact of declining oil prices was on the oil-related industries themselves, which had overexpanded when prices were high and now had to cut back severely. The sharpest declines in stock prices and reductions in capital expenditures and employment were in the capital goods industries supplying the oil industry, such as Offshore Drilling, Oil Well Equipment & Services, and Construction & Engineering.* The oil-related industries had a disproportionate impact on both the stock market and the general economy. They were almost 25% of the S&P 500 at the end of 1979 but only 16% at the end of 1984, and accounted for 28% of U.S. capital spending from 1981 to 1982 but only 18% in 1984. Changing oil prices also affected the finances of less-developed countries that were oil exporters, and affected in turn the commercial banks lending to them.

As the dollar strengthened 55% from 1980 to 1985, it had a severe impact on manufacturing industries heavily involved in exports, such as construction machinery and office equipment, or those exposed to significant import competition, such as autos, steel, aluminum, and machine tools. Other industries, such as metals mining, agricultural machinery, and pulp and paper, were affected more by declining commodities prices related to the strong dollar than by changes in foreign trade. Strong labor unions and excessively high wage rates in the auto, equipment manufacturing, and metals industries generally restricted adaptation to the changing pressures on them.

In most industries there were complicating factors that prevented ascribing their underperformance solely to oil prices, the dollar, or high wage costs. The oil industry was involved in manic overexpansion from 1979 to 1982. The auto industry used protection to price for returns above its Japanese competitors. The steel industry in the 1970s raised prices faster than inflation but did not generate the profits to modernize, instead buying labor peace with the highest wages in U.S. industry. Farm-

---

*Througout the text a capitalized industry refers to a stock market index published by Standard & Poor's Corp. or Value Line. The reader should be alert that the reference may be to the stock index itself or the underlying financial data.

ers greatly overexpanded under the impetus of high crop prices, and the chemical industry overexpanded as the oil companies integrated upstream after the 1973 oil crisis. Mainframe computers were struck by technological change, aluminum was affected by advances in recycling, and steel was affected by increased use of plastics in the auto industry, but the only industry in which technological changes were a primary cause of underperformance was the mainframe computer business.

There was also a general decline in capital spending between 1979 and 1984 that disproportionately affected the capital goods industries. A large part of the decline in capital expenditures related to declining oil prices. Direct oil capital expenditures declined from 28% to 18% of U.S. private capital expenditures between 1982 and 1984. Other factors affecting capital spending were the rise in real long-term interest rates from virtually zero under President Carter to over 7% under President Reagan, and limitations on the available capital caused by the increase in the 100 largest acquisitions from 19% to 66% of capital spending by the S&P Industrials between 1979 and 1984.

In this chapter I will first examine the underperforming industries in terms of stock prices, earnings, and dividends; then I will review the oil industry, the effects of the strong dollar, labor problems, and the general decline in capital spending. The last half of the chapter will provide a broad sense of the extent of fundamental decline in each industry and of the additional roles played by government, management, and other unique factors.

The Underperforming Industries: Definition and Summary Data

Tables 4.1, 4.2, and 4.3 categorize sixty-six industry indexes into three groups—underperforming, average, and overperforming—according to how their stocks performed within a twenty percentage point range relative to the S&P 500's growth of 55% between 12/79 and 12/84. Dividends are excluded. Twenty-one underperforming industries outlined in table 4.1 had stock prices that grew 35% or less. Fifteen average industries outlined in table 4.2 had stock prices that grew between 35% and 75%. Thirty overperforming industries outlined in table 4.3 had stock prices that grew 75% or more.[2]

The underperforming industries are ranked in table 4.1 in descending order of stock price performance.[3] Stock prices for fourteen of the twenty-one underperforming industries declined absolutely, not just relatively. The worst declines were in the industries dedicated to serving the oil industry's capital needs—Oil Well Equipment and Services, Construction and Engineering,[4] and Offshore Drilling. Value Line's Petro-

Table 4.1. The Underperforming Industries 1979–1984

Industry (In order of underperforming the S&P 500)	General Source	Number of companies	Change in stock price	Change in return on equity	Change in dividends
Col 1	Col 2	Col 3	Col 4	Col 5	Col 6
S&P Industrials[1]	S&P	400	55%	−11%	30%
Autos[3]	S&P	4	31%	24%	−26%
Banks (Money Center)	Value Line	8	27%	−53%	43%
Chemicals	S&P	8	9%	−36%	18%
Paper & Forest Products	Value Line	29	9%	−45%	−6%
Natural Gas Dist[2]	Value Line	27	2%	−17%	82%
Machinery—Industrial/ Specialty	S&P	8	1%	−42%	20%
Computers—ex IBM	S&P	13	−1%	−34%	6%
Copper (Mining)	S&P	3	−6%	−238%	−55%
Savings & Loans	S&P	4	−7%	−282%	−4%
Steel	S&P	8	−10%	−215%	−67%
Oil[2,4]	S&P	15	−12%	−33%	51%
Pipelines[2]	Value Line	20	−15%	−25%	38%
Machine Tools[5]	S&P	5	−16%	−84%	8%
Perfume & Cosmetics	Compustat	15	−17%	−39%	−5%
Aluminum	Compustat	5	−22%	−80%	−29%
Petroleum Producers[2]	Value Line	19	−33%	−39%	159%
Construction Machinery	Compustat	9	−43%	−144%	−39%
Agricultural Machinery	S&P	4	−47%	−239%	−73%
Offshore Drilling[2]	S&P	4	−51%	−100%	28%
Engineering & Construction[2]	Value Line	8	−55%	−73%	10%
Oil Well Equipment & Services[2]	S&P	7	−60%	−58%	60%
Averages excluding S&P Industrials			−15%	−88%	10%

[1]The S&P Industrials is used rather than the S&P 500 because of the underlying data available.
[2]Oil-related industries use a 1980 base rather than 1979.
[3]Uses 1977 base.
[4]Uses average of Petroleum-Integrated—Domestic and Petroleum-Integrated—International indexes.
[5]Uses 1980 base.

leum Producers index, which comprised most of the independents, was close behind. The only oil-related industry that didn't have an absolute stock price decline was Natural Gas Distribution, which had strong utility characteristics. The worst other industries were in machinery manufacturing, such as Agricultural Machinery, Construction Machinery, Industrial/Specialty Machinery, and Machine Tools, and in commodities-

Table 4.2. The Average Industries 1979–1984

Industry (In order of performance relative to the S&P 500)	General Source	Number of companies	Change in stock price	Change in return on equity	Change in dividends
Col 1	Col 2	Col 3	Col 4	Col 5	Col 6
Semiconductors	S&P	6	75%	−9%	26%
Electronics	Value Line	39	70%	−32%	1%
Air Conditioning & Heating	Compustat	13	67%	0%	51%
Insurance (non-life)[1]	S&P	11	56%	−72%	50%
S&P Industrials	S&P	400	55%	−11%	30%
Auto Parts: Replacement	S&P	4	55%	−9%	13%
Drugs	S&P	12	54%	8%	58%
Soap	Compustat	6	54%	−13%	45%
Computers	S&P	14	51%	−1%	34%
Conglomerates	S&P	8	49%	−24%	43%
Apparel manufacturers	S&P	6	45%	−19%	57%
Hospital Supplies	S&P	6	45%	−5%	102%
Telephones	Annual Reports	10	41%	10%	−26%
Building Materials	S&P	10	40%	−16%	2%
Entertainment	S&P	5	39%	−71%	33%
Electric Utilities[2]	Value Line	97	35%	29%	22%
Averages excluding S&P Industrials			51%	−15%	34%

[1]Average of Multiline Insurance and Property & Casualty Insurance indexes.
[2]Electric Utilities are included among the Average Industries despite a stock gain slightly more than 20% below the 58% of the S&P 500 because of their much higher dividend yield.

related industries such as Copper (mining), Steel, Aluminum, Chemicals, and Paper & Forest Products. Autos only barely fell into the category of underperforming industries, despite the industry's deep troubles during 1980–1982.

The underperforming industries suffered serious declines in their return on common equity from 1979 to 1984, although the economy had been recovering for two years by the end of 1984. The declines outlined in table 4.1 were rarely less than 30% and averaged 76%, versus 11% for the S&P Industrials.[5] Steel, Agricultural Machinery, Construction Machinery, Copper (mining), and Offshore Drilling had outright losses by 1984. By comparison, the average industries had a 15% decline in return on equity and the overperforming industries had a 10% improvement.

Changes in dividends, also outlined in table 4.1, provided only limited guidance with respect to industries that underperformed. On average, the underperforming industries increased dividends 10%, but this reflected that the energy industries had dividend increases beyond the average for the S&P 500 because of actions taken during 1980–1981 when

Table 4.3. The Overperforming Industries 1979–1984

Industry (In order of overperforming the S&P 500)	General Source	Number of companies	Change in stock price	Change in return on equity	Change in dividends
Col 1	Col 2	Col 3	Col 4	Col 5	Col 6
Engines & Turbines	Compustat	7	237%	71%	60%
Restaurants	S&P	5	219%	6%	235%
Hospital Management	S&P	4	204%	3%	286%
Publishing	S&P	6	169%	7%	59%
Beer	S&P	3	165%	99%	112%
Life Insurance	S&P	4	162%	−18%	106%
Drugstores	S&P	4	159%	−11%	120%
Department Stores	S&P	8	153%	14%	54%
Computer Services	S&P	3	151%	−25%	325%
Newspapers	S&P	5	148%	−12%	79%
Advertising	Compustat	8	142%	−16%	21%
Shoes (retailing)	S&P	4	133%	−22%	68%
Trucking[1]	Value Line	9	126%[2]	−14%	35%
Broadcast Media	S&P	6	124%	−34%	28%
Tobacco	S&P	3	121%	1%	97%
Household Furnishings & Appliances	S&P	7	120%	6%	20%
Foods	S&P	19	119%	33%	49%
Pollution Control	S&P	4	119%	34%	40%
Regional Banks	Value Line	67	111%	−9%	46%
Containers—Metal and Glass	S&P	3	110%	−21%	29%
Electric Equipment	Value Line	19	96%	−11%	48%
Grocery Stores	S&P	7	90%	7%	43%
Tire & Rubber[1]	S&P	4	90%	175%	7%
Hotel/Motel	S&P	4	86%	−3%	11%
Beverages—Soft Drinks	S&P	4	85%	−4%	38%
Aerospace	S&P	9	84%	3%	33%
Airlines	S&P	5	83%	42%	−32%
Retail: General Merchandising[1]	S&P	5	81%	22%	22%
Railroads	S&P	7	79%	−14%	47%
Auto Parts: Original Equipment	S&P	5	79%	−9%	8%
Averages			128%	10%	70%
S&P Industrials	S&P		55%	−11%	30%

[1]Industries that were underperforming over 1/77–12/84.
[2]S&P Truckers index.

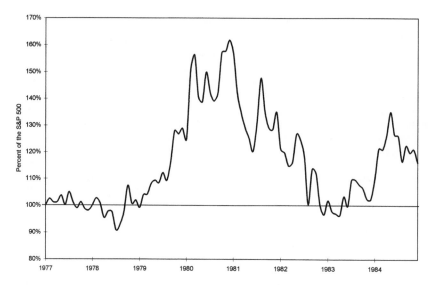

Figure 4.1 The S&P Oil Composite vs. the S&P 500. Source: Standard & Poor's Corp.

oil prices were rising that the companies were slow to reverse, while the commodities and machinery industries—such as Copper, Steel, Aluminum, Construction Machinery, and Agricultural Machinery—had dramatic dividend reductions. By comparison, the average industries had dividend increases of 34% and the overperforming industries had increases of 70%.

The underperforming industries were an unusually large segment of the stock market. Table 4.4 outlines the changing shares of the S&P 500 for the various underperforming nonfinancial industries grouped into broad categories. They made up 43% of the S&P 500 at the end of 1979 and only 30% by the end of 1984—a change so large that it supports the popular view that an unusual industrial decline occurred at this time. Although there were forty-one average or overperforming industries versus twenty-one underperforming industries, the underperforming industries were individually larger in stock market terms and constituted some of the largest sectors of the American economy. The effects of their decline were therefore widespread. The oil-related industries accounted for 61% of the decline. The metals industries (Aluminum, Copper, and Steel) accounted for a further 13% of the decline, and the machinery industries accounted for 15%.

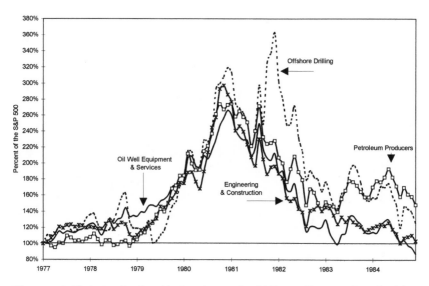

Figure 4.2 Various oil-related industries vs. the S&P 500. Sources: Standard & Poor's Corp. and Value Line.

The Oil-Related Industries

The decline in oil-related stocks between 1980 and 1984 reflected their sharp rise in 1979–1980, stimulated by rising oil prices, and their subsequent decline as overexpansion and conservation led to lower oil prices. When oil prices rose from $14.85 per barrel in 1978 to $40 in 1980, the S&P Oil Composite index,[6] outlined in figure 4.1, rose from approximately 100% to 162% of the S&P 500. Then, as oil prices declined modestly to $35 in 1981, the S&P Oil Composite dropped to 120% of the S&P 500 in six months, and was back to 101% by August 1982, when oil prices were down to $32. Lower oil prices were soon reflected in a drop in return on equity from 20.0% in 1980 to 13.4% in 1984 for S&P's two indexes for integrated oil companies. Merger activity in 1984 temporarily boosted the large oil companies' stock prices back up to 125% of the S&P 500.

Rising oil prices had a supercharged impact on stocks in S&P's Offshore Drilling index, S&P's Oil Well Equipment and Services index, stocks of the smaller, independent oil and gas companies,[7] and stocks in Value Line's Engineering and Construction index. These indexes relative to the S&P 500 are outlined in figure 4.2. They rose from 100% of the S&P 500 in 1/77 to 266–320% in 12/80, while the stocks of the large integrated oil companies only rose to 162%.[8] Once oil prices started to fall, however, the decline was as supercharged as the ascent. The stocks of

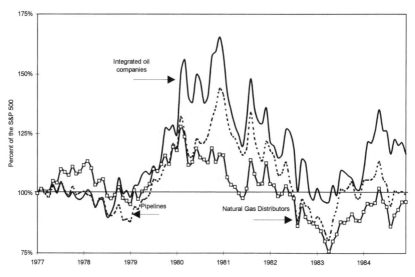

Figure 4.3 Integrated oil companies, Pipelines, and Natural Gas Distributors vs. the S&P 500. S&P's Oil-Integrated—Domestic and Oil-Integrated—International were averaged to create the integrated oil companies index. Sources: Value Line and Standard & Poor's Corp.

these oil-related industries were back to their 1977 relationships with the S&P 500 by 12/84, which constituted a substantial decline from 12/80. Return on equity also dropped precipitously—from 20.7% in 1980 to 8.7% in 1984 for S&P's Oil Well Equipment and Services companies; from 19.9% to 12.2% for Value Line's Petroleum Producers; and from 19.4% to 5.2% for Value Line's Engineering and Construction industry. S&P's Offshore Drilling industry incurred a loss in 1984. Subsectors of the oilfield services and equipment industry began to incur losses in 1983.[9]

The stocks of the pipeline and natural gas distribution industries had what can best be described as sympathetic reactions to oil prices. Their stocks rose relative to the general market in line with the integrated oil companies' stocks, as can be seen in figure 4.3. However, they had no corresponding improvement in earnings such as was experienced by the other oil-related industries. Pipelines' 1980 return on equity of 16.8% was only modestly above their 15.1% average in the prior five years.[10] The natural gas distribution companies' return on equity only rose from 15.1% in 1979 to 16.1% in 1981. Once oil prices began to fall, stocks of the pipelines and natural gas distributors fell in close unison with the decline in oil stocks, and were back to their relative 1977 levels by 1984.

The oil-related industries constituted a surprisingly large share of the stock market. They constituted 24.6% of the S&P 500 at the end of 1979,

Table 4.4. Changes in the Underperforming Industries' Share of the S&P 500 (% of the S&P 500)

Industries	1979	1984	% Chg
Aluminum	0.73	0.59	−19.2%
Steel	0.74	0.54	−27.0%
Copper	0.37	0.16	−56.8%
Metals Misc.	1.42	0.25	−82.4%
Metals Total	3.26	1.54	−52.8%
Chemicals	2.58	2.12	−17.8%
Chemicals (misc)	1.03	0.88	−14.6%
Cosmetics	0.75	0.62	−17.3%
Chemicals Total	4.36	3.62	−17.0%
Paper & Forest Products	2.48	1.81	−27.0%
Containers-Paper	0.15	0.07	−53.3%
Paper Total	2.63	1.88	−28.5%
Offshore Drilling	0.26	0.12	−53.8%
Oil-Crude Producers	0.97	0.48	−50.5%
Oil-Integrated—Domestic	8.16	6.38	−21.8%
Oil-Integrated—International	10.00	6.56	−34.4%
Oil Well Equipment & Services	3.13	1.56	−50.2%
Coal	0.24	0.10	−58.3%
Nat Gas Distributors	0.84	0.54	−35.7%
Nat Gas Pipelines	0.95	0.76	−20.0%
Energy Total	24.55	16.50	−32.8%
Autos (1977 base)	4.00	3.08	−23.0%
Machine Tools	0.15	0.08	−46.7%
Machinery-Agricultural	0.59	0.23	−61.0%
Machinery-Construction	0.83	0.32	−61.4%
Machinery-Industrial/Specialty	0.67	0.41	−38.8%
Computers-Ex-IBM	2.27	2.38	4.8%
Machinery Total	8.51	6.50	−23.6%
Totals	43.31	30.04	−30.6%

as we saw in table 4.4, and this understated oil's importance since many non-oil companies had significant oil and gas divisions or manufactured equipment and supplies predominantly for the oil and gas industry. This also meant that the U.S. economy, as reflected in the stock market, was not nearly as sophisticated and highly developed as its popular image, since the energy industries have a strong commodity component and a significant proportion of unskilled workers.

Oil was a classic commodities example of high prices eventually producing oversupply and conservation. High oil prices produced almost frenetic levels of activity in the search for oil. Domestic drilling expenditures between 1978 and 1982 tripled from $13 to $39 billion.[11] World-wide petroleum industry capital and exploration expenditures doubled from $72 billion in 1978 to $149 billion in 1981.[12] Much of this was spent in Arctic exploration, the North Sea, Indonesia, Nigeria, and South America, as capital expenditures of the fourteen largest U.S. oil companies shifted from 34% foreign during 1956–1975 to 45% foreign during 1976–1985. Within the U.S., oil and gas capital expenditures averaged 23% of all business plant and equipment spending between 1979 and 1982.[13]

Oil and gas exploration in the U.S. expanded beyond the traditional oil and gas areas of the Gulf of Mexico, Texas, Louisiana, and Oklahoma. A new oil and gas province was developed in the Western Overthrust Belt in Colorado, Wyoming, and along the border between Montana and North Dakota. Major oil discoveries were made offshore California at Arguello Point. Heavy oil deposits and oil sands suddenly looked economically attractive, as Shell Oil Company paid $3.65 billion in 1979 to acquire closely held Belridge Oil Company because of its heavy oil reserves in California. Most of the major oil companies undertook huge investments in projects to produce oil or gas from oil shale and coal, and both the U.S. and Canadian governments tried to foster Arctic and synthetic natural gas development.

Companies that were major consumers of oil and gas also participated in the exploration expansion. Many set up significant subsidiaries to explore for oil and gas. DuPont spent $6.8 billion buying Conoco in 1981 to hedge its heavy exposure to hydrocarbon supplies. Monsanto, Allied Chemical, and Dow Chemical invested heavily in oil and gas. Virtually all of the pipelines undertook significant gas exploration efforts, especially in the Gulf of Mexico, and many gas distribution companies also made exploration investments. Other companies that simply had a nose for high profits got into the oil and gas business, such as Esmark (the old Swift Packing Company), Penn Central Corp., and Northwest Industries, while the railroads began to exploit their large land holdings for oil and gas opportunities.

Private financial institutions, particularly The Prudential Insurance Company, Northwest Mutual Insurance Company, Metropolitan Life, John Hancock, and The Travelers set up special funds to coinvest in oil and gas exploration. Aetna Insurance even went so far as to acquire Geosource, an oil field services company.

Individual investors also swarmed into the oil business through tax-sheltered drilling funds that had formerly been the preserve of wealthy and sophisticated investors. The sharp rise in oil prices in 1979 made a great many people suddenly rich, and personal participation in oil and gas tax shelters became avid cocktail party conversation. The number of partners reported in drilling funds on IRS returns rose more than sevenfold, from 0.2 million in 1975 to 1.5 million in 1982, and the tax losses claimed rose from $1.7 to $13.2 billion.[14]

Texas, Louisiana, Oklahoma, Colorado, and Wyoming boomed, not only from sudden oil wealth and increased oil and gas capital spending, but also from the spillover effects as the oil companies created new skylines of great glass office towers and financed expansions in civic facilities, and oil executives bought expensive new homes and generally indulged in conspicuous consumption. Economic growth in Texas, Louisiana, Oklahoma, Colorado, and Wyoming was double the national average from 1979 to 1981.[15] The oil boom was a major source of national economic growth in 1979 and 1980, when expectations had been that there would be a recession.

The worldwide increase in oil production resulted in a decline in OPEC'S market share and thus of the organization's pricing power. OPEC had accounted for 51% of worldwide production in 1977—31.7 million barrels per day versus 30.9 million barrels per day outside of OPEC—but by 1982 OPEC accounted for only 35% of worldwide production. OPEC's daily production was down to 19.9 million barrels, while non-OPEC production was up to 37.1 million barrels. Mexico, the United Kingdom, and Norway increased their combined output by 166% in these five years, despite the worldwide recession in 1981 and 1982. This loss of OPEC market power promptly led to lower oil prices. Oil prices peaked at $40 per barrel in late 1980; they dropped to $35 by the end of 1981, $32 by the end of 1982, $30 by the end of 1983, and $29 by the end of 1984.

This price decline, modest as it may have been in absolute terms, produced a sharp contraction in oil-related capital expenditures. Nominal capital expenditures for the S&P Oil Composite leveled off in 1982, and dropped 23% in 1983. U.S. oil and gas capital and exploration expenditures dropped 28%.[16] The big synthetic fuels and frontier projects were canceled with few exceptions. Exxon canceled its participation in the Colony Shale Oil Project with Tosco despite having spent $1 billion. Sohio quit the $2 billion Hampshire Energy Project in Gillette, Wyoming. Ashland Oil withdrew from a $3 billion synfuels project in Kentucky. Consolidated Natural Gas and Panhandle Eastern canceled their plans to import LNG from Algeria, and Texas Eastern canceled its plans for a $3.6 billion coal slurry pipeline from Wyoming to Arkansas. The Northwest Energy consortium was forced to suspend work on its $40 billion project to bring natural gas from the North Slope of Alaska to the lower forty-eight states via the Alaska Highway. In Canada, Dome Petroleum faced bankruptcy, Imperial Oil canceled its Alberta synthetic oil project, and Shell Canada was forced to suspend its $13 billion Alberta oil sands project, while Hydro-Quebec cut its ten-year plans for additional hydroelectric capacity from $56 billion to $18 billion. Capital expenditures net of depreciation for the integrated oil companies declined 43% between 1980 and 1984, 71% for the independent Petroleum Producers, 72% for Oil Well Equipment and Services, 77% for Engineering and Construction, and 82% for Offshore Drilling. The much greater reductions in the industries serving the oil industry indicated their riskiness as capital goods suppliers. Employment was cut 12% in the oil and gas industry, 27% in engineering and construction, and 41% in oil well equipment and services.

There was an air of unreality about $30–40 oil prices right from the beginning, and in retrospect the boom only lasted three years, despite the magnitude of oil industry capital expenditures and the high profile that the Carter administration, business, and the general public gave to energy matters. The stock market valued the oil industry's growth potential very modestly, as can be seen in figure 4.4, which shows the S&P Oil Composite's return on equity (ROE) and market-to-book value ratio relative to the S&P Industrials from 1977 to 1984. When the oil industry's ROE rose to over 140% of the S&P Industrials in 1980 its market-to-book value ratio rose to only 95%. Over a longer period from 1979 to 1984, the S&P Oil Composite had a return on equity that averaged 124% of the S&P Industrials, but only 78% of its market-to-book value ratio.[17] By the end of 1984, the oil companies' absolute market-to-book-value ratio was only 103%—a modest incentive for capital expenditures. The integrated oil companies, which were the largest part of the S&P Oil Composite, were similarly undervalued, as can be seen in figure 4.5, which outlines their price-earning ratios. Their price-earnings ratios never expanded relative to the general market, despite their relative expansion in return on equity.

The adverse valuation of the integrated oil companies extended to a comparison with the independent producers' stocks, which were consistently higher even though their financial results were consistently poorer. This can be seen in figure 4.6, which compares Value Line's index for twenty-three independent petroleum producers with the average for S&P's Oil-Integrated—Domestic and Oil-Integrated—International indexes. Even though the independents' return on equity was only 92% of the S&P Integrated Oil index from 1979–1984 and their debt ratio was 162% (not shown), the independent producers' stocks had an average price-earnings ratio that was 228% and a market-to-book value ratio that was 202% of the S&P integrated oil companies'. Analysts and investors following the independent petroleum producers would respond that they were valued on the basis of oil and gas reserves rather than earnings and market-to-book values, but that simply begs the question. The stock valuations of the independent producers reflected either that they could always sell their assets to the integrated companies at prices unconnected to their own stock market valuations, or that the integrated oil companies' stocks were oddly valued relative to their earnings. Either way, it is a nice question about efficient markets.

The integrated oil companies' stock market valuations created strongly conflicting crosscurrents. On the one hand, the relatively low valuations

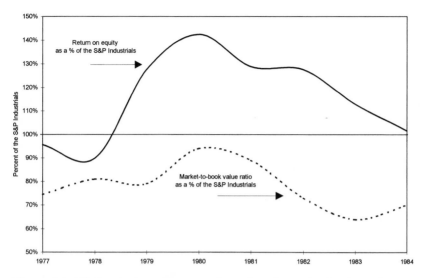

Figure 4.4 Oil Composite return on equity and market-to-book value ratio vs. the S&P Industrials. Source: Standard & Poor's Corp.

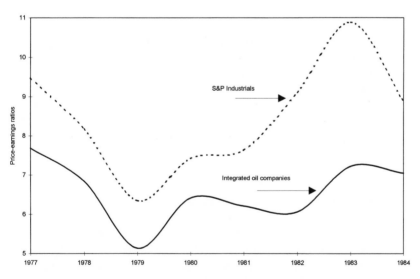

Figure 4.5 Price-earnings ratios for the integrated oil companies vs. the S&P Industrials. S&P's Oil-Integrated—Domestic and Oil-Integrated—International were averaged to create the integrated oil companies data. Source: Standard & Poor's Corp.

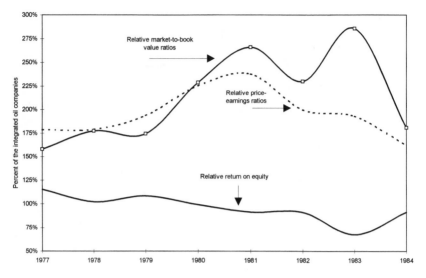

Figure 4.6 Independent Petroleum Producers valuations vs. the integrated oil companies. S&P's Oil-Integrated—Domestic and Oil-Integrated—International were averaged to create the integrated oil companies data. Sources: Value Line and Standard & Poor's Corp.

suggested that investors expected the companies' high earnings to be temporary and the industry's massive capital expenditures to be unproductive. On the other hand, the low valuations made "exploring for oil in Wall Street" cheaper than the real thing and led to a boom in oil industry acquisitions, which I will review in chapter 9. Industry outsiders also used the low stock price levels to acquire major asset positions rather than develop them, as when DuPont acquired Conoco for $6.8 billion in 1981 and U.S. Steel acquired Marathon Oil for $6.2 billion in 1982.

The Effects of the Strong Dollar

The 55% rise in the value of the dollar between mid-1980 and 1985 had a serious negative impact on many of the underperforming industries. Industries that had large exports or that were domestically competitive with imports—such as autos, construction machinery, agricultural machinery, machine tools, office equipment, chemicals, steel, aluminum, and paper and forest products—either lost foreign export markets or saw imports' share of the domestic market rise dramatically. Many of these industries were also selling to customers in the commodities industries, such as farming or metals mining, that were themselves contracting sharply because the strong dollar was slashing their prices. The strong

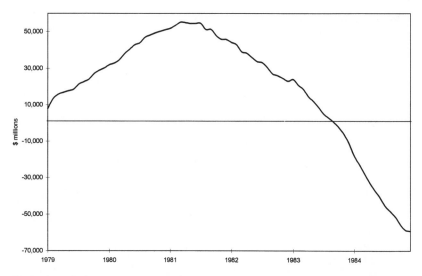

Figure 4.7 U.S. merchandise trade deficit (excluding petroleum) (rolling twelve-month totals). Source: Bureau of Economic Analysis.

dollar caused a shift from a $55 billion merchandise trade surplus (excluding petroleum products) in 1980 to a deficit of $58 billion in 1984, outlined in figure 4.7.[18] Since the machinery industries exported almost twice as much of their output as manufacturing generally, they felt the most impact.[19] The impact of foreign trade on the underperforming industries (other than oil-related) can be seen in table 4.5. Net exports of these industries declined 200% between 1979 and 1984 (column 2), and imports grew from 17% of domestic production in 1979 to 25% in 1984 (columns 4 and 5). Chemicals and perfume and cosmetics were not much affected by the strong dollar, but in the auto, office equipment, copper, and machine tool industries imports rose to over one-third of domestic production. These trade results would have been worse had it not been for import restrictions in the auto and steel industries.

Several of the industries with average stock performance—particularly semiconductors, electronics, and apparel manufacturers—also had adverse foreign trade experiences, as can be seen in table 4.6. Foreign competition was a longstanding problem for the consumer electronics and apparel industries, so that companies in these industries had already narrowed and specialized their functions before the dollar strengthened. The semiconductor industry fought foreign trade competition with technological innovations. Otherwise, the reader can see in table 4.6 that while the industries with average stock price performance had declines in their net exports larger than the underperforming industries (column 2), they were not as greatly affected because imports were a smaller share of their

Table 4.5. Changes in Foreign Trade of the Underperforming Industries 1979–1984 (Excludes Oil-Related and Financial Industries)

Industry	Change in Net Exports 1979–1984 (%)	Change in Net Exports 1979–1984 ($ millions)	1979 Imports as % of Dom. Prod'n.	1984 Imports as % of Dom. Prod'n.
Col 1	Col 2	Col 3	Col 4	Col 5
Autos[1]	−150%	−18,844	23%	35%
Chemicals	−12%	451	16%	15%
Paper & Forest Products	−87%	2,700	27%	22%
Computers-ex-IBM (Office Equipment)	−100%	−1,109	41%	58%
Copper (copper, lead, zinc, incl wire)	−47%	−900	24%	36%
Steel	−70%	−4,169	12%	23%
Machine Tools[2]	−333%	−1,000	19%	40%
Perfumes & Cosmetics	−87%	−151	1%	2%
Aluminum	−1,132%	−1,336	9%	14%
Construction Machinery[2]	−58%	−4,200	6%	14%
Agricultural Machinery[2]	−117%	−700	12%	19%
Averages	−200%	−35,560	17%	25%

Sources: U.S. Commodity Exports and Imports as Related to Output 1981 and 1980, 1986 and 1985, tables 3A and 3B, U.S. Dep't. of Commerce, Bureau of the Census, Government Printing Office.

Notes: Export and import SIC codes do not match exactly. Missing elements are assumed to be insignificant. Imports in the sourcebooks are calculated as a % of domestic output plus imports, but are converted here to a % of just domestic output.

[1]Uses 1978 base.
[2]Uses 1981 base.

domestic markets—6% excluding the above three industries versus 25% for the underperforming industries. This difference becomes exceedingly clear when we turn to the overperforming industries in table 4.7. Sixteen of these industries had virtually no foreign trade, while the other twelve had a decline in net exports of almost 300%, but imports' share of their market rose to only 8% in 1984, versus 25% for the underperforming industries.

Autos

In absolute dollars, the greatest impact of the strong dollar was on the auto industry, which suffered a $19.5 billion increase in net imports. The progression of this deficit is outlined in figure 4.8. It began to increase sharply in 1983, responding to the strength of the dollar rather than to falling gasoline prices. The deficit was $34 billion by 1985—26% of the merchandise trade deficit.

The rapid growth in auto imports reflected the combined effects of

Table 4.6. Changes in Foreign Trade of the Average Industries 1979–1984 (Excludes Oil-Related and Financial Industries)

Industry	Change in Net Exports 1979–1984 (%)	Change in Net Exports 1979–1984 ($ millions)	1979 Imports as % of Dom. Prod'n.	1984 Imports as % of Dom. Prod'n.
Col 1	Col 2	Col 3	Col 4	Col 5
Semiconductors	−900%	−4,086	35%	45%
Electronics	−335%	−7,584	57%	90%
Air-Conditioning & Heating	−36%	−476	2%	6%
Auto Parts: Replacement*	−256%	−2,313	9%	18%
Drugs	−1,765%	−18	1%	1%
Soap	−21%	−38	1%	2%
Computers	1%	78	0%	16%
Conglomerates	NA	NA	NA	NA
Apparel Manufacturers	−185%	−9,085	30%	41%
Hospital Supplies	42%	203	3%	3%
Telephones	0%	0	0%	0%
Building Materials	NA	NA	NA	NA
Electric Utilites†	−49%	NA	1%	2%
Averages	−319%	−23,319	14%	22%

Sources: U.S. Commodity Exports and Imports as Related to Output 1981 and 1980, 1986 and 1985, Tables 3A and 3B, U.S. Dep't. of Commerce, Bureau of the Census, Government Printing Office.

Notes: Export and import SIC codes do not match exactly. Missing elements are assumed to be insignificant. Imports in the sourcebooks are calculated as a % of domestic output plus imports, but are converted here to a % of just domestic output.

*All Auto Parts
†Electric Utility data based on kwh.

high oil prices and the strong dollar. The rise in oil prices in 1979 and 1980 resulted in an explosion in small cars' share of the market from 37% to 71% that increased imports' share from 16% to 27%.[20] Imports rose from 1.9 million units in 1978 to 2.5 million units in 1980, even while overall auto sales were declining. The rise was particularly significant for Japanese cars, which rose from 12.0% of the market to 22.6% between 1978 and 1982.[21] The 25% decline in oil prices from 1981 to 1984 might have led to a movement back into larger, domestically produced cars, except that the decline in oil prices was offset by a 46% rise in the value of the dollar that kept imported cars' prices unnaturally low. These offsetting forces are outlined in table 4.8. The result, when coupled with consumers' experience of the higher quality of imported cars, was a dramatic decline in brand loyalty to the U.S. car companies and the establishment of a strong dealer-distribution system by the Japanese that permanently changed the shape of the U.S. auto industry.

Table 4.7. Changes in Foreign Trade of the Overperforming Industries 1979–1984 (Excludes Oil-Related and Financial Industries)

Industry	Change in Net Exports 1979–1984 (%)	Change in Net Exports 1979–1984 ($ millions)	1979 Imports as % of Dom. Prod'n.	1984 Imports as % of Dom. Prod'n.
Col 1	Col 2	Col 3	Col 4	Col 5
Engines & Turbines	−23%	−381	9%	11%
Restaurants	0%		0%	0%
Hospital Management	0%		0%	0%
Publishing	34%	106	2%	2%
Beer	−82%	−301	4%	5%
Drugstores	0%		0%	0%
Department Stores	0%		0%	0%
Computer Services	0%		0%	0%
Newspapers	−442%	−53	1%	2%
Advertising	0%		0%	0%
Shoes (retailing)	0%		0%	0%
Trucking	0%		0%	0%
Broadcast Media	0%		0%	0%
Tobacco	21%	190	0%	1%
Household Furnishing & Appliances	−425%	−476	11%	9%
Foods	101%	−2740	8%	8%
Pollution Control	0%		0%	0%
Containers—Metal & Glass	−2,083%	−125	1%	1%
Electric Equipment	−110%	−1987	9%	15%
Grocery Stores	0%		0%	0%
Tire & Rubber	49%	−492	15%	19%
Hotel/Motel	0%		0%	0%
Beverages—Soft Drinks	−517%	−62	0%	0%
Aerospace	2%	220	4%	11%
Airlines	0%		0%	0%
Retail: General Merchandising	0%		0%	0%
Railroads	0%		0%	0%
Auto Parts: Original Equipment[1]	−256%	−2,313	9%	18%
Averages	−133%	−8,414	3%	4%
Averages for 12 industries with foreign trade	−287%		6%	8%

Sources: U.S. Commodity Exports and Imports as Related to Output 1981 and 1980; Ibid. 1986 and 1985, Tables 3A and 3B, U.S. Dep't. of Commerce, Bureau of the Census, Government Printing Office.

Note: Export and import SIC codes do not match exactly. Missing elements are assumed to be insignificant. Imports in the sourcebooks are calculated as a % of domestic output plus imports, but are converted here to a % of just domestic output.

[1] All Auto Parts

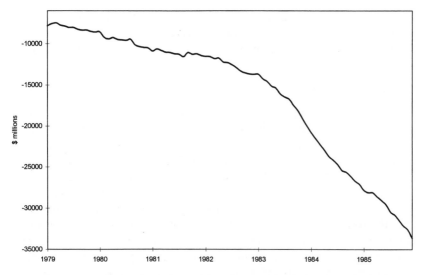

Figure 4.8 Net imports of autos, trucks, and related parts (twelve-month moving totals). Source: Bureau of Economic Analysis.

Auto imports would have been even higher had it not been for restrictions on Japanese imports. Ford and Chrysler began aggressive campaigns for protection in 1979 and petitioned the U.S. Trade Commission for limits on imports and a tariff of 20% just before the 1980 elections. Initial discussions with the Japanese on limiting exports were unproductive, but the tone changed when Reagan promised to seek voluntary import restrictions while campaigning in Michigan in 1980. Senators Lloyd Bentsen (Dem.-Tex.) and John Danforth (Rep.-Mo.) significantly increased the

Table 4.8. Factors in U.S.-Japanese Auto Competition

Year	Japanese Auto Imports Mkt. Share %[1]	Domestic Small Car Mkt. Share %[2]	WTI Oil Price[3]	Mgn 15 $[3]
1977	12.4%	24.9%	14.85	96.66
1978	12.0%	38.1%	14.85	89.76
1979	16.6%	37.1%	32.50	91.13
1980	21.3%	64.1%	37.00	91.98
1981	21.8%	70.7%	35.00	100.28
1982	22.6%	67.6%	32.00	111.26
1983	21.8%	65.7%	30.00	118.04
1984	20.2%	71.1%	29.00	129.46

[1]Includes U.S. production in 1983 and 1984 equal to 0.9% and 1.9%.
[2]Under 4.0 liters engine capacity.
[3]Year-end.

pressure by introducing highly popular legislation to set auto import quotas early in 1981. The Japanese announced on May 1, 1981 that they would restrain imports to 1.7 million units—7.7% below the prior year's volume.

Computers and Office Equipment

Net exports of computers and accessories soared from $3.3 billion in early 1979 to $6.7 billion in mid-1981, as can be seen in figure 4.9, but were stopped dead in their tracks in 1981 by the strength of the dollar and actually declined to $5 billion in 1983, even though worldwide computer spending continued to rise. From 1981 to 1985 there was no growth in computer net exports, while imports rose from zero to 16% of domestic production. This was a more subtle case of the strong dollar slowing down a key industry rather than the devastation wrought in the auto, steel, aluminum, mining, and equipment industries. Yet the computer industry was curiously quiescent about foreign competition. IBM's foreign assets between 1979 and 1984 actually dropped from 98% of U.S. assets to 54%, and none of its annual reports in this period even mentioned foreign competition.[22]

But the office equipment industry (excluding computers) was not so quiet. Imports were already 41% of domestic production in 1979 and rose to 58% by 1984 as net imports doubled, as outlined in table 4.5. The effect of the strong dollar on Xerox was devastating. Its international sales barely changed between 1979 and 1984. Its domestic sales grew over 50%, but only by extensive price-cutting which reduced its return on equity to under 10% as imports of duplicating machines rose from only $17 million to $788 million. Japan's Canon Corp. became an entrenched U.S. competitor at this time.

Steel

Despite the manifold problems of the steel industry, the change in its net import position was principally affected by the strong dollar. The 68% growth in steel net imports between 1979 and 1984 was fairly erratic due to the evolution of import restrictions, as can be seen in figure 4.10, but the change in trend in 1981 as the dollar began to strengthen is clear. Net imports rose in 1981 even though the economy was in a steep decline.

The steel industry responded similarly to the auto industry in seeking restrictions on import competition, but with more justification since many countries subsidized their steel industries for political objectives, whether it was developed countries—such as the United Kingdom, Belgium, Germany, and France, which tried to protect jobs—or less-developed countries like Brazil, Turkey, Spain, Taiwan, and Korea, that saw steel as an engine of industrial growth. U.S. Steel filed formal dumping

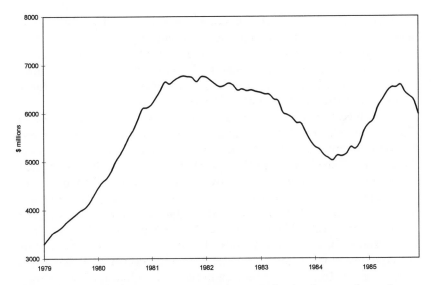

Figure 4.9 Net exports of computers and accessories (twelve-month moving totals). Source: Bureau of Economic Analysis.

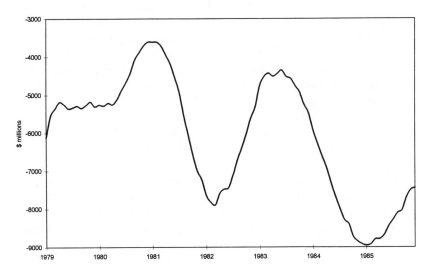

Figure 4.10 Net imports of iron and steel (twelve-month moving totals). Source: Bureau of Economic Analysis.

complaints against five European countries in 1979 under existing trade laws, much to the chagrin of the Carter administration. During the election campaign both candidates bid for the steel vote. President Carter announced new import restrictions and delays in pollution control requirements, and Ronald Reagan promised Pennsylvania steelmakers that he would take further action against imports.[23] Common market steel producers agreed to cut production and raise prices in mid-1981 based on direct negotiations with U.S. steel producers, but later in 1981, the federal government nonetheless began a probe of unfair trading practices by the European steelmakers in the first such instance of the government acting on its own without a filing by a steel producer.[24] When imports continued to rise, U.S. steelmakers filed 132 countervailing duty and antidumping petitions all at once under the unfair trade laws, mainly against European producers. The Commerce Department issued dumping findings against six European nations shortly thereafter. The Europeans agreed to restrain their carbon steel exports, and steel net imports dropped almost 50% in 1982, as can be seen in figure 4.10; but the battle simply moved to other producers. By 1984, imports were back to record levels, and the U.S. steelmakers filed unfair trade practice petitions against producers outside of Europe since four of the five largest production increases during 1980–1985 were in Brazil, China, Spain, and Turkey.[25] Bethlehem Steel and the United Steelworkers joined to file an escape clause petition under GATT rules for temporary import relief due to serious injury. These appeals were carefully timed for the 1984 presidential elections, and shortly thereafter U.S. Trade Representative William Brock negotiated steel import restrictions on all countries to hold finished steel imports at about 18.5% of the U.S. market versus 25.4% in the first ten months of 1984. Europe was to get 5.4% of the market, Canada 3%, and Japan, South Korea, Spain, Brazil, Mexico, South Africa, and Australia 10.1%.[26] As can be seen in figure 4.10, steel imports declined approximately 15% in 1985.

Unlike the auto industry, as we shall see later, import pressure did force a change in the steel industry's pricing policies. In the 1970s, iron and steel prices rose 10.2% annually versus 6.9% for the GNP deflator, but they were virtually flat from 1982–1986, while the GNP deflator rose 3.9% annually.[27]

Copper

The copper, lead, and zinc industries experienced import pressures similar to those felt by the steel industry, as well as even greater price pressures. Imports of copper, lead, and zinc rose from 24% to 36% of domestic production between 1979 and 1984, and net imports increased 47% (see table 4.5). The growth in the absolute level of net imports did

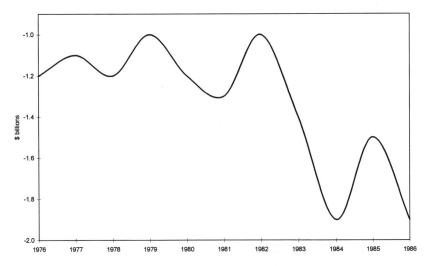

Figure 4.11 Net imports of copper, lead, and zinc (annual totals). Source: U.S. Dept. of Commerce, *Commodity Exports and Imports Related to Output 1981 and 1980*; Ibid. *1986 and 1985*, Tables 3A and 3B.

not show up during the recession but was abrupt once the economy began to recover, as can be seen in figure 4.11.

However, price pressures were the more debilitating aspect of the strong dollar for the metals mining industries. Copper dropped from an average price of $1.01 per pound in 1980 to 67 cents in 1984, lead from 53 cents per pound to 19 cents,[28] molybdenum from $9.00 per pound to $3.20.[29] Very few mines could operate profitably at these prices. Unlike the steel industry, no import restrictions or other federal government assistance was given to the mining industry, despite its appeals,[30] perhaps because the mines were principally situated in the West, which the Reagan forces considered already secure.

Agricultural Machinery

The strong dollar caused imports of agricultural machinery to rise from 12% to 19% of domestic production between 1981 and 1984, and net exports to decline 117%, as outlined in table 4.5. The change in trend of net exports of agricultural machinery lagged other machinery, not occurring until 1983, but was striking thereafter, as can be seen in figure 4.12. The strong dollar also had an important indirect effect on agricultural machinery sales through its impact on wheat, corn, soybean, and cotton prices, the principal products of the buyers of agricultural machinery. Wheat prices declined from a peak of $3.91 per bushel in 1981 to $2.42

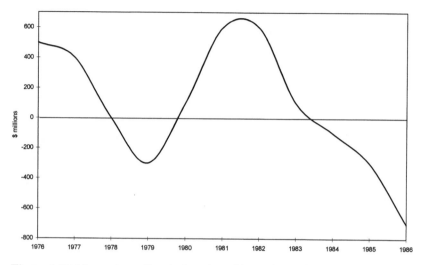

Figure 4.12 Net exports of agricultural machinery (annual totals). Source: U.S. Dept. of Commerce, *Commodity Exports and Imports Related to Output 1981 and 1980*; Ibid. *1986 and 1985*, Tables 3A and 3B.

in 1986, corn prices declined from $3.11 to $1.50, soybean prices declined from $7.57 to $4.78, and cotton prices declined from $0.75 to $0.52 per pound. Farm revenues from these four crops declined almost 39% between 1982 and 1986.[31] The financial status of the farm sector was further complicated by excessive debt and high interest rates, as we shall see below. Altogether these problems led to a 56% decline in domestic farm equipment purchases between 1979 and 1986. European farm producers suffered simultaneous price and financial problems.

Construction Machinery

The construction machinery industry experienced a 58% decline in net exports from 1981 to 1984 and imports increased from 6% to 14% of domestic production as a result of the strong dollar, as can be seen in table 4.5. Import penetration undoubtedly would have been worse had Caterpillar not made a determined effort to cut costs and meet import prices at the expense of $950 million in losses between 1982 and 1984. The change in trend in net exports in 1982 as the dollar strengthened is clearly illustrated in figure 4.13. Construction equipment industry net exports were $7.2 billion at their peak in 1980 and Caterpillar was the world's dominant manufacturer, exporting almost half of its 1981 U.S. production.[32] This U.S. dominance was sharply eroded by the strength of

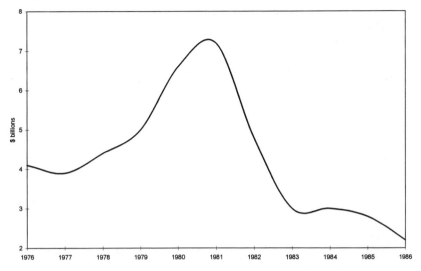

Figure 4.13 Net exports of construction machinery (annual totals). Source: U.S. Dept. of Commerce, *Commodity Exports and Imports Related to Output 1981 and 1980*; Ibid. *1986 and 1985*, Tables 3A and 3B.

the dollar in 1982–1984 as net exports dropped steadily to $2.2 billion in 1986. Japanese construction equipment manufacturers invaded the U.S. market in this period, pricing 50% below Caterpillar.[33] Komatsu in particular gained 18% of the U.S. market and was able to establish a significant dealer network.

The strong dollar also had a commodity price effect among customers of the construction equipment industry. Declining metals prices eliminated the domestic mining industry's role as a major buyer of construction equipment, while new capital projects among Latin American customers virtually ceased because of their dependence on dollar-denominated commodities exports. The decline in oil prices also ended the major energy construction projects and halted expansion in the coal industry. Abroad, the sudden change in Middle East oil cash flows sharply reduced their large construction projects (not just for oil production).

Machine Tools

Machine tool imports rose from 19% of domestic production to 40% between 1979 and 1984 as net imports rose 333% (table 4.5). The decline in net exports outlined in figure 4.14 was not manifest until 1984 when capital spending recovered, but from then through 1986 it was precipitous.

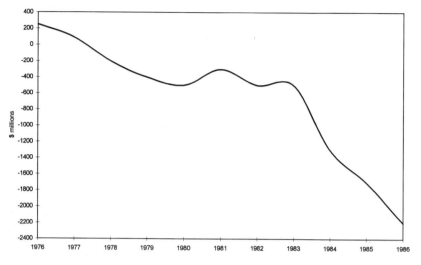

Figure 4.14 Net exports of machine tools (annual totals). Source: U.S. Dept. of Commerce, *Commodity Exports and Imports Related to Output 1981 and 1980*; Ibid. *1986 and 1985*, Tables 3A and 3B.

Labor Problems

The underperforming industries (other than oil-related industries) tended to have historically strong unions and high wage-benefit packages that hindered their competitive response to the low costs created for foreign competitors by the strong dollar. These industries tended to be among the older industries and had histories of labor strife. Many of the leading companies, such as General Motors, Ford, Chrysler, Caterpillar, Deere, Alcoa, U.S. Steel, DuPont, Dow, Phelps Dodge, Kennecott, and Anaconda, had also been entrenched in their markets for decades, which permitted a web of high direct labor costs, high benefits, and restrictive work rules to develop at the expense of their customers and stockholders. When the effects of the strong dollar disrupted these relationships, almost without exception the unions resisted reductions in wage-benefit packages and instead accepted significant declines in industry employment and extensive contracting out.

Table 4.9 indicates just how poorly these underperforming industries adjusted their wage costs. Their average direct hourly wages did not change from 133% of the national average for manufacturing between 1980 and 1984. Only steel and farm machinery industry wages dropped significantly, but steel still remained the highest paid U.S. industry. Table 4.9 does not indicate the costs of benefits in these industries, but they were broadly understood to be much above the national average. General

Table 4.9. Underperforming Industries Average Hourly Earnings of Production Workers (% of private sector average)

Industry	1980	1984
Private Sector Average	$6.66	$8.33
Steel	171%	156%
Autos	148%	153%
Oil & Gas Exploration and Refining	147%	152%
Alum-Cu-Lead-Zn Metal Fabrication	146%	147%
Metal Mining	138%	140%
Farm Machinery	132%	116%
Construction Machinery	129%	128%
Chemicals	125%	133%
Machine Tools	123%	122%
Paper & Forest Products	108%	110%
Computers	101%	107%
Average vs. Private Sector	133%	133%

Source: Statistical Abstract 1986, pp. 412–413.

Motors calculated that its hourly costs including benefits were $18.45 in 1980—87% higher than the $9.85 per hour used as the average for automakers in table 4.9. U.S. Steel similarly cited a cost of $17.93 in 1980—57% higher than the $11.39 used as the average for steel companies in Table 4.9.[34]

The auto industry was the natural leader to deal with the question of whether import competition would lead to a redefinition of labor's position. Political pressures were in that direction, as Congress insisted that labor contribute to the effort to save Chrysler before approving $1.5 billion in U.S. debt guarantees in 1980; but the labor contribution was only a modest slowdown in wage and benefit increases compared to those at General Motors and Ford. None of the auto companies challenged the U.A.W.'s position during this period. Instead, they continued a long history of collaboration in raising wages and benefits in return for labor peace, but at the expense of higher prices. Despite the industry's problems after 1979, the wage package continued to rise. For example, at Ford labor costs rose from $15.94 in 1979 to $24.57 in 1984—a compound annual rate of 9.0%. General Motors exacerbated the problem in 1984 by agreeing to what was billed as "lifetime job security."[35]

In the steel industry, which desperately needed wage relief both to gain market share and to avoid bankruptcy, management and labor instead joined together to seek import restrictions.

All of these industries needed to do something about wage costs because average unit labor costs outside the U.S. declined from 110% of U.S. costs in 1980 to only 74% in 1984, reflecting the stronger dollar.

Table 4.10. International Unit Labor Costs in Manufacturing (% of U.S. on a $ basis)

Country	1980	1984
United States (indexed)	130.5	145.6
Canada	89%	91%
France	118%	70%
Germany	113%	69%
Italy	108%	78%
Japan	86%	67%
Netherlands	102%	66%
Sweden	96%	53%
United Kingdom	166%	99%
Averages vs. U.S.	110%	74%

Source: Statistical Abstract 1986, p. 849.

This can be seen in table 4.10, which outlines the changes between 1980 and 1984 in unit labor costs for manufacturing in the leading industrialized countries. The competitive pressure did result in a considerable decline in U.S. strike activity as the days lost to work stoppages declined 58% between 1979 and 1984.[37] High wages and heavy unionization in the Atlantic and Midwestern states also drove an increasing number of manufacturing jobs to the South and West, where wages were lower and unions weaker,[37] but in general wages were not reduced. Most companies contracted out production as an alternative. Chrysler entered joint venture agreements to import small Japanese cars, while Ford made its Hermosillo, Mexico assembly plant into one of the most important in its system. Caterpillar entered manufacturing agreements with unaffiliated, lower-cost producers in Germany, South Korea, and the U.S. for sales under the Caterpillar name through its vaunted dealer network. Deere did similarly. U.S. Steel began importing steel bars, and Alcoa expanded foreign production while shutting down U.S. facilities. And companies (such as mining) for whom contracting out was not an alternative simply closed down.

The General Decline in U.S. Capital Spending

A further influence on the underperforming industries was the general decline in U.S. capital spending. Business expenditures for plant and equipment in 1972 dollars rose from $152 billion to $168 billion between 1979 and 1984—a compound annual rate of increase of only 2.0%, which was more than accounted for by increased imports of machinery. Real business spending on durable equipment other than computers de-

Figure 4.15 Real business purchases of producers durable equipment excluding computers (1987 dollars; rolling twelve-month totals). Source: Bureau of Economic Analysis.

clined from $230 billion in 1978 to $170 billion in 1982 and only recovered to $220 billion by 1984.[38] This measure, outlined in figure 4.15, more directly indicates the effect of reduced capital spending on the underperforming industries, although it too has to be adjusted for increased imports.

To some degree the decline in business capital spending simply reflected the problems in the industries we are considering here, which were themselves among the most capital intensive. Oil and gas domestic capital expenditures alone accounted for approximately 28% of U.S. capital spending in 1981–1982, at the tail end of the oil boom, but only 18% in 1984.[39] But other factors exacerbated the decline in capital spending. The high real interest rates caused by monetary policy discouraged capital spending. New-issue Aaa-rated corporate bonds bore real interest rates averaging 7.1% from 1981 to 1984 compared to −0.1% from 1977–1980. The federal government's own direct capital expenditures (excluding national defense) and grants to state and local governments for major physical investments declined in real terms between 1980 and 1984 from $35 billion to $32 billion, as the Reagan administration cut discretionary non-military expenditures. Net of depreciation these expenditures fell 36%.[40] The impact was particularly strong on the construction machinery industry as spending on interstate highways declined.

Mergers and acquisitions also competed for capital dollars on a new scale. The value of the Top 100 mergers rose from 19% of gross capital expenditures by the S&P Industrials in 1979 to 28% in 1981–1983 and 66% in 1984, which constrained corporate funds that otherwise could have been spent on new plant and equipment. Almost all of the money paid out for acquisitions went into further portfolio investments of individuals or fiduciary institutions, and very little of it found its way back into plant and equipment expenditures.

The Extent of Industrial Decline

The extent of decline between 1979 and 1984 varied among the underperforming industries. Some industries, such as oil, pipelines, natural gas distributors, chemicals, paper and forest products, construction equipment, and even autos, appeared strong enough to recover from their declines when the pressures on them subsided. Other industries, such as steel, mining, agricultural equipment, aluminum, and many of the oil-related industries, appeared to have closed so many plants, shrunk so far in employment and capacity, and had such low stock prices, that their potential for recovery was limited. In this section I will relate the extent of each industry's decline to its stock price relative to its book value, its return on equity, its decline in capital spending, and its decline in employment. While lower oil prices, the strong dollar, excessive labor costs, and the general decline in capital spending were the principal factors behind the underperforming industries, we will also develop a more nuanced impression of various industries' fortunes as we review the other factors at work, particularly management decisions, overexpansion, and government aid.

A market-to-book value ratio below 100% encourages gradual liquidation or a shift in assets through diversification, since newly invested capital is immediately discounted by the stock market. Ten industries— Autos, Chemicals, Natural Gas Distributors, Copper (mining), Steel, Aluminum, Construction Machinery, Agricultural Machinery, Offshore Drilling, and Engineering and Construction—had market-to-book value ratios below 100% as of 12/31/84, as can be seen in table 4.11. These low levels compared with 149% for the S&P Industrials, 175% for the average industries, and 207% for the overperforming industries, as outlined in tables 4.12 and 4.13.

An average market-to-book value ratio of only 101% for the underperforming industries reflected that their 1984 return on equity averaged only 4.9%. This was a very weak result for this stage of the business cycle. Eight of the underperforming industries in table 4.11 had returns on equity above 10%, which might be considered a measure of whether their potential for cyclical recovery remained, but five industries had losses and six others had returns below 10%. By comparison, the average

Table 4.11. The Extent of Decline Among the Underperforming Industries 1979–1984 (Excluding Financial Industries)

Industry (In order of underperforming the S&P 500)	Dec. 1984 Market-to-Book-Value Ratio[1]	1984 Return on Equity	Change in Net Capital Expenditures as % Capitalization 1979–1984[1]	Change in Employment 1979–1984
Col 1	Col 2	Col 3	Col 4	Col 5
Autos	97%	21.5%	−15%[2]	−17%[2]
Chemicals	91%	10.8%	−47%	−12%
Paper & Forest Products	109%	9.6%	−49%	−4%
Natural Gas Dist[3]	96%	12.3%	−53%	3%
Machinery— Industrial/Specialty	110%	9.3%	−103%	−31%
Computers ex-IBM	135%	10.3%	−42%	−11%
Copper (Mining)	67%	−18.1%	−75%	−26%
Steel	34%[5]	−4.9%	−75%	−42%
Oil[3,6]	103%	13.4%	−43%	−12%
Pipelines[3]	108%	12.6%	−67%	1%
Machine Tools[3]	128%	3.0%	−59%	−15%
Perfume & Cosmetics	176%	16.0%	−44%	16%
Aluminum	86%	7.0%	−50%	−12%
Petroleum Producers[3]	160%	12.2%	−71%	−12%[4]
Construction Machinery	86%[5]	−10.0%	−145%	−14%
Agricultural Machinery	42%[5]	−25.8%	−145%	−45%
Offshore Drilling[3]	88%	−0.1%	−82%	NA
Engineering & Construction[3]	91%	5.2%	−77%	−8%
Oil Well Equipment & Services[3]	118%	8.7%	−72%	−41%
Averages	101%	4.9%	−69%	−16%
S&P Industrials	149%	14.6%	−38%	6%

[1]From general sources cited in table 4.1 except for employment.
[2]1978 base.
[3]Oil-related and Machine Tool industries use 1980–1984.
[4]Decline from 1981.
[5]Uses 1979 book value because of such large subsequent writeoffs.
[6]Combines averages for S&P's Oil-Integrated—Domestic and Oil-Integrated—International indexes.

industries had a return on equity of 14.7%, which was only modestly below the 17.7% average for the overperforming industries.

The reader will note in tables 4.12 and 4.13 that Electric Utilities, Tire and Rubber, and Railroads also had market-to-book value ratios below 100%. If I had used the period from 12/77 to 12/84 to measure stock performance, both the Electric Utilities and Tire and Rubber industries would have been classified as underperforming. We can see here that the stock market discouraged further investment in them consistent with that interpretation. I will note later that Railroads' superior stock price perfor-

Table 4.12. Growth or Decline Among the Average Industries 1979–1984 (Excluding Financial Industries)

Industry (In order of underperforming the S&P 500)	Dec. 1984 Market-to-Book-Value Ratio[1]	1984 Return on Equity	Change in Net Capital Expenditures as % Capitalization 1979–1984[1]	Change in Employment 1979–1984
Col 1	Col 2	Col 3	Col 4	Col 5
Semiconductors	219%	17.7%	118%	19%
Electronics	170%	11.3%	−23%	12%
Air Conditioning & Heating	121%	15.0%	11%	3%
Auto Parts: Replacement	185%	15.3%	−13%	−17%[2]
Drugs	266%	22.1%	−18%	3%
Soap	183%	15.7%	22%	4%
Computers	219%	18.8%	−67%	32%
Conglomerates	112%	12.6%	−51%	NA
Apparel Manufacturers	158%	15.4%	−57%	−12%
Hospital Supplies	209%	16.4%	4%	25%
Telephone	116%	13.2%	−61%	−10%
Building Materials	121%	12.4%	−87%	NA
Entertainment	225%	6.1%	83%	0%
Electric Utilities	88%	13.9%	−17%	11%
Averages	171%	14.7%	−11%	7%
S&P Industrials	149%	14.6%	-38%	6%

[1]From general sources cited in table 4.2.
[2]All auto parts.

mance actually came from cutting back, so capital expenditures were also discouraged in this industry.

Industry in general reduced its capital spending between 1979 and 1984 as capital expenditures net of depreciation declined from 11.2% to 7.0% of capitalization for the S&P Industrials.[41] This ratio declined 83% between 1979 and 1984 for the underperforming industries, compared with a 10% decline for the average industries and growth of 2% for the overperforming industries. This represented a shocking contraction in many of America's largest, most capital-intensive industries. Industries with declines over 100%, such as Machinery-Industrial/Specialty, Construction Machinery, and Agricultural Machinery, were shrinking absolutely.

Changes in employment in the underperforming, average, and overperforming industries are outlined in tables 4.11, 4.12, and 4.13. This provides another measure of how extensively the underperforming industries contracted, as severe employment declines serve as a proxy for plant closings and permanent capacity reduction. While employment in the total private sector grew 6% between 1979 and 1984, employment in the underperforming industries declined 6%. In the average industries employment increased

Table 4.13. Growth or Decline in the Overperforming Industries 1979–1984
(Excluding Financial Industries)

Industry (In order of underperforming the S&P 500)	Dec. 1984 Market-to-Book-Value Ratio[1]	1984 Return on Equity	Change in Net Capital Expenditures as % Capitalization 1979–1984[1]	Change in Employment 1979–1984
Col 1	Col 2	Col 3	Col 4	Col 5
Engines & Turbines	131%	21.9%	−6%	−17%
Restaurants	248%	20.0%	−10%	13%
Hospital Management	232%	18.0%	23%	12%
Publishing	437%	28.4%	33%	13%
Beer	148%	15.9%	−33%	−10%
Drugstores	246%	16.3%	5%	9%
Department Stores	133%	14.3%	−68%	8%
Computer Stores	314%	20.2%	8%	77%
Newspapers	457%	30.8%	−55%	5%
Advertising	241%	20.4%	11%	23%
Shoes (retailing)	241%	13.5%	−48%	14%
Trucking	131%	13.8%	−7%	−1%
Broadcast Media	211%	19.6%	−54%	18%
Tobacco	314%	24.4%	−72%	−12%
Household Furnishing & Appliances	131%	15.7%	78%	−14%
Foods	211%	22.9%	26%	−3%
Pollution Control	314%	21.2%	197%	NA
Containers—Metal & Glass	102%	10.7%	−46%	−29%
Electric Equipment	167%	15.2%	−4%	−10%
Grocery Stores	150%	15.4%	88%	15%
Tire & Rubber	74%	10.3%	86%	−32%
Hotel/Motel	201%	15.9%	91%	25%
Beverages—Soft Drinks	318%	18.5%	−21%	−6%
Aerospace	175%	22.0%	−66%	5%
Airlines	116%	9.5%	−47%[2]	7%
Retail: General Merchandising	136%	14.6%	−2%	−15%
Railroads	83%	10.0%	−24%	−34%
Auto Parts: Original Equipment	138%	16.6%	−5%	−17%[3]
Averages	207%	17.7%	3%	2%
S&P Industrials	149%	14.6%	−38%	6%

[1]From general sources cited in table 4.3.
[2]Partly estimated
[3]All Auto Parts.

7% and in the overperforming industries it increased 2%. Employment declined over 25% in the copper, steel, agricultural machinery, industrial/specialty machinery, and oil well equipment and services industries.

The broad measures of stock price performance, return on equity, market-to-book value ratios, capital spending, and employment tell only part of the story of the decline in the underperforming industries. For example, the declines varied in timing. The oil-related industries entered a general contraction as oil prices declined from 1981 to 1984; but declines in the auto, agricultural equipment, and steel industries substantially preceded that of the oil industry and to some degree were caused by the initial rise in oil prices. Declines for the machine tool and aluminum industries did not occur until 1983-1984, and the auto industry was hit again by imports at this time. It will be helpful to briefly consider the course of events from 1979 to 1984 in some of the more important of these industries in order to appreciate the other factors, especially federal government and management actions, that affected these industries.

Autos

The auto industry declined ahead of the general economy as oil prices and interest rates rose in 1979, and it recovered as they declined and the economy surged during 1983–1984, but in the interim Chrysler almost collapsed and the industry underwent permanent market share changes due to the shift to smaller cars and the strength of the dollar. Domestic auto production peaked at an annual rate of 9.2 million units during 1977–1978, and was flat through the first half of 1979. However, when gasoline prices rose from 64 cents per gallon in 1978 to $1.33 in 1981[42] and the prime rate rose from 9% to over 20%, quarterly domestic production compared with the prior year dropped for eight quarters in a row to 6.3 million units. After a slight pickup in mid-1981, production dropped for five more quarters, ultimately bottoming out in 1982 at only 5.1 million units—55% of peak production.[43] The monthly trend can be seen in the Federal Reserve's index of motor vehicle production in figure 4.16. Capital expenditure requirements surged at the same time, as the companies rushed to develop small car designs and to comply with new federal mileage standards and emission regulations. These pressures would have bankrupted Chrysler had the federal government not agreed in June 1980 to guarantee $1.5 billion of new debt for it. Ford was forced to cut costs aggressively under similar pressures, but was saved by its profitable European operations and its stronger financial condition.

Chrysler was already in trouble before the rise in oil prices. Between 1976 and 1978 its market share dropped from 13.7% to 11.1%, and profits swung from $424 million to a loss of $205 million. Its market share dropped further to 10.1% in 1979 when it had a shattering $1.1 billion

Figure 4.16 Federal Reserve index of automobile production. Source: Federal Reserve.

loss, equal to 40% of its 1978 year-end common equity. Common stock dividends were eliminated.[44] Moody's Investors Service dropped the rating on Chrysler's bonds to Ba, a junk bond rating, in April 1979. The finance subsidiary's commercial paper rating was completely withdrawn in July 1979. By April 1980, in the midst of negotiations for a federal government debt guarantee, Chrysler's bond ratings were down to Caa—bankruptcy level—and all access to credit had disappeared.

Chrysler was only saved by federal debt guarantees of $1.5 billion and over $2.5 billion of contributions and "give-ups" by other interested parties. Its banks exchanged $1.3 billion of Chrysler debt for preferred stock and warrants and renegotiated the credit company's debt on the condition that Chrysler would ultimately sell control of it. Six other governments, including Canada and the province of Ontario, provided $657 million in loans or grants. The U.A.W. accepted $622 million in wage and benefit cuts, plus deferral of Chrysler's 1980 pension fund contribution of $220 million.

Even with this aid package, the outlook for Chrysler was unclear. Chrysler's sales in 1980 were only 1.2 million units versus 1.8 million in 1979—down 33%—and its market share dropped further to 8.8%—now down 36% from its peak. Its 1980 loss was $1.7 billion—even larger than in 1979—which wiped out its equity. Capital expenditures rose to $835 million, adding to the company's cash flow problems. Chrysler's year-end 1980 stock market value of only $326 million was basically no more than the option value of a bet on its recovery.

Chrysler nearly collapsed in early 1981 when it fell $350 million behind in payments to its suppliers and the federal government postponed guaranteeing a $400 million debt installment because suppliers, banks, unions, and other governments procrastinated in providing concessions. Borg Warner, a major supplier, balked at further price cuts, and several states began to complain that Chrysler's credit did not justify self-insuring for workmen's compensation. Chrysler's auditors refused to certify it as a "going concern" for its 1980 annual report, and its investment bankers made a merger proposal to Ford Motor Company. At one point in January 1981 when the company's cash was down to $8 million the lawyers wanted a release to file for bankruptcy, but Lee Iacocca simply refused. When the various parties finally knuckled under and the federal government guaranteed an additional $400 million in borrowings, it could only do so by waiving twelve different requirements that Chrysler could not meet, including expert outside opinions that it could survive and that its strategic plans were feasible.[45]

There was little improvement during the rest of 1981. Unit sales were stuck at 1.2 million, and the company engaged in severe price cutting by offering rebates of $300–$2,000 on slow-selling models. Losses in 1981 were $0.7 billion—$250 million over the company's projections to the government. Year-end book equity was negative $540 million, and the company's year-end 1981 stock market value shrank further to only $256 million. The company's liquidity was also perilous, as it had already borrowed $1.2 billion of the $1.5 billion in government guaranteed funds that were to cover cash shortfalls through 1983. Fortunately, capital expenditures dropped from $835 million the year before to only $456 million in 1981, and the company was able to raise cash by selling its Chrysler Defense subsidiary to General Dynamics.

The silver lining in 1981 for Chrysler was that its market share bounced back from 8.8% to 9.9%; its new K-cars were a popular success; it had introduced a new line of front-wheel drive cars that averaged forty-six miles per gallon on the highway; and it offered the first U.S. convertibles in six years. Operating costs had been slashed so that breakeven was only 50% of the sales level required in 1979.[46] Chrysler returned to profitability in 1982, earning $170 million, despite the fact that its sales were stuck at 1.2 million units for the third year in a row.

Chrysler made several crucial decisions during this period of great stress, the first of which was to hire Lee Iacocca, the ousted president of Ford Motor Company, in November 1978. Iacocca was the undisputed leader of all aspects of Chrysler's rescue effort. Operationally, he inherited the company's move toward a small front-wheel drive car—the K-car—in which it led the industry, probably because it had historically had greater profitability with small cars than the other companies. The K-car facilitated a 1980 commitment to go ahead with development of a minivan that ultimately became the company's strongest product. While at Ford in the 1970s, Iacocca had been involved in the argument over whether to develop a minivan. Ford had found a strong demand for it in customer surveys, but delayed a decision because it required a front-wheel drive platform for weight, mileage, and styling reasons—a platform Ford did not have. The decision was easier for Chrysler once it had the front wheel-drive K-car, although it was still a courageous move considering Chrysler's financial circumstances. Equally courageous was Iacocca's decision to revive Chrysler's five-year/50,000-mile warranty, which had been dead for ten years and was strongly opposed by the rest of upper management. The effect of Iacocca's decision was to force a beneficial company-wide emphasis on quality. The Chrysler marketing effort was also helped by the decision to make Iacocca the company's spokesman in its television ads—an unconventional move at the time, considering that he was an overweight, middle-aged man with a big nose and not much polish. But in the end Iacocca became a national hero and customers came to identify his personal pitch with personal commitment.[47]

Ultimately, the Chrysler aid package was vindicated by Chrysler's recovery. Chrysler's sales rose over 113%, from $9.2 billion in 1980 to $19.6 billion in 1984, as its domestic market share recovered from 8.8% to 10.3%. In March 1983 the company had a wildly successful stock offering for $430 million, which it used along with 3.2 million additional shares to swap its banks out of $1 billion in preferred stock that they had accepted in 1981. It repaid $400 million of its federally guaranteed debt in May 1983, and thereafter was able to borrow in the junk bond market to repay the remainder. The minivan was introduced in the fall of 1983 and was a sellout. The company had $1.4 billion in cash on hand at the end of 1983 and was able to afford a corporate jet again—the status symbol of successful corporations. (Treasury Secretary Miller had insisted that the company sell its jets in 1980.) Profits were an eye-popping $2.4 billion in 1984, and capital expenditures rose to $1.2 billion as the company was able to invest heavily in new products. Dividends were restored, and the company was so strong and sure of itself that it approved a program to buy back 20% of its common stock. Chrysler's stock market value rose from a low of $256 million at the end of 1981 to $4.0 billion at the end of 1984. The federal government sold the warrants it had received for guaranteeing Chrysler's debt back to the company in 1984 for $311 million. The government's resulting profit was approximately 27% of the $1.2 billion that it actually guaranteed.

The Ford Motor Company went through wrenching changes similar to Chrysler's but without federal aid. Its U.S. market share declined from 23.5% in 1978 to 16.6% in 1981 as its vehicle sales dropped from 4.5 million units to 2.3 million. Its net income swung from $1.2 billion in 1979 to three years in which losses were over $1 billion each, the worst year being 1982, when it lost $1.7 billion. These were Ford's first losses in thirty-four years. Losses in the U.S. and Canada began in 1979, but foreign operations had earned $1.4 billion in 1979 and still earned $0.7 billion in 1982. The common stock dividend was progressively cut from a high of $3.90 per share in 1979 until it was eliminated in 1982. Ford's stock dropped from a high of $30 in 1979 to lows between $10½ and $12 in 1980–1982. At the end of 1981, Ford's equity market value was only $2.0 billion, versus a book value of $6.0 billion.

Stringent cost cutting was implemented. Officers' compensation was cut 47% between 1979 and 1981, while the next level of salaried employees' compensation was cut by 28%. The number of employees dropped from a peak of 507,000 in 1978 to 379,000 in 1982. Three assembly plants were closed and plans for a new V-8 engine were canceled. Annual operating costs were reduced over $3 billion by the end of 1982 versus 1979 operating income of $700 million, and breakeven was possible at sales levels a third lower than in 1979.[48]

When recovery came it was dramatic as the auto companies benefited from declining gasoline prices, lower interest rates, and the general recovery in consumer incomes. Domestic car production rose from 5.1 million units in 1982 to 7.8 million units in 1984. The operating leverage in this sales increase was great since all of the companies had sharply reduced operating costs. In 1984, Chrysler earned $2.4 billion, Ford $2.9 billion, and GM $4.5 billion. Earnings for the S&P Auto index in 1984 were a record $25.39—over 50% higher than the prior peak in 1977—and represented a 26.7% return on equity. Total returns on auto stocks were 72% in 1982 and 37% in 1983,[49] versus slightly over 20% each year for the S&P 500. Chrysler and Ford's stocks rose 336% from trough to peak.[50] The industry's market-to-book value ratio rose from a low of 70% in 1980 to 97% at the end of 1984.

However, even when the auto industry recovered, the signs of decline were widespread. Business wasn't growing. The peak recovery in auto production in 1985 to 8.2 million units was still 11% below the 1977–1978 peak of 9.2 million units, and employment was down 17%. Various stock market indicators signaled the decline in the auto industry, despite the earnings recovery. The S&P Auto index lagged the S&P 500 by 30% over the eight years since January 1977, as can be seen in figure 4.17, and 1984 proved to be the peak in the industry's relative stock recovery for the decade. Rather ominously, the industry's average stock price in 1984 was only 3.8 times its prodigious earnings of that year, and its market-to-book value ratio was only 61% of the S&P 500 average.

The industry had survived, but only on the basis of extensive government action. The government had bailed out Chrysler Corp., negotiated restrictions on Japanese imports, and eased thirty-five different regula-

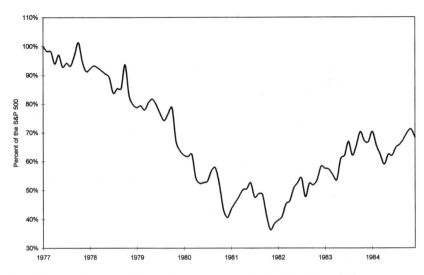

Figure 4.17 Autos vs. the S&P 500. Source: Standard & Poor's Corp.

tions affecting the auto industry, particularly those relating to air bags and 1984 emission standards.

The industry's real problem was competition with the Japanese auto makers. The U.S. companies were at a disadvantage versus the Japanese in labor costs, quality, and efficiency, all of which were exacerbated by the strength of the dollar, as well as financial strategy and Japanese home market protection. Protection from Japanese imports had become a key feature of the auto industry's strategy, but the Japanese were getting around it by building domestic production facilities and shifting to larger cars. Honda, the most reliant on the U.S. market of the Japanese manufacturers, opened its first plant for domestic production in 1982 in Marysville, Ohio, with capacity equal to 80% of its 1980 sales of 375,000 units. The other Japanese manufacturers soon followed on a scale that rendered the 1981 import restrictions insignificant.

Consumers' introduction to Japanese cars was spurred by lower prices and fuel efficiency, but familiarity quickly bred appreciation for Japanese quality advantages. The U.S. manufacturers had serious quality problems as the incidence of defects in standard U.S. cars was 50% greater than in Japanese cars, and 100% greater in luxury cars.[52]

The U.S. companies also had defects in their financial strategy vis-a-vis the Japanese. The U.S. companies operated with much greater capital intensity than the Japanese companies. Between 1977 and 1984, U.S. auto makers' capital expenditures averaged 15.4% of capitalization[52] while the Japanese companies' capital spending averaged only 9.7%,[53] partly because U.S. companies bore more of the burden relative to suppliers of designing new models (particularly small cars) and developing mandated fuel efficiencies.[54] The U.S. companies had to deal with a powerful union that had created very high labor costs, unlike the Japanese, which also made the U.S. companies more inclined toward capital intensity. The stock market's attitude toward such expenditures was particularly negative, as the industry's market-to-book-value ratios hovered between 56 and 69% of the averages for the S&P 500 from 1979 through 1982.

The U.S. auto makers also strove for higher returns on equity than the Japanese companies, rather than going head-to-head with them for market share. In the three years following the initiation of import restrictions, U.S. auto companies raised prices at almost twice the rate of the Consumer Price Index (27.5% vs. 14.3%).[55] In the two periods when profits were meaningful enough to make comparisons, 1977–1979 and 1983–1985, U.S. auto makers averaged returns on equity of 15.0% and 19.7% respectively, versus 11.3% and 12.5% for the Japanese companies. In 1984, when the auto companies' return on equity was highest, cutting it in half would have reduced prices by 4%—not a big advantage, but one they did not pursue.

Contrary to popular impression, the U.S. companies had a cost of capital advantage at this point due to lower income tax rates. In the profitable years between 1977 and 1979, the Japanese companies had an average operating profit margin of 10.1% versus 8.2% for the U.S. companies, and 10.7% versus 8.4% between 1983 and 1985, but the Japanese had lower returns on equity because their income tax rates averaged 54.3% in both periods versus 47.7% in 1977–1979 and 37.7% in 1983–1985 for the U.S. auto makers. Leverage—another point of comparison for capital costs—was similarly low in both industries.[56] The Japanese companies had the benefit of higher stock valuations than the U.S. companies, but it could hardly be said that stock market valuations were driving the U.S. companies' profit objectives. The stock market gave extremely low relative valuations to the US auto companies' peak 1983–1985 results, with price-earnings ratios and market-to-book value ratios that averaged only 39% and 53%, respectively, of the S&P 500.

The Japanese auto makers had an important sales advantage in their home market protection. They had the only domestic market among the developed countries in which auto imports were not a factor and therefore had complete pricing freedom in their largest market. Imports as a share of the Japanese market never exceeded 2%, while they reached peaks of 27% in Germany, 29% in the U.S., 36% in France, 41% in Italy, 58% in the United Kingdom, and 69% in Sweden.[57]

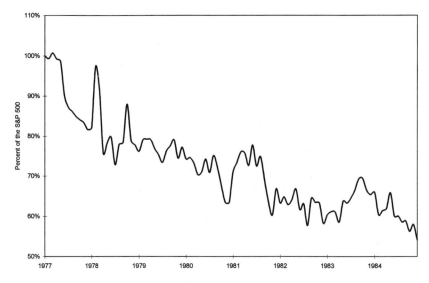

Figure 4.18 Chemicals vs. the S&P 500. Source: Standard & Poor's Corp.

Chemicals

The problems of the chemical industry reflected the impact of higher oil prices on commodities chemicals[58] and the overcapacity caused by extensive upstream integration by the major oil companies after the first oil crisis in 1973. Return on equity for S&P's Chemical stocks dropped from an average of 14.4% during 1977–1980 to only 9.5% during 1981–1984. There was very poor adjustment to these changes on the wage front as pay rose from 125% of the manufacturing average in 1979 to 133% in 1984. Capital expenditures, however, declined from 11% of sales in the 1970s to 7% from 1983 to 1985. Overcapacity, the strong dollar, and excessive wage costs set the stage for large-scale divestitures of these facilities in the mid-1980s as leveraged buyouts.[59]

Chemical stocks declined in an uninterrupted trend, outlined in figure 4.18. This contrasted with other commodities industries that had benefited from inflation in the 1970s. The three key chemicals markets—the energy industries, autos, and construction—were all underperforming industries.

Mainframe Computers and Business Equipment

The accepted image of computer innovation and sales growth is so strong that it is surprising to find the industry included in our discussion of underperforming industries. Overall sales of computers and peripheral equipment grew steadily from $7.5 billion in 1975 to $46.5 billion in

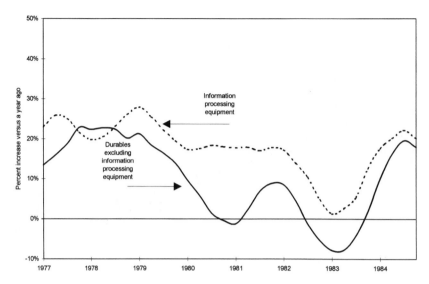

Figure 4.19 Changes in private purchases of nonresidential durable goods (moving four quarters vs. a year ago). Source: Bureau of Economic Analysis.

1984,[60] and the growth in business computer expenditures was particularly impressive in comparison with other business equipment expenditures—250% versus 105%. Figure 4.19 compares the two on a year-to-year basis. Business computer expenditures grew at approximately 20% annually from 1977 through 1981, and recovered to that level following the recession of 1981–1982.

However, the technological changes in the industry in the early 1980s, combined with the overvalued dollar, produced a very difficult period for the mainframe manufacturers other than IBM such as Burroughs, Control Data, NCR, and Sperry. The best stock index to illustrate this is S&P's Computer and Business Equipment—Excluding IBM which is outlined relative to the S&P 500 in figure 4.20. The index had a steady descent from approximately 115% of the S&P 500 in 1979 to only 75% in 1984. Return on equity for the industry dropped from 15.6% in 1979 to 10.3% in 1984. Dividends were reduced 6% between 1979 and 1984. The companies' capital spending net of depreciation declined 42% from 8–9% of capitalization during 1979–1981 to only 5% in 1984.

The stock market had been in the process of discounting the fortunes of the computer manufacturers other than IBM for some time. Their stocks peaked during 1972–1973 and had fallen 46% by 1979, despite a 220% increase in earnings per share. Their price-earnings ratios had declined from approximately 40 (or 225% of the S&P Industrials) throughout 1965–1974 to only 10 (or 120% of the S&P Industrials) by 1979, as

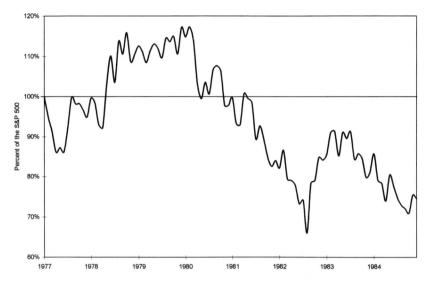

Figure 4.20 Computer and Business Equipment—Excluding IBM vs. the S&P 500. Source: Standard & Poor's Corp.

outlined in figure 4.21. Market-to-book value at the end of 1984 was only 135%—91% of the S&P Industrials. This stock market reevaluation, which included IBM as well, was one of the contributing factors to the large difference between the level of the S&P 500 indicated by the changes in interest rates and earnings during the 1970s and the considerably lower level that was realized.

Mainframe computer manufacturing was the one underperforming industry in which technological change was the driving force. The technological promise of the 1960s had turned into a very research-intensive industry in which R&D routinely ran 6–10% of sales—equal to a normal manufacturing profit margin. The result was only moderate returns on equity. Burroughs went through a complete reorganization under Michael Blumenthal in the early 1980s; NCR suffered losses in its semiconductor, personal computer, and office systems divisions; and Honeywell lost money in semiconductors and found the R&D burden of its computer business so heavy that it eventually sold the business.

The industry also had to cope with business's appetite for dispersed computing power at the expense of mainframes. To some extent this dispersion took place on network systems, such as those provided by Digital Equipment and Wang, but more important was the rapid growth of personal computers (PCs). The first PC was built in 1975 by MITS Corp. in Albuquerque, New Mexico, based on Intel's 8080 chip and using Microsoft BASIC software. It was 1977, however, before personal comput-

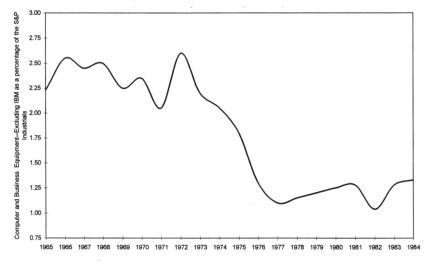

Figure 4.21 Price-earnings ratios for Computer and Business Equipment—
Excluding IBM relative to the S&P Industrials (based on average of annual high
and low prices). Source: Standard & Poor's Corp.

ers appeared at the National Computer Conference in Dallas, and even
then they were relegated to the basement. Commodore, Radio Shack,
and Apple all brought personal computers to market at approximately
the same time, but it was not until VisiCalc was demonstrated at the National Computer Conference Show in New York City in 1979 that it was
obvious that PCs had applications beyond games and home bookkeep-
ing. Two years later IBM announced its own PC with sixteen kilobytes of
RAM, one disk drive, a Microsoft MS-DOS operating system, and a
basic price tag of $1,565, although with options that could reach $6,000.
Upgrades of Microsoft's DOS system, the addition of hard disk drives,
and expansion of random access memory quickly expanded the applications of PCs. Lotus Development Corp. introduced the 1-2-3 spread-
sheet in November 1982 at the Compdex show in Las Vegas, exclusively
for use on an IBM PC with 256K of memory, and business use of the
PC was on its way. Sales of personal computers skyrocketed from 1.1
million units in 1981 to 3.5 million in 1982, 6.9 million in 1983, and 7.6
million in 1984.[61] *Time* magazine named the PC its "Man of the Year" in
its January 1983 issue.

Personal computer applications mushroomed throughout business, es-
caping the control of centralized computer mainframe departments.
Intel's 80286 chip, first used in the IBM PC in 1984, further expanded
the capability of PCs. The traditional business computer community was
thrown into disarray because PC development was so fast, the costs were

so modest compared to mainframes, and applications expanded so rapidly as users gained control of their own technology.

Steel

The U.S. steel industry was in terrible condition as it entered the 1980s. Plants and technology were old, lacking continuous casting, computerization, robot handling, and pollution controls. Productivity was one-third of Japan's. Labor relations were superficially fine because of an industry-wide no-strike agreement, but only at the price of an agreement to raise wages 3% annually, plus inflation, plus bonuses, plus supplemental unemployment benefits. Steel wage costs were 171% of the private sector average by 1980 and the highest of any U.S. industry. Imports had risen under this price umbrella from 4% of domestic consumption in 1970 to 15% in 1977.[62] This penetration also reflected heavy subsidies by European producers, Japanese and Canadian efficiency, and expansion of steel capacity in less-developed and newly industrialized countries, which the U.S. producers fought by seeking import controls rather than focusing on their costs. Profits were terrible as return on equity averaged only 6.5% throughout the 1970s, providing no economic justification for capital investment to improve operations. Management was weak and beaten down, and government relations were poor.

Entering the 1980s in this weakened condition, the steel industry was decimated by the steep recession, the strong dollar, and shifts to lighter materials. The decline in the steel industry in the 1980s was the most significant of any industry, taking into account its size and impact on concentrated regions. Capacity utilization dropped to 48% in 1982, and production in 1984 was still down 32% from 1979. The auto industry's steel purchases didn't rebound at all, dropping from 21.3% of steel shipments in 1978 to 12.9% in 1984 as the auto makers worked to reduce auto weights. Steel shipments to the oil and gas industry had actually grown in 1980 and 1981 when other uses were declining, rising from 3.7 million tons in 1979 to 6.2 million tons in 1981, but these sales dropped to 2.0 million tons by 1984. Capacity was cut from 154 million tons in 1980 to 112 million tons in 1987 as integrated companies closed twenty-one steel plants. Employment dropped from almost 400,000 in 1980 to only 163,000 in 1987—a far cry from the peak employment of 531,000 in 1970. Steel ghost towns began to appear in Pennsylvania and Ohio. Steel minimills picked up 12 million of the 42 million tons of capacity reductions, but almost totally in the South and West, far from the traditional steel manufacturing states.[63]

The financial decline of the steel industry was precipitous. The industry had five successive years of losses from 1982 to 1986 aggregating $11.5 billion. Stockholders' equity dropped from $15.4 billion to $2.4

Figure 4.22 Steel vs. the S&P 500. Source: Standard & Poor's Corp.

billion—a liquidation comparable only to the farm machinery industry. Dividends for the S&P Steel index were cut from $3.18 in 1979 to $1.05 in 1984, significantly lagging the decline in earnings, as in many other declining industries. Capital expenditures dropped from $2.7 billion to $1.2 billion, and net of depreciation dropped from 8.3% of prior year capitalization in 1982, when the industry was trying to fight back, to -2.4% in 1986, when it had given up. Further efforts to improve efficiencies mostly involved joint ventures with the Japanese where they put up the money, such as National Steel's joint venture with Nippon Kokan, and Wheeling-Pittsburgh's joint venture with Nisshin Steel.

Steel stocks declined unremittingly relative to the S&P 500 with no change in trend to reflect interest rates, recession, the dollar, or import restrictions. Standard & Poor's Steel index relative to the S&P 500, outlined in figure 4.22, declined from 100% in January 1977 to 53% at the end of 1979, 34% at the end of 1982, and 17% at the end of 1986. For five years before the great stretch of losses from 1982 to 1986 that cut the industry's book value by 75%, steel stocks averaged only 42–46% of book value, the lowest valuation of any industry. On a relative basis, Steel stocks' market-to-book value ratio hovered between 33 and 36% of the S&P 500 from 1979 to 1982. Small wonder that capital spending dried up in the industry and that the market leader, U.S. Steel, did its best to exit the industry by buying Marathon Oil and Texas Oil & Gas and changing its name to USX. In 1987 USX was taken out of the S&P Steel index.

The decline of the steel industry decimated the iron ore mining towns around the southern shore of Lake Superior in Michigan and Minnesota. U.S. iron ore production had been sustained at almost 90 million tons from 1970–1980, 90% of which was in the Lake Superior region. Iron ore production dropped to 70 million tons in 1980, and then to only 35 million tons in 1982. Seventeen of the thirty-seven mines closed permanently. Production was still only 41 million tons in 1986, and production from mines outside of the Lake Superior district had been reduced permanently to insignificance.

Aluminum

Aluminum looked like the wave of the future versus steel in the 1970s, but high energy prices, the 1981–1982 recession, the appreciation of the dollar, and the movement to recycling changed the trend of the aluminum industry and made it look more like the steel industry by 1984. Production, capacity, employment, profits, and stock prices all reversed trend from the late 1970s and entered into sharp declines. Primary production of aluminum fell from 4.7 million tons in 1980 to 3.3 million tons in 1982, and fell yet further to only 3.0 million tons in 1986 when the economic recovery was far advanced. At first aluminum prices did not fall, as they did in other metals industries, but rather rose from 71.6 cents per pound in 1980 to 77.8 cents in 1983,[64] partly due to the sharp rise in electricity prices the industry had to bear as higher oil prices worked through to other forms of energy. These high prices stimulated expansion in the Canadian aluminum industry, with its low-cost hydroelectric base, and when imports doubled in early 1984, aluminum futures prices dropped from 80 cents to 50 cents per pound, obliterating profits. Secondary recovery, which was much less energy-intensive, was also stimulated, rising from 27% of primary production in 1980 to 49% in 1985.[65]

The industry was slow to reduce capacity after a decade of expansion, but capacity was cut from a peak of 5.5 million tons in 1981 to 5.0 million tons in 1983, 4.7 million tons in 1985, and 4.0 million tons in 1986.

It was also slow to face its labor problems. Employment declined 25% between 1979 and 1984, but nothing was done about the high wage rates in aluminum. Not only were they among the highest in U.S. manufacturing at 146% of the national average, but they actually rose to 147% by 1984, as shown in table 4.9. It was not until 1986 that the industry was able to negotiate a 95-cent-per-hour wage reduction amounting to 4% of all-in labor costs.

The industry's finances entered a period of extended turmoil under such stress. Aluminum stocks, outlined in figure 4.23, reversed trend from 1977 to 1980, when they outperformed the S&P 500 by over 30%,

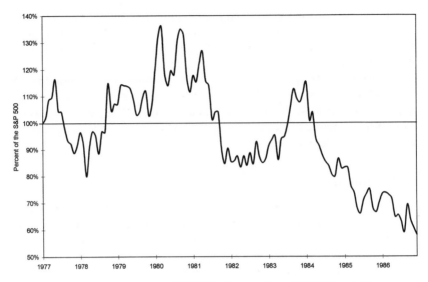

Figure 4.23 Aluminum vs. the S&P 500. Source: Standard & Poor's Corp.

and by 12/84 were down 22% from 12/79. Return on equity declined 80%, dividends declined 29%, and net capital expenditures as a percentage of capitalization declined 50%. The industry's market-to-book value ratio was 86% in 12/84, which greatly discouraged investment in expansion and modernization.

The comparison between 12/79 and 12/84 actually makes the industry look better than it really was. Earnings for the S&P Aluminum index were negative in 1982, break-even in 1983, 7% on equity in 1984, and negative again in 1985. Dividends were cut from a peak of $8.72 per share in 1981 to ultimately $3.90 in 1986. Capital expenditures net of depreciation over the same period fell to virtually zero. S&P's Aluminum stock price index deteriorated further to only 58% of the S&P 500 in December 1986. The only valuation ratio that was useful in light of the industry's losses was market-to-book value, which was only 61% of the S&P Industrials in 1980, but sank further to 52% in 1982 and 46% in 1986—among the lowest valuations of any industry.

The aluminum industry could not justly be likened to the steel industry, despite this sharp decline. Aluminum product use continued to grow, and the book values of aluminum stocks never suffered attrition on the scale of the steel industry. Nonetheless, the industry had suffered a permanent shock in its production capacity, employment, and stock market valuation under the pressures of higher energy prices, recession, and a strong dollar.

Copper (Mining)

The non-ferrous metals mining industry also reversed trend in production, capacity, employment, and stock prices from 1981 to 1984, following the growth it experienced in the inflationary atmosphere of the late 1970s. Whereas U.S. copper mining expanded 250,000 tons (20%) and refined copper production expanded almost 400,000 tons (23%) between 1975 and 1981, which was almost double the growth in world production, both sectors contracted almost 500,000 tons by 1984 while world production continued to grow.[66] Never a strong industry, by 1985 the U.S. metals mining industry was permanently decimated. The decline is less evident in the stock market because many of the leading mining companies were acquired in the late 1970s. General Electric acquired Utah International in 1976, Anaconda was acquired in 1977 by Atlantic Richfield, Cyprus Mines in 1979 by Amoco, Kennecott Copper in 1981 by Standard Oil Company (Ohio), and St. Joe Minerals in 1981 by Fluor. The S&P Copper index provides some insight into the mining industry, but it only included Asarco and Phelps Dodge as domestic companies. The S&P Metals-Misc. index is even less satisfactory, relying mostly on Amax, a coal and molybdenum producer, among domestic companies for this period. I am forced to supplement these indexes with broad industry data and the divisional reports of larger companies to illustrate the severe losses and substantial contraction of the industry as the environment shifted from inflation to the pressures of recession in 1981 and 1982 and the strong dollar from 1981 to 1985.

Over slightly varying dates between 1977 and 1986, copper production dropped over 30%, lead production dropped 47%, zinc production dropped 55%, and molybdenum production dropped 58%. These production declines carried over into huge losses, especially for the oil companies. Arco's metals division, which included both Anaconda and aluminum smelting, had EBIT (earnings before interest and taxes) losses totaling $841 million between 1980 and 1984. Losses at Sohio's Kennecott division totaled $504 million, and Amoco's mining division had EBIT losses totaling $275 million.

Among the independent mining companies, Amax's income from molybdenum mining dropped from $425 million in 1980 to a loss of $143 million in 1982, and total losses were $394 million from 1982 to 1984. Phelps Dodge had $354 million in EBIT losses in 1982–1984, while Asarco's EBIT losses totaled $295 million between 1980 and 1984.

These losses led to extensive closings of facilities throughout the industry. Arco closed Anaconda's historic mine in Butte, Montana, its Carr Fork mine in Utah, and its molybdenum mine in Nevada. It also sold its aluminum interests to Alcan Aluminum, and announced plans to divest the rest of its metals business. Sohio closed Kennecott's great Bingham

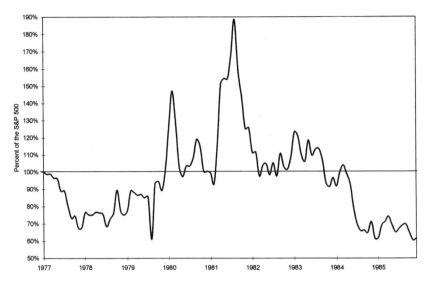

Figure 4.24 Copper vs. the S&P 500. Source: Standard & Poor's Corp.

Pitt mine in Utah—America's largest copper mine—its lead mines in Missouri, and its Nevada smelter. Amoco spun off its metals business to shareholders. Amax closed its three molybdenum mines, including the Climax mine in Henderson, Colorado. Asarco closed smelter facilities in Tacoma, Washington, Corpus Christi, Texas, and Helena, Montana, as well as mines in Sacoton, Arizona, Newfoundland, and New Brunswick. Employees in metal mining dropped 43% from 98,000 in 1980 to 56,000 in 1984.[67] This drop was severe but did not represent huge numbers, except that the job losses were concentrated in the western mountain states and in mining towns where there were few other opportunities. Hardship was particularly severe in Arizona, where over two-thirds of all U.S. copper was mined, and in Utah, Montana, and Nevada. In Missouri, where over 90% of U.S. lead production occurred, production dropped almost 40% between 1980 and 1986 and its value 68%. In the broader metals industries, which included mining and primary metal fabrication, employment dropped 26% (table 4.11).

S&P's Copper index mirrored the roller coaster of the metal industry's brief allure in the inflationary environment of the late 1970s and bleak outlook thereafter, as can be seen in figure 4.24. From 1/77 to 8/81 the S&P Copper index outperformed the S&P 500 by 89%, then declined to only 62% of the S&P 500 by 12/85. The index's market-to-book value ratio was historically poor, averaging only 75% in 1979–1980 when industry earnings peaked—59% of the S&P Industrials. By 1985 it was only 49% of the S&P Industrials and 67% of absolute book value.

Phelps Dodge, the country's largest copper producer, provides an excellent illustration of what the mining industry went through. After earning $111 million in 1979 and $91 million in 1980, the company went into a steep slide, losing $74 million in 1982, $64 million in 1983, and $268 million in 1984. Its bond rating was cut by Moody's in 1982 from A to Baa, and then in 1985 to Ba—a junk bond rating. Its stock dropped from a high of $48½ in 1981 to under $13 in 1984.

The company initiated a fierce battle for survival. The common stock dividend was eliminated in 1982 and not restored until 1987. The total number of employees was cut 48%, including a 45% reduction in headquarters staff. Two of four smelters and one mine in Arizona were closed, and capital spending was cut from an average of $125 million annually in 1980 and 1981 to $76 million annually in 1982 and 1983 and $40 million annually in 1985 and 1986. The company's 40% share of Consolidated Aluminum Company was sold to Alusuisse, and minor investments outside the copper industry were sold off to raise cash. The one bright light was the company's commitment to a new solvent extraction/electrowinning process to produce copper from low-grade ore and tailings that eliminated the concentrating, smelting, and electrolytic refining stages of traditional copper production. By 1985 its Tyrone, New Mexico plant was producing copper at costs under 30 cents per pound and the company earned $30 million. Similar facilities were installed in Arizona, but it was not until 1987, when the dollar had declined substantially, that the company earned more than its 1979 peak of $111 million.[68]

Agricultural Machinery

The Agricultural Machinery industry contracted permanently in the early 1980s, in an abrupt change of trend from the late 1970s, but there is no simple explanation for its fate. The strong dollar hurt farm equipment net exports, and high interest rates hurt farmers' financial condition; but farmers had also accumulated excessive debts previously, and European agriculture was extremely depressed.

Machinery purchases were one of the easiest costs for farmers to defer as their business declined. Combined purchases of motor vehicles and farm equipment fell almost 30% from $14.3 billion in 1979 to $10.2 billion in 1981, principally due to high interest costs and high oil prices. This was before debt liquidation began and before land prices started to fall. Vehicle and machinery purchases fell a further 32% from 1984 to 1986 to $6.3 billion when $39 billion of farm debt was liquidated out of peak borrowings of $207 billion.[69] Farm purchases of most types of field equipment other than trucks and tractors fell over 75% between 1979 and 1986.[70]

There had been an improving trend in the agricultural machinery industry in the 1970s, when high commodities prices buoyed farm incomes. Farm purchases of motor vehicles and farm equipment rose 192% between 1972 and 1979, and the Agricultural Machinery industry's return on equity almost doubled to an average of 11.5%. The Agricultural Machinery industry's capital spending during 1975–1979 was up over 140% from 1970 to 1974, as capital expenditures net of depreciation rose to 4% of prior year's capitalization.

After farmers' good fortune peaked in 1979, the Agricultural Machinery industry deteriorated quickly. At the first sign of a downtown in equipment sales in 1980, the industry recorded losses equal to 6.2% of equity. Between 1980 and 1984 the industry recorded losses every year, as losses in 1982 alone wiped out over 40% of the industry's accumulated lifetime equity, and by 1985, the industry's book value per share had declined 92%. Dividends dropped from $4.00 per share in 1980 to $0.96 in 1985. Capital spending dropped to less than depreciation, and showed the sharpest decline relative to capitalization of any industry. There was little wonder in this, since the industry's 12/84 stock price was only 42% of 1979 book value—a strong incentive to draw capital out of the industry. Employment declined 42% from 1979 to 1984 as numerous plants were closed (see table 4.11). Wages were cut throughout the industry as average hourly earnings dropped from 132% of the private sector average in 1980 to 116% in 1984.[71]

Stock prices for the Agricultural Machinery industry reflected the change in trend for the industry and its subsequent problems. The S&P Agricultural Machinery index, outlined in figure 4.25, rose to 116% of the S&P 500 between 12/77 and 12/79, declined to 82% in May 1980 in the midst of a major strike at International Harvester, then fell to 42% in August 1982 as the farm industry's credit problems became acute and even Deere & Co. began to suffer. In 1985, as farm purchases of equipment fell to less than 50% of 1979 and the dollar reached its peak, Agricultural Machinery stock prices dropped further to 27% of the S&P 500. At that point, S&P discontinued the index. Agricultural Machinery stock prices had one of the worst performances of any industry.

Construction Machinery

Construction machinery was one of America's most prominent industries during the 1970s as its big machines were in demand around the world for the oil industry, infrastructure projects in the Middle East and South America, and mining expansion. The industry severely reversed course in the 1980s, however, as oil prices fell, the dollar strengthened, and construction needs turned toward smaller machines manufactured by Europeans and the Japanese.[72] The change in trend is quite apparent in S&P's Construction Machinery index, outlined in figure 4.26. It slightly outper-

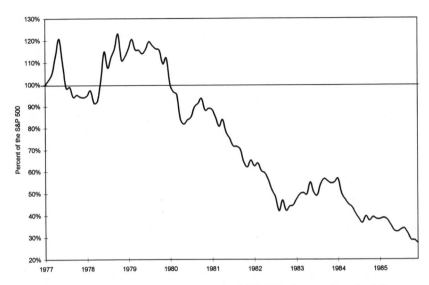

Figure 4.25 Agricultural Machinery vs. the S&P 500. Source: Standard & Poor's Corp.

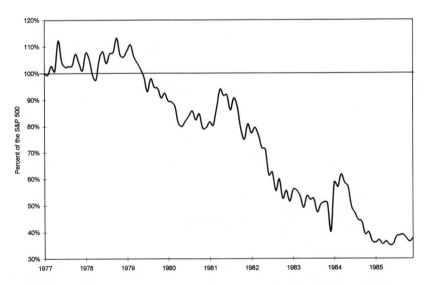

Figure 4.26 Construction Machinery vs. the S&P 500. Source: Standard & Poor's Corp.

formed the S&P 500 during 1977–1978, when the oil and commodities industries were booming, but began to decline as energy prices rose from 1979 to 1980, even though big energy projects proliferated. The Construction Machinery index failed to participate in the stock market recovery of 1982–1983 because of the negative effects of declining oil prices and the rising dollar. It dropped from 90% of the S&P 500 in early 1981 to only 50% in mid-1983, and thereafter declined further to less than 40% of the S&P 500 in 1985. Over the same period its relative market-to-book value ratio declined from 100% of the S&P 500 in 1979 to 71% in 1985, as book value itself declined by over 30% between 1981 and 1985. The index was only 86% of 1979 book value at the end of 1984.

This bleak situation was reflected in a 145% decline in capital expenditures net of depreciation between 1979 and 1984 and a 74% decline in gross capital spending. Capital spending in 1984 was less than half of depreciation.[73] Employment dropped 14% (See table 4.11).

The change in the construction equipment business was vividly played out at Caterpillar, one of the finest capital equipment companies in the world. Caterpillar's net income rose steadily through the late 1970s, and return on equity was over 20% in 1977–1978 and 16–17% in 1979–1981; but the company lost $180 million in 1982 —its first loss since 1932. It lost $345 million in 1983 and $428 million in 1984. Profits in 1985 and 1986 were small. The common stock dividend was cut over this period from $2.40 per share to 50 cents, and Caterpillar's stock dropped from a high of $73 in 1981 to a low of $30 in 1984. Capital expenditures were cut from $836 million to $229 million, and capital expenditures net of depreciation were negative from 1983 on. Plants were closed in Mentor (Ohio), San Landro (California), Burlington and Davenport (Iowa), Milwaukee (Wisconsin), Dallas (Oregon), Newcastle (England), and Glasgow (Scotland). Employees dropped from 89,300 in 1979 to 54,000 in 1987.[74] Costs were cut 22% through salary reductions, layoffs and early retirements, plant consolidations, and manufacturing efficiencies. Heavy price pressure was put on suppliers, worldwide sourcing was instituted, and 25% of production was moved abroad.[75] Manufacturing agreements were struck with unaffiliated lower cost producers in Germany, South Korea, and the U.S. for sales under the Caterpillar name through its vaunted dealer network.

However, the company did not seek protection, nor did it go for higher leverage. It kept its debt below 40% of capitalization throughout this period, and although its bond rating was cut from Aa to A by Moody's in 1982, it was able to maintain an A rating thereafter. It also kept up a strong research and development effort around 3.5% of sales, although in absolute terms R&D took cuts like everything else. Caterpillar represented a premier U.S. company buffeted by macroeconomic forces beyond its control and planning horizon. It maintained its leading industry position by cutting prices and avoiding excessive leverage, but only at the cost of large losses, great human stress, downsizing, and a permanent change in its approach to supplier sourcing.

Machine Tools

The machine tool industry suffered the sharpest change of trend of any industry as it shifted in 1981 into permanent secular decline. Sales dropped almost 40% between 1981 and 1983 and never recovered to their 1981 peak during the 1980s. Net imports rose from $200 to 400 million annually during 1978–1983, to $700 million in 1984, and to $1.5 billion in 1986, due to the strength of the dollar and to U.S. customers' interest in flexible manufacturing systems using robots and highly automated metal-cutting techniques, in which German, Japanese, and Swedish machine tool manufacturers were superior. Foreign competitors also stimulated sharp price cutting. Return on equity dropped from an average of over 16% from 1977 to 1981 to losses in 1983 that persisted through 1989, except for two years near breakeven. The industry entered a period of sustained liquidation as net worth declined 37%, and capital expenditures net of depreciation dropped from an average of over 6% of prior year's capitalization between 1979 and 1982 to 1.8% from 1983 to 1985 and were negative from 1986 to 1988. Employees were cut during the decade from 31,000 to 20,000. Research and development rose steadily from 3.4% of capitalization in 1979 to 6.9% in 1989,[76] which was a substantial relative commitment to R&D, but it was born of desperation rather than opportunity, and simply represented an additional cost for the beleaguered industry.[77]

Machine Tool stocks to some degree present a confusing image of this decline because they performed spectacularly from 1977 to 1981, when S&P's Machine Tools index rose by over three times the S&P 500, as outlined in figure 4.27. Even from 1982 to 1983, the decline in machine tool stocks was not greatly more than the S&P 500, and was less than one-third of the great gains previously; but beginning in 1984 the relative decline was persistent and precipitous, from 350% of the S&P 500 in 1/84 to 230% in 12/84, 170% in 12/85, 140% in 12/86, and eventually only 40% in 12/91. Even in absolute terms, machine tool stocks declined steadily from 1983 through 1989, and at the end of the decade averaged only 46% of their peak 1981 price. The industry's market-to-book value ratio relative to the S&P Industrials declined from approximately 120% in 1980–1981 to 106% in 1984, and only 60% in 1989.

The industry provided an interesting case study for the role of dividends in stock valuation and as a signal of management expectations, since dividends were cut so slowly that in 1986 they were still 85% of their 1982 peak, despite four years of losses or breakeven results.

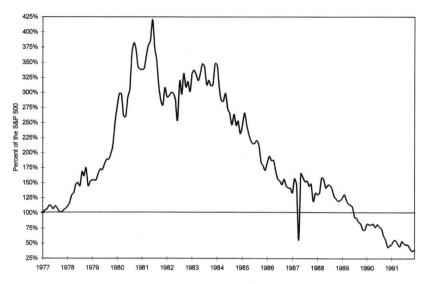

Figure 4.27 Machine Tools vs. the S&P 500. Source: Standard & Poor's Corp.

Summary

The price of the new regime's success in lowering inflation was a wrenching decline in the oil-related, commodities, auto, and equipment manufacturing industries, which at the beginning of the decade had accounted for 43% of the S&P 500. They had an 80% decline in return on equity, 69% decline in net capital expenditures relative to capitalization, and 16% decline in employment. The largest component of this decline related to the decline in oil prices. Oil-related industries declined from 25% to 16% of the S&P 500 between 1979 and 1984, and their capital expenditures declined from 28% to 10% of the U.S. total. The change was particularly difficult for those industries supplying the oil industry, such as oil and gas drillers, oil field services, engineering and construction, and steel tubing. The industry's decline also spread into the financial industry, creating bad debts for the banking industry, real estate problems for the savings and loan industry, and credit problems for the less-developed countries and the banks that lent to them.

The second major factor was the 55% rise in the dollar, which severely hurt the auto, steel, construction and farm machinery, machine tool, steel, aluminum, mining, pulp and paper, commodity chemical, and even the computer and office equipment industries. These industries' net exports declined 200%, as many switched to becoming net importers and imports rose from 17% to 25% of domestic production. Japanese manufacturers of autos, construction machinery, and office equipment gained first-time footholds in American markets.

The problems of these industries were not solely related to factors particular to the new regime. Adjustment in most of these industries was hampered by excessively strong unions that restricted work practices and sustained direct wage rates that were 33% above the national average in manufacturing. The oil and farm industries had also engaged in classic commodities overexpansion in the 1970s. The general level of capital spending also declined, reflecting the oil industry's contraction, the high level of real interest rates, and the rise of more consumer-oriented industries. Some industries, notably the auto industry, followed poor management strategies, placing too much emphasis on protection against imports and on high profits and capital intensity, and not enough emphasis on design assistance from suppliers. The net effect was contractions in the oil, mining, pulp and paper, commodities chemical, aluminum, steel, auto, and heavy equipment industries that created a rust belt in the midwest and declines in the oil and mining states that justified the public's concern over the deindustrialization of America.

Fortunately, while these industries suffered, the traditionally smaller media- and consumer-oriented industries and a variety of industries subject to specific government expansionary influences grew strongly, as we shall see in the next chapter, setting the stage for a very different economy by the end of the decade.

Appendix 4.1   A Note on the Selection of Industry Indexes

Stock market data and much of the fundamental financial data on the industries analyzed in this chapter and the succeeding chapter on overperforming industries were selected from industry indexes compiled by Standard & Poor's, Value Line, and Compustat. Unfortunately, a broad industry picture cannot be achieved from just one source. The preferred source was Standard & Poor's both because of its popularity among investors and because of the comprehensive financial data available. For many reasons, however, Standard & Poor's alone is inadequate, It lacked certain industry indexes in 1979, such as Engineering and Construction and Advertising. Some of its industry indexes, such as Electronic— Major Companies and Electrical Equipment, include too few companies. Some industries were poorly defined: for instance, Forest Products and Paper were separated, while Natural Gas Distributors and Pipelines were combined. I found S&P's separation of the integrated oil companies into international and domestic sectors to be unhelpful as well, but handled it by combining the averages for the two indexes. S&P also lacked background financial data for the transportation industries prior to 1983 and has none for the financial industries. It also included foreign companies in some indexes, which I tried to minimize.

When these objections arose I turned to Value Line or Compustat for alternatives. These were second choices, because Value Line industry indexes are limited by lack of public stock price data, frequent inclusion of foreign companies, and less information on the historic changes in the composition of their indexes. Compustat is limited by its inclusion of too many foreign companies, large gaps in data prior to the mid-1980s, and breakdown into too many industries to facilitate exposition. None of these services had a telephone index that included the period prior to the breakup of AT&T in 1984. Therefore, I constructed my own index of AT&T (before and after the breakup), the regional holding companies, GTE, and United Telecom.

I excluded a few industry indexes that I considered too small in both number of companies and market capitalization: they include Distillers (also too foreign), Communications Equipment (also too foreign), Gold (also too foreign); Coal, Fertilizer, Hardware, Home-building, Leisure, Manufactured Housing, Misc. Retail, Textile Products, Toys, and Air Freight. Their aggregate market capitalization at the end of 1979 was only 3.1% of the S&P 500.

Some readers may object to the comparison of stock market industry indexes with SIC-based data on imports, exports, employment, and other broad-based industry data. Obviously the definitions are not consistent. The ideal comparison would be with SIC-based stock market industry indexes such as Compustat prepares. I received extensive industry data back to 1979 courtesy of Compustat, but did not use it versus S&P because complete historical data was lacking for too many industries, too many foreign companies were included, and because Compustat defined so many industries that exposition was hampered. Therefore I accepted the inconsistencies between stock indexes and SIC-based data.

In several instances of changes in industry employment between 1979 and 1984 I used data for a specific company as a proxy for the industry because the available SIC data was inadequate. For example, SIC data for the oil industry acceptably reflects conditions in the exploration and production functions but captures nothing of the refining, chemical, and marketing changes in the major integrated oil companies, so I used Exxon. There is no SIC code that accurately reflects the heavy construction, hospital management, oil field services, or industrial/specialty machinery companies that I am dealing with, so I used proxy companies in these instances. I tried to select companies that had not changed through acquisitions.

The reader needs to bear in mind when the text makes comparisons of stock prices and industry data that there will be inconsistencies, but I have done my best to minimize them. The alternative was to avoid comment in critical areas such as foreign trade and employment. Comments on the oil industry also relied extensively on industry data not truly consistent with the stock indexes; contemporary financial observers had the same problems.

5

The Overperforming Industries

The overperforming industries reflected the new regime in that they were heavily consumer-oriented, thereby benefiting from the lower taxes and higher confidence of the Reagan administration, and unaffected by foreign trade competition and therefore untouched by the strong dollar. Many of the overperforming industries, such as Aerospace, Pollution Control, Hospital Management, and the transportation industries, were also highly influenced by specific government policies, in contrast to the hands-off attitude of government toward most of the underperforming industries.

Thirty industries whose stocks overperformed the S&P 500 by at least twenty percentage points between 12/79 and 12/84 were previously outlined in table 4.3 in chapter 4. Most of them fell into six categories: media, retailing, foods, transportation, various capital goods, and new industries. Their strong stock price performance raised their share of the S&P 500 from 16.6% in 1979 to 23.1% in 1984, as can be seen in table 5.1. By 1984 they equaled the underperforming oil, capital goods, and commodities industries, which five years previously had 2.4 times their weighting.

Some of the overperforming industries had cyclical recoveries in 1982–1984 rather than secular long-term overperformance. This was true of the large retailers in General Merchandising and Groceries, Airlines, Truckers, and virtually all of the capital goods industries: Engines and Turbines, Household Furnishings and Appliances, Containers, Electric Equipment, Tire and Rubber, and Auto Parts. Based on a broader time period of 1/77–12/84, among these industries all but Engines and Tur-

Table 5.1. Changes in the Overperforming Industries' Share of the S&P 500

Industries	Percentages of the S&P 500		
	1979	1984	% Chg
Brewers	0.26%	0.37%	42.3%
Foods	2.63	3.45	31.2%
Soft Drinks	0.98	1.14	16.3%
Tobacco	1.41	1.71	21.3%
Food Total	5.28	6.67	26.3%
Publishing	0.52	0.94	80.8%
Publishing (Newspapers)	0.61	1.03	68.9%
Radio-TV/Broadcast Media	0.59	0.72	22.0%
Media Total	1.72	2.69	56.4%
Restaurants	0.47	0.55	17.0%
Retail-Department Stores	0.69	1.02	47.8%
Retail-Drug	0.21	0.36	71.4%
Retail-Food	0.51	0.69	35.3%
Retail-General Merchandise	1.56	2.12	35.9%
Shoes	0.21	0.29	38.1%
Retail Total	3.65	5.03	37.8%
Air Transport	0.38	0.52	36.8%
Railroads	1.42	1.68	18.3%
Truckers	0.16	0.23	43.8%
Transportation Total	1.96	2.43	24.0%
Aerospace	1.84	2.38	29.3%
Auto Parts: Original Equipment	0.61	0.57	−6.6%
Tire & Rubber	0.26	0.38	46.2%
Containers-Metal & Glass	0.39	0.31	−20.5%
Electrical Equipment	0.60	0.65	8.3%
Household Furnishings & Appliances	0.20	0.31	55.0%
Capital Goods Total	2.06	2.22	7.8%
Hospital Management		0.73	
Hotel/Motel		0.43	
Computer Services		0.18	
Pollution Control	0.13	0.30	130.8%
Misc. Total	0.13	1.64	
Totals	16.64	23.06	38.6%

bines, Containers, and Electrical Equipment ceased to qualify as over-performing, and Truckers, Tire and Rubber, and Retail—General Merchandise actually became underperforming industries. This helps to refine the general picture of secularly improving industries to media, foods, specialty retailers, new industries, and just a few capital goods producers. It removes all connection to the auto industry, and narrows the benefits of transportation deregulation to Railroads.

The stock price performance of the overperforming industries reinforces the broad point that a change in regime took place in the early 1980s. Stocks of seventeen of the thirty industries reversed either negative or neutral trends to become overperforming industries. They also substantiate my assertion that the effects of the change in regime occurred over several years rather than quickly.

The Factors Behind the Overperforming Industries

The overperforming industries had clearly superior financial performance. It suffices here to summarize in table 5.2 the averages for the overperforming, average, and underperforming industries that were treated in detail in tables 4.1–4.3 and 4.11–4.13 in chapter 4. The overperforming industries had a 10% improvement in return on equity between 1979 and 1984 versus declines of 15% and 88% for the average and underperforming industries. In absolute terms, 1984 return on equity was 18%, versus 15% and 5% respectively. Dividends increased 70% for the overperforming industries versus 34% and 10% for the average and underperforming industries. These results produced a 207% market-to-book value ratio for the overperforming industries versus 171% and 101% for the average and underperforming industries.

The factors behind the superior financial results of the overperforming industries were frequently in direct contrast to those affecting the underperforming industries. The underperforming industries were closely related to energy production and capital goods, while the overperforming industries were heavily oriented toward consumer nondurables or services. Twenty of the thirty overperforming industries were in consumer nondurables or services, versus only one of the average or underperforming industries. When interest rates declined sharply in the second half of 1982, it was housing starts that recovered early and strongly rather than capital spending, providing a strong stimulus to consumer spending. As consumer confidence and employment recovered, consumer credit expanded even faster than disposable income, providing further stimulus to the consumer sector.

The overperforming industries were insensitive to foreign trade compared to the underperforming industries (see table 5.2). Imports for the overperforming industries only rose from 3% to 4% of domestic production between 1979 and 1984, whereas they rose from 14% to 22% for the average industries and from 17% to 25% for the underperforming industries. For twenty of the twenty-eight overperforming industries such as retailing, media, and transportation, foreign trade was less than 2% of their market. Only five of the overperforming industries had imports greater than 10% of domestic production in 1984, and they were all cap-

Table 5.2. Averages for Underperforming, Average, and Overperforming Stocks (1979–1984)

Ratios *Col 1*	Underperforming *Col 2*	Average *Col 3*	Overperforming *Col 4*
Change in Stock Price	−15%	51%	128%
Change in ROE	−88%	−15%	10%
Change in Dividends	10%	34%	70%
Change in Net Exports	−178%	−319%	−133%
Imports % 1979 Domestic Production	17%	14%	3%
Imports % 1984 Domestic Production	25%	22%	4%
12/84 Market/Book Value ratio	101%	171%	207%
1984 ROE	5%	15%	18%
Change in Net Capital Expenditures as % of Capitalization	−69%	−11%	3%
Change in Employment	−16%	7%	2%

ital goods industries: engines and turbines, electric equipment, tire and rubber, aerospace, and auto parts (original equipment). The thirteen overperforming industries that had any foreign trade suffered a 133% increase in net imports that was almost as large as the 178% change for the underperforming industries, but it was not very destructive since imports were such a minor proportion of domestic production.

Most of the overperforming industries lacked the problems associated with historically entrenched strong unions and high wages that plagued the underperforming industries. As can be seen in table 5.3, the hourly wages of production workers in the overperforming industries averaged 112% of the private sector average in 1980 and 116% in 1984, compared to 133% in both years for the underperforming industries (table 4.9 in chapter 4). But even in the overperforming industries, high wages were not sheltered by the lack of foreign trade. Thirteen industries had declines in employment, and in nine wages were over 125% of the national average. The only industries that had employment growth with wages over 125% of the national average were computer services and advertising, which had very strong winds to their backs.

The overperforming industries were greatly affected by government policy actions, in contrast to the hands-off attitudes that prevailed toward the underperforming industries other than steel and autos. The overperformance of Airline, Railroad, and Trucking stocks reflected expectations regarding the outcome of deregulation. The Aerospace industry benefited directly from greater federal defense expenditures. Hospital Management companies expanded under the impetus of President Carter's 1978 reimbursement caps on Medicare and Medicaid expenditures. Pollution Control companies grew to meet the needs of industries affected by environmental legislation that restricted local dump sites and

Table 5.3. Hourly Wages in the Overperforming Industries as a Percentage of the Private Sector

Industry	1980	1984	Employment Growth
Total Private Sector	$6.66	$8.33	6%
Engines & Turbines	146%	155%	−17%
Restaurants	55%	52%	13%
Hospital Management	91%	103%	12%
Publishing	113%	113%	13%
Beer	122%	130%	−10%
Life Insurance	94%	102%	2%
Drugstores	NA	NA	9%
Department Stores	NA	NA	8%
Computer Services	108%	128%	77%
Newspapers	116%	114%	5%
Advertising	121%	127%	23%
Shoes (retailing)	NA	NA	14%
Trucking	137%	126%	−1%
Broadcast Media	112%	116%	18%
Tobacco	139%	164%	−12%
Household Furnishings & Appliances	104%	108%	−14%
Foods	103%	101%	−3%
Pollution Control	NA	NA	NA
Regional Banks	74%	79%	12%
Containers—Metal & Glass	148%	150%	−29%
Electric Equipment	107%	110%	−10%
Grocery Stores	94%	92%	15%
Tire & Rubber	146%	155%	−32%
Hotel/Motel	67%	65%	25%
Beverages—Soft Drinks	122%	130%	−6%
Aerospace	139%	148%	5%
Airlines	NA	NA	7%
Retail—General Merchandising	72%	68%	−15%
Railroads	149%	160%	−34%
Auto Parts: Original Equipment	NA	NA	−17%
Averages	112%	116%	

Source: Statistical Abstract 1986, pp. 412–414.

required licensed disposal of industrial wastes. And the media industries were stimulated by relaxed antitrust rules.

Technology played an important, but still modest, role in the stock performance of the overperforming industries. Technology affected the media industries, especially the expansion of cable television, satellite use, and the computerization of publishing and business information services, but the big impacts were still to come—the VCR and cellular telephones had barely entered the market in 1984. The Food industry gained dramatic new product opportunities from diet-conscious consumers and the spread of microwave ovens. High technology was prominent in Aerospace, although it is not clear that it played a role as a growth factor except in the airlines' emphasis on acquiring larger, more fuel-efficient airplanes. Computer Systems benefited from the huge increases in computer power. Interestingly, Semiconductors and Electronics were overperforming industries if the comparison period is changed from 12/79–12/84 to 1/77–12/84, but by the early 1980s it had become clear that in the industries where technology was most prominent—Semiconductors, Electronics, Drugs, and Computers—it was not necessarily a source of investment profits, at least among the large companies. Heavy research and development expenditures were as much a cost of staying competitive as a source of profit, and the high technology industries other than Drugs were particularly vulnerable to price cutting as new technology spread and economies of scale were achieved. The stock price benefits of technology advancements were limited to the small capitalization companies in the computer and biotech industries.

The Media Industries

The media stocks—Broadcasting, Publishing, and Newspapers—enjoyed a highly consistent secular overperformance from 1/77–12/84, rising to 180–240% of the S&P 500, as can be seen in figure 5.1. Their share of the S&P 500 more than doubled from 1.2% to 2.6%. This overperformance reflected returns on equity that averaged 31% for the three industries (unweighted) for 1979–1984 versus 14% for the S&P Industrials, and continued earnings growth during the recession of 1981–1982. The effects of these superior earnings were augmented by a steady rise in the relative price-earnings ratios of the media industries from 84% of the S&P 500 in 1977 to 138% by 1984. The fundamentals underlying these superior returns and the rising price-earnings ratios were a confluence of real media advertising growth that was 70% greater than GNP between 1977 and 1984 (4.8% versus 2.8%), improved cable television and computer technology, deregulation, and frequent acquisitions. These industries were also insulated from the effects of the strong dollar.

The relative valuation of media stocks is an interesting example of being able to buy growth cheaply. While media returns on equity rose from approximately 1.5 times the S&P Industrials during 1972–1976 to over 2.0 times in 1978–1984, media price-earnings ratios only rose from 1.0 times the S&P Industrials to 1.4 times, as can be seen in figure 5.2.[1] In other words, relative price-earnings ratios for media companies were only 60% of their relative return on equity quite consistently over thirteen years. This meant investors were buying substantially higher media earnings growth than the S&P Industrials for the same dollar, as long as

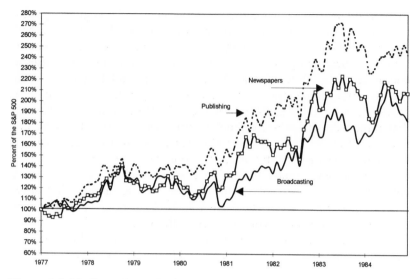

Figure 5.1 Media stocks vs. the S&P 500. Source: Standard & Poor's Corp.

media return on equity was maintained over a significant number of years. The eventual inferred decline in media return on equity had to be significant to justify this discrepancy.

The most concrete factor affecting the media industries was advertising growth. Real media advertising growth was 70% greater than real GNP growth from 1977 to 1984, and less volatile. The only down year in advertising was 1980, when the Carter administration's anti-inflation program virtually rationed consumer credit. Otherwise, advertising even grew 2.9% in 1982 when GNP fell 2.5%, and in the economic recovery atmosphere of 1983–1984 real advertising expenditures grew 11% annually.[2] Such advertising revenue growth had a potent impact on media company profits because of the operating leverage inherent in broadcasting, magazines, and newspapers. Marginal production and distribution had insignificant costs, resulting in marginal revenues coming down almost completely to the bottom line.

Numerous technological changes were also heavily impacting the media industries. Cable was sweeping the television industry, spurred by coaxial cable innovations that allowed over 100 channels into a home and by pay-channels initiated by Home Box Office in 1975. Cable television's penetration rose dramatically from 20% of television homes in 1980 to 43% in 1985. Cable subscription revenues doubled from $3.4 billion to $7.0 billion between 1981 and 1984, and cable advertising revenues surged eightfold from a low base.[3] The networks' share of the TV audience dropped from 93% in 1977 to 74% in 1985.[4]

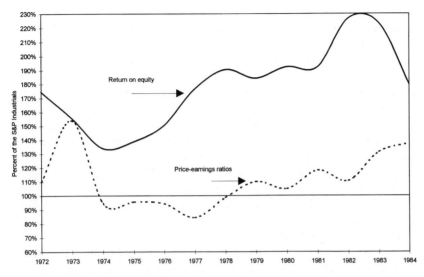

Figure 5.2 Media return on equity and price-earnings ratios vs. the S&P Industrials. Media data averages of the broadcasting, publishing, and newspaper indexes. Source: Standard & Poor's Corp.

Publishing was especially affected by computer technology. When union barriers could be overcome, newspaper and magazine production costs could be cut substantially by desktop publishing and other applications of computer technology. Desktop publishing permitted the profitable growth of a host of specialized magazines as the number of titles grew from 1,018 in 1977 to 1,707 in 1987.[5] There was also an explosive growth in business newsletters, which could be organized at minimal expense by only a few reporters armed with telephones and personal computers.

Computerized databases also opened up new demands and opportunities for business information. Public information in this area is very limited, but revenues appear to have grown 30% in 1982–1984 alone.[6]

Further technological change was also pending, such as using satellites for broadcasting and printing. By 1984, cellular telephones and the VCR were just beginning to enter the markets.[7]

At the same time that technology was sweeping the media industries, the federal government was evolving related policies that encouraged free-play of market forces. In 1981, the Federal Communications Commission (FCC) raised from seven to twelve the number of AM radio, FM radio, and television stations that one company could own, and in 1984 it eliminated both the fairness doctrine and advertising limits in television. Newspapers benefited from similar freedom when antitrust regulations were relaxed in 1982 to allow newspapers in the same market to merge, giving many companies a local monopoly and the ability to raise advertising rates faster.

The government's lenient antitrust attitude had a major impact on the media companies' opportunities for growth because the basic trends in radio, television, and newspapers provided only limited opportunities for reinvestment. Neither the number of television stations nor the number of television viewers were growing faster than the general economy, and newspaper readership was actually declining. The incremental investment required for plant and equipment in both industries was modest. Acquisitions were the principal way to grow. Media companies consistently ranked among the most frequent acquirers between 1979 and 1984. When the FCC lifted the 7-7-7 limit on AM/FM radio and television stations, radio and television station acquisitions jumped from 461 in 1980 to 1,875 in 1985.[8]

The same antitrust attitude carried over into the cable industry. Showtime and The Movie Channel, two struggling pay-TV channels, were allowed to merge in 1983, despite the fact that HBO had 60% of the market, and Viacom and ABC/Hearst were allowed to put together their units to form the Lifetime channel. Ted Turner felt the antitrust climate was open enough to discuss a bailout of his money-losing CNN channel with the networks. Cable television was deregulated in 1984, taking cable rates out of the hands of local governments.

Technology, deregulation, and acquisitions made the media companies remarkably similar by 1984 as broadcasters, publishers, and newspapers moved into one another's industries; the extensive overlap among the industries can be seen in table 5.4. By 1984, most of the radio and TV broadcasters were also in publishing; most of the newspaper companies were also in radio and TV broadcasting, publishing, and business information services; and most of the publishers were also in radio and TV broadcasting and business information services. The principal distinction among the sixteen media companies was that only the broadcasters got into entertainment but they did not get into business information systems, and most of the publishers did not get into cable, with the important exception of Time, Inc.

Among the broadcasters, CBS created a successful records business that had operating income of $124 million in 1984 and a publishing business with operating income of $59 million. The two combined represented 45% of broadcasting operating income—but CBS also lost $82 million in frivolous investments in toys and musical instruments.[9] ABC tried publishing on a more modest scale, amounting to only 8% of broadcasting operating income in 1984, and lost $44 million on forays into video production, motion pictures, and scenic attractions.[10] Capital Cities Broadcasting built an outstanding growth record by acquiring net-

Table 5.4. Media Companies Representation in Various Industries, 1984

Company	Broadcasting	Publishing	News-papers	Enter-tainment	Business Information	Cable	Cellular
Broadcasting							
CBS	X	X		X			
ABC	X	X		X			
Capital Cities	X	X				X	X
Metromedia	X			X			X
Cox	X	X		X		X	X
Taft	X			X		X	
Newspapers							
Gannett	X	X	X		X		
Times Mirror	X	X	X		X	X	
Dow Jones	X	X	X		X	X	
Knight Ridder	X		X		X		
Publishing							
Time Inc.		X	X		X	X	
Dunn & Bradstreet	X	X			X		
McGraw-Hill	X	X			X		
HBJ	X	X	X				
Macmillan		X			X		
Meredith	X	X	X		X		

work radio and television stations, which it operated with minimal overhead, and by acquiring shopping guides and specialized trade publications such as *Women's Wear Daily* and *Institutional Investor*. Capital Cities' 1984 operating income was up 149% over 1977 in broadcasting and up 202% in publishing, and the two sectors were almost equal. By 1984 Capital Cities also had small investments in cable television and cellular telephones.[11] Metromedia also had dynamic operating income growth from acquiring independent radio and television stations, outdoor advertising businesses in twenty-one states, and entertainment businesses such as the Ice Capades and the Harlem Globetrotters. During 1982–1983 it began making acquisitions in the paging and cellular telephones businesses, acquiring seven companies.[12] Cox Broadcasting and Taft Broadcasting both doubled operating income between 1980 and 1984 and had substantial investments in cable and programming. Cox owned "Lifestyles of the Rich and Famous," "Star Search," and "Solid Gold Radio," while Taft owned Hanna Barbera Productions.[13]

The newspaper companies moved into broadcasting well before the 1980s. The competition of radio and television with newspapers for the local consumer's attention and the resulting allocation of local advertising expenditures between the three media was too obvious for aggressive companies to miss. The FCC broadening of the 7-7-7 rule to 14-14-14 and the opportunities in computerized business data provided further substantial growth for the newspaper companies. By 1980 Gannett had already acquired seven television stations and fourteen radio stations, the Louis Harris & Associates research company, and had put together a major business in outdoor advertising. Between 1980 and 1984 it made eighteen more acquisitions, and by 1984 broadcasting and outdoor advertising were 36% of newspaper operating income.[14] It was, however, the only company to introduce a new newspaper during the decade when it launched *USA Today* in 1982. Times Mirror in 1984 had operating income from books, television stations, cable television, information services, and other investments equal to 59% of its operating income from newspapers. Dow Jones got over 80% of its operating income from the *Wall Street Journal,* but it had substantial investments in books, local newspapers, the Telerate quotation system, and cable television. Knight Ridder had large investments in business information services and broadcasting. In some respects newspapers, despite no growth in circulation, had advantages over television in that they benefited from similar earnings leverage as advertising revenues increased, but also achieved substantial production economies as printing was computerized and satellites allowed remote printing, nor were antitrust controls as strict as in broadcasting. Gannett Company owned over 100 local newspapers, and was therefore able to obtain significant economies of scale as well as to introduce more professional management into its frequent newspaper acquisitions. Dow Jones and Knight-Ridder had less expansive variations on the same theme.

Although publishers did not buy into the newspaper industry, they overlapped with broadcasting and newspapers in their cable operations and data services. Time, Inc. made more money from its cable television operations ($212 million) than its magazines, even though it was the largest publisher in the U.S. and its magazines division (*Time, Fortune, People,* and *Sports Illustrated*) increased operating income 169% between 1979 and 1984 ($70 million to $188 million). Its cable subsidiary, American Television and Communications, was the second largest and most profitable operator of local cable systems in the country and also owned Home Box Office. At Dun & Bradstreet, publishing shifted from 57% of income in 1979 to only 40% by 1984 because of extensive acquisitions, the most notable being its $1.3 billion acquisition of A. C. Nielsen, the television rating service.

McGraw-Hill had a similar expansion as it mixed publishing, broadcasting, and information services. The company had a strong base in traditional textbook publishing, magazines (*Business Week*), and broadcasting, and it capitalized heavily on the demands of business for computerized information by strengthening its existing operations and acquiring others. Dodge Construction Industry reports and other weekly or monthly specialized industry reports were acquired, computerized, and better marketed. Standard & Poor's greatly expanded its output and its focus on

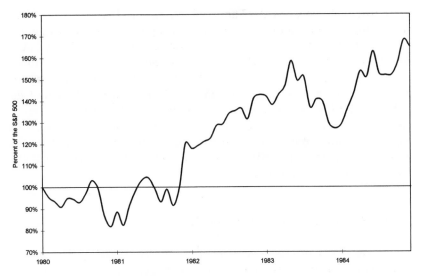

Figure 5.3 Advertising stocks vs. the S&P 500. Sources: Compustat and Standard & Poor's Corp.

profitability. Otto Eckstein's Data Resources Inc. was acquired and used as a base for expanded economic information services. McGraw-Hill's operating income from its information systems and financial and economic information divisions expanded 154%, from $52 million in 1979 to $132 million in 1984, versus only 28% for its publishing and broadcasting divisions.[15]

The other publishing companies, such as Harcourt Brace Jovanovich, Macmillan Inc., and Meredith Corp., followed similar patterns of frequent acquisitions and strong growth in related areas of broadcasting and business information services. Harcourt Brace Jovanovich, best known as an education publisher, strongly emphasized the software elements of its publishing activities and saw its operating income from business publishing, graphics, and broadcasting grow from $8 million in 1977 to $27 million in 1984.[16] Macmillan Inc. was stimulated by an unfriendly tender offer in 1979 and by a new chief executive into a strategic restructuring that involved divesting eight subsidiaries in 1981 and making nineteen acquisitions between 1982 and 1984. Pretax income from specialized business publications grew from an unrecognized level in 1979 to $21 million in 1984.[17]

The advertising industry benefited from many of the same trends that propelled the superior stock performance of the media industries. Stocks in Compustat's Advertising industry composite[18] rose to over 160% of the S&P 500 by the end of 1984, as outlined in figure 5.3. As real advertising rose 4.8% between 1977 and 1984 versus GNP growth of 2.8%,[19] advertising revenues surged 203%, far outstripping revenue growth in the other media industries. The advertising companies were too labor-intensive, however, to get as much profit growth out of the increase in revenues as the other media companies. Technology had little impact on the industry, although some agencies made efforts to develop technologically-based information services in promotions and direct mail. Return on equity remained constant at 145% of the S&P Industrials, whereas the media companies' return on equity rose from 150% to 200%, and the rise in Advertising stocks to 160% of the S&P 500 was below the 180–240% for the other media industries.

The Recovery of the Consumer Sectors

The recovery in consumer stocks in 1979–1984 reflected cyclical factors, long-term demographics, and the end of earlier fears of the effects of high inflation on food stocks. It would be a neat economics story if the overperformance was related to the significant consumer stimulus of the Reagan administration's income tax cuts and the negative capital spending effects of high real interest rates, but this scenario simply doesn't hang together. Too many other important factors intervened, such as oil prices, inflation, recession, and the strong dollar. Between 1977 and 1984 growth in GNP, disposable personal income, consumer credit, and business plant and equipment spending was surprisingly similar at 90%, 90%, 100%, and 101%, respectively. Plus, the Social Security amendments of 1983 offset part of the personal income tax cuts in the 1981 tax act.[20]

Foods

A meaningful part of the overperformance of consumer stocks between 1979 and 1984 reflected that several sectors sharply underperformed the stock market during the Carter administration and then recovered back into line with the market by 1984. Sharp changes in inflation between 1977 and 1984 made this particularly true of Food stocks,[21] outlined in figure 5.4. They declined shaprly in 1979–1980 to 64% of the S&P 500 as CPI inflation accelerated from 7% to over 14% and investors expected the food companies to have difficulty passing through their rising costs. Food stocks then recovered in advance of the general rise in the stock market, and as inflation declined to 4%, they rose further to 119% of the S&P 500 by the end of 1984. This was the beginning of a trend that carried Food stocks to 206% of the S&P 500 by the end of 1989.

The psychological element in the Food stocks' decline and recovery reflected investors' fears that the food industry would come under mar-

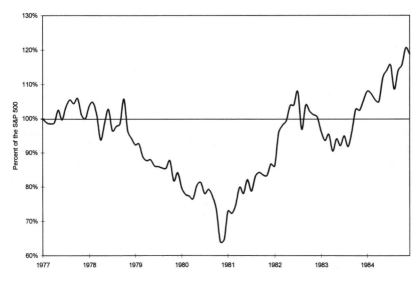

Figure 5.4 Food stocks vs. the S&P 500. Source: Standard & Poor's Corp.

gin pressure from rising commodities costs; but in fact the industry had been improving the value-added aspects of its products, its production and distribution efficiency, and its profit margins for thirty years. Profit margins rose steadily from approximately 7.5% in the 1960s to over 9% by the end of the 1970s, and over 10% by 1984. Return on equity rose from 110% of the S&P Industrials throughout 1977–1981 to over 150% throughout 1983–1986 without any change in leverage.

Industry growth was sparked by new product opportunities for diet-conscious consumers and working mothers who were attracted to quick preparation of foods. Annual new product introductions soared from approximately 2,000 in 1977–1980 to 5,400 in 1984.[22] Companies such as H. J. Heinz, Sara Lee, Conagra, and McCormick showed impressive dynamism.

Stocks of the Soft Drink and Beer industries performed similarly to the Food industry, including the sharp decline in valuation in 1979–1980, the recovery in 1981–1982, and the overperformance in 1984.

Retailing

All of the retailing industries overperformed the S&P 500 between 1979 and 1984; however, the traditional merchandisers in S&P's Retail: General Merchandise index—Sears, J. C. Penney, K-Mart, and Woolworth (Walmart was only added in 1982)—were declining, while discounters and specialty stores grew at their expense. Although I have included the

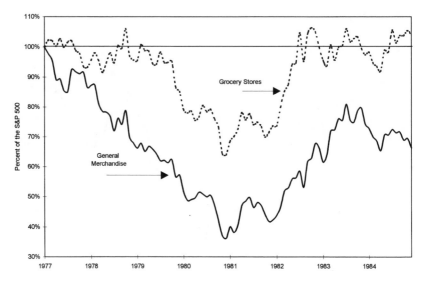

Figure 5.5 General Merchandise and Grocery Stores vs. the S&P 500. Source: Standard & Poor's Corp.

General Merchandise index as an overperforming industry, this would not have been the case had the period been 1/77–12/84, as can be seen in figure 5.5. These companies' stocks suffered a steep decline relative to the S&P 500 during 1977–1980 to only 35% of their 1/77 value. The index recovered to 80% of its 1/77 relative value in early 1983, but by 12/84 was at only 70%. This would have qualified the industry as an underperforming industry. Since the General Merchandise index was over 60% of the S&P Retail Composite, the reader can appreciate the magnitude of the opportunity presented to other retailers. This laid the base, as we shall see in volume 2, for the first substantial change in the companies dominating U.S. retailing in over fifty years.

Earnings for these General Merchandise retailers declined almost 25% between 1978 and 1981, and were still slightly behind the S&P Industrials by 1984, but their price-earnings ratios contracted from approximately 150% of the S&P in the early 1970s to 98% in 1984. Trapped by old managements, old stores, and consumers pinched by inflation, and poorly adapted to market to the baby boomer generation, these traditional retailers were rapidly losing market share to discounters such as Walmart, Price Club, and Levitz Furniture, and to specialty retailers such as The Limited, Gap, Toys "R" Us, and Home Depot. These dynamic new beneficiaries of the changing retail climate do not appear in the stock indexes of this period.

Grocery Stores also declined relative to the S&P 500 from 1977 to 1981, as can also be seen in figure 5.5. While Grocery Stores recovered

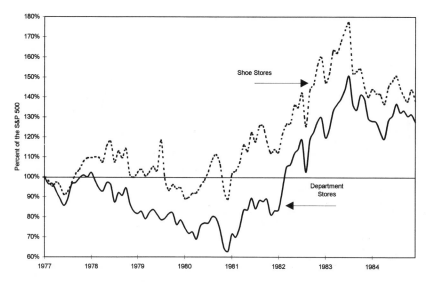

Figure 5.6 Department Store and Shoe Store stocks vs. the S&P 500. Source: Standard & Poor's Corp.

to 105% of the S&P 500 by the end of 1984, they would not qualify as an overperforming industry if the period was 1/77–12/84.

The remaining sectors of retailing clearly overperformed the S&P 500, irrespective of a 1/77 or 12/79 starting point. As outlined in figures 5.6 and 5.7, the Department Stores index at the end of 1984 was 130% of the S&P 500, the Shoe Stores index was 140%, the Drugstores index was 180%, and the Restaurants index (which I include because the consumer buying decision became so similar to a grocery decision) was 220%, mostly reflecting McDonald's.

Even these industries, however, were depressed relative to the S&P 500 during 1978–1980 by investors' persistence in anticipating greater negative effects on retail sales and earnings than occurred—an anticipation that was part of the general undervaluation of the stock market in these years, as we have seen in chapter 3. There was no decline in earnings for the Department Store, Shoe Store, Drug Store, or Restaurant indexes.

These investor anticipations appeared closely tied to changes in consumer confidence. Figure 5.8 shows the S&P Retail Composite and the University of Michigan Consumer Confidence Index with both indexed to 1/77 = 1.00. Their confluence is obvious except for the bump up in consumer confidence surrounding the presidential elections in 1980 and 1984—as if the stock market discounted the effects of political rhetoric at these times. Each of the six retail stock indexes began to recover relative to the S&P 500 in 1981, once consumer confidence rose—well before easier monetary policy stimulated the general stock market in the last

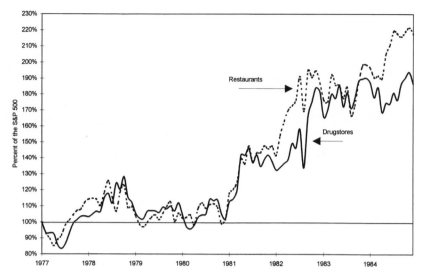

Figure 5.7 Drugstore and Restaurant stocks vs. the S&P 500. Source: Standard & Poor's Corp.

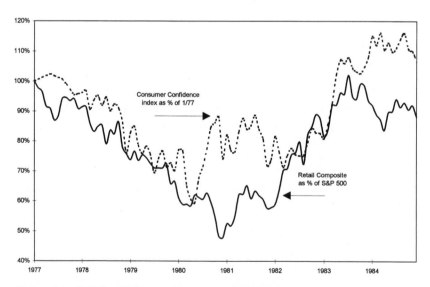

Figure 5.8 S&P Retail Composite vs. the S&P 500 and consumer confidence. Sources: Standard & Poor's Corp. and the University of Michigan.

half of 1982. In the general market recovery of 1982, all of the six retail indexes substantially outperformed the S&P 500.

Airlines, Railroads, and Trucking

Congress substantially deregulated the airline, railroad, and trucking industries between 1978 and 1980, and the stocks of the three industries outperformed the S&P 500 between 1979 and 1984. Economists' reviews of these industries at mid-decade generally considered deregulation a success, as prices came down and customer choices expanded; however these reviews did not reflect changes in stock market values, perhaps because it is difficult to separate the new competition and pricing freedom achieved by deregulation from the sharp increase in fuel costs, high interest rates, and prolonged recession that accompanied deregulation. Over the period 12/79–12/84 the three industries' stocks did outperform the S&P 500, but as we shall see, the only industry with secular overperformance was Railroads, and that was mostly due to its advantage under high energy prices. Airline earnings were so poor that it is difficult to make sense of their stock prices, and Truckers stocks over a 1/77–12/84 period (which covers the beginning of the deregulation debate) actually qualified as an underperforming industry.

In all three industries, historically powerful unions that had negotiated superior wage and benefit packages were put under great pressure to reduce them as competition increased and prices came down. But there the similarities ended. The airline industry saw many new entrants and further erosion in its already weak finances. The trucking industry became more concentrated in the less-than-truckload sector, where large operational efficiencies were possible, and less concentrated in the truckload sector, where non-union, owner-operated truckers, who could get into business with just a permit, a down payment on a tractor, and insurance, cut prices. Only the railroads were able to stabilize their finances and market share by merging, cutting back employees and track, and introducing operating efficiencies.

Airline stocks rose 83% between the end of 1979 and the end of 1984, and had a 42% improvement in return on equity, but it is a stretch of the term to call Airlines an overperforming industry. Over the broader period of 1977–1984 Airline stocks fluctuated widely with no upward trend versus the S&P 500, as can be seen in figure 5.9, and would have been categorized as an average industry.[23] The industry had inadequate earnings, a market-to-book value ratio of only 116% at the end of 1984 that approximated the average for the underperforming industries of 101%, and many of the major carriers were perennially close to bankruptcy.

The heyday of the airline industry was in 1966–1967, when it earned

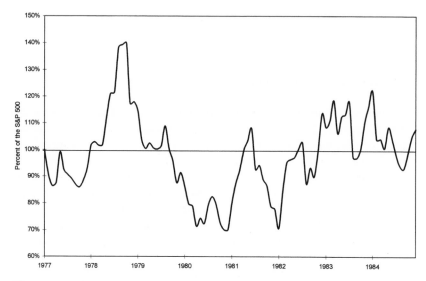

Figure 5.9 Airline stocks vs. the S&P 500. Source: Standard & Poor's Corp.

a 13–14% return on equity, its credit was strong, and the S&P Airlines index hit a high of 304.50—a price it would not reach again until the merger mania of 1989. In 1966 and 1967, respectively, Airline stocks at their peaks sold at 22.8 and 20.6 times current year earnings, 134% and 109% of the price-earnings ratios for the S&P Industrials, and 145% and 125% of the market-to-book value ratios of the S&P Industrials. After that it was all downhill. Rising fuel prices throughout the 1970s doubled the share of fuel in airline costs from 15% to 30%. Labor was 35% of costs, and under poor control. Thanks to strong unions and a 144% growth in employees between 1970 and 1980, airline real wage costs rose over 25% in the 1970s, while real wage costs for all U.S. industry declined 8%.[24] Fares and flight economics simply did not keep up with these rising costs, and as a result the industry averaged less than 5% return on equity between 1968 and 1976, and had a 65% reduction in dividends. Despite poor returns, capital expenditures net of depreciation stayed high at almost 13% of capitalization as the industry spent to create a more fuel-efficient fleet.

There was a substantial improvement in airline results in 1976–1978 as the economy improved. Revenue passenger miles grew 9.8% in 1976, 7.8% in 1977, and an astounding 17.6% in 1978, so that load factor rose from 53.7% to 61.5%. This growth fell quickly to the bottom line, and industry net income rose from zero in 1975 to $1.2 billion in 1978. Return on equity rose to 13.0%. Airline stocks responded enthusiastically, with the S&P Airline index outperforming the S&P 500 by 40% between 1977 and

1978, as can be seen in figure 5.9, but Airline stocks still averaged only 79% of book value in 1978—66% of the average for the S&P Industrials.

Unfortunately, airline economics began to deteriorate again after Congress passed an airline deregulation bill in October 1978. Some industry observers anticipated greater flexibility and speed of response, more pricing freedom, and more efficient operations as hub-and-spoke route configurations accelerated. Instead, deregulation was accompanied by rising fuel prices, inflation, sharp recession, and increased competition from new discount carriers that obliterated profits, almost destroyed the industry's credit, and made airline stocks a roller coaster.

Revenue passenger miles and total revenues continued to grow by over 15% in 1979, as did load factor, which hit a peak of 63.0%, but the airline industry adapted poorly to the sharp increase in fuel prices from 40 cents per gallon to 85 cents, raising airline operating costs by approximately $3 billion. Airline net income dropped from $1.2 billion to only $0.4 billion. United Airlines lost $101 million in 1979, Braniff $38 million, Hughes Airwest $23 million, and Continental $13 million. Airline finances got even worse in the early 1980s. The industry operated at breakeven in 1980, but as traffic declined during the recession it lost $0.3 billion in 1981 and $0.9 billion in 1982. Growth did not begin again until 1983 when revenue passenger miles exceeded 1979 by 7.6%, but the industry still lost $0.2 billion.[25]

An unanticipated effect of deregulation was the rapid expansion from thirty-four carriers in 1978 to 86 in 1985.[26] Prior to 1978, an airline wishing to provide new route service had to be "required by public convenience and necessity." From 1979 to 1981 it had to be "consistent with public convenience and necessity," and thereafter the carrier only had to be "fit, willing, and able." The first new carrier was Midway Airline, which began discount service between New York's LaGuardia airport and Midway airport in Chicago in November 1979. It was followed by New York Air in 1980, People Express and Muse Air in 1981, and a host of others. Of course, established carriers began new route services as well. Competition into the large and medium-sized hubs increased dramatically. The number of carriers increased 78% on routes from non-hubs to large hubs, 73% from small hubs to large hubs, 58% from small hubs to medium hubs, 38% from medium hubs to large hubs, 32% from large hubs to large hubs, and 20% from medium hubs to medium hubs. This competition immediately showed up in prices as discounted tickets rose from approximately 58% of business in 1980 to over 80% in 1983.[27]

The most dramatic new entrant among the airlines was People Express. Founded with venture capital funds in 1980, and operating out of Newark Airport with used planes, People Express provided a youthful, bare-bones, discount service to similarly youthful customers traveling between New York, Buffalo, Columbus, and Norfolk. There were no reservations, and tickets were sold only on the planes. Discounts averaged 40–55% during peak hours and 65–75% in off-peak hours, with extra charges for meals, drinks, and baggage. Founded by Donald Burr, the disgruntled ex-president of Texas International Airlines, not one of the company's original officers was over forty, and all employees were stockholders. Students in particular flocked to the airline, and waiting areas took on the atmosphere of college weekends as people sat on the floor, brought their own meals and drinks, back-packed their luggage, and participated in a general hum of conversation with each other and the attractive, enthusiastic People Express personnel. As People Express expanded service to other cities its fares were truly fantastic. The New York-California fare was $99 in 1982, versus $478 on a major carrier. Chicago-Miami was $114, New York-Dallas $149. Discount service to London was begun in 1983 at only $149 one-way with load factors as high as 90%. The public's response to discount rates was enormous, with People Express planes flying at a 75% load factor, versus an industry average of 61%. Service was quickly expanded so that by mid-1984 the company was serving nineteen cities with forty-two planes and had 1,300 employees. By 1984 People Express was the twelfth-ranked U.S. carrier, carrying 12 million passengers—29% of industry leader United Airlines.

Revenues went from $38.4 million in the first nine months of service in 1981 to $287 million by 1983. Load factor in 1983 was 75%, versus an industry average of 61%, in an industry where the final 1% had a great impact on profits. The company went from a loss of $9.2 million in 1981 to profits of $10.4 million in 1983, and its stock price went from $3.50 to $25.50. Morgan Stanley & Co. signed on as the company's underwriter to get it the capital necessary to quickly expand the People Express style of business to as many routes as possible.

Unfortunately, People Express ran headlong into the effects of over-expansion. By the end of 1984 it was serving forty-nine airports out of Newark, of which twenty-seven had been added since mid-1984. Available seat-miles had expanded 124% in one year. It was also trying to keep seventy-eight used planes in good repair. The result was chaos. On-time arrivals dropped to 55% of flights, bags constantly went astray, phone lines were jammed, and the huge crowds in the constricted space of the old Newark airport were frightening and dangerous. Equipment problems were constant: twice I personally witnessed plane engines bursting into flames on the way to Burlington, Vermont.

The major airlines also began to fight back with their own discount fares. Continental Airlines filed for bankruptcy in September 1983 with the intent of reopening as a discount carrier, relieved of its labor agreements so that it could cut wages. Once Continental's strategy was confirmed by the courts, United Airlines matched Continental's discount fares in seventy-nine different cities without restrictions, and discounting promptly spread throughout the major airlines to all parts of the country. People Express was hard hit by the competition. Its load factor had already dropped from 78% to 68% in the fourth quarter of 1983 when it raised its own prices, and in 1984 it reported a loss of $4 million even though its revenues had doubled. Braniff entered bankruptcy, and Eastern Airlines, TWA, Western Airlines, Republic, Frontier, and Pan Am all suffered serious losses that threatened them with bankruptcy. Numerous small feeder lines went bankrupt in 1984, including Capitol Air, Air Florida, and Pacific Express.

The highly leveraged nature of the Airline industry's finances and operations made the S&P Airlines index 35% more volatile than the S&P 500 between 1/77 and 12/84. The Airlines index varied between 140% and 70% of the S&P 500 as if all influences had a super-leveraged impact, whether it was the positive effects of improved earnings and deregulation in 1978; airlines' vulnerability to $40 oil prices in late 1980, then benefits from declining oil prices after 1981; the negative effect on travel of the recession of 1981–1982, then the positive effect of the economic recovery of 1983–1984; or the spread of discount fares in 1984.

This volatility partly reflected the multiple forms of leverage in the airline industry. The industry had very high operating leverage, as the cost of serving the marginal customer was virtually zero and the industry operated very close to breakeven. The industry was also highly leveraged financially. Not only was its common equity ratio as low as 43% of capitalization in 1982, most companies had additional lease obligations for planes and airport gates. For example, American Airlines had debt and capitalized leases equal to 62% of capitalization, but it also had operating lease rentals of $115 million that if capitalized raised its debt ratio to 72%.

In many respects, airline stocks' volatility reflected the fact that they were simply speculative vehicles since their leverage was so high and there was so little in the way of earnings or even operating income to which stock prices could be tied. The industry's outlook was made even more negative by its capital expenditure requirements, which net of depreciation averaged 12% of capitalization from 1979 to 1984[28]—133% higher than the S&P Industrials. As we shall see in volume 2, airline stocks in 1984 still did not fully reflect the negative effects of discounting and route competition that were to grow out of deregulation.

Trucking industry stocks were ranked as an overperforming industry, but their 1979–1984 growth actually reflected a recovery from inferior performance during 1977–1979, as can be seen in figure 5.10. Over the period 1/77–12/84, S&P's Truckers index actually ranked as a declining industry. It declined from 100% of the S&P 500 at the beginning of 1977 to almost 50% in 1980, reflecting both the energy crisis and the impact of deregulation on the truckload carriers; but once gasoline prices began to decline the

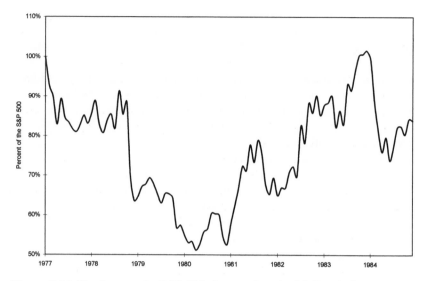

Figure 5.10 Truckers vs. the S&P 500. Source: Standard & Poor's Corp.

Truckers index rose steadily to over 100% of the S&P 500 at the end of 1983, before slipping back to 84% in 1984. Earnings for S&P's Truckers index declined steadily from $10.99 in 1978 to $9.02 in 1982 under the impact of higher gasoline prices and the recession, but rose to approximately $15.00 in 1983 and 1984, only to fall again to $8.29 in 1985.

The impact of deregulation on the industry proved hard to judge. The substantial market share growth of the 1950s and 1960s, in which trucking had gone from 5% of intercity freight traffic to 22%, had stalled in the 1970s,[29] but the Motor Carrier Act of 1980 and piecemeal predecessor legislation of the late 1970s offered the possibility of large market share gains for the larger trucking companies, provided they were nonunion.

Two outcomes of trucking deregulation were fairly clear. In the truck-load market, where "over the road" costs were 60–70% of revenues, freedom to set competitive rates and freedom of market entry would open up the business to small nonunion operators at the expense of Teamster-affiliated companies. In the less-than-truckload market, where "over the road" costs were only 25–30% of revenues and captive carriers handled 55–60% of all freight, the large carriers gained the opportunity to create real efficiencies once freed of restrictive regional rate-setting bureaus and given routing freedom. The large carriers moved vigorously in the late 1970s to set up hub-and-spoke terminal operations and to take over captive carrier operations. Value Lines' Trucking industry net capital expenditures averaged 22.4% of prior year capitalization from 1977 to 1979 — one of the highest capital expenditure levels in U.S. industry.

The oil crisis disrupted this positive outlook from 1979 to 1980, driving return on equity down from 17% during 1977–1979 to 13% in 1980. Declining oil and gasoline prices from 1981 to 1982 should have raised earnings, but the unionized public companies in the truckload business came under great competitive pressure from low-cost owner-operated truckers. McLean Trucking, a prominent unionized company, went bankrupt in 1982.

The economic recovery in 1983–1984 had a very positive impact on Truckers earnings as they rose from approximately $9 to $15, but this was short-lived despite the persistence of the recovery. Competition between new nonunion truckers and the unionized companies, even in the less-than-truckload sector, cut earnings almost in half in 1985. Other than stockholders, the other losers in truck deregulation were the Teamsters.

The railroad industry entered into deregulation from a different position than either the airlines or the trucking industry as the poor cousin of U.S. transportation, and yet was the only transportation industry for which stocks enjoyed secular overperformance. The railroads' market share of intercity freight had declined from 75% in 1929 to 56% in 1950 and 40% in 1970. Their passenger traffic had been almost totally lost to airplanes and automobiles. Most of the Northeastern lines, notably Penn Central Corporation, had gone bankrupt during 1969–1970, and industry return on equity in 1970 was a mere 0.4%. Labor practices were hopelessly inefficient, and direct labor costs were almost $25,000 per employee plus substantial benefits.[30] Some improvement occurred in the 1970s, but it was minimal, and regulation held a heavy hand over the industry. Northeast passenger and freight operations were reorganized into Amtrak and Conrail, but only because of bankruptcies and with heavy subsidies.

The Staggers Act of 1980, which deregulated the industry, promised significant gains in efficiency. It allowed the railroads to abandon lines that were uneconomic, provided for setting rates quarterly to truly recover projected costs including inflation, allowed unregulated rates for contract shipments, set strong limits on rate challenges by shippers, and created an atmosphere favoring mergers.

The railroads took aggressive advantage of these new freedoms. Employees were cut almost 30% between 1980 and 1983, from 458,000 to 322,000 and track mileage was cut 5%. The volume of freight under negotiated price contracts rose from 25% to 50%. Five major mergers took place between the Chesapeake & Ohio and Seaboard Coast Line systems, the Union Pacific and Missouri Pacific/Western Pacific systems, the Burlington Northern and St. Louis & San Francisco Railway systems, the Norfolk & Western and Southern Railway systems, and the Santa Fe and Southern Pacific systems. Efficiencies began to show up quickly in the form of lower revenue per ton-mile which began a steady decline that

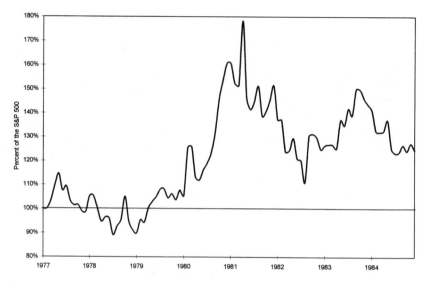

Figure 5.11 Railroads vs. the S&P 500. Source: Standard & Poor's Corp.

amounted to 40% by the end of the decade. Railroads stopped losing market share and stabilized at 37% of intercity freight transportation. The new regulatory freedom also appeared to induce a surge of management initiatives to improve productivity, such as longer trains, larger freight cars, "hump" assembly, centralized traffic control, hub-and-spoke traffic patterns, and computerized billing. "Piggyback" volumes rose by one-third. Claims for lost and damaged freight dropped from 1.08% of revenues in 1980 to 0.46% by 1984. Return on equity—never adequate—at least recovered into the 7–9% range.[31]

The performance of railroad stocks relative to the S&P 500 is outlined in figure 5.11. From 1/77 to 12/79 Standard & Poor's Railroad index moved more or less in line with the S&P 500, then moved up briefly to 178% of the S&P 500 in early 1981. This strong move reflected both the energy crisis and the anticipated effects of deregulation. The energy crisis benefited railroad stocks as investors anticipated that railroads, being less energy-intensive than trucking, would gain freight traffic, as well as increased western coal shipments to utilities shifting from oil and gas. Coal shipments were already 35% of railroad tonnage, and a highly efficient, long-haul product. Investors also expected railroads' mineral rights on their extensive land holdings to finally pay off.

The optimism about the industry was short-lived, however. Oil prices began to fall in 1981, the outlook for large gains in freight and mineral rights revenues diminished, and coal shipments increased very gradually, only reaching 40% of railroad tonnage in 1984.[32] S&P's Railroad index

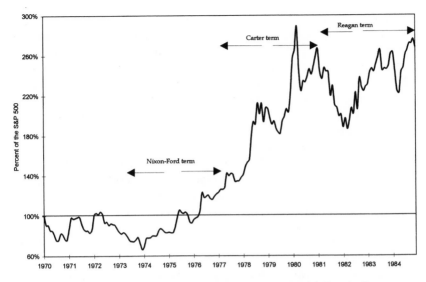

Figure 5.12 Aerospace vs. the S&P 500. Source: Standard & Poor's Corp.

was only 124% of the S&P 500 at the end of 1984, but the gain from pre-deregulation prices was still substantial.

The Defense Industry

S&P's Aerospace index, which is our best proxy for the defense industry, rose 84% between 12/79 and 12/84, outperforming the S&P 500 by 36 percentage points, as aerospace sales to the Department of Defense more than doubled between 1980 and 1984 from $22.8 billion to $46 billion.[33] However, growth in Aerospace stock prices, earnings, and capital expenditures was much greater under President Carter than President Reagan, indicating how broad and early the political support for increased defense expenditures was. In 1978, President Carter had promised our European allies that the U.S. would increase real defense expenditures at least 3%—a commitment that was strengthened when the Russians invaded Afghanistan in 1979 and it appeared that they might invade Poland in 1980 because of the success of the Solidarity movement. The humiliation of U.S. forces in trying to retrieve the Iranian embassy hostages in 1980 added public pressure. As can be seen in figure 5.12, the Aerospace index outperformed the S&P 500 by 45% between 1/73 and 12/76 (Presidents Nixon and Ford's term) by 110% between 1/77 and 12/80 (President Carter's term), and did not outperform it at all from 1/81–12/84 (President Reagan's first term). Stock price growth corresponded to similar gains in fundamentals. Capital expenditures net of depreciation averaged 4.2% of capitalization between 1973 and 1976, 12.0% of capitalization between 1977 and 1980, and 7.5% of capitalization between 1981 and 1984. Return on equity rose from 12.0% from 1973 to 1976 to 17.5% from 1977 to 1980, and remained at 17.7% from 1981 to 1984.

Aerospace stocks sold at price-earnings ratios averaging only 92% of the S&P 500 between 1977 and 1984, which appears inconsistent with extreme notions that the U.S. economy was dependent on the defense infrastructure or that there was a dominating industrial-military complex.

Commercial aviation had two sharply conflicting trends while defense expenditures were rising so rapidly. Commercial aircraft orders were basically stable throughout 1977–1984 at approximately three hundred units annually. Private aircraft orders, however, plummeted 30% in 1980 in response to high fuel costs and the recession, and dropped a further 45% in 1981 and 37% in 1982. They never recovered in the rest of the 1980s. By 1987, private aircraft orders were only 6% of their 1978 level. Cessna, Beech Aircraft, Gates Learjet, and Piper Aircraft were all virtually squeezed out of the turbo aircraft business except for parts and maintenance. Only a modest executive jet business remained. Commercial helicopter orders followed a similar trend.[34]

Other Industries

The overperforming industries not yet discussed require little comment. Among the capital goods industries, Household Furnishings and Appliances, Tires, and Auto Parts were not secularly overperforming industries when looked at over 1/77–12/84; my 1979–1984 period simply caught the "up" phase of their frequent cyclicity. The other industries illustrated no particular general theme.

Among the other overperforming industries, Computer Services, Hospital Management, and Pollution Control reflected secular long-term trends of cheapening computer power, private management of health care facilities, and increased environmental regulation, that appear obvious in retrospect. The Hotel/Motel industry had a long-term record of overperformance dating from the recovery from the oil crisis of 1973–1974 that reflected the continuing consolidation of a highly fragmented industry.

Small Capitalization Stocks

Small capitalization stocks are not an industry, but the attention to them as an investment strategy is so intense that they merit discussion here.

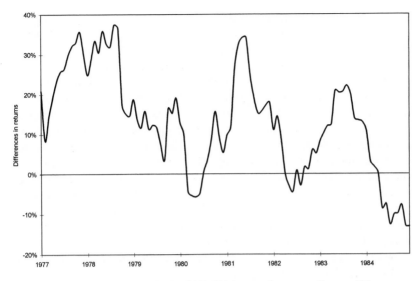

Figure 5.13 Small Cap minus the S&P 500 log total returns. Source: Ibbotson Associates.

Small capitalization stocks had a total return 67 percentage points better than the S&P 500 between 1979 and 1984 that continued their superior performance of the 1970s, when their total return was 2.6 times that of the S&P 500.[35] However, as can be seen in figure 5.13, which charts the difference between returns on small cap stocks and the S&P 500, this superior performance failed to occur periodically in early 1980, 1982, and 1984, presaging the remainder of the decade, in which small cap stocks consistently underperformed the S&P 500.

Numerous studies have documented a dramatic change in the relative earnings of small cap companies in the early 1980s.[36] Fama and French found that the return on equity for small companies selected on the basis of market capitalization plunged from 10% during 1978–1979 to losses during 1982–1983 and only 2% in 1984. They also found a sharp decline for small cap companies selected on the basis of book assets. They summed up earnings results for small cap companies as follows:

> In short, the 1980s qualify as a depression for the profitability of small firms. The depression is worse for small market-equity firms than for small book-asset firms . . . . The post-1980 period is nevertheless an earnings disaster for small book-asset firms as well as for small market-equity firms.[37]

There has been considerable investor and academic attention to this change in the performance of small cap stocks. Investors are curious as to whether there will be a reversal of fortunes, returning small cap stocks to their apparent long-term trend of overperformance. Fama and French express surprise that small cap stocks' price-earnings ratios and market-to-book value ratios remained high, leading them to conclude that "In every year after 1979 . . . the market is continuously fooled by the low (often negative) equity earnings of small firms during the 1980s."[38]

The performance results and underlying financial data for small cap stocks may, however, reflect overly generalized statistical data rather than results that can be ascribed to small cap stocks per se. More research is needed to determine whether the relative performance of small cap stocks from 1960 to 1990 was associated with results in three different stock market sectors—marginal NYSE companies in the 1960s, oil-related companies in the 1970s, and high-tech initial public offerings (IPOs) in the 1980s. Unfortunately, such research is hampered by data problems. There is no Compustat data on NASDAQ stocks prior to 1973, and there is no public access to some of the better, more recent data in this respect, particularly the Russell 2000 Index, which excludes the one thousand largest companies, and the Wilshire Next 1750, which excludes the 750 largest companies.

Because of the lack of Compustat data on NASDAQ stocks prior to 1973, students of earlier periods are forced to define small cap stocks as the smallest capitalization NYSE stocks. These stocks, however, have a strong bias toward what might be called "fallen angels," (to borrow a term from the junk bond market) rather than companies that are initially small. Two-thirds of the NYSE stocks in the lowest quintile by market capitalization declined into that category from a higher quintile; their return on assets from 1966–1984 was only 68% and their interest coverage was only 58% of the top NYSE quintile's; over one-quarter of the companies had dividend reductions in the prior year versus 0.5% for the top quintile.[39] These lowest quintile NYSE companies are failed companies, relatively speaking, rather than growing small companies. Investment results for them reflect an extreme form of "value investing," rather than small cap performance.

Using the lowest NYSE quintile as a measure of "small cap" reflects that the notion of small cap companies is somewhat confused. Small historic capitalization measures are more likely to capture the greater ease of high growth from a small base as well as the virtues of being smaller, such as lack of overhead and bureaucracy, greater entrepreneurship, and greater flexibility. The Russell 2000 and the Wilshire Next 1750 are also selected based on market capitalization rather than book capitalization.

After 1973, further research is needed to determine whether small cap stock performance was predominantly influenced by the energy crises of the 1970s. There is no NASDAQ energy index by which we can determine the impact of energy stocks on the overall NASDAQ market, but the American Stock Exchange's Natural Resources Index rose from 58 at the end of 1974 to 356 at the end of 1980, which surely provides consid-

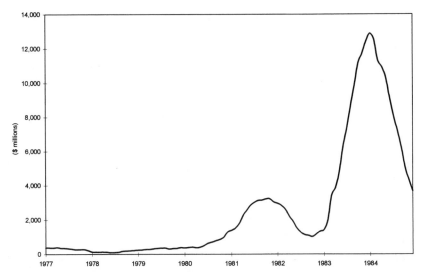

Figure 5.14 Initial public offerings ($ millions). Source: Securities Data Company Inc.

erable insight into the NASDAQ market.[40] In 1979, twenty-three energy stocks accounted for 56% of the trading volume in the fifty most active NASDAQ stocks.[41]

In the early 1980s, the surge in initial public offerings was so great that it transformed the NASDAQ market and made comparisons with the 1970s inapposite. IPOs, outlined in figure 5.14, went from an annual average of approximately $0.5 billion during the late 1970s to $3.2 billion in 1981, to almost $13 billion in 1983. This changed the small cap market in two important ways. First, the number of firms in the NASDAQ Composite Index jumped from a stable, decade-long level of approximately 2,600 in 1982 to 3,751 by the end of 1984,[42] making small cap performance oversensitive to the systematic underpricing that occurs in IPOs. The S&P New Issues Index, outlined in figure 5.15, enjoyed a run from 140% of the S&P 500 in October 1982 to over 360% in July 1983, coinciding with small cap 1983 overperformance.[43] When the New-Issues Index declined in 1984, and IPO volume declined to $3.7 billion, so did the measures of small cap stock performance.

Secondly, the IPO surge transformed the small cap market from one heavily influenced by the oil-related industries to one dominated by the high-tech and bio-tech industries. Fueled by the rise of the personal computer industry, high-tech public offerings rose from an annual average of $0.5 billion from 1977 to 1979, to over $4.2 billion in mid-1981, to almost $11 billion in mid-1983, as can be seen in figure 5.16.[44] Bio-

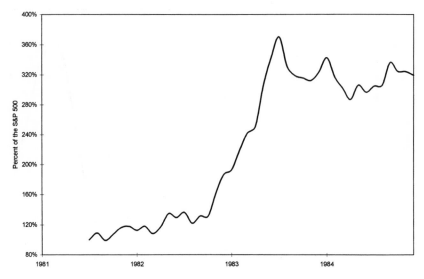

Figure 5.15 S&P New-issues index vs. the S&P 500. Source: Standard & Poor's Corp.

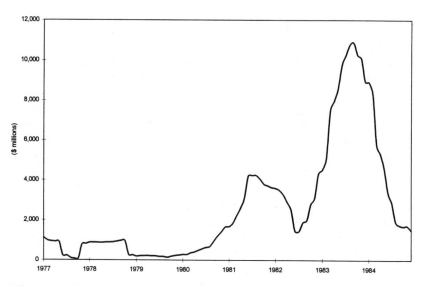

Figure 5.16 High-tech common stock offerings ($ millions). Source: Securities Data Company Inc.

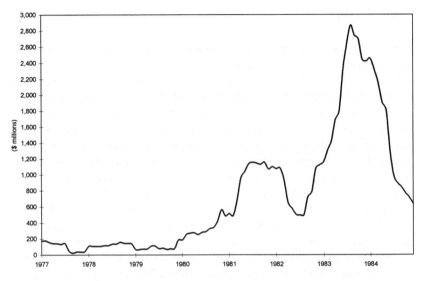

Figure 5.17 Health, drug, and biotech common stock offerings ($ millions).
Source: Securities Data Company Inc.

tech and health care offerings, outlined in figure 5.17, rose from an annual average of $100 million in the late 1970s to $1.2 billion in mid-1981, to almost $3 billion in mid-1983, fueled by advances in molecular biology and the spread of private health-care institutions. The two sectors constituted approximately 25% of the Russell 2000 at the end of 1984.[45]

High-tech stocks dropped sharply in 1984, reflecting that IBM had immediately vaulted to the top of the personal computer market, but also that IBM had became much more aggressive in pricing and marketing after its antitrust case was dropped in 1982. The Amex High Technology Index dropped from 525 at the end of 1983 to 375 at the end of 1984, giving some indication of what must have happened in the NASDAQ market.[46] Health care stocks were also battered by the first stage of phasing in the prospective payment system, beginning in October 1983, created in the Carter administration's earlier effort to control Medicare and Medicaid costs. These high-tech and health care problems created a corresponding sharp underperformance by small cap stocks in 1984.

The growth in high-tech and bio-tech IPOs also radically changed the financials and market-based ratios of small cap stocks. Many of these new companies were research efforts that generated large losses that may have created the very low earnings results that Fama and French found for small cap stocks in general. On this basis, the stock market probably was not "fooled" at all in the valuations that it gave to small cap stocks.

Summary

Just as the underperforming stock groups reflected the new regime, so did the overperforming ones, which in just a few years went from being only 40% of the size of the oil, capital goods, and commodities industries in the S&P 500 to being their equal. Twenty of the thirty overperforming industries were in consumer nondurables or services, versus only one among the average and underperforming industries, and seventeen of the thirty changed their trend from previous average or underperformance. This reflected the positive impact of lower income taxes, higher consumer confidence, and the lack of serious impact from the strong dollar. The retailing stocks were particularly sensitive to the improvement in consumer confidence, and all of the industries were insensitive to imports. Imports only rose from 3 to 4% of domestic production in the overperforming industries, versus 22–25% for the average and underperforming industries.

The most prominent overperforming sector was the media industries which benefited from an increase in advertising 70% greater than GNP, the end of advertising limits in radio and television, technological developments in computerization and cable television, and antitrust freedoms to add radio and television stations, consolidate competing newspaper operations in the same city, and merge cable operations. Radio and television acquisitions quadrupled from 461 in 1980 to 1,875 in 1985, and the broadcasting, publishing, and newspaper industries became highly overlapping.

The other secularly overperforming industries were the Food industry, which benefited from reduced inflation and a huge increase in new diet-oriented and microwave products, specialty retailers, industries stimulated by government actions such as the Aerospace, Pollution Control, and Hospital Management industries, and a few technologically oriented capital goods producers. Small capitalization stocks continued to overperform, but their character was greatly changed by the record volume of IPOs for high technology computer and biotechnology companies, which proved to be short on earnings and high on volatility. Most of the other overperforming industries, particularly those in transportation or related to the auto and capital goods industries only enjoyed cyclical recoveries. Railroads were unique among the transportation industries, in truly benefiting from deregulation as they got to negotiate freight rates on 50% of their volume and to cut employees by 30%. The airlines, by contrast, were plagued with price cutting from startup discount carriers such as People Express and New York Air, as were the truckload truckers.

The division of American industry into under- and overperforming stock groups had a parallel in the separation of the corporate bond market into declining and improving credits; but before turning to it I will first look at the treasury market to establish the great influence of the Federal Reserve and the administration on interest rates and to show how they supercharged the mortgage securities market into new prominence.

6

U.S. Treasury Markets

Nowhere was the impact of the new regime, particularly monetary policy, more obvious than in the U.S. treasury markets. After a decade in which monetary policy appeared subservient to political goals, it became the principal government policy lever to control inflation, and the actions of the Federal Reserve were so aggressive in this respect that they overrode many of the other influences on interest rates. The academic literature gives little attention to the institutional role of the Federal Reserve in determining interest rates, especially long-term rates, but between 1979 and 1984 it was dominant. Insofar as the direction of long-term rates varied from monetary policy pressures, it reflected the prospect of a dramatic increase in the federal deficit during the 1981 budget debate and its ultimate long-term financing, which began in 1983.

In this chapter I will review the course of the treasury markets and the influence on them of the Federal Reserve, the budget deficit, inflation, economic growth, and the dollar. I will then examine how the volatility, size, and high returns of the treasury market made it a hothouse for the development of derivatives products and highly leveraged speculation.

The Direction of Interest Rates

The early 1980s were a fulcrum point at which the Federal Reserve's aggressive fight against inflation altered the trend of returns on long-term treasuries from a long period of negative nominal and real returns that

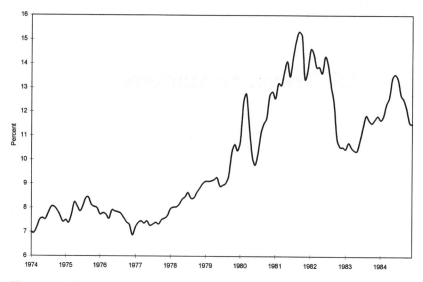

Figure 6.1 Ten-year treasury rates. Source: Federal Reserve.

stretched from 1968 to 1981 to attractive returns thereafter. But before I get to the broader question of why interest rates moved as they did, it will be helpful to review the chronology of movements in long-term rates, using ten-year treasuries as a proxy.[1] I have already reviewed the path of short-term rates, particularly federal funds, in chapter 2.

Ten-year treasury rates, outlined in figure 6.1, only varied between 7–8% from 1974 through 1977, but rose steadily to 9% during the first half of 1979. Rates rose sharply to 10.3% when the Federal Reserve changed monetary policy in October 1979, and then to 12.4% in the inflation crisis of February 1980. They fell to 9.8% in June 1980 following the introduction of President Carter's anti-inflation program, as the economy declined and monetary policy eased, then rose again to 12.8% by December 1980 as the economy recovered and inflation revived, and the Federal Reserve began to tighten credit again. Federal funds rates were more or less stable around 18% from January through August 1981, but ten-year treasury rates continued to rise to a peak of 15.3% in September 1981, in reaction to the massive deficit increase implicit in the negotiations over the Reagan tax and defense programs.

Long-term bond investors were exceedingly discouraged by 1981. Total returns on long-term treasuries, outlined in figure 6.2,[2] averaged only 5.5% annually in the 1970s. There were periods of substantial losses from 1973 to 1974 and 1978 to 1979, but 1980–1981 returns were excruciating. In the worst twelve-month period, through February 1980, total returns were almost 20% negative, and the losses kept building thereafter through the

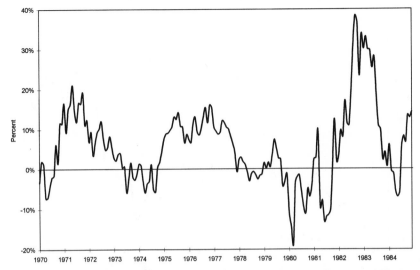

Figure 6.2 Total log returns on twenty-year treasuries (rolling twelve months). Source: Ibbotson Associates.

summer of 1981, when in four successive months the monthly losses ranged between 7.7% and 13.1% (not shown).

Long-term investors' disillusionment can be easily imagined by studying figure 6.3, which outlines total returns on long-term treasuries on an index basis. The index, which is based on 12/68 = 100, was flat around 170 for most of 1977–1979, and at its worst declined from 175 in June 1979 to 139 in September 1981. From 1976 to mid-1982, long-term treasury investors had six years of virtually no positive return. The comparison with common stocks was particularly galling. From the beginning of 1979 to the end of 1981, stocks averaged an annual return of 14.3%, versus losses averaging 1.1% for long-term treasuries.[3]

Real returns on long-term treasuries were even worse. Rolling twelve-months total returns on twenty-year treasuries, adjusted for CPI inflation, are outlined in figure 6.4. These returns were persistently negative for over five years from November 1977 through January 1982. At the lowest point, for the twelve months ending March 1980, the real return was −32.5%, and for the extended period from January 1980 through September 1981 real returns consistently approached −20%.

The cumulative effect of these real returns can be seen in index terms in figure 6.5. The index is based on 12/68 = 100, but it conveniently returned to 100 in 12/76. Thereafter, it dropped steadily to its lowest point of 52 in September 1981, which is to say that investors had lost virtually half of their funds with no return on capital since 1968 or 1976.

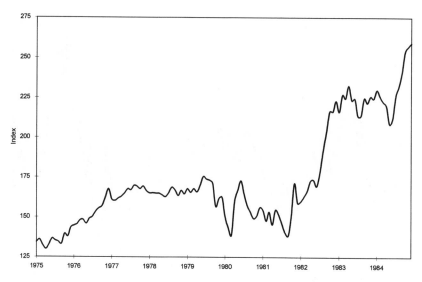

Figure 6.3 Twenty-year treasury total return index. Source: Ibbotson Associates.

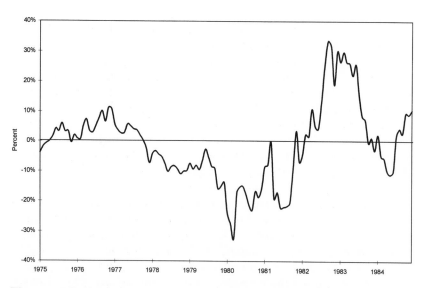

Figure 6.4 Real total log returns on twenty-year treasuries (rolling twelve months). Monthly total log returns minus monthly log CPI inflation. Source: Ibbotson Associates.

Figure 6.5 Real total return index for twenty-year treasuries. Source: Ibbotson Associates.

These dismal bond market returns were permanently reversed in the second half of 1982 when the Federal Reserve's dramatic efforts to ease credit translated into a total return on long-term treasuries of 40.4%. The index of nominal long-term treasury returns (figure 6.3) rose from a low point of 138.5 in September 1981 to a recovery peak of 232.7 in April 1983. On a real basis (figure 6.5), the treasury index recovered from 52% to over 80% of its 1976 value.

When the Federal Reserve twice tightened credit again in 1983–1984, the yield on the ten-year treasury at first rose from 10.5% to 11.8% (figure 6.1), where it stayed through February 1984, then rose again to 13.6%. Investors who had participated in the great 1982 rally got a profound sense of whiplash. However, amid the Continental Illinois crisis and dissipating inflation fears in the last half of 1984, the Federal Reserve eased credit and ten-year rates dropped from 13.6% to 11.5%. The total return on long-term treasuries was only 0.7% in 1983, but it was 15.4% in 1984 and even higher in the next two years. Since inflation was just under 4% from 1982 to 1984, real returns were correspondingly high. The attractions of bond investing had been restored.

The Federal Reserve's Impact on Interest Rates

The Federal Reserve had an overwhelming impact on interest rates from 1979 to 1984 because it controlled one of the principal policy levers, and

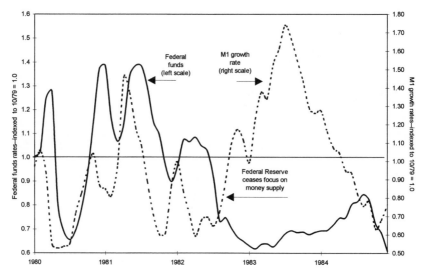

Figure 6.6 Federal funds and M1 growth rate (both indexed to 10/79 = 1.0).
Source: Federal Reserve.

during the Reagan administration the only policy lever, to reduce inflation. The other factors reducing inflation were fortuitous, such as the strong dollar and declining oil prices. We will see below that the Federal Reserve determined federal funds and treasury bill rates during this period, and that it and the budget deficit determined long-term bond rates. Thus, treasury rates reflected the institutional forces of the Federal Reserve and the budget rather than the traditional factors of inflation, the state of the economy, or the dollar.

The federal funds rate is the best variable for tracking the Federal Reserve's impact on interest rates because it was controlled by the Federal Reserve. The course of this rate was remarkably simple between October 1979, when the Federal Reserve announced its new policy of focusing on money supply, and late 1982, when it gave up this policy. The rate simply followed year-to-year M1 growth rates, as can be seen in figure 6.6. As Paul Volcker said early in his tenure as Federal Reserve chairman, the Federal Reserve's policy position had to be kept simple to be effective.

Both series in figure 6.6 have been indexed to 10/79 = 1.0. Federal funds rates usually lagged upward changes in M1 by one to three months and lagged the downward changes with more variability, particularly in 1982, when the Federal Reserve was determined not to repeat what seemed to be earlier errors of reversing credit constraint too quickly. No wonder market professionals devoted huge efforts to predicting money supply reports at this time.

It should be emphasized, however, that money supply changes did not

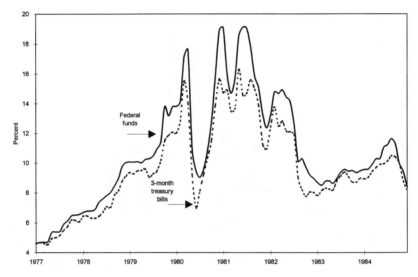

Figure 6.7 Federal funds and treasury bill rates (monthly averages). Source: Federal Reserve.

change federal funds rates—Federal Reserve policy actions did. The reader will note in figure 6.6 that in mid-1982, when the Federal Reserve stopped linking its actions to money supply growth, the connection between money supply and federal funds rates disappeared. When M1 growth skyrocketed in 1983 it had no impact on federal funds, and when federal funds rose in 1984, M1 growth was in sharp decline.

The Federal Reserve's control over the federal funds rate translated into virtual control over treasury bill rates, as can be seen in figure 6.7. It was very difficult for the Federal Reserve to justifiably claim that its policies followed the markets when federal funds yielded more than treasury bills throughout 1977–1984, as can be seen in figure 6.8.[4] It is unlikely that this relationship implied continuous expectations that federal funds rates would decline below treasury bills. More realistically, the relationship reflected a market constantly distorted by Federal Reserve actions.

The Federal Reserve's impact on short-term rates makes intuitive sense, but its impact on long-term rates is not widely appreciated. The notion runs counter to traditional economic emphasis on inflation and economic growth; but figure 6.9 shows the strong relationship between changes in federal funds, which were under Federal Reserve control, and ten-year treasury rates. Both rates have been indexed to 1/79 = 1.0 to facilitate comparison. Federal funds rates were more volatile than ten-year treasury rates, but the latter generally tracked the Federal Reserve's actions in the federal funds market.

Sorting out the relative impact of Federal Reserve actions, inflation,

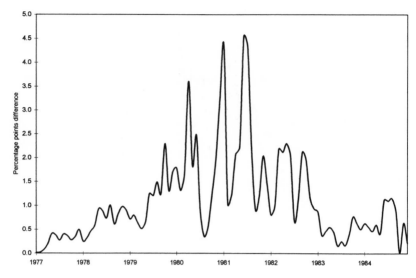

Figure 6.8 Federal funds minus three-month treasury bill rates. Source: Federal Reserve.

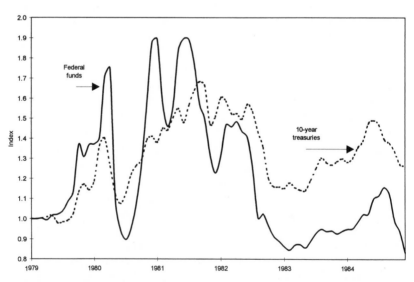

Figure 6.9 Federal funds and ten-year treasury rates (indexed to 1/79 = 1.0). Source: Federal Reserve.

Table 6.1. Major Moves in Ten-Year Treasuries 1979–1984

Period (Col. 1)	Ten-Year Change (basis pts.) (Col. 2)	Federal Funds Change (basis pts.) (Col. 3)	% Change Industrial Production (Col. 4)	% Change CPI[1] (Col. 5)
Oct. 1979	1.00	2.40	0.0%	17.2%
Feb.–Mar. 1980	2.00	3.40	0.7%	−22.8%
Mid-1980	−3.00	−8.60	−5.8%	−11.5%
Second Half 1980	3.00	9.90	5.8%	22.8%
Summer 1981	1.80	−3.20	2.5%	−37.0%
Year-end 1981	0.90	1.50	−2.6%	−38.9%
Second Half 1982	−3.80	−5.20	−3.8%	−78.5%
Summer 1983	1.50	0.90	6.8%	−2.1%
First Half 1984	1.90	1.40	2.7%	−25.5%
Second Half 1984	−2.10	−3.20	−0.7%	2.9%
Coincident Indicator		9	7	4

[1]Moving six-month average anticipating three months.

and the economy on long-term interest rates is complicated by their tendency to overlap, and anticipations of changes in these factors are even more difficult to ascertain. However, a good sense of these factors' influence can be had from table 6.1, which compares their directions at the time of the ten largest movements in ten-year treasury rates between 1979 and 1984. Changes in the monthly average for federal funds rates are used as an indication of Federal Reserve actions, changes in the monthly industrial production index are used to indicate economic growth, and the rolling average of six-month changes in the Consumer Price Index is used for inflation. Ten-year treasury rates followed the direction of changes in monetary policy 9 out of 10 times, except in Summer 1981 during the budget debate. They followed changes in the economy seven times, but two of those times the change in industrial production was very minor—less than 2%. Rates only followed changes in inflation four times.

The assertion that the Federal Reserve caused the principal changes in long-term treasury rates opens the question of how policy actions in the money markets were transmitted to long-term markets. It was not as a result of direct open market operations. As the reader can see in table 6.2, open market transactions were mostly confined to treasury bills. The Federal Reserve only sold longer treasuries once between 1979 and 1984, and then only $300 million in 1984 (col. 8) when interest rate changes were not dramatic.[5] We can safely assume that Federal Reserve purchases other than treasury bills were portfolio balancing transactions at treasury auctions, unrelated to monetary policy.

Federal Reserve purchases at treasury auctions provided another possible avenue of influence. As can be seen in table 6.3, Federal Reserve auction purchases of bonds were very substantial from 1978 to 1980, ac-

Table 6.2. Federal Reserve Actions in Open Market Treasuries ($ Billions)

Year	Treas. Bills		Coupons <1 Yr		Coupons 1>5 Yrs		Coupons >5 Yrs	
	Bought (Col. 1)	Sold (Col. 2)	Bought (Col. 3)	Sold (Col. 4)	Bought (Col. 5)	Sold (Col. 6)	Bought (Col. 7)	Sold (Col. 8)
1979	16.6	7.5	3.2	0.0	2.1	0.0	1.0	0.0
1980	7.7	7.3	0.9	0.0	2.1	0.0	1.5	0.0
1981	13.9	6.7	0.3	0.0	1.7	0.0	0.8	0.0
1982	17.1	8.4	0.3	0.0	1.8	0.0	0.7	0.0
1983	18.9	3.4	0.5	0.0	1.9	0.0	1.3	0.0
1984	20.0	8.6	1.1	0.0	1.6	0.0	1.0	0.3

Source: Federal Reserve annual reports.

counting for between 14% and 28% of the net increase in marketable treasury bonds. However, these purchases declined substantially under the Reagan administration to between 3% and 10% of the net increase — not much of an influence.

The simple explanation of the Federal Reserve's impact on long-term rates is its impact on investors' expectations. When the Federal Reserve telegraphs the direction in which it wants interest rates to go, investors have a powerful incentive to follow since most long-term bond investors have a major timing element in their transaction decisions. Changes in short-term rates can also affect long rates as banks, savings and loans, insurance companies, and mutual funds adapt their portfolios, but these changes take months and are generally anticipated by the markets.

Professional arbitrage also moves short-term market influences out along the yield curve. Sometimes arbitrage is only implicit, such as when insurance companies and many other traditional long-term investors shortened their maturity focus from 25–30 years to 7–10 years in the early 1980s, but professional arbitrage became a major force in this period. Investment bankers developed much larger fixed income arbitrage activities in the 1980s than they ever had before, facilitated by the growth of the futures and repurchase markets, which I will discuss below. They thereby provided quite formal, massive, and fast-acting arbitrage pressures.

This emphasis on the Federal Reserve's impact on long-term rates runs counter to theories of the term stucture of interest rates — that long-term rates equal the average of anticipated future short-term rates plus some constant premium. Terms structure theory does not accord well with the Federal Reserve's impact on the expectations of active, performance-oriented debt managers who are focused on total returns (yield plus price changes) as the tradeoff against short-term interest rates.

Table 6.3. Federal Reserve Share of the Net Increase in U.S. Treasury Bonds ($ billions)

	1975	1976	1977	1978	1979	1980	1981	1982	1983	1984
Federal Reserve U.S. treasury bond holdings	-	6.7	8.8	12.5	14.6	16.9	18.4	18.6	20.8	23.0
U.S. treasury bonds outstanding	38.6	40.6	47.0	60.0	74.7	85.4	99.9	104.6	133.7	167.9
Federal Reserve share of increase		-	33%	28%	14%	21%	10%	4%	8%	6%

Sources: Federal Reserve Annual Report 1979, p. 315; 1980, p. 254; 1982, p. 216; 1984, p. 226, and Annual Statistical Digest, 1970–1979, pp. 219–220; 1980–1989, pp. 183–184.

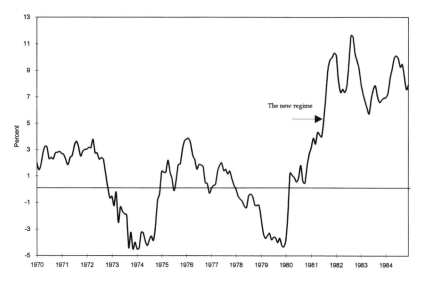

Figure 6.10 Real ten-year treasury rates (ten-year rates minus six months' average CPI inflation). Sources: Federal Reserve and Bureau of Labor Statistics.

Real Interest Rates

The Federal Reserve's impact on interest rates between 1979 and 1984 and the advent of a new regime is well illustrated by the profound disjunction in real interest rates compared with the 1970s. Figure 6.10 shows inflation-adjusted ("real") interest rates for ten-year treasuries.[6] Real ten-year treasury rates were never over 4% in the 1970s, but rose to 11½% in 1982. They averaged 6.2% in 1981, 9.2% in 1982, 7.0% in 1983, and 8.7% in 1984. These yields compared with the mean real yield on long-term treasuries from 1946 to 1980 of only 1.0%.

There was a similar change in the real yields on treasury bills that are outlined in figure 6.11. They rose from negative levels throughout the 1970s to over 7% from August 1981 through November 1982, 4.5% in 1983, and 5.9% in 1984. These real yields contrasted with the mean real treasury bill return from 1926 to 1980 of −0.1%, and were the highest since 1930–1932.

These high real interest rates reflected the Federal Reserve's determination to use interest rates as an instrument to squelch inflation rather than following it down between late 1980 and 1984. Figure 6.12, which indexes CPI inflation rates and nominal ten-year treasury rates to 1/77 = 1.0, reveals the sharp divergence between the two series beginning in late 1980. Co-movement between ten-year interest rates and inflation was not particularly close even before 1980, but a radical difference occurred when ten-

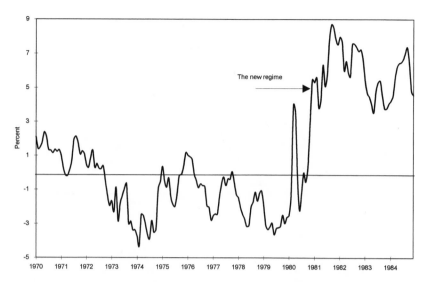

Figure 6.11 Real treasury bill rates (three-month treasury bills minus six months' average CPI inflation). Sources: Federal Reserve and Bureau of Labor Statistics.

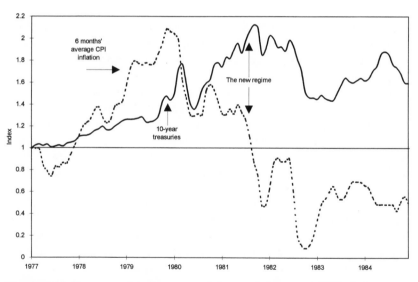

Figure 6.12 Ten-year treasury rates and six months' average CPI inflation (indexed to 1/77 = 1.0). Sources: Federal Reserve and Bureau of Labor Statistics.

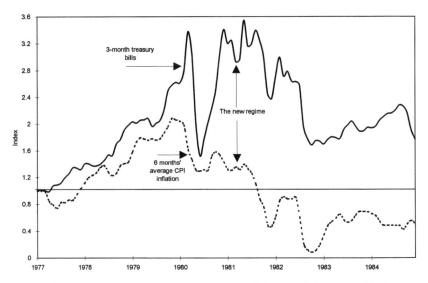

Figure 6.13 Three-month treasury bill rates and six months' average CPI inflation (indexed to 1/77 = 1.0). Sources: Federal Reserve and Bureau of Labor Statistics.

year interest rates stayed high through 1981 and the first half of 1982, while the CPI inflation rate declined from 12.4% in 1980 to 3.8% in 1982.

Figure 6.13 similarly plots CPI inflation rates and nominal treasury bill rates, indexed to 1/77 = 1.0. Co-movement between the two series was very close from 1/77 to mid-1980, contrary to the case for ten-year treasuries, but similar divergence occurred in mid-1980 through 1984.[7]

It is not my purpose to review foreign interest rates here, but I should note that high real long-term interest rates prevailed in Germany, Japan, and the U.K. as well. When Margaret Thatcher was elected Prime Minister in the U.K. in 1979 she introduced a shift in monetary policy almost contemporary with that in the U.S. to controlling money supply and bringing down inflation. High real rates there were new. They were not new in Germany and Japan, which had strong histories of monetary discipline. The U.S. movement to high real interest rates was nonetheless unique in that U.S. real rates on ten-year treasuries went from being 300–500 basis points lower than the average for Germany, Japan, and the U.K. during 1977–1980 to 100–400 basis points higher during 1981–1984, as can be seen in figure 6.14.

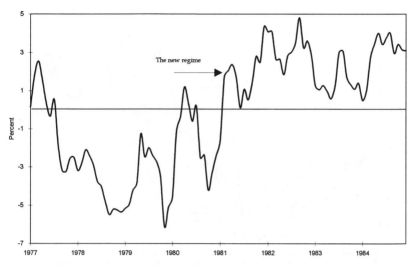

Figure 6.14 Real ten-year U.S. treasury rates minus the average of real ten-year rates in Germany, Japan, and the U.K. Inflation rates are six months' averages for CPI inflation. Sources: Federal Reserve, Bureau of Labor Statistics, Deutsche Bundesbank, Bank of Japan, Bank of England, and U.K. Central Statistical Office.

Interest Rates and the Federal Deficit

The increase in the federal budget deficit from 1982 to 1983 to almost $200 billion from the $30–70 billion range that prevailed in the Carter administration has been cited frequently as the cause of the shift to historically high real interest rates in the 1980s. Figure 6.15 compares the deficit as a percentage of GNP with real ten-year treasury rates for 1977–1984, and intuitively suggests that the relationship between the two factors was strong under both President Carter and President Reagan.

We can trace the deficit's influence quite specifically under President Reagan. During the budget debate in 1981, ten-year rates moved at odds with federal funds rates (which in a simple way controls for monetary policy effects), consistent with market anticipation of the rising deficit. While federal funds were 19% in January and 19% in June and July, ten-year treasury rates moved up from 12.6% to 13.5% (90 basis points); as the budget debate climaxed in the summer of 1981, federal funds rates fell from 19.1% in June to 15.9% in September, but ten-year treasury rates rose from 13.5% to 15.3% (180 basis points). During these last months of the debate, Republicans and Democrats were vying to see which party could produce the biggest tax cut, and the administration gave up trying to pare back Social Security.[8] Thus, in 1981 ten-year treasury rates rose 270 basis points independently of federal funds rates, or

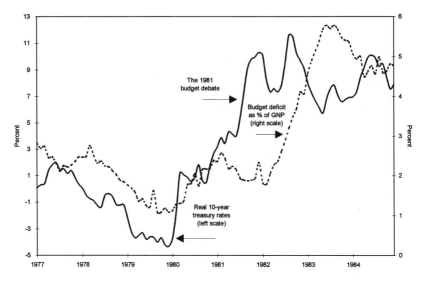

Figure 6.15 Real ten-year treasury rates and the budget deficit as a percentage of GNP. Sources: Federal Reserve, Bureau of Labor Statistics, and Bureau of Economic Analysis.

even more if we presume that ten-year rates should have fallen with federal funds rates in the summer. Real ten-year treasury rates also rose from 4.0% to 9.0% at this time. When the actual increase in the deficit occurred between May 1982 and May 1983, there was a perverse movement in ten-year treasury rates as they dropped from 13.6% to 10.4%. The increase in the deficit had, of course, already been anticipated in the market and other forces were at work, particularly the Federal Reserve's aggressive efforts to lower rates to stimulate the economy and relieve stress in the financial system.

The impact of the actual increase in the deficit on long-term interest rates from 1982 to 1983 was also muted by the Treasury's decision to reduce new issues of treasury bonds in favor of shorter maturities. This was a time-honored political maneuver, as can be seen in figure 6.16. The Nixon administration actually reduced treasury bonds outstanding—not just their rate of increase—in an effort to reduce interest rates. The Carter administration worked assiduously to correct this by steadily increasing the proportion of bonds in treasury financing until at the peak in April 1979 treasury bonds outstanding had increased 30% in twelve months; but the Carter administration also reduced the rate of increase as the elections approached. The Reagan administration dropped the rate of increase to only 4.6% over the twelve months ending November 1982 to help push interest rates down.

When the volume of treasury bonds outstanding finally began to rise

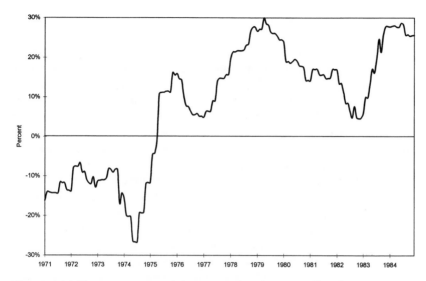

Figure 6.16 Year-to-year growth in treasury bonds outstanding. Source: Monthly statement of the public debt of the U.S.

substantially in the second and third quarters of 1983, there was a corresponding increase in ten-year rates. The Federal Reserve also acted to raise interest rates from May to August 1983, so both influences on interest rates were acting together, but we can judge the effect of the increase in treasury bonds by comparing the rise in ten-year rates with the rise in federal funds rates. Ten-year treasury rates rose 148 basis points from May to August 1983, while federal funds only rose 93 basis points, whereas in each prior phase of Federal Reserve credit tightening since 1979, federal funds rates rose approximately three times as much as ten-year rates. On this simple three-to-one ratio, 117 basis points of the increase in ten-year rates was due to the increased volume of long-term treasury bonds. Monthly inflation rates were quite stable at this time and not an influence on long-term rates.

A year later in March-August 1984, when the Federal Reserve raised interest rates for the second time in twelve months and the rate of increase in outstanding long-term treasuries was unchanged, federal funds rates rose 205 basis points and ten-year treasuries rose only 88 basis points, reflecting the earlier 3-1 relationship.

The combined effects of the deficit on ten-year treasury rates during the budget debate (270 basis points) and when the volume of long-term bonds began to increase (117 basis points) was 387 basis points. This was half of the difference between the average real interest rate on ten-year treasuries from 1981 to 1984 of 8.7% and the average real interest rate from 1946 to 1980 of only 1.0%.

Speculation in U.S. Treasuries

The U.S. treasury market became a magnet for speculation in the early 1980s, fostered by the growth in marketable treasury debt from $531 billion at the end of 1979 to $1.2 billion at the end of 1984, the record volatility of interest rates, and the growth in the futures and repurchase markets where one could control huge investments with very little capital.* Investment banking firms, hedge funds, and some extremely marginal promoters were attracted to the treasury market's speculative opportunities on a scale that presaged the wider speculative activities of the last half of the decade. In the early 1980s this speculative element was a minor side effect of the new regime's tough monetary policy and expanded deficit, but in the last half of the decade speculation played a fundamental role in the stock market crash of 1987, the savings and loan debacle, the collapse of the junk bond market, and the restructuring of much of American industry.

The increase in interest rate volatility ushered in by the Federal Reserve's October 1979 change to a focus on money supply provided the basic speculative opportunity. The annual standard deviation of three-month treasury bill rates outlined in figure 6.17 more than quadrupled, from an average of 0.68 percentage points in the 1970s to a peak of 3.0 percentage points in early 1981, and was still triple the 1970s in 1982 and early 1983 after rates came down. The annual volatility of ten-year treasury rates, also outlined in figure 6.17, also quadrupled from an average of .31 percentage points in the 1970s to over 1.25 percentage points in early 1980, and rose further to a peak of 1.5 percentage points from January to April 1983. In price terms, 1.5% represented $8–9 on a $100 bond. Volatility of total returns was very similar to that for yields.

The increased volatility of interest rates led to a dramatic increase in the use of financial futures, as can be seen in table 6.4. Trading volume in treasury bill and treasury bond futures languished originally when they were established in 1976 and 1977, respectively, but the learning experience with futures that traders developed out of necessity in the turbulent markets of 1979–1980 introduced them to a new speculative tool. Trading volume between 1978 and 1982 rose by 8.6 times for treasury bill futures (col. 5) and by 12.5 times for the three long-term contracts—treasury bond, GNMA, and treasury note futures (col. 4).[9] Of course, the

---

*Of course, the treasury market had always had speculative elements. A notable earlier example was First Pennsylvania Bank & Trust's effort in 1979 to bolster its subnormal earnings by investing in $1.2 billion of long-term bonds to gain the interest rate differential versus its short-term sources of funds. These bonds suffered sharp price erosion as interest rates rose in 1980 and the bank reported a loss of $164 million, leaving its equity at only $216 million. The FDIC had to provide $500 million of new capital to rescue the bank.

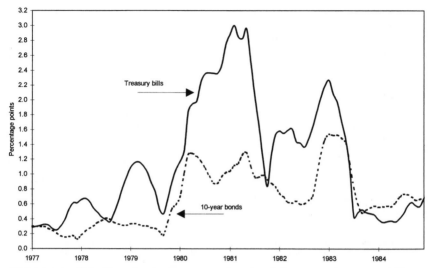

Figure 6.17 Volatility of ten-year treasury bond and three-month treasury bill rates (standard deviation of monthly rates over rolling twelve months). Source: Federal Reserve.

outstanding volumes of the underlying securities also rose, but the increase in volume relative to the underlying securities was profound. The underlying principal for the monthly volume of treasury bill futures contracts rose 4.4 times from 40% of outstanding treasury bills in 1978 to 176% in 1982. The underlying principal for the monthly trading volume in treasury bond and GNMA futures rose almost sevenfold, from 9% of combined marketable treasury bonds and mortgage pool securities outstanding in 1978 to 61% in 1982.

Table 6.4. Futures Volumes (Thousands of contracts)

Year	T bonds (Col. 1)	GNMA (Col. 2)	Notes (Col. 3)	Total Long-term Volume (Col. 4)	T bills (Col. 5)
1978	553	953	0	1,506	769
1979	2,060	1,371	0	3,431	1,931
1980	6,490	2,326	0	8,815	3,319
1981	13,908	2,293	0	16,201	5,631
1982	16,740	2,056	0	18,795	6,598
1983	19,551	1,692	0	21,243	3,791
1984	29,964	861	1,662	32,487	3,294

Sources: Commodities Research Bureau, Inc., *Commodity Year Book 1981*, pp. 183, 185, *1986 CRB Commodity Year Book*, pp. 124–126, 130.

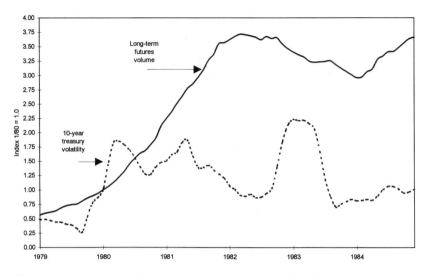

Figure 6.18 Long-term futures volumes and the volatility of ten-year treasury bond rates (both series indexed to 1/80 = 1.0). Futures are relative to treasury bonds outstanding plus mortgage pools; volatility is standard deviation of monthly rates over twelve months. Sources: Commodity Research Bureau and *Annual Statistical Digest 1970–1979*; Ibid. *1980–1989*.

The learning effect in futures, which led to their use beyond the increases in volume and volatility, stands out clearly in figure 6.18, which indexes both relative futures volume and volatility to 1/80 = 1.0. Futures volume relative to the growth in debt rose in line with rising volatility through 1980, but then as volatility leveled out or declined, futures volume continued to rise until it had risen 2.7 times more than volatility. It was as if the learning experience had breached a barrier.

Futures volume in figure 6.18 is the rolling twelve-months trading volume in the three long-term contracts—treasury bonds, treasury notes, and GNMA futures—relative to the publicly held principal of treasury bonds and mortgage-backed securities pools.[10] It is necessary to combine the treasury and mortgage-backed markets because there was substantial crossover in their use of futures. Volatility is the rolling twelve-months standard deviation for monthly ten-year treasury constant maturity index rates.

The complicated relationships between treasuries and futures, other derivatives such as options, strips or zero coupons, and related securities such as agencies or mortgage securities presented great opportunities for the thirty-five primary treasury dealers. Energetic and gifted traders supported by capital and investment in analytical tools could profit enormously from distortions in these relationships, especially when they were due to bureaucratic forces such as Treasury financing or foreign central

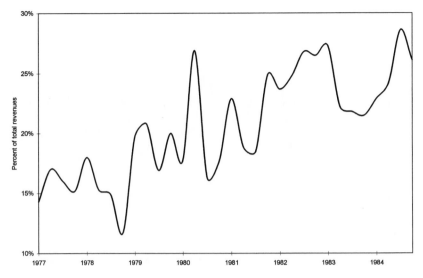

Figure 6.19 Brokerage firms' trading gains as a percentage of revenues (quarterly). Source: Securities Industry Association member data.

banks' activities. The primary dealers' trading volume grew fivefold between 1979 and 1984 from $10.5 billion per day to $52.8 billion, while treasury debt only doubled. The annual trading profits in treasuries for a typical large firm rose steadily from insignificant levels during 1977–1978 to approximately $100 million by 1984.

Salomon Brothers, which was the leading firm in all sectors of bond trading, provides an excellent example of the changes that took place in fixed income trading generally and treasury trading specifically. Salomon increased its net worth from $256 million in 1980 to $1.5 billion in 1984. This increase represented virtually 100% retained earnings except for a $300 million infusion when it was acquired by Phibro Inc. Salomon's results were achieved with dramatic growth in assets. It increased its U.S. treasury, agency, and repurchase inventories from $3 billion in 1978 to $38 billion at the end of 1984—over six times the growth in the overall treasury market. And the growth was achieved with very high leverage. At the end of 1984, Salomon's assets were thirty-one times its net worth, and at one point in 1980 they were forty-nine times![11]

Salomon Brothers' example was reflected on a lesser scale for the investment banking industry as a whole. The industry's annual revenues from trading rose from $1.1 billion in 1977 to $11.3 billion in 1984, and from 17% of total revenues to 28.5% (figure 6.19). Leverage almost doubled from 11 times net worth to 21.5 times (figure 6.20).[12]

The largest commercial banks also expanded their treasury trading.

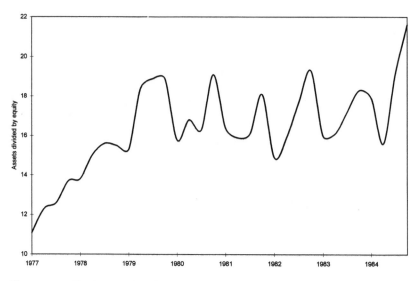

Figure 6.20 Brokerage firms' asset/equity ratios (quarterly). Source: Securities Industry Association member data.

The top ten banks' revenues from bond trading rose from $132 million in 1979 to $461 million in 1982, but these revenues were only 6–8% of the investment banking industry's.[13]

The unique inability of the Treasury to call its outstanding debt, despite the fact that it was being issued at historically high interest rates, created the stripped treasury market, which was a huge speculative arena as well as the precursor of the collateralized mortgage obligation (CMO) market. By contrast, virtually all corporate and municipal bonds could be called and refunded after five or ten years, and mortgage-backed securities could be refunded from their inception. Under the high rates and extreme volatility that prevailed in the early 1980s, reinvestment rates for both interest and principal became of crucial importance to investors, and dealers were uniquely able to satisfy this need with non-callable treasury bonds by "stripping" their principal and interest components into zero-coupon securities.* In mid-1982, Salomon Brothers and Merrill Lynch developed trademarked versions called CATS and TIGERS, which they created by placing regular coupon treasuries with a trustee and then

---

*The bond market traditionally used yield to maturity as its comparison methodology, but returns at 12% versus 6% interest were greatly affected by the assumed reinvestment rate for the coupon payments. Duration, which measures average life of combined principal and interest cash flows, became an important alternative tool in bond market valuation.

selling participation certificates in the interest payments at a discount as zero-coupon serial bonds and the ultimate principal payment as simply a larger and deeper discount zero-coupon bond.

There were substantial profits in this stripping procedure. When there was a rising yield curve, the yield on a regular bond assumed that all of the interest payments were discounted at the long term yield, but the intermediate term coupon payments could be stripped off and sold at lower yields (higher prices) without changing the yield on the remaining longer cash flows. Indeed, rather perversely, the longer cash flows could sometimes also be sold at lower yields (higher prices) to investors emphasizing long-term duration. When this opportunity was first recognized, dealers capitalized on it in the crudest fashion by literally cutting the coupons off bearer treasury bonds, and selling coupons and principal separately. Using a trustee was much more efficient, and soon treasury dealers established a generic program called Treasury Receipts that facilitated trading the resulting securities. Eventually the Treasury formalized stripping treasuries with its own STRIPS program, which made the market more efficient, and the yield curve for stripped treasuries became different from that for coupon treasuries. Eventually, stripping treasuries became highly mechanical trades with limited profit opportunities.

There was a huge corporate pension demand for stripped treasuries because they carried real rates of interest as high as 7–8% compared to actuaries' assumed real growth rates for liabilities of 3–4%. With reinvestment rates already provided for at these high levels through the zero-coupon mechanism, there was an accounting opportunity to reduce annual pension payments. Treasury dealers developed highly sophisticated computer programs to match projected pension obligations with bond portfolio cash flows in "dedicated" or "immunized" portfolios that minimized annual pension accounting charges. International Harvester, Firestone Tire & Rubber, Colt Industries, and B. F. Goodrich all made large investments of this type for their pension funds in 1982, and in mid-1984 Chrysler Corp. made one of the most celebrated switches when it moved all of its pension plan from stocks to a dedicated portfolio in a transaction valued at $1.1 billion. Many of the recently independent Bell system regional holding companies made similar pension switches. A Goldman Sachs analyst estimated that the eighteen largest such transactions in 1984 amounted to $6.4 billion and that $50–75 billion of dedicated portfolios was amassed between 1982 and 1984.[14]

Individuals also had a substantial appetite for stripped treasuries. Sometimes they were impressed simply by how fast money compounded at such high rates or by the ease of providing for some future need by a one-time smaller initial payment; others looked for tax advantages (legal or otherwise) in not receiving cash interest payments and thereby postponing tax payments until the combined principal and interest ultimately came due together; some, of course, understood the true mechanics of locking in reinvestment rates at historically high real returns.

The demand for stripped treasuries from pension funds and individuals reflected generally legitimate investment objectives, but it nonetheless produced highly speculative responses among treasury dealers. These pension transactions dwarfed historic secondary market transactions and their esoteric structures were incompatible with traditional dealer inventories; therefore, dealers had to either build up inventories in anticipation of transactions or accept enormous short positions in the course of them. Stripping treasuries also left dealers with large, unsold positions in the resulting intermediate-term securities, typically between twelve and twenty-five years. The shorter maturities were easy to sell, as were the longest ones, but demand in the middle maturities has always been lacking in the bond market. The profits in stripping treasury bonds were dramatic at first—sometimes three or four points—and probably justified the risks in the resulting positions and such hedges as were attempted, but once stripping became more mechanical the speculative risk and leverage in stripped treasuries remained but the profits were gone. Stripped treasury positions were also difficult to hedge as there was no history from which to make hedging judgments. The prices of stripped treasuries moved with much greater volatility than conventional treasuries and were less predictable. Their novelty, plus the new experience of such high interest rates and volatility, meant that the full implications of these factors were often not well understood, even by primary treasury dealers. The Bank of America had a well-publicized $10 million loss in treasury trading in the second quarter of 1983 that led management to sharply curtail trading activities, and Merrill Lynch had a similarly publicized loss in treasury and mortgage-backed securities trading in the second quarter of 1984. Such losses did not restrain dealers in general, however, nor did it deter them from carrying the same trading techniques over into mortgage-backed securities (chapter 7) where the risks were appreciably greater.

The investment world was not about to leave the speculative opportunities in U.S. treasuries to the thirty-five primary dealers. The largest hedge fund managers, such as George Soros and Michael Steinhardt, took huge leveraged treasury positions—long or short—and borrowed either funds or securities in the repurchase market alongside the dealers. Boutiques specializing in treasury trading proliferated—some very sophisticated and some very cynical—dealing in the treasury and repurchase markets either through dealers or directly with investors.

The U.S. treasury market offered unparalleled leverage to primary dealers and speculators alike. Very little capital was required in the treasury futures markets to control very large positions, but there were none-

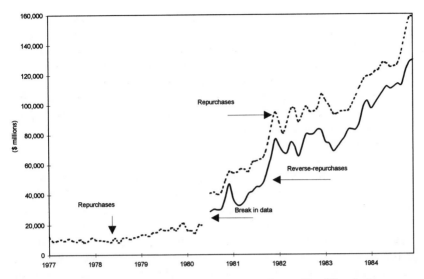

Figure 6.21 Dealer repurchases and reverse-repurchases ($ millions). Source: Federal Reserve.

theless firmly enforced rules on margin requirements and marking-to-market. The leverage available in the repurchase market, however, was unique to the treasury market. Almost no cash was needed to control large positions in the repurchase market. It had originally developed as a call loan market in which large institutions, mostly banks, could invest day-to-day surplus funds and dealers could finance their inventories. The participants were so familiar with one another and so sophisticated, the collateral so liquid and the time horizons so short, that practices were very rough and ready. Loans against short-term securities were often at par, and collateral for borrowed securities ignored accrued interest. This meant that net capital could sometimes be generated—the opposite of requiring margin—by borrowing par for a short-term treasury issue that was actually selling at a discount, or by collecting large amounts of accrued interest on borrowed securities in between borrowing and returning them.

The repurchase market grew dramatically from approximately $10 billion during 1977–1978 to $159 billion by the end of 1984, as can be seen in figure 6.21. This $159 billion was over 1.5 times dealers' total securities inventories, including equities and spot commodities. Speculators and other borrowers had obviously bloated the repurchase market far beyond its original purpose of financing dealers' inventories. The largest part of this growth reflected the fact that dealers began lending to their customers to finance purchases in the reverse repurchase market, also outlined in figure 6.21. This practice meant that customers were buying treasuries on margin from dealers who were reborrowing in the repurchase market against their customers' collateral.[15] The expansion of the reverse repurchase market also reflected that dealers began to borrow treasuries on a day-to-day basis as they went short to hedge their positions or to lend in the federal funds market, where rates were invariably higher. Major institutions found loans of securities in the reverse repurchase market an attractive source of additional income, which involved little risk if collateral was adequate.

In many respects the repurchase market was being set up for a fall. It was essentially unregulated, and only became subject to the oversight of a special unit at the Federal Reserve Bank of New York in 1982. Borrowing practices were so loose, and speculative positions among both dealers and non-dealers so large, that someone was bound to get hurt. Plus there was the overarching aura of dealing in conservative, safe U.S. treasury securities to lure the gullible. As a result, numerous abuses arose in the treasury market that were the earliest examples of overaggressive pursuit of profits without adequate managerial control or even knowledge—a theme that evolved into horrendous losses and outright corruption in the last half of the 1980s.

The first publicity about large treasury losses occurred on Monday, May 17, 1982 when Drysdale Government Securities collapsed. Drysdale Government Securities had been set up only three months previously as a subsidiary of Drysdale Securities Inc. with apparent capital of $20.8 million. The new subsidiary's president, Richard Taaffe, was an ex-Shearson-Loeb Rhoades bond salesman who wanted a more "risk-oriented" environment. Its head trader was David Heuwetter, a temperamental workaholic who had gone twenty-three years without a holiday, wouldn't share business details with colleagues, and wasn't above an occasional fistfight in downtown bars. Together they ran up positions as high as $5 billion on their $20.8 million equity. Their demise occurred when they could not pay more than $270 million in accrued interest that they had collected on borrowed securities.[16] They had been borrowing treasury securities in the reverse repurchase market with large amounts of accrued interest, but only putting up collateral equal to par under the market's lax practices. They received the accrued interest immediately by selling the borrowed securities, but still had to pay it back when they repaid their loans. For a while they had been able to pyramid their "borrowings" of accrued interest.

Various firms had sensed trouble when Drysdale Government Securities was set up. Almost immediately Morgan Stanley, Donaldson Lufkin, Manufacturers Hanover, and U.S. Trust got tough with Drysdale, and either stopped dealing with them or got very exacting about collateral. Drysdale's business contracted under scrutiny, but it still remained large and borrowings naturally moved along the path of least resistance. That path happened to lead to Chase Manhattan Bank.

Chase Manhattan Bank had seen an opportunity for substantial revenues in the burgeoning repurchase market, and had installed nine commission salesmen in a sub-basement department who were generating large fees by lending and borrowing treasury securities in the repurchase market. These salesmen had taken Chase's repurchase business from zero to billions of dollars in just two years. Drysdale alone was borrowing approximately $2 billion in treasuries through Chase from thirty different lenders.

It is doubtful that Chase management really knew much about what was going on in this area. There was very little supervision, no credit officers checking on borrowers, and when Drysdale defaulted Willard Butcher, Chase's president, met with major treasury dealers at the Federal Reserve Bank of New York to tell them that Chase was just an agent and not liable for the accrued interest Drysdale owed. Chase had to back down within the week as Manufacturers Hanover Trust and New York Trust accepted liability for loans through them.

"There was nothing sinister here," a former Chase executive said of Chase's involvement with Drysdale. "They just didn't know what they were doing." But there was something sinister going on. Drysdale's Heuwetter had piled up large losses in 1981 and earlier by pursuing aggressive trading strategies in the treasury market. Setting up the treasury securities subsidiary had been a facade behind which to hide, and hopefully recover, these losses. Arthur Andersen & Co. ultimately had to pay approximately $50 million to Chase and $17 million to Manufacturers Hanover Trust for its role as Drysdale's accountant/consultant in setting up the subsidiary and certifying its financial statements. The Arthur Andersen partner who advised Drysdale was eventually accused of fraud by the SEC. The two top officers of Drysdale in 1984 pleaded guilty to "stealing more than $270 million from two major banks by means of computer fraud and other schemes." They had paid bribes of $25,000 over two years to a night supervisor at Depository Trust, a widely accepted industry depository for securities, to falsely credit Drysdale with delivering securities.[17]

Many things therefore came together in Drysdale's collapse. Drysdale originally was attracted by the speculative appeal of the huge treasury market, where large positions could be controlled with very little capital. Once financial losses occurred, the effort to conceal and overcome them turned to fraud. The lack of effective regulatory oversight gave Drysdale free rein until something serious went wrong. A substantial and sophisticated intermediary like Chase Manhattan Bank was attracted by the rapid growth in revenues possible and gave unsupervised authority to relatively junior people in an area that top management only superficially understood. When the financial losses finally had to be realized, it was a substantial burden to be shared by unwitting participants rather than just Drysdale. This was a pattern that was repeated in various markets throughout the 1980s.

The collapse of Drysdale Government Securities led to a searching review of similar boutiques and to the collapse of several. Lombard-Wall Inc. filed for bankruptcy in August 1982. It had assembled a treasury portfolio of $2 billion on equity of only $3.1 million before being forced to reduce its positions by the unwillingness of lenders to continue with it after the Drysdale collapse. Chase Manhattan Bank was caught again, this time for $45 million, but so were the New York City Housing Development Agency for $130 million, the New York City Health and Hospital Corporation for $30 million, and the New York State Dormitory Authority for $55 million.

What were public institutions doing in this business? A lot, it would turn out. These institutions had developed a practice of putting their surplus cash up for competitive bids in the treasury repurchase market. Overnight loans collateralized by treasuries appeared very conservative in principle, but over time the practice developed of allowing the collateral to be pooled and held by the borrower. This practice offered such flexibility and opportunities to cut corners that naturally the bidding became concentrated in those firms that could use this flexibility most. At one point, the New York State Dormitory Authority had over $300 million in loans to Lombard-Wall.[18] Here was another theme that would be repeated in various markets throughout the 1980s. Public institutions in control of very large sums of both short-term and pension funds invested them with a relative lack of supervision and sophistication in the trendy financial markets, sometimes with happy returns and sometimes with disastrous results.

Three other small firms got in trouble in this period. Comark Securities on the West Coast had to close because of collateral disputes. Edward G. Markowitz was prosecuted for tax fraud in partnerships he sold to the public promising 10-to-1 and 15-to-1 tax deductions. At one point in 1981, the Markowitz partnerships had $5 billion in repurchases based on only $5 million of equity capital. Sentinel Government Securities was prosecuted on the same basis. In Sentinel's case, George Sharffenberger, the chairman of City Investing, was a substantial investor. He was financially very sophisticated, and City Investing was large and well staffed. Chase Manhattan Bank was not alone among the sophisticated victims.[19]

If anyone believed there were only two or three sophisticated victims in the treasury markets, Charles Agee Atkins exploded that thesis. Atkins set up shop in New York City in 1978; he was only twenty-four, but he was backed by his prominent father, chairman of Ashland Oil Orin Atkins. Based on enormous personal flair and the promise of tax deductions of four times the investment, Charles Atkins attracted funds from

Michel David-Weill, the chairman of Lazard Freres ($1.8 million), William Salomon, the chairman of Salomon Brothers ($0.9 million), Larry and Robert Tisch ($1.5 million), the Estee Lauder family ($2.8 million), and various movie stars and politicians. The implicit stamp of approval from such illustrious financial sophisticates induced less sophisticated investors to come along. By 1981, Atkins's company had assets of $21 billion, mostly in treasury securities, based on $85 million of paid in capital and approximately $340 million in recourse agreements with his investors.

Once he was successful, Atkins ran riot. His holding company bought New York Hanseatic Co., an old and reputable treasury primary dealer, an oil and gas company, and a California savings and loan. For his own account, he borrowed $35 million from the holding company and bought the New York City office building in which his company was located, land in Colorado, a Long Island estate, and an apartment on New York's elegant Sutton Place. His lifestyle expanded to match. He bought art and antiques, imported Savile Row suits, maintained limousines, ran a big tab at Twenty-One Club, New York's ultimate macho restaurant, and even paid $1 million for an option to buy it.

But the dream eroded quickly. The 1981 tax laws wiped out Atkins's original business and left his partners with large taxes to pay. When the Federal Reserve Bank of New York ordered Atkins' New York Hanseatic to substantially reduce its leverage after the Drysdale bankruptcy, it incurred $29 million in trading losses. Then the oil markets deteriorated and Atkins's oil company went into bankruptcy. Finally his savings and loan, Southern California Savings & Loan Association, came under the scrutiny of the Federal Home Loan Bank of San Francisco because of $39 million in losses between 1980 and 1982. The Federal Home Loan Bank demanded that Atkins repay approximately $13 million in loans from the savings and loan that were backed by dubious collateral. Atkins couldn't pay, and his business quickly unraveled. In mid-1983 Atkins estimated that his investors would get back 30 to 60 cents on the dollar, plus tax bills. He was still only twenty-nine years old. In 1988 he was found guilty of tax evasion, conspiracy, and fraud and was sentenced to two years in prison.[20]

Mishaps continued in the treasury market in 1984 when interest rates rose somewhat. Lion Capital, which was set up similarly to Atkins' firm to generate tax losses, went into bankruptcy in May 1984. At one point it had assets of $2.7 billion on $28 million of equity capital. The losers were mostly school districts and other public agencies that had lent to Lion Capital in the repurchase market. Fifty million dollars worth of securities collateral was in dispute at Bradford Trust Company, which claimed it as collateral for its own loan, but which the other lenders thought was theirs.[21] As other bankruptcies arose, the phrase "the collateral is at Bradford Trust" became worth as little as "the check is in the mail."

The same rise in interest rates caught Marsh & McLennan, the prominent insurance broker, by surprise, causing $165 million in pretax losses. Marsh & McLennan initially made an $11 million gain speculating in treasuries, mostly in the "when-issued" market, by committing for newly-issued bonds but selling them before the company had to take delivery and pay for them.[22] Emboldened by success, the company's commitments in the first quarter of 1984 reached $2 billion, but as rates rose and it incurred losses it had to take delivery of the bonds and borrow against them. Its losses rose further and became a scandal. The company insisted that the trading was unauthorized.

There was a scandal, too, in Memphis at the Public Housing Authority, which borrowed approximately $19 million to buy $24.5 million of treasuries and lost $2 million, as well as $1 million in interest that it should have earned by investing more safely.[23]

Even Continental Grain Company, which knew as much about risk as anyone, incurred large losses for a second time at its subsidiary, Conti-Commodity Services Inc. Earlier in 1980, Continental Grain was forced to inject $81 million in additional capital into ContiCommodity when it had large losses in the silver market debacle that caught the Hunts. The losses in 1984 were such that Continental Grain virtually gave the subsidiary away to Refco Inc.[24]

The list of sophisticated losers in the treasury markets could go on in terms of individuals and institutions and over time. For example, it was not until 1991 that we learned that the Pakistan-based Banque du Credit et Commerce Internationale lost nearly $1 billion between 1977 and 1985 speculating in financial futures and options.[25] There was always a substantial speculative element in the U.S. treasury market, attracted by its size, leverage, and lack of regulation. The speculators' problems had little effect on either monetary policy or interest rates, other than temporarily, but these speculative elements were precursors to strong speculative movements in stocks, junk bonds, mortgage securities, and foreign exchange in the second half of the decade.

Summary

Interest rates in the treasury market between 1979 and 1984 were dominated by Federal Reserve policies and the budget deficit. The Federal Reserve alone controlled short-term rates in four stages as it raised rates in 1980-1981, eased them in the second half of 1982, raised them twice in 1983 and 1984, and then eased them in late 1984. Its aggressive efforts to reduce inflation determined market expectations for long rates, overwhelming traditional influences on long-term rates such as inflation and the economy. The only other meaningful influence was the budget deficit, which pushed long-term rates up contrary to the Fed's direction during the Reagan administration's first budget debate in mid-1981 and again in mid-1983 when the Treasury finally began to increase the proportion of long-term bonds in its financing. As a result, the United States had the highest real interest rates since the Depression.

At first, Federal Reserve policies worsened the record of disastrous returns in the long-term treasury market in the 1970s, at the worst point in 1981 reducing an index of real treasury returns to only 52% of its value in 1976. But when the Fed brought down rates in the second half of 1982, long-term treasury returns skyrocketed to 42% and were generally high for the rest of the decade. This evolution had several unintended side effects, however. Volatility in both short-term and long-term interest rates was unprecedented, which induced market learning experiences in interest rates futures and derivatives such as stripped treasuries that led to increased speculation and lack of appreciation for the risks involved. Expansion of the repurchase market led to greatly increased leverage, speculation, lax institutional awareness and oversight, and corruption, which were harbingers of similar trends in other markets later in the decade.

Despite the success of Federal Reserve policy in reducing inflation and ultimately restoring the health of the bond market, there was a price in the severe credit problems of the savings and loan industry and important sectors of American industry, as we shall see in the next two chapters. These problems led to huge expansion in the mortgage-backed securities and junk bond markets, where the speculative activities and lack of institutional oversight were of significantly greater magnitude and import than in the treasury market.

7

The Mortgage Securities Market

An unintended effect of the high interest rates of 1981–1982 was the virtual bankruptcy of the savings and loan industry. The industry had considerable support in Congress, however, which led in 1980 and 1982 to legislation designed to save the industry by broadening its investment powers, increasing its federal deposit guarantee to $100,000, and weakening its accounting. These changes stimulated the growth of the mortgage securities market into one of the most dynamic markets of the late 1980s, and fostered speculative investment activities that precipitated the savings and loan debacle. This chapter will only deal with the beginning of these two developments.

Federal government involvement in home financing began during the 1930s, when the Federal Home Loan Bank System was established to support the thrift industry, the Federal Housing Agency (FHA) was set up to guarantee home mortgages, and the Federal National Mortgage Association (FNMA or "Fannie Mae") was set up to assist secondary markets in mortgages guaranteed by the FHA or the Veterans Administration (VA). In 1968, in an effort to bring the efficiencies of the securities markets to housing, Congress created the Government National Mortgage Association (GNMA or "Ginnie Mae") to guarantee pass-through securities backed by FHA and VA guaranteed mortgages, and the Federal Home Loan Mortgage Corporation (FHLMC or "Freddie Mac") to guarantee pass-through securities backed by conventional mortgage loans originated according to specific, limited criteria.[1] At the same time, provisions were made to transfer ownership of FNMA to the private mortgage market participants using it.

Table 7.1. New Issues of Mortgage Related Securities ($ millions)

Year	GNMA MBS[1]	FHLMC PCs[1]	FNMA MBS[1]	Agency Total	CMOs[1]	Private MBS[2]
1970	452	0		452		
1971	2,702	65		2,767		
1972	2,662	494		3,156		
1973	2,953	323		3,276		
1974	4,553	46		4,599		
1975	7,447	450		7,897		
1976	13,764	960		14,724		
1977	17,440	4,057		21,497		226
1978	15,358	5,712		21,070		706
1979	24,940	3,796		28,736		446
1980	20,647	2,526		23,173		213
1981	14,257	3,529	717	18,503		133
1982	16,012	24,169	13,970	54,151		253
1983	50,496	19,691	13,340	83,527	4,680	1,585
1984	27,857	18,684	13,546	60,087	10,765	236

[1]*M-B-S Statistical Annual 1988*, p. 3.
[2]*Mortgage Market Statistical Annual for 1991*, pp. 75–79.

Both the GNMA and the FHLMC began issuing mortgage-backed securities in the early 1970s, the former for federally guaranteed mortgages and the latter for conventional mortgages. Annual new-issue volume for both agencies is outlined in table 7.1. Early new-issue volume for GNMA and FHLMC was modest until 1976, when it doubled to $14.7 billion due to a surge in mortgage activity when interest rates declined from the high levels of 1973–1975. Volume rose further to approximately $20 billion in 1977, but stabilized there through 1981. Much of this volume did not reach the public markets, however, as many thrifts simply exchanged their mortgages for collateralized securities. This accounted for 54% of Freddie Mac's participation certificates in 1977, and even more in prior years.[2] The certificates were more liquid and more favorably treated for regulatory purposes than outright mortgages. The market was well on its way to efficiency, however, as over two-thirds of all FHA and VA mortgages were packaged in GNMA pools.[3]

New-issue volumes of mortgage securities quadrupled between 1981 and 1983 to almost $84 billion in response to the savings and loan industry's financial problems, new legislation, FNMA's entry into conventional mortgage financing, and a surge in housing starts and mortgage refundings as interest rates came down. These securities did reach the public markets and turned mortgage finance into a vast public market with intense competition, frequent innovations, and considerable potential for trouble. The growth potential was enormous since residential and commercial mortgage debt equaled half of all U.S. private debt, reflecting that half of all private capital expenditures were on real estate.

Table 7.2. Savings & Loan Data ($ Billions)

Year	Cost of Funds[1] % Col 1	Mortgage Holdings Yield[2] % Col 2	Net Margin Col 3	Regulatory Profits[3] Col 4	Change in Tangible Net Worth[4] Col 5
1976	6.4	8.0	1.6	2.3	
1977	6.4	8.3	1.9	3.2	
1978	6.7	8.5	1.8	3.9	
1979	7.5	8.9	1.4	3.6	3.5
1980	8.9	9.3	0.4	0.8	0.7
1981	10.9	9.9	−1.0	−4.6	−6.9
1982	11.4	10.7	−0.7	−4.3	−21.6
1983	9.8	11.2	1.4	2.0	−0.2
1984	10.0	11.7	1.7	1.1	

[1]Office of Thrift Supervision, *Savings & Home Financing Sourcebook* 1988, p. A-22; average annual rate.
[2]Ibid. p. A-23; avg annual rate.
[3]*87 Savings Institutions Sourcebook*, p. 50.
[4]Larry White, *The S&L Debacle*, p. 78; reflects GAAP treatment of asset sales.

The Savings and Loan Crisis

The growth in mortgage-backed securities in 1982–1983 was principally due to the management failures of the savings and loan industry and FNMA, and to the efforts of regulators and Congress to compensate for the resulting problems. Savings and loans had a radical mismatch between assets and liabilities that was vividly exposed by the high interest rates of 1979–1982. Almost all of their assets were thirty-year fixed-rate residential mortgages with an embedded average yield in 1979 of less than 9%. These mortgages were financed by short-term deposits, the cost of which was approximately 6.5% from 1974 to 1978, but which rose to 11.4% in 1982. The trends of these rates and the resulting profits or losses are outlined in table 7.2. The industry's spread between mortgage yields and deposit rates swung from 180 basis points in 1978 to −100 basis points in 1981 and losses were over $4 billion in 1981 and 1982 (columns 3 and 4). The loss based on generally accepted accounting principles was $21.6 billion in 1982, and the industry's tangible net worth dropped from 5.7% of assets at the end of 1979 to only 0.5% at the end of 1982.[4] "Tangible net worth" is actually a misnomer that only reflects adjustments for goodwill, deferred assets, and other intangibles. If savings and loan assets had been marked to market to reflect the value of 9% mortgages in a 15% environment, savings and loans' net worth would have been drastically negative. Virtually all thrifts were similarly affected as the percentage of thrift industry assets held by money-losing institutions rose from 4% to 90% between 1979 and 1981.[5]

Depositor confidence in the industry eroded sharply—net new retail savings declined $33 billion in 1981 and at a $26 billion annual rate in the first three quarters of 1982. These combined outflows were equal to 12.6% of 1979 deposits.[6] Savings and loan borrowings from the Federal Home Loan Bank Board rose from $40.4 billion (6.9% of total assets) in January 1980 to $67.0 billion (9.7% of total assets) in July 1982. The savings and loan industry began a strenuous pursuit of liquidity, selling off $54 billion of mortgages in 1982, while it made new mortgage loans of only $24 billion, and aggressively building up cash and investments from $48.3 billion (8.3% of total assets) in January 1980 to $85.4 billion (12.1% of total assets) at the end of 1982.[7]

Fannie Mae was equally disrupted by the rise in interest rates in 1980–1981 because it invested in fixed-rate thirty-year mortgages, and the average maturity of its debt was only 3.25 years. Fannie Mae also gave mortgage originators free four-month options to put their mortgages to Fannie Mae. Thus, when Fannie Mae's cost of new funds surged from 10.7% in 1979 to 16.22% in 1982, its portfolio yield only rose from 8.75% to 9.85%, and originators put 100% of their mortgage commitments to it. Its net interest margin (interest on assets minus interest on borrowings) dropped from over $300 million each year from 1977 to 1979 to losses of approximately $500 million in 1981 and 1982. At the worst point, in the third and fourth quarters of 1981, Fannie Mae had negative net interest margins of over $170 million.[8] Annualized, this equaled negative net margins of approximately $700 million, and although commitment fees and income tax recoveries ameliorated these losses, the losses were very threatening compared to Fannie Mae's 1981 net worth of only $1.2 billion. Investor confidence in the value of Fannie Mae's federal agency status waned, and the yield on its debentures rose to 200–240 basis points over comparable U.S. treasuries versus 30–45 basis points historically.[9]

Fannie Mae's experience was in sharp contrast to Freddie Mac's. Privately owned by the thrift industry and very conservatively run, Freddie Mac began issuing mortgage pass-through certificates ("participation certificates" or PCs) in 1971, but the securities were sold exclusively to thrifts in exchange for mortgages. By dint of experimentation and perseverance, however, Freddie Mac created a mortgage pass-through certificate acceptable to Wall Street. By 1978, less than a third of Freddie Mac's PCs were exchanged with thrifts. When high interest rates hit in 1979, Freddie Mac bore very little disintermediation risk. Two-thirds of its portfolio was financed with PCs that passed all of the financing risks to investors. Freddie Mac only guaranteed full payment. While Fannie Mae struggled, Freddie Mac hardly stumbled. Freddie Mac's 1981 net income of $31 million was only modestly below 1979's record $36 million.[10] Freddie Mac's model of financing mortgages with pass-through securities in the public markets was clearly the one for others to follow.

Congress and the thrift regulators did all they could to ameliorate the deterioration of the savings and loan industry, and many of the remedies pushed it toward the mortgage-backed securities market. In September 1981, Congress gave thrifts the power to carry tax losses back ten years and the Federal Home Loan Bank Board permitted savings and loans to amortize the losses on mortgage sales over the life of the original loan, contrary to generally accepted accounting principles, which would have written off the losses immediately. Under generally accepted accounting principles, savings and loans' losses would have been unsustainable if they had sold their low coupon mortgages, but under the new regulations savings and loans could sell mortgages, reinvest in mortgage-backed securities, and enjoy current high rates on the reinvestment while only recognizing the losses gradually.

There were also good economic reasons for savings and loans to shift from holding mortgages to securitizing them. It enabled savings and loans to pass on interest rate risks to third parties while retaining the servicing fees and the margins between rates on raw mortgages and mortgage securities. Mortgage-backed securities also had greater collateral value and greater liquidity because they traded promptly within narrow bid-asked price ranges. Under these incentives, annual mortgage-backed securities issues surged from approximately $20 billion in the prior five years to $54 billion in 1982. Freddie Mac alone swapped $25 billion of its mortgage-backed securities with savings and loans for mortgages in 1982.[11]

Numerous regulations also pushed the savings and loans to expand their assets, leading to increased mortgage-backed securities investments. The Depository Institutions Deregulation and Monetary Control Act of 1980 set the stage for massive growth in brokered deposits by phasing out Regulation Q limits on deposit rates, raising federal deposit insurance from $40,000 to $100,000, and authorizing reduced net worth requirements as low as 3%, which the Federal Home Loan Bank Board set as a standard by 1982. The Garn-St. Germain Depository Institutions Act of 1982 expanded powers further to permit 30% of savings and loans' assets to be invested in credit card and construction loans, 40% in commercial real estate loans, 11% in commercial loans, and 3% in direct equity investments. Under these rules, savings and loans' total assets expanded 27% in the next two years.[12]

Fannie Mae's role in the mortgage-backed securities expansion began when new management was brought in under David Maxwell in mid-1981 at the height of the agency's financial problems. He quickly got Congress to lift the restrictions limiting FNMA to financing only FHA and VA guaranteed mortgages and got the power to guarantee conventional mortgage-backed securities in competition with Freddie Mac. Fannie Mae issued $700 million of mortgage-backed securities in 1981, and $13–14 billion each year from 1982 to 1984.

Table 7.3. Relative Size of Mortgage-Backed New Issues ($ Millions)

Year	Agency Total[1]	1–4 Family Originations[2]	Corporate Public Issues[3]	Agencies as % of Originations	FNMA & FHLMC as % of Corporate Issues[1]
	Col 1	Col 2	Col 3	Col 4	Col 5
1978	21,070	185,037	21,459	11.4%	29.9%
1979	28,736	187,195	22,605	15.4%	18.8%
1980	23,173	133,103	36,601	17.4%	7.5%
1981	18,503	98,322	40,773	18.8%	10.7%
1982	54,151	96,952	45,751	55.9%	83.9%
1983	83,527	201,862	37,760	41.4%	91.7%
1984	60,087	203,704	81,866	29.5%	39.7%

[1]*MBS Statistical Annual 1988*, p. 3.
[2]HUD data.
[3]IDD data.

Maxwell also had a strategy of growing FNMA's assets at the current high interest rates in order to reduce the proportion of its low-rate assets. In 1982, the Secretary of HUD raised Fannie Mae's permissible ratio of debt to capital from 15-to-1 to 30-to-1, and FNMA aggressively bought adjustable rate mortgages, second mortgages, and short-term investments. These securities helped to offset the short term of FNMA's financing—$2\frac{1}{4}$ years. Fortunately, interest rates began to decline sharply in the last half of 1982, and Fannie Mae's stock rose from a low of $7\frac{1}{8}$ to a high of $27\frac{1}{4}$, indicating the expected change in its fortunes as the negative interest margin on its portfolio almost disappeared in 1983.

A sense of proportion for the huge expansion in mortgage-backed securities from 1982 to 1984 can be had from table 7.3. Mortgage pools, guaranteed by the three federal agencies and backing new mortgage securities, surged from an average of $23 billion from 1978 to 1981 to $54 billion in 1982 and $84 billion in 1983 (column 1). In these two years, agency-guaranteed mortgage-backed securities amounted to 46% of all new 1–4 family mortgage originations compared to under 15% in the five prior years (column 4), although not all mortgage pool securities were based on new mortgages. New issues of just FNMA and FHLMC mortgage-backed securities grew from 17% of corporate bond underwriting during 1980–1981 to 63% during 1982–1984 (column 5).

The Structure of the Mortgage-Backed Securities Market

Table 7.4 outlines the investing sectors whose purchases financed the dramatic expansion in mortgage-backed issues from 1982 to 1984. Sav-

Table 7.4. Increases in Mortgage-Backed Securities Holdings 1982–1984 ($ Billions)

Year	New Issues of MBS[1]	All Savings Institutions[2]	%	Life Insurers[3]	%	Pension Funds[3]	%	State & Local Pensions[4]	%	Commercial Banks[4]	%	Money Market Mutuals[4]	%	Total	%
1982	54.2	29.2	54%	4.3	8%	6.4	12%	10.0	18%	7.5	14%	1.6	3%	59.0	109%
1983	83.5	28.0	34%	7.2	9%	11.6	14%	5.0	6%	0.8	1%	1.4	2%	54.0	65%
1984	60.1	21.2	35%	11.0	18%	-4.3	-7%	4.0	7%	-1.3	-2%	3.6	6%	34.2	57%
Total	197.8	78.4	40%	22.5	11%	13.7	7%	19.0	10%	7.0	4%	6.6	3%	147.2	74%

Sources: [1] *MBS Statistical Annual 1988*, p. 3. New issues—no provision is made for retirements.
[2] OTS, *Savings & Home Financing Sourcebook 1988*, p. A-2.
[3] Flow of Funds data for agencies.
[4] Federal Reserve, *Annual Statistical Digest 1980–1989* for agencies, pp. 252–257, 263–267.

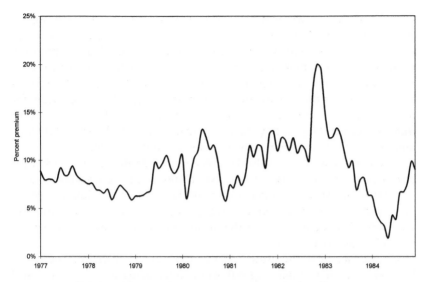

Figure 7.1 GNMA yield premiums over ten-year treasuries. Current coupon GNMA yields. Source: Federal Reserve and Goldman, Sachs & Co.

ings institutions were the dominant investors, purchasing 40% of the new issues. This reflected the sharp expansion in their assets during 1982–1984, the earnings incentive to swap old mortgages for new securities, and regulatory requirements that treated mortgage-backed securities as home mortgages. The next largest sectors, life insurance companies, state and local pension funds, and private pension funds, reflected a straightforward search for higher yields. Independent money managers in particular directed their funds into mortgage-backed securities in search of better comparative performance.

The yield attractions of mortgage-backed securities appeared self-evident. The assets backing the securities were guaranteed by federal agencies and the yields were regularly 7–12% over treasuries, as can be seen in figure 7.1, which outlines the yield premium for GNMA pass-through securities on thirty-year mortgages versus ten-year treasuries. The mortgage borrower's prepayment option had to be factored into this premium, but the simple point of higher yield appeared to hold straightforwardly.

The growth of the mortgage securities market was still restrained, however, by traditional bond buyers' reluctance to absorb the risk inherent in mortgage borrowers' option to refund at par when interest rates fell. This risk was substantially modified in June 1983 when First Boston Corp. sold the first Collateralized Mortgage Obligation (CMO) for Freddie Mac. A CMO split the cash flows of the underlying mortgages into several tranches, to which mortgage prepayments were allocated preferentially. Each tranche was made to look more like a traditional bond thereby, including semiannual interest payments rather than the monthly payments on the actual mortgages. Under a reasonable band of prepayment assumptions, the probable average lives of the tranches could be estimated at two to three years for the shortest tranches, five to ten years for the medium-term tranches, and fifteen to twenty years for the long-term tranches, depending on how many tranches were employed. CMO volume surged to $4.7 billion in the remaining months of 1983.

The ease of access to GNMA collateral made the CMO market instantly competitive. During 1983, federal mortgage agencies issued 36% of CMOs, investment bankers using special purpose subsidiaries issued 32%, builders issued 22%, and mortgage companies issued 10%. In 1984 the market broadened even further as insurance companies issued 12%, thrifts 7%, and banks 5%.[13]

On the face of it, the growth of the mortgage-backed securities market was a credit to financing efficiency, intermediaries' ingenuity, and improved matching of assets and liabilities in the savings and loan industry. Efficiency was achieved by facilitating the flow of funds into regional markets and broadening the market reach of the most efficient operators. The ingenuity of intermediaries progressively crafted debt vehicles that attracted traditional bond investors to the market despite the immediate call provision granted to home borrowers. And the savings and loan industry was kept afloat until interest rates fell, and thereafter encouraged to securitize its mortgage loans so that assets and liabilities matched better.[14]

There was a dark side to the expanded mortgage-backed securities market, however. Its expansion reflected the growth in savings and loans' assets under the new powers granted by Congress, and that growth in turn reflected heavy use of the reverse repurchase market and brokered deposits rather than growth in deposits within the savings and loans' market areas. A handful of savings and loans were particularly aggressive about speculating in mortgage-backed securities.

Charlie Knapp's American Savings & Loan Association in California held no mortgage-backed securities at the end of 1982, but had $6.6 billion (35% of total loans) by June 30, 1984. In a bet on interest rates, Knapp bought $2.1 billion of GNMA pass-through certificates between February and May 1984 and financed the purchase under a reverse repurchase agreement. By June 30, 1984 their value declined $188 million because the Federal Reserve raised interest rates, and Charlie Knapp was on the way out.[15]

Tom Spiegel, as part of his headlong expansion at Columbia Savings & Loan, also in California, raised mortgage-backed securities holdings in three years from $53 million to $1.8 billion and 28% of assets. Trading gains on mortgage loans were 25% to 50% of Columbia's pretax income between 1982 and 1984.[16]

David Paul at Centrust, a Miami savings and loan, came to the party slightly later. After he took over in November 1983 he raised Centrust's mortgage-backed securities holdings from $311 million to $847 million a year later (26.0% of total assets), while cutting mortgages held outright from $1.0 billion to $300 million.[17] Other thrifts followed these activities on a lesser scale.

The leading investment banking firm in the mortgage-backed securities market was Salomon Brothers. They alone took the market seriously when it was a backwater. Salomon first set up a formal department dedicated to mortgage securities in 1978 under Lewis Ranieri. When housing volume fell off in 1979, and new mortgage volume fell similarly, the number of firms dealing in mortgage-backed bonds dropped from over thirty to five or six, but Salomon Brothers actually continued to expand its efforts. Ranieri built a 135-man department by 1983 with six partners and an emphasis on strong research. His department managed almost 50% of the huge mortgage-backed volumes of 1982–1983, earned approximately $200 million after taxes (40% of Salomon's total profits), and he joined the firm's management committee at the age of thirty-six.[18]

Such prominent success, plus the transparency of the new laws and regulations governing savings and loans, attracted virtually every significant investment banking firm into the market, despite their lack of experience with it. Access to GNMA, FHLMC, and FNMA collateral was easy and mortgage securities trading and underwriting volumes were sufficient for even these latecomers to experience revenues of $40–50 million in 1982. There was a concentrated, but ultimately not very successful, effort to expand securitization to private mortgages (as distinct from those of the federal housing agencies). Salomon Brothers, MGIC, and Norwest Mortgage set up Residential Funding Corp. in 1982 to issue bonds backed by mortgages ineligible for agency guarantees, and Sears Roebuck, Citicorp, Bear Stearns, and Shearson-Lehman set up similar devices.

Analyzing the new securities these various firms were creating could be blindingly complex. Analysts at Goldman Sachs had to rent time on two Cray supercomputers to run simulations of mortgage securities' cash flows under different interest rate scenarios. The applicable theory was complex and incomplete, especially for valuing the long-term put option given to the borrower. Experience with the volatility of various CMO tranches under different interest rate scenarios was nonexistent. Nor did anyone know whether lending standards, appraisals, legal procedures, title searches, and loan servicing would be applied with the same care as when a mortgage was not sold off to third parties.

These risks received varying recognition from the new market participants during 1982–1984 as savings and loans, money managers, investment bankers, and other mortgage market participants swarmed into the market. All aspects of the mortgage market were likely to be pushed to their limits when there was intense competition, most of the participants were new to the market, and borrowers and lenders were dealing with each other anonymously through unknown loan servicers. On the political level, federal politicians and regulators were anxious for any remedy that appeared likely to staunch thrift industry losses and rebuild equity through increased competitiveness. As Larry White, a former FHLBB director, has pointed out, "virtually everyone within the Washington policy community (and outside it as well) was mesmerized by the hemorrhaging of the thrifts and focused myopically on measures that would stop the bleeding."[19] This myopia was not merely among the politicians, but among some of the market participants as well. Charlie Knapp at American Savings & Loan was just the first big loser.

Summary

This brief description of the inception of the mortgage-backed securities market points out the crucial roles in its growth played by government efforts to offset the stresses of monetary policy on the savings and loan industry and Fannie Mae. Such rapid growth carried with it speculative excesses and poor institutional controls that became important in the second half of the decade. The mortgage securities market was not alone in being supercharged by government efforts to save the savings and loan industry, however. As we shall see in the next chapter, the savings and loan industry was also vital to the growth of the junk bond market, and there was a similar ignorance of the growing risks associated with it.

8

The Corporate Bond Market

The new regime of high interest rates, a strong dollar, declining oil and other commodities prices, and steep recession achieved lower inflation and ultimately steady economic growth at the price of profound credit distress in important sectors of American industry and the farm community. In many respects, the corporate bond market bore the brunt of the unintended negative effects of the new regime as industries accounting for 53% of the publicly issued, nonfinancial, corporate debt either had severe credit declines or passed through unusual credit crises. Most of the problem industries were the same ones that we saw as underperforming industries in the stock market.

Very little attention has been paid to this credit decline because of the more obvious credit decline in the late 1980s, when corporate America made heavy use of debt for acquisitions and related corporate restructurings. In many respects, the 1979–1984 decline was more fundamental, caused by declining returns on invested capital due to the strong dollar and declining commodities prices, especially oil. Increased leverage was a minor factor in this corporate credit decline, and in general management did not have the power to reverse it, in contrast to the credit decline of the late 1980s, which reflected strategic decisions to increase leverage. To a considerable degree, the decisions of the late 1980s, were reversible by future strategic decisions, such as selling equity, selling assets, or taking a leveraged buyout public again. In contrast, the oil, metals, agricultural, and machinery industries experienced permanent negative effects on their credit in the early 1980s. And two of the largest industries, autos and electric utilities, went through credit crises that required government aid. While the problems of all of these industries were partially offset by credit improvements in other industries, the declining industries were much larger issuers of debt. Including the electric utility and auto industries, these industries accounted for 53% of the public debt issues of nonfinancial companies from 1970 to 1984.

I will also review the growth of the junk bond market in this chapter. In part, it was an outgrowth of the new regime, particularly the deposit and investment expansion of the savings and loan industry and the merger boom (see chapter 9). The 50% decline in interest coverage ratios for new junk bond issues in 1983 that powered their subsequent growth in merger financing also paralleled a similar decline in credit ratios for banks' merger loans that was prompted by the intense deposit competition that accompanied deregulation of bank deposits. But the growth in junk bonds also reflected a natural investor response to an extended period of superior junk bond returns in the 1970s. The junk bond market's effect on increasing corporate leverage was only beginning at the end of the period under review. Its greatest impact was felt in the last half of the 1980s, which will be covered in volume 2.

The Decline in Corporate Credit Quality

The overall decline in corporate credit quality in the early 1980s was evident in macro data. The number of business failures rose from twenty-eight per ten thousand in 1979 to 107 in 1984.[1] Corporate tax data, outlined in table 8.1, indicates a sharp decline in earnings before interest and taxes (EBIT) from 2.1 times interest in 1979 to 1.3 times in 1982, and a recovery to only 1.4 times in 1984—a decline of 33%. There was no further recovery in 1985. This decline was not due to higher leverage. Debt-to-capitalization ratios barely changed between 1979 and 1984, hovering around 43–45%. Nor was the decline due to higher interest rates. If interest rates had held constant between 1979 and 1984, EBIT coverage of interest in 1984 would still have been only 1.7 times—a decline of 19%. The problem was rooted in the decline in unleveraged corporate return on capitalization. EBIT as a percentage of capitalization was 17.9% in 1979, but only 14.7% in 1984—a decline of 18%, and during 1985–1986 it was even lower. The one mitigating credit measure was improvement in funds from operations (after-tax income plus depreciation) as a percentage of debt. It improved slightly from 10.9% in 1979 to 11.8% in 1984, reflecting lower corporate tax rates and heavy investment in short-lived computer equipment.

Income tax data covers a much larger corporate population than that issuing securities, which is our concern, but bond rating changes by

Table 8.1. Corporate Credit Ratios from Income Tax Returns

Credit Ratios	1979	1980	1981	1982	1983	1984	1985
EBIT/Interest	2.1	1.7	1.4	1.3	1.4	1.4	1.4
EBIT/Capitalization.	17.9%	17.0%	17.8%	15.3%	14.0%	14.7%	13.5%
Debt/Capitalization.	43.8%	43.4%	42.3%	43.4%	44.1%	45.0%	45.0%
EBIT/Interest at 1979 rate	2.1	2.0	2.2	1.8	1.6	1.7	1.5
Funds from Operations as a % of Debt	27.3%	23.2%	19.1%	16.4%	17.5%	17.8%	16.6%

Sources: IRS, *Statistics of Income*, Vol. 4, no. 1 (Summer 1984), p. 128; Vol. 6, no. 2 (Fall 1986), pp. 104–105; Vol. 7, no. 3 (Winter 1987), pp. 92–93; Vol. 9, no. 4 (Spring 1990), pp. 165–166.

Moody's Investors Service showed a similar trend of credit deterioration. The percentage of rated issues downgraded a full letter grade rose from 2–3% annually in 1975–1979 to 8% in 1982–1984. The 1982–1984 reductions of 8% compared with prior recession peaks of 4% in 1971 and 5% in 1975.[2]

The S&P Industrials, which are more reflective of the bond-issuing population, also experienced sharp credit declines, as can be seen in table 8.2. EBIT coverage of interest declined 36% from 7.7 times in 1979 to 4.9 times in 1984.[3] It would have declined 27% if interest rates had been constant. The decline in unleveraged earnings was the fundamental factor, as in the tax data, as EBIT declined from 24.0% of average capitalization in 1979 to 20.4% in 1984. Book common equity ratios declined only modestly from 65.8% to 61.4%. Unlike the tax data, funds from operations (net income plus depreciation plus deferred taxes) dropped sharply from 59% of debt to 44%. The average for the five ratios, giving half-weight to each of the two capitalization ratios, was a decline of 20%.

An element of severe dislocation among the weakest companies in the

Table 8.2. Credit Ratios for the S&P Industrials

Credit Ratios	1979	1980	1981	1982	1983	1984	Decline
EBIT/Interest	7.7	6.1	5.0	4.0	4.7	4.9	−36.4%
Funds as % of Book Value Debt	59.2%	57.4%	54.2%	33.9%	45.3%	43.9%	−25.8%
Book Value Common Ratio	65.8%	65.5%	64.4%	62.3%	64.1%	61.4%	−4.4%
Book Value Debt % Market Value Equity + Book Value Debt	32.0%	30.0%	32.0%	36.0%	28.0%	31.0%	−1.0%
EBIT/Average Capitalization	24.0%	22.2%	21.1%	17.0%	18.1%	20.4%	−15.0%
Average[1]							−20.0%

[1]The third and fourth ratios are only given half-weight in the average.

Figure 8.1 Proportions of the S&P Industrials with "Z Scores" below 1.81.
Source: Professor Edward Altman, NYU Stern School of Business.

S&P Industrials was reflected in Edward Altman's Z score predictor of bankruptcies, outlined in figure 8.1. The percentage of companies in the S&P Industrial Index with a Z score below 1.81, which historically predicted bankruptcy with high accuracy, rose from 3% to almost 8% between 1979 and 1984. The reader will note that the percentage of companies with Z scores at the bankruptcy level did not decline after 1984 as it did after the deep recession of 1974–1975.[4]

Bernanke and Campbell found similar trends for a larger group of public companies using Compustat data. They found that EBITD coverage of interest declined 22% from 7.1 times to 5.6 times between 1979 and 1984, and that severe dislocation was reflected in a 43% decline in EBITD coverage of interest for companies in the 90th percentile from 2.1 times to only 1.2 times. They also found that the only improvement was a decline in the debt ratio based on market values, which was also the case for the S&P Industrials.[5]

By and large, the macroeconomic approach to corporate credit quality establishes that a 20–30% decline in credit ratios took place between 1979 and 1984, but the data is too general to reveal the true depths of the credit problems that arose out of the new regime. The macro data reflects what were ultimately offsetting improvements in the regulated, auto-related, retailing, and electronics industries and it misses the credit crises experienced by the auto and electric utility industries in 1980–1981.

A clearer appreciation of the severe decline in corporate credit quality can be had by examining industry data chosen from Standard & Poor's,

Compustat, government agencies, and trade associations[6] that indicates that the lower quartile had a 74% decline in interest coverage, a 58% decline in unleveraged return on capitalization, and an average decline of 52% in five selected credit ratios. These are declines of great magnitude without even taking into account the credit crises in the auto and electric utility industries, which by 1984 actually ended up in the category of improved credits.

The data for these industries is outlined in tables 8.3, 8.4, and 8.5, which group fifteen declining, thirty-two stable, and fifteen improving industries, ranked according to their average change in five credit ratios between 1979 and 1984 (column 3). The average unweighted decline for the sixty-two industries was 8.3%, with a standard deviation of 34.7%. Those industries that had average credit changes within one-half standard deviation of the 8.3% average decline were ranked as stable credits. Those above and below this range were ranked as improving or declining credits. The result was to divide the sixty-two industries approximately into quartiles, with one quartile in each of the declining and improving categories.

The credit ratios were defined as follows:

1. EBIT/Int (col 4)—earnings before interest and income taxes divided by interest;
2. Funds % BV Debt (col 6)—net income plus depreciation plus deferred taxes as a percentage of book value debt;
3. BV Common Ratio (col 8)—book common equity as a percentage of total capitalization (this ratio is given only half weight because there are two capitalization ratios);
4. BV Debt % MV Equity + BV Debt (col 10)—book value debt as a percentage of market value equity plus book value debt (this ratio is also given half-weight as the second capitalization ratio);
5. EBIT/Avg Cap (col 12)—earnings before interest and income taxes as a percentage of average capitalization for the current and prior year.

The extreme problems of the lower quartile stand out clearly in its averages. Interest coverage declined 74% versus only 25% for the average industries and a rise of 32% for the improving industries. Funds from operations as a percentage of debt declined 67% versus no change in the average industries and a rise of 75% in the improving industries. Neither book-value nor market equity ratios declined severely, however, only dropping 9–11% versus almost no change among the average industries and only 7–12% increases among the improving industries. The most important ratio was return on capitalization[7]—EBIT/Avg Cap—which fell 58% for the lower quartile, only 10% for the average industries, and rose 28% for the improving industries. If return on capitalization is adequate, capitalization ratios and interest and cash flow coverages are in many respects optional, since management has unrestricted access to the capital markets. But return on capitalization itself is not optional.

Table 8.3. Declining Corporate Credits 1979–1984

Industry (Col 1)	Year (Col 2)	Avg Credit Chg (Col 3)	EBIT/ Int (Col 4)	Chg (Col 5)	Funds % BV Debt (Col 6)	Chg (Col 7)	BV Common Ratio (Col 8)	Chg (Col 9)	BV Debt % MV equity +BV debt (Col 10)	Chg[5] (Col 11)	EBIT/ Avg Cap (Col 12)	Chg (Col 13)	General Source (Col 14)	Number of Companies (Col 15)
Airlines[4]	1978		2.5		64.0%		59.8%		42.6%		12.2%		ATA	30
	1984	-32%	1.4	-45%	18.7%	-71%	48.1%	-12%	48.1%	-6%	11.8%	-3%		
Paper & Forest Products[3]	1979		5.8		50.3%		65.9%		33.2%		18.9%		S&P	15
	1984	-33%	3.4	-42%	30.5%	-39%	61.4%	-5%	37.6%	-4%	10.5%	-45%		
Steel	1979		2.5		29.9%		68.4%		52.4%		5.8%		S&P	8
	1984	-34%	0.9	-64%	13.4%	-55%	40.2%	-28%	59.4%	-7%	5.7%	-1%		
Beverages—Soft Drinks	1979		12.6		100.0%		77.4%		11.9%		30.4%		S&P	5
	1984	-35%	4.5	-64%	49.2%	-51%	64.0%	-13%	18.5%	-7%	25.8%	-15%		
Integrated Oil[1,2]	1980		11.1		104.9%		73.6%		26.2%		32.5%		S&P	15
	1984	-36%	4.9	-56%	61.4%	-41%	65.2%	-8%	33.0%	-7%	20.1%	-38%		
Oil Well Equipment & Service	1980		8.7		111.1%		76.4%		8.0%		27.0%		S&P	7
	1984	-45%	3.0	-65%	59.7%	-46%	75.1%	-1%	18.9%	-11%	10.1%	-63%		
Aluminum	1979		6.4		50.3%		60.0%		36.7%		21.5%		Compustat	5
	1984	-47%	2.0	-69%	20.5%	-59%	54.5%	-5%	44.2%	-8%	9.9%	-54%		
Heavy Construction[2]	1980		11.6		102.0%		78.0%		9.2%		31.4%		Compustat	10
	1984	-48%	3.4	-71%	47.0%	-54%	76.0%	-2%	23.0%	-14%	12.3%	-61%		
Cosmetics	1979		15.2		122.6%		82.9%		8.0%		34.6%		S&P	6
	1984	-49%	4.4	-71%	38.9%	-68%	62.8%	-20%	25.0%	-17%	21.6%	-37%		
Offshore Drilling[2]	1980		3.2		43.9%		55.0%		26.9%		18.4%		S&P	4
	1984	-51%	1.2	-63%	15.3%	-65%	44.2%	-11%	56.3%	-29%	8.2%	-56%		

Table 8.3. (*continued*)

Industry (Col 1)	Year (Col 2)	Avg Credit Chg (Col 3)	EBIT/ Int (Col 4)	Chg (Col 5)	Funds % BV Debt (Col 6)	Chg (Col 7)	BV Common Ratio (Col 8)	Chg (Col 9)	BV Debt % MV equity +BV debt (Col 10)	Chg[5] (Col 11)	EBIT/ Avg Cap (Col 12)	Chg (Col 13)	General Source (Col 14)	Number of Companies (Col 15)
Machine Tools[6]	1980		8.0		57.7%		70.4%		21.8%		27.5%		S&P	7
	1984	-52%	1.7	-78%	32.5%	-44%	77.3%	7%	16.8%	5%	2.2%	-92%		
Entertainment	1979		10.8		109.0%		81.0%		13.0%		28.6%		S&P	4
	1984	-53%	2.5	-77%	39.6%	-64%	57.8%	-23%	26.9%	-14%	13.0%	-55%		
Agricultural Machinery	1979		2.2		32.1%		57.2%		47.9%		17.8%		S&P	4
	1984	-70%	.04	-82%	0.2%	-99%	22.4%	-35%	57.2%	-9%	3.8%	-78%		
Construction Machinery	1979		5.9		57.4%		69.6%		24.3%		19.2%		Compustat	9
	1984	-73%	0.0	-100%	5.6%	-90%	70.5%	1%	32.3%	-8%	0.0%	-100%		
Copper	1979		4.7		44.0%		67.0%		42.0%		11.8%		S&P	3
	1984	-120%	-2.8	-160%	-23.0%	-152%	62.0%	-5%	37.0%	5%	-7.9%	-167%		
Averages		-51.9%		-73.6%		-66.7%		-10.7%		-8.7%		-57.6%		

[1]Uses average of Petroleum-Integrated—Domestic and Petroleum-Integrated—International indexes.
[2]Oil-related industries used a 1980 base rather than 1979.
[3]Uses an average of S&P Paper and Forest Products indexes.
[4]Uses 1978 because it was a peak year. Market Equity estimated from S&P Index. No allowance for deferred taxes in cash flow.
[5]A reduction in debt is reflected as a positive percentage and vice versa.
[6]Uses 1980 because it was a peak year.

Table 8.4. Average Corporate Credits 1979–1984

Industry (Col 1)	Year (Col 2)	Avg Credit Chg (Col 3)	EBIT/Int (Col 4)	Chg (Col 5)	Funds % BV Debt (Col 6)	Chg (Col 7)	BV Common Ratio (Col 8)	Chg (Col 9)	BV Debt % MV equity +BV debt (Col 10)	Chg[5] (Col 11)	EBIT/Avg Cap (Col 12)	Chg (Col 13)	General Source (Col 14)	Number of Companies (Col 15)
Telephone	1979	8%	3.9	-8%	31.0%	39%	55.0%	3%	48.8%	5%	14.6%	-5%	FCC	76
	1984		3.6		43.0%		58.0%		44.1%		13.9%			
Grocery Stores	1979	5%	3.8	-10%	33.1%	19%	52.2%	1%	43.8%	6%	15.7%	9%	S&P	7
	1984		3.4		39.5%		53.0%		37.7%		17.1%			
Containers (Metal & Glass)	1979	5%	3.8	-21%	40.1%	41%	59.0%	8%	46.8%	13%	13.0	-12%	S&P	5
	1984		3.0		56.7%		66.6%		33.4%		11.4%			
Aerospace	1979	4%	9.9	-11%	108.0%	24%	71.0%	7%	20.0%	6%	23.0%	-3%	S&P	8
	1984		8.8		134.0%		78.0%		14.0%		22.4%			
Shoes–Retailing	1979	1%	11.1	-6%	63.2%	21%	67.5%	9%	24.4%	9%	28.7%	-19%	S&P	4
	1984		10.4		76.8%		76.1%		15.3%		23.2%			
Hospital Mgt	1979	1%	6.1	-48%	19.0%	17%	34.0%	9%	50.0%	13%	17.0%	22%	S&P	4
	1984		3.2		22.3%		43.1%		36.5%		20.7%			
Electric–Major Companies	1979	1%	6.3	-20%	71.9%	32%	71.7%	3%	23.7%	8%	19.7%	-13%	S&P	3
	1984		5.1		95.0%		74.3%		16.2%		17.1%			
Textile Products	1979	0%	4.7	-17%	42.0%	17%	69.0%	2%	51.0%	17%	13.1%	-8%	S&P	7
	1984		3.9		49.0%		71.0%		34.0%		12.0%			
Publishing–Newspapers	1979	-4%	18.0	-14%	130.0%	4%	83.0%	-1%	10.0%	2%	33.2%	-6%	S&P	4
	1984		15.5		135.0%		82.0%		8.0%		31.3%			
Drugs	1979	-4%	16.6	-15%	93.3%	9%	79.0%	0%	10.5%	0%	29.2%	-9%	S&P	12
	1984		14.1		101.7%		79.4%		10.0%		26.5%			
Conglomerates	1979	-4%	3.3	-27%	29.0%	21%	49.0%	8%	52.0%	12%	16.9%	-18%	S&P	8
	1984		2.4		35.0%		57.0%		40.0%		13.9%			
Pipelines[1,3]	1980	-5%	3.6	-13%	30.5%	-2%	43.5%	2%	45.5%	-3%	18.2%	-6%	Compustat	32
	1984		3.2		30.0%		45.0%		48.5%		17.0%			

Table 8.4. (*continued*)

Industry (Col 1)	Year (Col 2)	Avg Credit Chg (Col 3)	EBIT/ Int (Col 4)	Chg (Col 5)	Funds % BV Debt (Col 6)	Chg (Col 7)	BV Common Ratio (Col 8)	Chg (Col 9)	BV Debt % MV equity +BV debt (Col 10)	Chg[5] (Col 11)	EBIT/ Avg Cap (Col 12)	Chg (Col 13)	General Source (Col 14)	Number of Companies (Col 15)
Foods	1979		7.2		55.5%		68.4%		28.3%		22.4%		S&P	21
	1984	-5%	4.8	-33%	69.0%	24%	60.3%	-8%	23.6%	5%	20.0%	-11%		
Soap	1979		12.6		80.8%		77.1%		18.37%		25.6%		Compustat	6
	1984	-5%	7.8	-38%	96.7%	20%	80.3%	3%	12.5%	6%	23.5%	-8%		
Advertising	1979		14.6		117.0%		80.0%		14.0%		37.0%		Compustat	7
	1984	-6%	9.5	-35%	150.0%	28%	82.0%	2%	9.0%	5%	30.0%	-19%		
Hospital Supplies	1979		10.0		85.6%		78.8%		11.8%		18.7%		S&P	6
	1984	-8%	6.3	-38%	81.9%	-4%	76.8%	-2%	12.2%	0%	20.6%	10%		
Chemicals	1979		5.6		60.3%		64.8%		34.8%		18.0%		S&P	6
	1984	-9%	3.9	-30%	60.0%	-1%	68.8%	4	31.6%	3%	16.8%	-7%		
Computer Services[2]	1979		19.0		170.0%		78.3%		7.4%		44.7%		S&P	4
	1984	-9%	17.4	-8%	169.2%	0%	83.6%	5%	8.0%	-1%	30.8%	-31%		
Hotel & Motel	1979		5.5		29.0%		55.0%		37.0%		19.5%		S&P	4
	1984	-9%	3.2	-42%	30.0%	3%	49.0%	-6%	35.0%	2%	20.0%	3%		
Semiconductors	1979		13.8		141.0%		80.0%		11.0%		32.6%		S&P	5
	1984	-11%	11.7	-15%	140.0%	-1%	80.0%	0%	9.0%	2%	22.9%	-30%		
Auto Parts–After Market	1979		21.4		128.2%		86.4%		9.1%		28.8		S&P	4
	1984	-12%	21.6	1%	81.5%	-36%	87.8%	1%	7.3%	2%	25.0%	-13%		
Autos[4]	1978		13.4		179.0%		83.0%		19.0%		30.2%		S&P	4
	1984	-12%	8.5	-37%	150.0%	-16%	77.0%	-6%	25.0%	-6%	33.1%	10%		
Gas Distributors	1979		3.4		21.0%		43.0%		48.0%		15.0%		Compustat	40
	1984	-12%	2.4	-29%	20.0%	-5%	45.0%	2%	49.0%	-1%	12.8%	-15%		
Industrial Machinery	1979		6.9		55.2%		70.5%		27.5%		24.5%		S&P	8
	1984	-15%	5.0	-28%	60.9%	10%	79.4%	9%	19.5%	8%	12.4%	-49%		

Table 8.4. (continued)

Industry (Col 1)	Year (Col 2)	Avg Credit Chg (Col 3)	EBIT/ Int (Col 4)	Chg (Col 5)	Funds % BV Debt (Col 6)	Chg (Col 7)	BV Common Ratio (Col 8)	Chg (Col 9)	BV Debt % MV equity +BV debt (Col 10)	Chg[5] (Col 11)	EBIT/ Avg Cap (Col 12)	Chg (Col 13)	General Source (Col 14)	Number of Companies (Col 15)
Drugstores	1979		20.0		109.4%		81.9%		10.8%		29.9%		S&P	4
	1984	-17%	12.4	-38%	96.1%	-12%	76.9%	-5%	9.4%	1%	24.7%	-17%		
Retail–General Merchandise	1979		3.0		23.5%		58.3%		44.6%		15.7%		S&P	5
	1984	-18%	2.2	-26%	13.5%	-43%	40.5%	-18%	52.5%	-8%	17.3%	10%		
Oil–Crude Producers[1]	1980		5.4		81.1%		64.0%		19.4%		27.0%		S&P	5
	1984	-20%	4.4	-18%	46.1%	-43%	43.1%	-21%	37.0%	-18%	27.5%	2%		
Broadcast Media	1979		7.1		79.0%		74.0%		19.0%		30.4%		S&P	6
	1984	-20%	5.9	-17%	53.0%	-33%	71.0%	-3%	19.0%	0%	22.1%	-27%		
Building Materials	1979		5.0		41.8%		59.2%		41.2%		18.3%		S&P	12
	1984	-20%	3.0	-39%	29.6%	-29%	55.5%	-4%	38.9%	2%	16.2%	-12%		
S&P Industrials	1979		7.7		59.2%		65.38%		32.0%		24.0%		S&P	400
	1984	-20%	4.9	-36%	43.9%	-26%	61.4%	-4%	31.0%	1%	20.4%	-15%		
Computers	1979		16.9		136.0%		81.0%		10.0%		31.1%		S&P	12
	1984	-24%	9.1	-46%	97.0%	-29%	74.0%	-7%	14.0%	-4%	26.8%	-14%		
Air Conditioner Manufacturers	1979		8.4		63.0%		72.0%		25.0%		19.9%		Compustat	16
	1984	-25%	4.3	-49%	44.0%	-30%	62.0%	-10%	33.0%	-8%	17.3%	-13%		
Averages (excl S&P Industrials)		-8.2%		-25.1%		0.7%		-0.5%		2.6%		-9.5%		

[1] Oil-related industries used a 1980 base rather than 1979.
[2] 1979 data is partially estimated.
[3] Uses average of Compustat Gas Distribution & Transmission and Gas Transmission.
[4] Uses 1978 because it was a peak year.

Table 8.5. Improving Corporate Credits 1979–1984

Industry (Col 1)	Year (Col 2)	Avg Credit Chg (Col 3)	EBIT/ Int (Col 4)	Chg (Col 5)	Funds % BV Debt (Col 6)	Chg (Col 7)	BV Common Ratio (Col 8)	Chg (Col 9)	BV Debt % MV equity +BV debt (Col 10)	Chg[1] (Col 11)	EBIT/ Avg Cap (Col 12)	Chg (Col 13)	General Source (Col 14)	Number of Companies (Col 15)
Engines & Turbines	1979		5.1		41.0%		65.0%		40.0%		17.7%		Compustat	7
	1984	87%	9.4	84%	117.0%	185%	77.0%	12%	20.0%	20%	28.4%	62%		
Tires and Rubber Goods	1979		1.9		21.0%		55.9%		62.6%		10.1%		S&P	4
	1984	75%	3.4	81%	55.4%	164%	60.2%	4%	33.0%	30.0%	13.9%	38%		
Electrical Equipment	1979		7.1		39.3%		62.6%		30.0%		21.5%		S&P	6
	1984	65%	12.9	81%	93.2%	137%	79.1%	16%	11.6%	18%	27.0%	26%		
Publishing	1979		13.6		63.0%		67.0%		19.0%		21.3%		S&P	6
	1984	53%	15.8	16%	139.0%	121%	82.0%	15%	7.0%	12%	34.6%	62%		
Truckers[2]	1979		16.3		143.8%		82.4%		14.8%		19.6%		Annuals	4
	1984	49%	27.2	67%	306.6%	113%	90.5%	8%	9.2%	6%	21.6%	10%		
Beer	1979		6.5		61.8%		76.3%		25.5%		13.5%		S&P	3
	1980	34%	7.2	11%	106.0%	72%	71.2%	-5%	19.2%	6%	20.8%	54%		
Household Furnishings & Appliances	1979		8.7		74.3%		77.6%		21.4%		21.4%		S&P	7
	1984	29%	9.4	8%	87.8%	18%	80.4%	3%	15.0%	6%	39.7%	85%		
Restaurants	1979		4.7		33.0%		50.0%		38.0%		21.0%		S&P	4
	1984	28%	6.0	28%	52.0%	58%	62.0%	12%	22.0%	16%	23.9%	14%		
Pollution Control	1979		4.6		48.0%		60.6%		31.4%		17.0%		S&P	5
	1984	26%	6.2	33%	62.2%	30%	68.4%	8%	19.0%	12%	22.0%	29%		
Electric Utilities	1979		2.1		13.4%		37.2%		54.6%		9.2%		EEI	100+
	1984	22%	2.5	19%	17.1%	28%	41.6%	4%	50.6%	4%	12.8%	39%		

Table 8.5. (*continued*)

Industry (Col 1)	Year (Col 2)	Avg Credit Chg (Col 3)	EBIT/ Int (Col 4)	Chg (Col 5)	Funds % BV Debt (Col 6)	Chg (Col 7)	BV Common Ratio (Col 8)	Chg (Col 9)	BV Debt % MV equity +BV debt (Col 10)	Chg[1] (Col 11)	EBIT/ Avg Cap (Col 12)	Chg (Col 13)	General Source (Col 14)	Number of Companies (Col 15)
Tobacco	1979		6.1		41.0%		55.6%		35.9%		23.7%		S&P	3
	1984	19%	7.1	15%	55.7%	36%	63.9%	8%	22.7%	13%	26.8%	13%		
Electronics (Instruments)	1979		22.2		88.2%		79.2%		10.2%		28.0%		S&P	4
	1984	17%	31.7	43%	135.9%	54%	87.0%	8%	5.4%	5%	18.3%	-35%		
Auto Parts–Original Equipment	1979		6.6		55.6%		69.1%		33.9%		22.3%		S&P	6
	1984	15%	7.1	9%	77.5%	40%	74.7%	6%	21.7%	12%	22.5%	1%		
Railroads	1979		4.3		31.7%		53.0%		43.7%		14.1%		Compusat	13
	1984	11%	4.2	-2%	44.0%	39%	54.7%	2%	39.0%	5%	14.5%	3%		
Department Stores	1979		4.9		39.5%		66.2%		38.5%		18.4%		S&P	8
	1984	10%	4.4	-9%	49.4%	25%	65.3%	-1%	27.9%	11%	22.3%	21%		
Averages		36.0%		32.2%		74.6%		6.7%		11.8%		28.2%		

[1] A reduction in debt is reflected as a positive percentage and vice versa.

[2] Size-weighted data from annual reports of the four companies in the S&P Truckers index. EBIT/Avg Cap uses 1979 and 1984 capitalizations only.

The fifteen declining industries in table 8.3 fell into four sectors—oil-related, metals related, machinery manufacturers other than those related to electronics, and miscellaneous. I have already examined most of these industries in chapter 4 as underperforming common stocks. I can summarize here that the credit problems of the oil and metals industries were caused by declining commodities prices as the inflationary atmosphere abated, and that the decline in the machinery manufacturing industries reflected the strength of the dollar, union problems, and a general fall in noncomputer capital spending. For most of these industries, the decline was an abrupt change in trend from the inflationary prosperity of the 1970s.

The fifteen improving industries in table 8.5 fall into four sectors—regulated, auto-related, electronics, and consumer-related industries. These industries also had superior common stock performance, as we saw in chapter 5. The trends that stand out in these improving industries are improved regulation in the electric utility, trucking, and railroad industries, technological advances in the electronics industries, a cyclical recovery in the auto-related industries, and strong consumer spending.[8]

The improvement in the electric utility industry's credit more than offset the declining credit of the commodities and equipment industries because of the capital intensity and heavy reliance on debt of the electric utility industry. But a correct sense of proportion for the credit stress of the early 1980s requires that the electric utility and auto industries be included with the declining credits because of the crises they went through. On this broad basis, industries accounting for 53% of the publicly issued, nonfinancial corporate debt between 1970 and 1984 declined or went through severe crisis. Table 8.6 outlines the annual public bond issues by these industries and provides a sense of proportion for various industries, particularly the size of electric utility issues (28%) and commodities issuers (19%).

The Oil-Related Industries

The most important credit decline was in the oil-related industries, such as the Integrated Oil companies, Oil Field Services and Equipment, Offshore Drilling, and Heavy Construction (mostly for energy projects). The oil-related industries were the largest industrial sector, as can be seen in table 8.7. They accounted for 24.3% of the S&P 500 in 1979—four times the share of the telephone industry and six times the auto and electric utility industries. Profit relationships were similar. The oil sector's debt of $70 billion was only 73% of the electric utility industry's debt, reflecting the latter's much higher leverage, but was 155% of the telephone industry's and almost five times the auto industry's (excluding their credit companies). Oil-related capital expenditures of $36.5 billion equaled those

Table 8.6. Public Bond Issues by Declining and Crisis Credits 1970–1984

Year	Total Non-fin'l Issues ($ mils)	Electric Utilities ($ mils)	Autos ($ mils)	Commodities Issuers ($ mils)	Machinery Issuers ($ mils)	Airlines ($ mils)	Total ($ mils)
1970	19,649	5,646	460	3,563	478	249	10,396
1971	17,548	5,061	225	2,463	363	103	8,215
1972	11,397	4,455	75	713	70	0	5,313
1973	10,053	4,046	315	1,383	50	0	5,794
1974	20,985	7,207	485	2,654	530	0	10,876
1975	27,773	7,619	735	4,551	1,033	0	13,938
1976	19,872	6,320	110	3,485	203	183	10,300
1977	15,464	5,349	0	2,704	455	53	8,561
1978	12,625	4,543	215	1,114	355	27	6,254
1979	17,141	5,045	350	2,375	250	90	8,110
1980	28,022	6,658	1,425	4,747	1,160	0	13,990
1981	28,077	7,690	600	7,907	1,410	90	17,697
1982	27,027	7,179	0	4,781	1,150	188	13,298
1983	21,380	5,500	0	7,219	500	411	13,629
1984	27,605	4,300	12	8,875	542	483	14,212
Totals	304,617	86,617	5,007	58,533	8,549	1,876	160,582
		28%	2%	19%	3%	1%	53%

Source: Securities Data Company.

of the electric utility and telephone industries combined, although a substantial part of the oil sector's capital spending was outside of the United States.

The largest part of the oil industry, the major integrated oil companies, suffered a 36% decline in credit ratios between 1980 and 1984 as oil prices fell and the industry sharply reversed direction from the easy profits of the 1970s. EBIT coverage of interest declined from 11.4 times in 1980 to 4.9 times in 1984, and funds from operations declined from 105% of debt to 61%, reflecting a decline in EBIT return on average capitalization from 32.5% to 20.1%. These 1984 ratios were not life-threatening, however, and the major oil companies had modest leverage by any standard. They were also cutting back capital expenditures by two-thirds, as net capital expenditures fell from 10.3% of prior year's capitalization in 1980 to only 3.5% in 1984.

Some of the smaller industries closely related to the oil industry were in trouble, however, since their business was a function of the major oil companies' capital expenditures. The Offshore Drilling industry's credit ratios declined 51% to untenable levels. EBIT coverage of interest declined to 1.2 times, as EBIT return on capitalization dropped to 8%. Funds from operations were down to a bare 15% of total debt in 1984. The industry's book common equity ratio was only 44%, and a powerful

Table 8.7. Relative Size of the Largest Industries (1979)

Industries	% of S&P 500 12/79	Capital Expenditures ($ bill.)	Employees (000)	Profits ($ bill.)	Debt Outstanding ($ bill.)
Oil-Related Industries[1]					
Refining	18.2%	30.2	1,227.0	27.1	55.0
Crude Petroleum Prod[2]	1.0%	2.0	NA	0.7	1.7
Drilling	0.3%	0.5	22.3	0.2	1.3
Oil & Gas Field Services	3.1%	0.7	88.3	0.7	1.0
Natural Gas Transportation	1.0%	1.6	30.8	0.6	6.3
Natural Gas Transportation & Distribution	0.8%	1.6	63.0	0.7	4.9
Totals	24.3%	36.5	1,431.4	30.0	70.2
Auto-Related Industries[1]					
Autos[2]	2.6%	9.6	1,510.0[5]	3.0	6.4
Industrial Trucks	0.1%	0.1	36.5	0.1	0.7
Motors & Generators		0.1	60.4	0.2	0.3
Engines & Turbines		0.2	77.6	0.2	0.7
Motor Vehicle Parts	0.8%	0.7	221.4	0.6	2.2
Tires	0.3%	0.4	132.0	0.2	1.8
Totals	3.8%	11.2	2,037.8	4.4	12.0
Electric Utilities[3]	3.7%	24.4	576.0[6]	7.6	96.3
Telephones[4]	6.0%	13.2	1,071.0[6]	6.5	44.9

[1] Compustat data.
[2] S&P data.
[3] EEI data.
[4] FCC data.
[5] *Ward's Automotive Yearbook 1986*, p. 183
[6] *Employment & Earnings*, U.S. Dept of Labor

indicator of trouble was the rise in its market-based debt ratio from 27% in 1980 to 56% in 1984.

Credit ratios for the Oil Field Services and Equipment and Heavy Construction industries declined a steep 45% and 48%, respectively. Their EBIT returns on capitalization of only 10.1% and 12.3% were approximately half that of the major oil companies, indicating the greater vulnerability of these industries' dependence on oil industry capital expenditures; but these two industries were much less troubled than the drilling industry because of their modest leverage.

The independent Crude Oil Producers suffered a 20% decline in credit ratios—not enough to place them among the declining industries—and even that reflected increased leverage rather than lower EBIT returns on capitalization. To a considerable degree, they were protected by their heavy investment in domestic natural gas, prices for which had not fallen by 1984. Pipelines had a similar benefit.

The oil-related industries' credit problems reflected a classic commodities boom and bust. The high prices of 1980–1981, which reached a peak of over $40 a barrel and stimulated projections that prices would reach as high as $100 a barrel by the year 2000, led to rising costs, excessive capacity expansion, mega-projects that look like pipe dreams today, and customer conservation and substitution. Just a modest decline in oil prices to $29 a barrel from 1982 to 1984 led to a sharp decline in profitability, steep reductions in oil and gas exploration activity, and questions about the feasibility of the large pipeline and synthetic fuels construction projects. I have already examined these fundamental factors in chapter 4.

The Metals Industries

The metals industries suffered an abrupt change in direction from the inflationary 1970s as they were buffeted by recession, the strong dollar, and only a modest recovery in traditional capital spending. Many of the metals industries' credit ratios dropped to unsustainably low levels.

Copper industry credit ratios dropped 120%, as EBIT return on capitalization turned to a negative 7.9% in 1984. The Copper industry did not even have EBITD earnings sufficient to cover interest payments, and funds from operations as a percentage of total debt were also negative. We have already seen in chapter 4 that most of the major copper and lead mines in the country were closed at this time.

The Steel industry was already sick in 1979, before the recession, when its EBIT return on capitalization was only 5.8%, but it incurred a further 34% decline in its credit ratios by 1984 because of ill-advised capital expenditures. Despite its low returns (the lowest of any industry in 1979 and less than 25% of the S&P Industrial average), and funds from operations after dividends equal to only 60% of its capital expenditures in 1979, the industry continued to make large capital expenditures and acquisitions, which it financed with debt. This led to a decline in the industry's book value equity to only 40% of capitalization in 1984. Due to no change in returns, EBIT coverage of interest declined from a meager 2.5 times in 1979 to an unsustainable 0.9 times in 1984, and funds from operations declined from 29.9% to 13.4% of total debt. Both 1984 ratios were crisis levels.

The Aluminum industry averaged a severe 47% decline in its credit ratios, but fared better than Copper and Steel because it started from a better base in 1979, when its EBIT return on capitalization was 21.5% and EBIT coverage of interest was 6.4 times. Its 1984 EBIT return on capitalization of 9.9% and EBIT coverage of interest of 2.0 times were absolutely low, but still above bankruptcy levels.

The metal industries were profoundly affected by the strength of the dollar. Between 1980 and 1984, copper imports rose from 14% to 23% of domestic consumption; steel imports rose from 18.5% of net domestic shipments to 35.6%; and aluminum went from a net-exporting industry to importing 17% of domestic requirements, as imports doubled and exports were halved.[9] The price of copper, which was widely traded without restrictions in world markets, dropped from $1.01 per pound to 67 cents, and aluminum fell from 85 cents to 45 cents. Whereas prices and production should have recovered significantly in these industries in 1983 and 1984 as the economy recovered, they did not principally because of the pressure from imports. Circumstances were similar in other metal industries such as lead, zinc, molybdenum, iron ore, and mercury. Only gold mining had a different story due to higher gold prices, but this almost exclusively benefited Canadian and other foreign companies at the time.

These metal industries were trapped in a vicious cycle of economic decline. Their return on investment and credit condition dictated sharply reducing capital expenditures. They also had historically strong unions that kept wages far above the manufacturing average, as we saw in chapter 4. But they could only compete against lower-cost imports and reduce the impact of their high wage costs if they modernized intensively. Return on investment criteria won, as net capital expenditures dropped 50–75% as a percentage of prior year's capitalization between 1979 and 1984, with all of the attendant implications for these industries' future competitiveness and growth.

Other commodities industries suffered severe reversals from their prosperity in the 1970s due to the strength of the dollar, high interest rates, and higher energy prices than the 1970s. Credit ratios in the Paper and Forest Products industry declined an average of 33%, as EBIT return on capitalization dropped from an already uncompetitive 14.2% in 1979 to only 11.7% in 1984. EBIT coverage of interest declined from 5.8 to 3.8 times, and funds from operations as a percentage of debt declined from 57% to 40%. The industry was weak but it wasn't going broke. Various commodities industries not covered in my tables suffered similarly, such as fertilizers, farming, and commodity chemicals.

The Machinery Industries

Credit ratios for the various nonelectrical machinery industries were ravaged between 1979 and 1984 and reached crisis levels for many companies. Credit ratios in the Machine Tool industry declined 52%, as EBIT coverage of interest dropped from 9.1 to 1.7 times, and funds from operations dropped from 65% of debt to 33%. The industry had very little leverage throughout 1979–1984, but this was no protection to the industry's credit as its EBIT return on capitalization dropped from an attractive 28.1% in 1979 to only 2.2% in 1984. Few industries illustrated so well the shift from prosperity to depression between the 1970s and the 1980s.

The prosperity of the Construction Machinery industry suddenly disappeared in the early 1980s and its credit ratios declined 73% as many large energy projects were eliminated and the strong dollar fostered foreign competition. Energy projects and exports accounted for a huge share of the industry's sales. EBIT return on capitalization dropped from 19.2% to zero, its EBIT coverage of interest dropped from 5.9 times to zero, and funds from operations declined from 57% of debt to only 7%. Caterpillar, the quintessential American construction machinery company, lost almost $1 billion between 1982 and 1984, cut costs sharply, and moved 25% of production abroad. Its bond rating was cut from Aa to A, but held there. The lesser companies, such as Clark Equipment and Rexnord, went through greater distress.

The Farm Industry

The Agricultural Machinery industry experienced a disastrous 70% decline in credit between 1979 and 1984 that was an abrupt change of trend from the late 1970s, when inflation was fostering farm prosperity. The decline merits a brief digression here because in the course of the decade not only the Agricultural Machinery industry but the whole farm economy and the financial institutions connected with it went through prolonged credit-related contractions. Problems in the federally sponsored Farm Credit System had not shown up by the end of 1984, but will form a dramatic element of the government bond market story in volume 2.

Farmers suffered twice from federal government policies to fight inflation, as can be seen in table 8.8, first as high interest rates raised the interest costs of this highly leveraged sector, and then as the strong dollar sharply reduced wheat, corn, soybean, and cotton prices and the U.S. share of world agricultural trade. Farm interest costs rose relentlessly from $10.9 billion in 1978 to $25.7 billion in 1981 (columns 4 and 5), as the prime rate rose from an average of 9% in 1978 to 19% in 1981.[10] Just as interest costs began to decline in 1982, wheat, corn, soybean, and cotton prices began a prolonged decline related to the strength of the dollar so that farm revenues from these crops dropped from $47 billion in 1981 to $33 billion in 1987.[11] U.S. agricultural exports also dropped as world agricultural trade stalled and the U.S. share of world agricultural trade dropped from approximately 28% during 1972–1981 to 20% in 1986.[12] Revenues from livestock and fruits, vegetables, and other crops continued to rise slowly, but farm income before interest, taxes, government payments, and imputed income declined from $36.7 billion in 1981 to only $10.8 billion in 1983 and was still only $29.1 billion by 1986 (column 6).

Table 8.8. Farm Finances ($ Billions)

Year	Total Income[1] Col 1	Total Income Excluding Govt Payments & Imputed Income Col 2	Total Debt[2] Col 3	Mortgage Interest[3] Col 4	Non-mortgage Interest[4] Col 5	Earnings Before Interest, Taxes Government Payments & Imputed Income Col 6	Interest Coverage Col 7
1977	20	10	119	4.3	3.7	18.0	2.3
1978	25	13	137	5.1	5.8	23.9	2.2
1979	27	15	162	6.2	9.5	30.7	2.0
1980	16	3	179	7.5	12.5	23.0	1.2
1981	27	11	195	9.1	16.6	36.7	1.4
1982	24	7	203	10.5	13.7	31.2	1.3
1983	13	–10	207	10.8	10.0	10.8	0.5
1984	32	11	204	10.7	11.0	32.7	1.5
1985	32	12	188	9.9	8.1	30.0	1.7
1986	37	14	168	9.1	6.0	29.1	1.9
1987	46	19	153	8.2	5.4	32.6	2.4

[1]Before taxes, including imputed income and government payments; *Agricultural Statistics 1988*, p. 412.
[2]Excluding CCC loans; Ibid. pp. 424, 429.
[3]Ibid., p. 428.
[4]Non-mortgage debt at average annual prime rate.

The combined effect of high interest rates and the dollar-related decline in wheat, corn, soybean, and cotton prices had a punishing effect on farm finances. Farm net income, excluding imputed rent and consumption and Federal payments to farmers (column 2), fell from an average of $13 billion during 1977–1979 to $7 billion in 1982 and a loss of $10 billion in 1983. Obviously the trend for wheat, corn, soybean, and cotton farmers was even worse than this. Farm income as calculated by the Department of Agriculture (column 1) showed approximately 50% declines in 1980 and 1983, but otherwise indicated a generally rising trend from approximately $25 billion in the late 1970s to $32 billion in the mid-1980s. This data reflected imputed rental income from buildings and farm consumption and from government payments. My data is more reflective of the earning power farmers could rely on to service debt.

Interest coverage on my basis dropped from 2.3 times in 1977 to 1.2 times in 1980 and 0.5 times in 1983 (column 7). This reflected not just declining incomes and rising interest rates, but also increased debt. Farmers had gone on a borrowing spree in the last half of the 1970s that raised their total debt from $103 billion in 1976 to $207 billion in 1983 (column 3) as land prices rose. Land values securing this debt began to drop in 1983 and by 1987 were down 27% nationally to $599 per acre.

These problems carried over into the Farm Credit System, which held $70 billion of farmers' $212 billion of debt. Dating back to the New Deal, the Farm Credit System was loosely organized with twelve regional cooperative banks, various land and intermediate credit lenders, and 387 local credit associations that were essentially controlled by the farm borrowers. The system used homemade accounting rules that were not subject to audit, and was hesitant to recognize bad debts, yet it operated with high leverage in the short-term credit markets like a federal agency. Worries about it were rising in 1984 but burst into a full-scale bankruptcy crisis in 1985, just beyond our purview in this volume. The system had to be totally reorganized, infused with government capital, given access to a line of credit with the U.S. Treasury, and congressionally mandated to make accounting and lending reforms. The building pressure on the Farm Credit System in 1984 and the terms of its reorganization after 1985 resulted in a wholesale liquidation of farm debt from a peak of $207 billion in 1983 to $153 billion in 1987 (column 3) that put the industry through the credit wringer.[13] A similar liquidation occurred among the small rural banks that existed alongside the Farm Credit System.

The Agricultural Machinery industry deteriorated quickly under these conditions. Even when farmers were prospering, the industry was weak because of excessive leverage. It had an adequate 1979 EBIT return on capitalization of 17.8%, but its book equity ratio was only 47% of capitalization (versus 66% for the S&P Industrials), which resulted in EBIT coverage of interest only 2.7 times and funds from operations equal to only 32% of its debt. At the first sign of a downturn in equipment sales in 1980, the industry recorded losses equal to 6.2% of equity. Between 1980 and 1984, the industry recorded losses every year, and losses in 1982 alone wiped out over 40% of the industry's accumulated lifetime equity. The industry's credit ratios declined 70%, as EBIT coverage of interest dropped to only 0.4 times in 1984, and EBIT return on capitalization dropped to only 3.8%.

This dismal performance was exacerbated at International Harvester —one of the most prominent companies in the industry—by serious errors made by its new chief executive, Archie McCardell, an overly optimistic sales type hired from Xerox in 1978. The company had earned a record $346 million in 1979 as both farm equipment and large truck sales boomed, but in 1980 it took a six-month strike with the U.A.W. just as rising interest rates and energy prices cut equipment sales. The company had a 1980 loss of $210 million and found itself seriously strapped for cash because it had not cut capital expenditures. External financing in 1980 was $980 million—over 25% of its $3.5 billion capitalization—and over $600 million of the financing was floating rate bank debt, the costs of which were about to rise to over 20%! The crunch came in 1981 as the company operated at only 40-50% of capacity and led an industry move to general price cutting, but McCardell did little to cut costs. The company had a negative EBIT of $433 million for 1981 before an interest charge of $362 million!

The financial markets revolted. Harvester's bond ratings were cut from Ba to Caa, and both the parent company and its credit subsidiary lost access to the commercial paper market. Its stock had been as high as $45½ in 1979 and was still at $31½ at one point in 1981, but dropped to a low of $2¾.

McCardell was fired in May 1982, and Louis W. Menck, a director and the ex-chairman of Burlington Northern, took over as chairman and chief executive and began to cut costs. The number of employees dropped from 98,000 in 1979 to 43,000 in 1982, and the number of manufacturing sites was consolidated from 41 to 18. Cash was raised by selling the Solar Turbines division to Caterpillar for $505 million, the construction equipment division to Dresser Industries for $100 million, and the axle and transmission business to Dana Corp. Various smaller activities were sold or closed. Capital spending was cut from $325 million in 1981 to $108 million in 1982—$48 million less than depreciation. A debt restructuring program was worked out with the banks under which they deferred part of interest and principal payments and converted $350 million of debt to equity, provided that suppliers, dealers, and public debtholders each met specified targets for their contributions to the restructuring. The unions signed a new agreement designed to save $200 million over twenty-nine months.

There was a natural tendency to see parallels between International Harvester and Chrysler, but the general economic recovery in 1983 brought no relief to International Harvester. Both its truck sales and agricultural equipment sales reached new lows in 1983. EBIT was still negative $277 million. Interest costs had only been reduced from a peak of $362 million to $252 million, despite the extreme efforts to raise cash and the general decline in interest rates. Employees dropped further to thirty-two thousand—now less than one-third of peak employment— capital spending was only $31 million, research and development was cut from over $200 million to $114 million, and the process was begun to sell the company's agricultural equipment business to Tenneco's J. I. Case division in 1984.

International Harvester was eventually reduced to manufacturing medium and large trucks under the strict control of its banks with total employment of fifteen thousand—approximately 15% of its 1979 peak. In 1986 its name was changed to Navistar—a meaningless public relations concoction.

Massey-Ferguson, the major Canadian agricultural machinery manufacturer, went through similar problems and was only kept out of bankruptcy by Canadian government intervention.

Other Industries

The airline industry had a 32% decline in credit ratios between 1979 and 1984 that resulted in a near-crisis level of only 1.4 times EBIT coverage of interest in 1984. This gives a much more meaningful image of the industry's trouble than the categorization of Airline stocks as an overperforming industry in chapter 5. We have already seen in chapter 5 how the industry was buffeted by higher fuel costs and by new discount airlines fostered by deregulation. Unfortunately, the airlines still needed to maintain capital spending for larger, more fuel-efficient planes. The industry began a descent into financial distress that was still at work in 1994 when this was written.

The other industries classified as declining credits between 1979 and 1984 were Cosmetics, Entertainment, and Soft Drinks. All of these industries continued to have acceptable absolute credit ratios. And they were not affected by the major variables, such as oil prices, high interest rates, the strong dollar, or weak capital expenditures, that were causing credit deterioration in the other declining industries. Rather, their credit trends reflected individual factors of management quality, leverage choices, and acquisitions. These industries' importance lies in their relative insignificance compared to the large industries cited above.

The Auto industry appears in these tables as an average industry, but it experienced a credit crisis during 1980–1982 that almost bankrupted

Chrysler, Ford, and American Motors, as we have already seen in chapter 4. Had it not been for federal government aid to Chrysler, restriction of Japanese imports by the Reagan administration, and a relaxation of gas mileage and environmental requirements, the industry would surely have undergone a tumultuous credit-related contraction. Its appearance of credit stability was therefore not a free market result.

The Improving Industries

Fifteen industries showed improvement in their five credit ratios between 1979 and 1984 averaging one-half standard deviation or more relative to the average decline of 8.3%. Important improvement occurred in the auto-related, regulated, electronics, and several consumer-oriented industries. Ten of the fifteen industries were subject to little or no foreign competition—a topic that I examined in chapters 4 and 5, and which was in sharp contrast to the commodities and machinery industries among the declining credits. Six of the industries provided direct consumer products or services, which was a sharp contrast to the capital orientation of the commodities, metal, and machinery industries, and an additional three had intense government involvement (Electric Utilities, Railroads, and Trucking) versus the free-market environments of the declining industries.

Electric Utilities

The most important change within the improving industries was for the electric utility industry, which was the largest issuer of debt in the country. It issued $115 billion in debt in 1981, approximately twice the amount of the integrated oil companies or telephone companies and ten times any other industry. The electric utility industry's credit ratios rose 22% between 1979 and 1984 as its EBIT return on capitalization rose 39%. However, this improvement only occurred after the industry faced the greatest threat to its credit since the 1930s and got almost $10 billion in indirect aid from the government through the Rural Electrification Administration.

The industry was struck from many directions at the turn of the decade. Higher oil and coal prices during 1979–1982 produced a sharp rise in fuel costs, particularly in the East and West Coast metropolitan areas, and for gas-burning utilities in the Southwest. High inflation hit hard at the industry because of its capital intensity (it is the most capital-intensive industry in America) as new fossil fuel plant costs rose 155% between 1977 and 1982.[14] High interest rates had a strong influence on the industry because of its high leverage—in 1979 it had a 37% common equity ratio versus 66% for the S&P Industrials. The slowdown in economic growth also burdened the industry with excess capacity that was placed under construction five to ten years earlier when higher growth rates were anticipated.

The industry needed to pass all of these higher costs through to consumers quickly because, despite its high historic credit ratings, financially it operated on a thin edge. In 1979 it raised 79% of its capital expenditures externally versus only 10% for the S&P Industrials, and it had interest coverage of only 2.1 times versus 7.7 times for the S&P Industrials. The public was highly unsympathetic, however. It, too, was battered by inflation, high oil prices, and weak economic growth. It also felt considerable disaffection for government and regulation in other respects and its antagonism produced a corresponding reaction among utility regulators.

These problems were exacerbated by an accident in March 1979 at General Public Utilities' Three Mile Island nuclear generating plant, which came close to a nuclear meltdown. General Public Utilities almost went bankrupt, and the accident had a substantial impact on the burdens placed on other utilities that were constructing nuclear generating plants. Federal and state regulators, courts, and the general public became dramatically more opposed to nuclear power even though both the Carter and Reagan administrations generally favored it. Nuclear plants were subjected to intensive regulatory review, new technical requirements, extended construction periods, and much higher costs. Annual nuclear construction budgets escalated from $9.9 billion in 1979 to $18.2 billion in 1983.[15] The planned costs of nuclear generating units rose from $586 per kilowatt of capacity in 1979 to $2,445 in 1985, and kept on rising to a peak of approximately $4,500 in 1990.[16] In response, electric utilities canceled sixty-seven nuclear generating units between 1979 and 1984, equal to 76,438 megawatts of capacity and 13% of 1979 nationwide electric utility generating capacity, forever casting the die against any further domestic construction of nuclear power plants.[17] But these cancellations still left the companies with serious problems of cost recovery, which was reflected in 60% of the bond ratings for AA and A rated nuclear utilities being downgraded between 1970 and 1989 versus only 21% for nonnuclear utilities.[18] Many companies faced financial crises.

The electric utility industry's problems with inflation and nuclear power were reflected in a decline in its EBIT coverage of interest from an already low 2.4 times in 1978 to 1.9 in 1980 and 1981;[19] but the industry had a more subtle credit problem that troubled industrial companies rarely shared. Because electric utilities financed 70% of their construction programs with externally raised funds, they were dependent on selling new shares frequently, some companies semiannually, and therefore maintained very high dividends—75% of earnings compared to 36% for the S&P Industrials. But dividends were not enough to sustain their stock prices, which were very sensitive to both high interest rates and the industry's problems. Electric utility stocks sold as low as two-thirds of book value in 1980 and 1981, and the most troubled companies sold even lower. Low stock prices and the need to keep selling stock created talk of a "death spiral" for the industry, but the companies had little choice except to push ahead. There was nothing to be gained from half-finished generating plants. For the most troubled companies, however, a serious cash crisis threatened, and both the stock and bond markets were frightened of bankruptcies.

An important aspect of resolving this crisis was the Reagan administration's use of the Rural Electrification Administration as a channel to fund nuclear power plant construction. Rural electric cooperatives were encouraged to purchase partial interests in unfinished power plants all around the country, and ultimately provided $9.75 billion for seventeen plants by early 1984—equal to over 7% of the electric utility industry's total debt at the time and 82% of 1983 industry cash flow after dividends. Companies that in the past had bitterly opposed the expansion of rural electric coops, especially in the Southeast, received major cash infusions from them, permanently ending their antipathy.[20]

The worst funding crisis for nuclear power occurred in the municipal power sector for the Washington Public Power Supply System (WPPSS) in the Pacific Northwest. WPPSS had five nuclear units under construction to service a region that was experiencing strong conservation and severe industrial contraction due to the recession and the effect of the strong dollar on aluminum and mining. The cost of the five units was also escalating wildly, up 38% in just a few months in mid-1981 to $24 billion. Faced with no need for the projected power and very weak markets for its bonds, WPPSS delayed or canceled four of the units and focused on completing its number 2 unit, which was already 94% done.

This set off battles in the courts and in the political arena among the ultimate customers and the various participants in the plants—the Bonneville Power Authority (BPA), five investor-owned utilities, and eighty-eight municipal utilities in three states. Approximately $6.8 billion of tax-exempt bonds were already outstanding on the five units that someone had to service. Matters were greatly complicated when courts in the three states with municipal participants ruled differently on their responsibility to pay. Bonneville Power Authority was forced into a 58% rate increase in 1982 and a further 27% in late 1983 to cover its obligations to the project. And the investor-owned utilities split among themselves over what to cancel and what to continue. In May 1983 WPPSS defaulted on the $2.25 billion of bonds issued for units 4 and 5, and in June the Washington supreme court ruled that the contracting municipalities had exceeded their powers and did not have to pay their share of debt service. Ratings on the bonds for units 1, 2, and 3, which were backed by the Bonneville

Power Authority and hence the federal government, had been Aaa as recently as 1982 but were reduced to Baa because of the "strain on BPA"—a new low point for federal debt ratings.

Elsewhere around the country, regulators responded to the electric utility industry's credit crisis by granting record rate increases, but other factors such as reduced inflation, lower oil prices and interest rates, and the entry of new generating plants into service also acted to raise the industry's credit ratios 18% by 1984. EBIT coverage of interest rose from a low of 1.9 in 1979 to 2.5 in 1984. Funds from operations minus dividends rose from 30% of capital expenditures in 1980 to 51% in 1984, as construction expenditures leveled off and funds from operations kept growing. Anticipations in this respect were even better, as capital expenditures were due to decline by almost one-third in the next five years, which was well understood by most observers since all companies in the industry provided five-year forecasts. Common equity ratios rose from 37.2% in 1979 to 41.6% in 1984.[21]

The improving trend was reflected in bond ratings. Moody's ratings changes shifted from 16 net downgrades in 1982 (44 down, 28 up) to 39 net upgrades in 1984 (81 up, 42 down).[22]

Railroads and Truckers

Railroads, the oldest regulated industry, improved its credit ratios 11% between 1979 and 1984 thanks to deregulation, the energy crisis, and environmental strictures. The Staggers Act of 1980 allowed the railroads to set economic rates after decades of inadequate returns just as the energy crisis favored the low energy requirements of rail transportation and as environmental regulations pushed utilities into using low-sulfur Western coal. I examined the Railroad industry in detail in chapter 5, and only note here that its principal credit improvement was in cash flow as a percentage of debt, rather than other ratios.

Truckers had the most substantial credit improvement among the regulated industries, as their credit ratios rose 49%. They were alone among the regulated industries in being modestly leveraged. Their improvement reflected both the decline in energy prices after 1982 and the flexibility of deregulation for truckers specializing in less-than-truckload shipments. Four of the five companies in the S&P Truckers index in 1979 were in this category. By contrast, the one truckload company in the index, McLean Trucking, and other companies like it, experienced severe credit deterioration due to price-cutting and excess capacity as new, small truckers entered their market. McLean was acquired in 1982 and removed from the index.

Auto-Related Industries

Several auto-related industries had cyclical credit quality recoveries between 1979 and 1984 that qualified them as improving industries: engines and turbines, Auto Parts—Original Equipment, and Tires and Rubber Goods. The apparent 87% improvement in credit ratios for the engines and turbines industry was fortuitous, reflecting unusual profits in 1984. A comparison between 1979 and 1985 would have produced an improvement of 23%. However, in either case its credit ratios were strong. Auto Parts—Original Equipment also had a meaningful improvement and absolutely strong ratios across the board. The Tire and Rubber Goods industry, however, only looked up because it had been down so far. It had never recovered from the energy crisis and deep recession of 1974–1975. Return on equity was under 10% every year from 1973 to 1983 and averaged only 6%. It exceeded 10% in 1984, when EBIT return on capitalization was still a weak 13.9%, and was followed by a deficit in 1985. The industry was contracting throughout 1978 to 1984 as its total assets declined 23% despite high inflation. Fortunately its debt declined 53%, which produced improved credit ratios, but the industry was hardly an improving credit.

Other Industries

Two electronics industries—Electrical Equipment and Electronics (Instrumentation)—showed significant credit improvement. Despite these industries' dependence on capital spending, their improvement was secular rather than cyclical, reflecting technological developments and a high incidence of strong management. Both industries had modest leverage.

Five consumer-related industries had improving credits: Restaurants, Department Stores, Beer, Tobacco, and Household Furnishings & Appliances. Restaurants reflected McDonald's expansion and the general spread of fast food outlets. Department Stores had a cyclical recovery, as I have already noted in chapter 5. The Beer industry's ratios reflected the improved management brought to Anheuser-Busch by August Belmont III. The Tobacco industry's ratios reflected the management dynamism of Philip Morris. Household Furnishings & Appliances had a cyclical recovery.

The Junk Bond Market

Junk bonds played a very modest role in lowering corporate credit ratios between 1979 and 1984. The pioneering public issues of junk bonds were in 1977 when Lehman Brothers underwrote issues for LTV, Pan American Airlines, Zapata Corporation, and Fuqua Industries. In the subsequent terminology of this market, these were "fallen angels"—once creditworthy companies that were now in financial distress. There had always been a market for such issuers, but traditionally it had been privately with major insurance companies that could negotiate highly protective covenants as part of the financing. Lehman Brothers' innovation was to recognize the appetite for high yields in the public market at a time when credit was easy and interest rates were low; but Lehman was serving established clients and was not motivated to turn junk bonds into a new line of business.

It took Michael Milken to do that. Prior to 1977, Milken's group at Drexel Burnham was focused on secondary markets rather than underwriting. Milken had carved out a unique niche in the low-grade bond world. He was one of a relatively small group of bankruptcy investors, an esoteric but established investment practice, and steeped in the credit values of the "chinese paper" issued by conglomerates such as Leasco, Rapid American, and LTV in the takeover wave of the 1960s—a much more unique investment area with few if any competitors. Thus, his knowledge crossed over from the bankruptcy market, where expertise was based on evaluating court procedures, recapitalization plans, and business projections, to low-grade credits, where values were based on very careful research and a good sense of the odds of business continuity. David Durand had pointed out years earlier in his exhaustive study of the corporate bond market that institutions were very resistant to holding bankrupt or near-bankrupt bonds, which made the market imperfect and the returns in the two years following bankruptcy filings approximately 25%. Milken saw that this was also true of "chinese paper" and other low-grade bonds issued in the merger market. He was clearly the best in this business. He was already earning $5 million a year in 1977, and had attracted some of the shrewdest investors, such as Larry Tisch of Loew's Corporation, Saul Steinberg of Reliance Insurance, and Carl Lindner of American Financial Corp.

The returns in Milken's business were not based on the simple mathematics of higher interest rates for higher risk, nor was he promoting long-term investing. He was essentially in the risk arbitrage business, investing for capital gains—the quicker the better—based on intensive research (for which he became famous) and careful understanding of bankruptcy laws and procedures. His was a trading business, much more like equities than bonds. Reorganizations, recapitalizations, debt exchanges, liquidations, and bets on the economic recovery of highly leveraged companies were his basic business—not an adjunct to it. I do not know enough about his early business to describe the details of it, but I can easily surmise from the practices of other successful firms in that market and the investors he attracted that his portfolios were highly leveraged, and that his returns probably exceeded 30% per annum.

In 1977, when Michael Milken linked up with Fred Joseph, then head of Drexel Burnham's corporate finance department, to underwrite junk bonds for small, previously unrated companies, he was personally branching out into a new and simpler business of higher interest rates for higher risk, rather than arbitrage; but in a narrower sense he was simply transferring business from the private to the public markets. There had always been a private placement market for such companies, mostly with insurance companies. The *Private Placement Directory* of the *Investment Dealers Digest* in the 1970s is replete with transactions from $500,000 to $20 million for companies without bond ratings whose names evoke little public recognition, many of them privately owned. The Prudential Insurance Company in the 1960s and 1970s had a regionally dispersed sales force dedicated solely to calling on such companies, not to sell them insurance, but to lend them money. These were the companies for which Drexel Burnham now sought to sell bonds publicly. There was also a large number of companies in financial trouble in the early 1980s, as we have already seen, providing a ready market for Milken's bankruptcy investing skills. Bringing low-rated and distressed companies' bonds to the public market simply required a minor firm that could present credible public underwriting capability in competition with the traditional private placement activities of the major firms. Milken and Drexel Burnham provided that capability.

Drexel's combination of Milken's skills and a focus that other firms did not have quickly led Drexel to the top spot as lead underwriter of junk bonds in 1978 with 34% of the market. Thereafter, Drexel dominated junk bond underwriting. It ranked first as lead underwriter of junk bond issues every year from 1978 to 1989 except 1980, and its share of the market was unlike any other investment banking market. Most years it led 50% of the offerings, and occasionally 70%, while the changing second-ranked firms rarely managed over 15%. Leadership of this market at the turn of the decade was of modest significance, however. New-issue underwriting volume averaged only 2.8% of total corporate bond underwritings from 1980 to 1982.

The early junk bond issuers offered a sensible balance of risk and reward. Over 25% of the earliest junk bonds issued in 1978 and 1979 were sold in unit offerings in which investors also received equity participation. The equity participation declined from 1980 to 1982, but the credit ratios were sustainable, as can be seen in table 8.9.[23] EBIT coverage of interest was approximately 2.0 times, funds from operations (net income plus depreciation plus deferred taxes) was approximately 19% of debt, and common equity was approximately 36% of capitalization. These early issuers were predominantly weak manufacturers such as LTV, Republic Steel, Jim Walter Corp., Mattel, and General Tire; lesser oil and gas companies such as Petro Lewis, Global Marine, and Forest Oil; en-

Table 8.9. Pro-forma Credit Ratios for New-Issue Junk Bonds

Year	Amount ($B)	EBIT/Int	Funds from Operations as % Debt	% Common Equity	% for M&A
1980	0.9	2.0	17%	39%	11%
1981	1.2	2.0	22%	35%	5%
1982	1.5	2.1	18%	18%	13%
1983	3.6	0.8	13%	13%	22%
1984	7.4	1.1	7%	7%	45%

Source: Barrie A. Wigmore, "The Decline in Credit Quality of New-Issue Junk Bonds," *The Financial Analysts Journal*, September/October 1990, Table 1.

tertainment and gambling companies such as Twentieth Century Fox, Lorimar, and Golden Nugget; numerous cable television companies such as Storer Broadcasting; MGM/UA, Telecommunications Inc., and Turner Broadcasting; airlines such as Eastern Airlines, Pan Am, and Texas International; and health care companies such as Humana and Charter Medical. The amount of junk bond financing for acquisitions was only $100–200 million from 1980 to 1982.

It was not until 1983 that credit ratios for junk bond new issues declined to unsustainable levels. EBIT coverage of interest dropped to 0.8 times—less than enough to cover current interest obligations—and only 1.1 times in 1984. Funds from operations dropped from 19% of debt from 1980 to 1982 to 7% in 1984. At the same time, issues for acquisition purposes rose from 10% of new issues during 1980 to 1982 to 22% in 1983 and 45% in 1984. I will examine in detail in chapter 9 how these low coverage ratios stimulated the merger boom.

The concept of higher yield for higher risk was meaningful in the late 1970s, and the roughly 6% returns in conventional debt and equities during the 1970s made investors susceptible to the search for higher returns. Six percent was a historically low return, and exceedingly discouraging in light of CPI inflation averaging 7.4%.[24] Junk bonds that had rates 5–6% above treasury returns and an annual default experience of only 1.5%[25] looked like a viable alternative that might actually beat inflation.

Investors had a successful example of this approach in a group of mutual funds that invested in lower grade bonds and achieved attractive absolute and relative returns as interest rates declined and the economy recovered during 1975 to 1976. Among the earliest participants in the junk bond market, First Investors Fund for Income earned 39.2% in 1975 and 40.4% in 1976, Lord Abbett's Bond-Debenture Fund earned 29.8% and 30.9%, and Keystone's Discount Bond Fund (B-4) earned 25.1% and 26.8%. These returns greatly exceeded the contemporaneous returns of 9.2% and 16.8% in long-term government bonds and 14.6% and 18.6% in long-term corporate bonds, and equaled the 37.2% and 23.8% returns

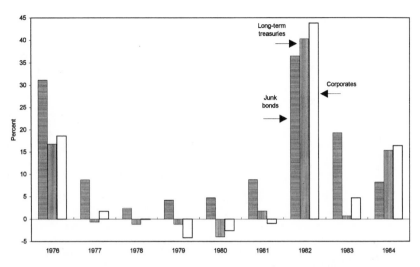

Figure 8.2 Comparative bond returns. Sources: Ibbotson Associates and Weisenberger Investment Companies Service.

in common stocks.[26] In response, assets of First Investors Fund for Income surged from $43.4 million in 1974 to $363 million by the end of 1977. Keystone's Discount Bond Fund grew from $237 to $477 million. Lord Abbett's Bond-Debenture Fund grew from $102 to $182 million.

This success led mutual fund organizations and investment bankers to sponsor a rash of new mutual funds specializing in junk bonds between 1977 and 1979: American Capital High Yield, Cigna High Yield, Dean Witter High Yield, Federated High Income, Fidelity High Income, Merrill Lynch High Income, Oppenheimer High Yield, PruBache High Yield, Putnam High Yield, United High Income, and Vanguard High Yield. Drexel Burnham managed offerings of two funds (High Yield Securities Inc. and Kemper High Yield Fund Inc.), but they only aggregated $175 million, which was not particularly significant.

Returns for this expanded universe of junk bond funds suffered along with the general bond market during 1979–1981, but the funds still outperformed the corporate and treasury markets, as can be seen in figure 8.2. Returns on junk bond mutual funds averaged 10.0% from 1976 to 1981, versus only 1.9% on long-term governments and 2.1% on long-term corporates.[27] The 36.5% return in 1982 was modestly lower than returns on corporate bonds and long-term treasuries, but the 19.3% returns in 1983 were dramatically above the returns of 0.7% on long-term treasuries and 4.7% on corporate bonds. It was not until 1984 and 1985, when junk bond volume was surging to finance mergers, and when credit quality of new-issues was declining sharply, that junk bond mutual fund returns fell below corporate bonds and long-term treasuries—7.5% in

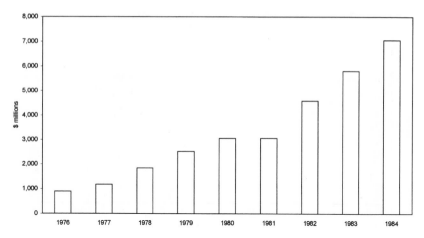

Figure 8.3 Junk bond mutual fund assets (year-end). Source: Weisenberger Investment Companies Service.

1984 versus 16.4% and 15.5%, respectively, and 20.1% in 1985 versus 30.9% and 31.0%, respectively. The returns for individual funds are outlined in appendix 8.2 at the end of this chapter.

Investments in the established junk bond mutual funds rose steadily, as can be seen in figure 8.3. Junk bond mutual fund assets grew from approximately $894 million in seven funds in 1976 to $7.1 billion in twenty-six funds in 1984.[28] Assets for the individual funds from 1976 to 1985 are outlined in appendix 8.3 at the end of this chapter.

Mutual funds were a vital part of the junk bond story, but one insurance company stood out among junk bond investors—Fred Carr's Los Angeles-based First Executive Corp., which held $4.8 billion of junk bonds by the end of 1984.[29] Carr had been a superstar stockpicker at Enterprise Fund in the "go-go years" of mutual fund management in the late 1960s, but left in disrepute as the fund suffered in performance and was temporarily closed down by the SEC. He took over First Executive Corp. in 1974 when it was on the verge of bankruptcy, and led it into super growth by selling high-yielding single premium deferred annuities through retail brokers such as E. F. Hutton, Dean Witter Reynolds, and Shearson/American Express, and investing the proceeds in junk bonds.[30] Single premium deferred annuities were essentially a scheme to earn tax-free corporate bond yields through the untaxed vehicle of life insurance. Carr spiced this up by offering high yields based on junk bonds. First Executive's premium revenues soared from $20 million in 1976 to $1.1 billion in 1981, its assets rose from $91 million to $1.1 billion, and net income rose from $424 thousand to $35 million.

Carr's investment strategy was simple—buy junk bonds for yield and hold money market assets for liquidity. His junk bond holdings rose from $385 million in 1980 to $4.8 billion in 1984, which was 82% of his total portfolio. Short-term investments were more variable. They were $1.2 billion and 36.7% of the portfolio at the end of 1982, when First Executive's liquidity was threatened by the credit problems of its principal competitor, Baldwin-United. By the end of 1984, when the portfolio was larger and the business felt secure, short-term investments were down to $534 million and 9.5% of the portfolio.[31] First Executive was unusual in its close relationship with Drexel Burnham. It kept an employee on Drexel's Los Angeles bond desk and apparently gave Drexel total discretion over junk bond transactions.[32]

Other important insurance companies investing in junk bonds were The Prudential, CNA Insurance, Reliance Insurance, American Financial, and Presidential Life. These insurance companies were no pawns of Drexel, however. The Prudential was one of America's leading insurance companies, and Larry Tisch, Saul Steinberg, and Carl Lindner, who ran the three casualty companies, were highly independent, sophisticated, and diversified investors. But Carr dwarfed the junk bond investment activities of these companies. Their junk bond investments probably aggregated only $600 million at the end of 1984.[33]

Savings and loans entered the junk bond market several years after the initial mutual fund and insurance company participants when two acts of Congress set the stage for massive savings and loan expansion. In 1980, the Depository Institutions Deregulation and Monetary Control Act raised all deposit insurance to $100,000 and lowered minimum capital requirements from 5% to 3%.[34] In 1982, the Garn-St. Germain Depository Institutions Act permitted savings and loans to invest up to 11% of their total assets in corporate debt,[35] 30% in credit card and consumer loan receivables, and 40% in commercial real estate loans. In case thrifts didn't get the expansion message, the act created a set of regulatory accounting rules inconsistent with GAAP accounting rules that treated subordinated debentures and loans from the Federal Home Loan Banks as net worth, permitted long-term amortization of losses on the sale of low-yielding mortgages, and encouraged writing up headquarters assets to market value. The stage was set for large-scale expansion of both brokered deposits and unconventional assets such as junk bonds, mortgage-backed securities, and commercial real estate.

Tom Spiegel's Columbia Savings & Loan (California) was the first savings and loan to invest massively in junk bonds. Purchased by his father in 1974 when its assets were only $42 million, Columbia was in serious trouble by 1981 when it lost $3 million and the two Spiegels personally bought $43 million of a $60 million issue of equity-linked subordinated debentures to maintain the company's capital. Freed in 1982 of Regulation Q restrictions on its deposit rates, and armed with a $100,000 FSLIC guarantee, Columbia set out on a massive growth strategy, marketing high-yield, multiyear deposits nationwide through brokers and funding the deposits with junk bonds and mortgage pass-through securities. Between 1981 and 1984, its assets grew from $373 million to $6.4 billion, its junk bond investments grew from under $46 million to $1.7 billion, and its net earnings grew from a $3 million loss to $44 million in profits. Columbia's return on equity soared to 114% in 1982 and 81% in 1983.[36]

Tom Spiegel, like Fred Carr at First Executive Corp., was particularly under Michael Milken's sway. We do not have the details of Columbia's junk bond portfolio, but the issues cited in the 1984 annual report were all Drexel Burnham issues: Lorimar, MCI, McCrory, Occidental Petroleum, Trans World Airlines, Blue Bell, Days Inns of America, and Metromedia Broadcasting Corp.[37]

Just as other mutual funds in the late 1970s followed the leaders into junk bonds, the example of Columbia's high returns had irresistible appeal to the more aggressive managers in the savings and loan industry. Gibraltar Savings & Loan had $532 million in junk bonds at the end of 1984, and Imperial Savings & Loan had $142 million. David Paul, who gained control of Miami-based Centrust Savings Bank in November 1983 after three years of losses totaling $63 million, expanded Centrust's assets almost 50%, established junk bond holdings of $626 million, and moved from a $10 million loss in 1983 to apparent profits of $93 million and an 89% return on equity in 1985.[38] Charles Keating took over Lincoln Savings & Loan in February 1984 and switched virtually all of its activities to real estate development and speculative investments, including $183 million worth of junk bonds at the end of 1984.[39] Other savings and loans invested in junk bonds on a lesser scale. In aggregate, savings and loans held approximately $3.5 billion of junk bonds by the end of 1984—half that of the mutual funds—but they were distinctive for the control Milken appeared to exercise over their junk bond investments and their insensitivity to buying some of the riskiest of these issues.

There were other investors in junk bonds, especially as time went on and intermediaries were forced by competitive pressures to offer high-yield products, but the investors outlined above accounted for almost all of the market, as can be seen in table 8.10. The mutual fund, insurance, and savings and loan sectors held $16.8 billion at the end of 1984,[40] which equaled 116% of the $14.6 billion of underwritten issues from 1980 to 1984. Of course, there were junk bonds that were placed privately rather than underwritten, as well as the "fallen angels" and "chinese paper" of the original junk bond market, but new issues accounted for most of the market by 1984.

There were frequent rumors about the fabulous size of Drexel's junk bond inventory, but at the end of 1984 it is unlikely that Drexel held more than $900 million of junk bonds, assuming they were 75% of

Table 8.10. Major Holders of Junk Bonds (1984)

Institution	$ Bill.	% of U/W Issues 1980–1984[1]
Mutual Funds	7.1	48.6%
Insurance Companies[2]	5.4	37.0%
Savings & Loans	3.5	24.0%
Drexel Burnham[3]	0.9	5.9%
Totals	16.9	115.5%

[1]Total of $14.6 billion.
[2]Assumes 20% of corporate bond investments of CNA, Reliance, American Financial, and Presidential Life were junk, and all of Executive Life's.
[3]Assumes 75% of Drexel's corporate bond inventory was junk.

Drexel's reported corporate bond inventory of $1.1 billion. This was only 6% of new-issue volume between 1980 and 1984.

The surge in junk bond investments sharply reduced the relative yields on junk bonds, as can be seen in figure 8.4, which outlines the premium over Moody's index of Baa corporate bond yields for monthly average offering yields (unweighted) on straight B/B rated junk bond new-issues on a rolling six-month basis.* B/B rated issues were approximately two-thirds of all junk bond new issues. The yield premiums on B/B new issues declined from 2.5 to 3.0 percentage points in 1979 (in 1978, too, which is not shown), to 2.0 percentage points from 1980 to 1982, and to only 1.5 percentage points in 1984. In 1983 the premium was down to .5 percentage points, or less. The volume of funds available also encouraged a decline in credit standards as I have already noted above. This was only the first stage of an explosion in junk bond issues that had the attributes of a mania, and that profoundly affected American industry, as we shall see in volume 2.

How much the surge in junk bond new-issues in 1983 and 1984 was due to expanded savings and loan powers and the merger boom and how dependent it was on under-the-table incentives to money managers will probably never be resolved. At the same time that academics were praising the logic of a new market that provided higher returns for higher risk, competitors were gossiping about Drexel's hold over the largest junk bond investors, its insistence that junk bond issuers invest some of their proceeds in other Drexel issues, and the personal rewards it was providing to issuers and money managers. I myself heard frequent accusations

---

*I created the B/B index using the unweighted monthly average of the offered yields on all underwritten new issues rated B/B (subscripts are ignored) of any maturity. Convertibles, unit offerings, and floating rate notes are excluded. Numerous months had no issues. The number of issues rose dramatically in 1983 and 1984.

Figure 8.4 B index yield spreads over Baa rates (percentage points—moving six-month averages). Sources: IDD Data and author.

that Drexel's junk bond prowess depended on associations with a small circle of key investors who were willing to buy very poor credits because of side deals they received personally. It was difficult at the time to distinguish between the truth and sour grapes. Milken was subsequently convicted of six securities felonies, and the prosecutors cited thirty-nine criminal transactions in his sentencing proceedings; however, only four of these citations were for events prior to 1985 and none of them involved junk bonds.[41] Milken's conviction depended heavily on evidence from Ivan Boesky, who was himself convicted on insider trading charges in 1986.

The key event in Drexel's transition into illegal activities appears to have been its November 1983 decision to use its junk bond skills to foment corporate takeovers. The Drexel-Boesky relationship, which relied on inside information about mergers, began the following month. No corruption prior to 1984 is suggested by Connie Bruck in her critical book *The Predators' Ball*, or by Dan Stone in *April Fools*, his inside account of Drexel, or by James Stewart in *Den of Thieves*.

The corrupt side deals that later became evident, particularly in unit deals in which Milken reserved the equity participations for himself and others, were barely visible prior to 1984. Drexel Burnham only managed ten unit deals between 1978 and 1982 and showed no particular propensity for them. The earliest side deal with investors that I can document was in 1983, when Fred Carr and Saul Steinberg invested in a Milken partnership for the leveraged buyout of Harris Graphics from Harris Corp.[42]

However, it may well be that Milken simply wasn't caught at this early stage. The SEC launched three separate investigations into Drexel's practices in 1979, 1982, and early 1984, based on frequent rumors of corrupt relationships. The findings of these investigations are not available.

A broader view suggests that Drexel's junk bond prowess was based on expertise. Prior to 1984 most outstanding bonds were "fallen angels" or "chinese paper" from the 1960s merger boom. Research and judgment counted for more than inside information, and the new-issue business was not large enough to dominate the investment opportunities in the secondary market. The principal investors in junk bonds were also too diverse and independent a group to suggest that their activities involved widespread corruption. The twenty-six mutual funds dedicated to junk bonds by 1984 were sponsored by many of the most prominent money managers in America, such as Cigna, Dean Witter, Federated Funds, Fidelity Investments, Kemper, Keystone, Lord Abbett, Mass Financial, Merrill Lynch, Oppenheimer, PruBache, Putnam Funds, Shearson, United Funds, and Vanguard Funds. The Prudential and CNA Insurance were equally unsusceptible to corruption. Saul Steinberg at Reliance Insurance and Carl Lindner at American Financial had reputations for treading a fine legal line, but they were astute investors whose personal fortunes were tied up in their insurance companies and who were unlikely to be seduced into investments from which they didn't expect to profit.

Based on the government's case against Michael Milken, most of his illegal acts were related to mergers rather than junk bonds. None of the thirty-nine crimes cited in the government's sentencing memorandum involved junk bonds directly, three appear to have involved stripping warrants out of issues for self-enrichment, but twenty-four involved stock market transactions related to mergers.

Corporate Bond Returns, Yield Spreads, and Maturities

I need to digress momentarily from my broad theme of the relationship between the elements of the new regime and the bond market to consider three technical aspects of the corporate bond market: the difficulty in determining corporate bond returns when they are not adjusted for changing bond ratings, the tendency for Baa yield spreads to widen when risk was declining rather than vice versa, and the general shortening of corporate bond maturities.

As the reader would expect, corporate bond returns tracked treasury returns quite closely during 1977–1984. Total returns (log basis) on Sa-

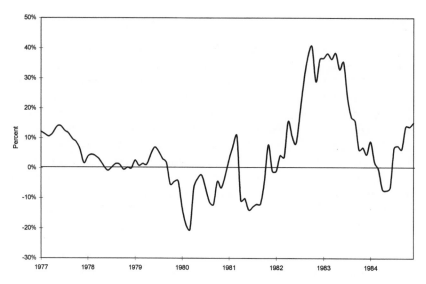

Figure 8.5 Corporate bonds log total returns (rolling twelve months). Source: Ibbotson Associates.

lomon Inc.'s High Grade Bond Index, outlined in figure 8.5, were zero or slightly negative from 1978 to 1981, then surged to 36% in 1982 as the Federal Reserve lowered interest rates. Returns dropped to 4.6% in 1983 as the Federal Reserve raised rates again, and then recovered to 15.2% in 1984 as it reduced them.

The index in figure 8.6 shows the persistent drought for corporate bond investors from 1/77 to 6/82, during which there were no returns at all, even on a nominal basis. The index was 173 in December 1976 and still 172 in June 1982. On the face of it, however, corporate bond returns were superior to treasury bonds between 1979 and 1984. Salomon Brothers' long-term high-grade corporate bond index indicated a compound annual return of 11.1% versus a return of 9.8% on long-term treasuries. On an index basis for this period, corporates rose 81% versus 72% for long-term treasuries. Returns in 1982 were equal to 74% of the total returns between 1979 and 1984, as can be inferred from figure 8.6.[43]

However, the actual returns on corporate bonds between 1979 and 1984 are more complicated to analyze than this data suggests. The Salomon Brothers index covers almost all Aaa and Aa corporate bonds, but removes bonds whose ratings were reduced below this. Altman and Kao have shown that a large proportion of high-grade issues were downgraded during this period. For new issues during 1977–1982, 46.7% of the Aaa bonds experienced ratings reductions within the next five years, as did 32.8% of the Aa bonds. Reductions over ten years were 73.9% for Aaa bonds and 53.7% for Aa bonds.[44] Thus, taking ratings changes out

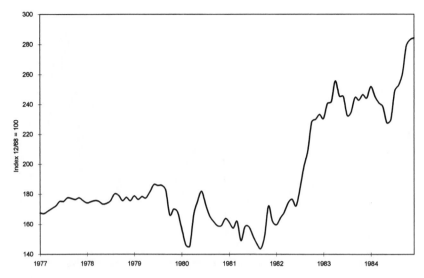

Figure 8.6 Corporate bond total return index (12/68 = 100). Source: Ibbotson Associates.

of total return results is severely misleading for calculating long-period returns.

Ratings changes also affected returns on Baa-rated issues, although in this case they benefited from numerous ratings upgrades. Over 16% of Baa-rated new issues between 1977 and 1982 were upgraded within the next five years and 47.0% were upgraded within ten years.[45] Since Baa-rated issues carried 10–20% yield premiums over Aaa issues, and had substantial net upgrading advantages, they obviously outperformed other high-grade corporate issues. Unfortunately, we do not have a total return index for Baa-rated issues for this period, let alone an index that is adjusted for ratings changes.

Yield Spreads

The traditional lore among both investors and academics is that the rates for lesser credits rise relative to better credits in periods of tight credit, reflecting the greater risk environment. In market parlance, yield spreads widen. The reader can see in figure 8.7 that there were pronounced peaks in the absolute spreads for Baa over Aa corporate bond yields during 1970–1971, 1974–1975, in 1980, and in 1982. The peak yield spreads were approximately 100 basis points in 1970, 170 in 1975, 130 in 1980, and 180 in 1982. There is a natural tendency in looking at figure 8.7 to assume that the higher yield spreads reflected increased risk due to the Federal Reserve's tight money policies. However, all of these peaks oc-

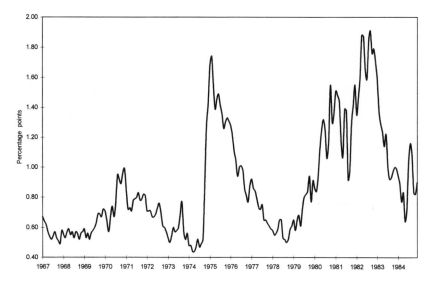

Figure 8.7 Baa yield spreads over Aa rates (seasoned bonds—percentage points). Source: Moody's Investors Services, Inc.

curred when rates declined after periods of tight money, rather than when rates were rising; in other words, peaks occurred when the risk environment was declining. Similarly, the periods of lowest spreads in 1974, 1978, and 1984 occurred when rates were rising sharply and the risk environment increasing. Therefore, Baa-Aa yield spreads reflected the lag between the better and lesser credits rather than changing risk perceptions. Baa rates consistently lagged Aa rates because of technical factors, such as smaller Baa issues, less well known issuers, fewer buyers (especially among state and local retirement funds), and smaller dealer inventories.

Corporate Maturities

There was a profound secular change in the average maturities of corporate bonds during the early 1980s, as can be seen in figure 8.8. In the 1970s, America was rightly celebrated for having the last truly long-term bond market. In 1978, the volume-weighted average life of corporate bond new-issues in the United States was over twenty years,[46] whereas European bond markets were limited to five- to seven-year maturities. In the ensuing years, maturities in the United States were shortened dramatically to an average of 10.6 years in 1982. They remained at this level until 1987, when they began to shorten even further until they stabilized at approximately six years during 1989–1990. This change reflected that U.S. corporations began to issue bonds more heavily in the Eurobond market, and that the medium-term note (MTN) market expanded from

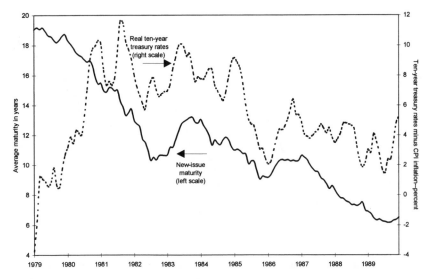

Figure 8.8 Average maturities (rolling twelve months) of corporate new issues and real ten-year treasury rates. Sources: IDD Data, Bureau of Labor Statistics, and Federal Reserve.

a small, private placement market into a large public market, facilitated by SEC "shelf" regulations that allowed issues to be sold on a continuous basis at varying prices. The combined share of total corporate public debt funding from the Eurobond and MTN markets, outlined in figure 8.9, rose from 11% in 1979 to a peak of 34% in 1982 in concert with rising interest rates; but then after a decline to 20% in 1983 when interest rates were lower, Eurobond and MTN issues surged to 43% of new issues in 1985 and approximately 50% from 1988 to 1990.

I have no explanation for the decline in corporate bond maturities. It may have been related to the very high real interest rates that prevailed in 1980 to 1985, as can be seen in figure 8.8 as well, but as these rates declined in 1985–1989, maturities perversely declined also. Declining maturities were not related to the decline in corporate credit quality; it was the highest quality issuers that were shortening their maturities. The Aaa and Aa issuers dominated the Eurobond and medium-term note markets, while Baa and lesser-rated issuers had only token participation. It is also difficult to explain the trend in terms of corporate treasurers selecting shorter maturities because of expectations of lower future interest rates. Unlike treasury securities, almost all corporate bonds were callable after either five years (utilities and telephones) or ten years, so there was very little logic in giving up the options of a long maturity if rates rose but calling the bonds if rates declined. Unfortunately, we do not have a theoretical framework in which to expeditiously assess the

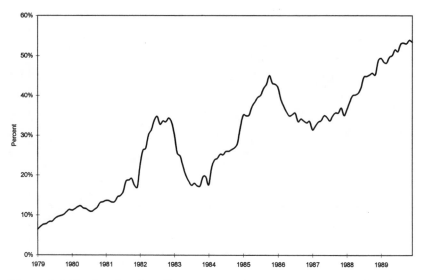

Figure 8.9 Eurobond and medium-term note issues as a percentage of total corporate new issues. Source: IDD Data.

economics of issuing consecutive medium-term securities versus callable long-term securities, nor did corporate treasurers have one at the time they made their decisions.*

The shift in corporate maturity preferences made the Eurobond market more competitive with the U.S. bond market than it had ever been before. The Eurobond market also offered the efficiency of no regulatory procedures. This put great pressure on U.S. investment banking firms to build up their European operations, and on the SEC to streamline its procedures, and was the first stage in the dramatic internationalization of securities markets, which I will note in volume 2.

---

*A corporate treasurer had to evaluate successive medium-term issues with bullet maturities, such as five-year issues rolled over every five years, at interest rates 50–150 basis points below long-term rates, versus a twenty-five- or thirty-year issue callable at a premium after five or ten years, but also subject to sinking fund redemptions of 4–5% annually at par beginning in the sixth or eleventh year. These sinking funds usually could be increased 100–150% at the issuer's option, providing additional issuer flexibility if rates had fallen. In practice, issuers confronted these options by considering the present value costs under three or four interest rate scenarios and making an intuitive choice. I have never seen the substantial option value inherent in both the call provision and the discretionary increase in the sinking fund quantified in practice.

Summary

The corporate bond market bore the brunt of the price that was paid in getting inflation down to 4%. Macroeconomic industrial credit ratios as reflected in tax data, Compustat, or Standard & Poor's Industrial index indicated a 20–30% decline in credit ratios, but the lowest quartile of industries suffered a 52% decline. Their interest coverage declined a shocking 74%. The same oil-related, metals, commodities, and heavy equipment industries dominated this group that appeared in the underperforming stock group. There were also credit crises in the auto, electric utility, and farm industries. All told, the fifteen industries making up the lowest quartile of declining credits and the auto and electric utility industries accounted for 53% of publicly issued, nonfinancial corporate debt between 1970 and 1984.

Recovery from these crises was not a free-market result. Chrysler Corp. received a $1.5 billion federal loan guarantee on the condition of $2.5 billion in additional benefits from other governments, banks, suppliers, dealers, and unions, and the whole auto industry was aided by auto import quotas and reduced gas mileage and environmental requirements. The electric utility industry received almost $10 billion in indirect aid for nuclear power plant construction through the Rural Electrification Administration and substantial rate relief from state regulators. In the case of the Washington Public Power Supply System, where rate relief wasn't available, there was a record $2.25 billion bankruptcy. The farm industry's problems totally disrupted the Farm Credit Administration, which had to be reorganized and refinanced in 1985.

The junk bond market evolved in this period from its early arbitrage origins, when credit measures were sustainable and returns superior to treasuries and other corporate bonds into a merger-financing tool with credit ratios barely half of those previously. As we shall see in the next chapter, it and the changing circumstances in the oil industry were catalyzed into a fourfold expansion of the merger market by the Reagan administration's historic relaxation of the antitrust regulations.

Appendix 8.1   Technical Notes on the Industry Credit Comparisons

Industry data for the above credit comparisons are drawn from industry aggregates in the Standard & Poor's 500 and Compustat, trade associations, and government reports. All of the data sources have inconsistencies and inconveniences, but these can be minimized by choosing carefully among sources. The Standard & Poor's data was the preferred source because of its popularity among investors, easy accessibility for readers, and comprehensive history. It also rarely includes foreign companies, whereas the Compustat industry aggregates frequently did. For simplicity's sake, two S&P industries were combined by simply averaging their credit ratios for Oil-Integrated—Domestic and Oil-Integrated—International, and for Paper and Forest Products.

Standard & Poor's alone was inadequate, however. It lacked certain industries, such as Heavy Construction and Advertising. Some industries were inartfully defined, such as Natural Gas Distributors. It also lacked balance sheet and income statement data for the transportation industries prior to 1983, and created a new Telephone index in 1984. In these cases other sources were used.

Compustat data was not used as a first choice, despite the fact that Compustat generously provided me with extensive industry data back to 1979. Compustat is disaggregated into too many industries—261—for my broad purposes. It also includes too many foreign companies, and there is frequently no data for the early 1980s.

I have tried to maintain consistent data sources between the credit and stock market industry comparisons of this and prior chapters, but this was not possible when the stock comparisons used Value Line. Value Line does not provide data for credit comparisons.

A few Standard & Poor's industries were excluded from the comparisons because they were small—Distillers (also too foreign), Communications Equipment (also too foreign), Coal, Fertilizer, Gold (also too foreign), Hardware, Homebuilding, Leisure, Manufactured Housing, Miscellaneous Retail, Toys, and Air Freight. Their aggregate market capitalization at the end of 1979 was only 3.1% of the S&P 500.

Neither Standard & Poor's nor Compustat have leveraged buyouts in their data, which skews it towards less leverage than occurred in the larger economy.

There is no alternative to the lack of data on cable TV, cellular telephones, computer software, and biotechnology at this stage of my study.

All industry aggregates involve companies entering and disappearing from the industry. For my purposes, this is not a disadvantage. I want to capture changes of this type in a particular industry. It is more problematic when meaningful industry aggregates disappear due to acquisitions, leveraged buyouts, or economic decline. This almost happened to the metal mining industry, and did happen after 1984 to Tire and Rubbber Goods, Fertilizers, Agricultural Machinery, Textile Products, and Homebuilding.

Comparisons of credit quality over time should be between similar phases of the business cycle. Most comparisons were between 1979 and 1984, which was from a cyclical peak to a relatively full recovery. The justification for treating 1984 as a cyclical peak was more fully outlined in

Appendix 8.2. Junk Bond Mutual Fund Returns (% per annum)

Fund	1976	1977	1978	1979	1980	1981	1982	1983	1984	1985
AGE High Income				4.0	1.4	6.0	27.7	17.5	8.2	18.4
American Capital High Yield				2.2	1.4	5.7	30.2	16.4	8.7	25.1
Bull & Bear High Yield									7.9	20.9
Bullock High Income Shares						7.8	24.5	19.5	6.4	15.4
Cigna High Yield Fund				3.3	1.0	7.1	31.7	17.5	9.8	23.5
Colonial High Yield	22.8	-1.6	4.6	7.7	0.3	6.4	24.6	20.4	10.5	21.8
Dean Witter High Yield					1.8	6.5	36.1	14.8	5.7	23.0
Federated High Income			1.0	6.6	2.7	3.9	32.5	14.5	10.8	21.7
Fidelity High Income			3.8	4.6	4.4	6.9	35.8	18.5	10.5	25.5
First Investors Fund for Income	41.4	12.0	0.2	6.6	4.9	8.0	19.8	13.2	2.1	20.0
High Yield Securities			0.4	4.5	3.5	7.3	30.5	19.4	5.6	17.9
Kemper High Yield Fund				2.4	-0.9	8.7	39.7	17.7	10.2	23.1
Keystone Discount Bond Fund	26.9	7.6	4.5	1.9	8.6	10.3	31.9	15.6	4.9	20.5
Lord Abbett Bond-Debenture Fund	30.9	6.9	2.9	7.0	8.9	5.3	27.5	16.6	5.0	21.0
Mass Financial High Income				6.8	5.3	7.3	35.8	26.7	6.4	23.1
Merrill Lynch Corporate Bond				2.4	3.0	6.6	23.1	18.3	8.6	21.6
Oppenheimer High Yield Fund				4.2	1.2	6.3	28.8	14.7	3.5	18.8
Phoenix High Yield						8.0	28.5	13.4	7.9	21.0
Pilgrim High Yield	26.2	10.0	0.6	3.2	0.4	7.8	30.0	11.7	10.6	14.6
Prudential Bache High Yield					4.9	4.0	28.1	15.7	10.2	20.6
Putnam High Yield Trust				2.8	7.0	5.3	38.9	15.6	7.7	19.9
Shearson High Yield						5.1	33.2	14.8	9.8	18.8
United High Income					7.8	5.3	32.7	14.0	9.6	23.3
Vanguard Fixed Income (HYP)				5.5	3.4	9.4	27.4	15.4	7.9	22.0
Averages	24.7	5.8	2.0	4.2	3.4	6.5	29.1	15.9	7.5	20.1
Weighted Averages	31.2	8.7	2.4	4.2	4.7	8.7	36.5	19.3	8.2	24.5

Source: Weisenberger Investment Companies Service, 1985 Edition.

Appendix 8.3. Junk Bond Mutual Fund Assets ($ millions)

Fund	1976	1977	1978	1979	1980	1981	1982	1983	1984	1985
AGE High Income	2.6	2.5	2.2	3.8	7.1	10.5	35.1	70.4	101.0	287.3
American Capital High Yield			103.6	205.8	236.7	233.5	327.5	365.5	395.4	504.4
Bull & Bear High Yield	2.9	2.9	2.8	2.8	3.6	3.2	4.4	5.3	4.4	6.3
Bullock High Income Shares					14.7	23.4	46.9	72.0	90.3	142.8
Cigna High Yield Fund			51.5	53.4	47.3	43.5	48.7	70.2	89.7	147.1
Colonial High Yield	35.9	29.8	25.4	27.2	35.8	41.2	62.5	75.3	94.9	132.3
Dean Witter High Yield				139.4	177.6	165.3	352.2	418.2	478.0	649.0
Federated High Income		36.6	47.4	55.1	57.6	57.2	96.3	155.2	162.3	251.4
Federated High Yield										17.3
Fidelity High Income			56.3	84.7	1.6.4	109.7	186.2	257.0	390.4	839.3
Financial Bond Shares High Yield										18.3
First Investors Fund for Income	222.6	362.8	443.8	522.4	565.4	540.6	650.7	851.2	968.7	1363.8
GIT Income Trust—Max Income			10.4					1.8	5.8	10.9
High Yield Securities		78.4	86.2	106.8	100.0	88.6	97.4	95.9	87.5	88.0
IDS Extra Income								2.6	280.2	587.2
Investment Portfolios High Yield										65.1
Kemper High Yield Fund			86.0	103.1	106.8	114.7	160.8	186.8	198.1	248.4
Keystone Discount Bond Fund	449.3	476.6	461.3	408.8	388.1	360.7	408.5	410.8	432.7	988.5
Lord Abbett Bond-Debenture Fund	174.8	181.9	182.1	180.1	176.3	163.0	186.7	203.3	203.1	299.3
Mass Financial High Income				43.0	113.8	113.3	223.3	326.5	375.8	567.6
Merrill Lynch Corporate Bond			111.8	173.1	239.0	215.1	228.7	244.2	238.9	327.1
Oppenheimer High Yield Fund			47.8	87.8	113.6	125.3	277.8	422.8	413.5	521.7
Paine Webber Fixed Inc High Yield										155.0
Phoenix High Yield					7.4	14.3	26.3	39.9	49.7	72.5
Pilgrim High Yield	5.4	6.4	6.2	6.7	6.8	6.5	7.3	7.7	9.8	12.4
Prudential Bache High Yield				52.8	63.6	62.5	172.5	225.1	257.9	687.4
Putnam High Yield Trust			112.9	216.2	268.4	277.3	441.1	570.2	757.8	1664.1

Appendix 8.3. (*continued*)

Fund	1976	1977	1978	1979	1980	1981	1982	1983	1984	1985
T. Rowe Price High Yied										357.7
Shearson High Yield					83.4	63.6	105.6	151.8	162.7	311.6
United High Income			44.6	128.3	217.9	396.4	478.7	588.6	939.8
Vanguard Fixed Income (HYP)				3.4	9.1	13.4	42.8	98.1	215.1	591.8
Totals	893.5	1,177.9	1,837.7	2,521.0	3,056.8	3,064.3	4,586.1	5,806.5	7,052.3	12,855.4
Count	7	9	17	21	24	24	24	26	26	31

Source: Weisenberger Investment Companies Service, 1985 Edition.

chapter 1. I used a 1978 base year for three S&P industries—Autos, Tire and Rubber Goods, and airlines—because results were superior to 1979. I did not have 1978 Compustat industry data. The oil-related industries peaked in 1980 because of rising oil prices, and I accordingly used 1980 data as their base year.

I have tried to focus on credit ratios that are used by rating agencies and financial market participants, although my ratios are more simply defined than those used by these professionals. The definitions are as follows:

1. EBIT—earnings before interest and taxes (after depreciation). Other nonoperating income was excluded. For utilities, the various forms of allowance for funds used during construction (which changed during the period) were excluded.
2. Interest—reported annual long and short-term interest. No adjustments were made for capitalized interest except for electric utilities, where it was excluded from operating income and included in interest. Capitalized interest, or AFUDC (allowance for funds used during construction), became so large for electric utilities, that financial market participants focused carefully on it and tended to treat it this way.
3. Capitalization—year-end short-term plus long-term debt, plus preferred stock, plus common equity. Deferred taxes and other liabilities were not included.
4. Funds from operations—annual net income for common stockholders plus depreciation and amortization plus deferred taxes.
5. Capital expenditures—annual capital expenditures as reported by S&P in *S&P's Analyst's Handbook,* from the flow of funds statement for Compustat, and as reported by trade associations or federal regulators.
6. Net capital expenditures—annual capital expenditures minus depreciation.
7. Market value equity—the twelve-month average of monthly closing common stock prices as reported by Standard & Poor's *Security Price Index Record.* For Compustat industries the monthly average was based on closing stock prices multiplied by year-end shares outstanding.
8. Common equity ratio—year-end common equity as a percentage of year-end capitalization including short-term debt.

Captive financial companies were not consolidated into parent company data until 1988. Therefore these subsidiaries' debt and interest do not enter into the 1979–1984 comparisons.

There was no effort to adjust for leases as a form of leverage, although they undoubtedly increased disproportionately in the 1980s.

Lower corporate income tax rates in this period should have lowered pretax credit ratios if competitive market forces led companies to pass on the benefits to consumers. No effort has been made to adjust for this effect.

9

The Merger and Acquisition Market

The sixfold growth in merger and acquisition volume from $25 billion in 1979 to $156 billion in 1989 was one of the most dynamic and noteworthy trends of the decade.[1] Similar merger explosions only occurred at the turn of the century, in the 1920s, and in the 1960s. The academic literature has debated whether the motives behind it were rationalizing industry and displacing inefficient management or executive self-aggrandizement or wealth transfers that created stockholder value at the expense of other stakeholders such as bondholders, employees, and communities. I propose to leave this issue until volume 2, when I can deal with the decade as a whole, and for the moment focus on the forces that struck practitioners at this early stage—a dramatic change in antitrust regulations by the Reagan administration, the dynamics of the oil industry, unprecedented leverage opportunities offered by the banks and the junk bond market, and the peculiar American institution of corporate raiders.

The new antitrust atmosphere permitted the number of mergers of $1 billion or more to rise from three in both 1979 and 1980 to nine in 1981 and nineteen in 1984, while the number of public companies acquired during 1981–1984 was actually 8.5% fewer than under President Carter. Among the ten largest transactions in 1984, 84% by value would have been subject to antitrust challenge without a change in the government's attitude.

Mergers and acquisitions related to the oil industry rose from 11% to almost one-third of the merger activity between 1979 and 1984 and were the hothouse for techniques employed elsewhere. At first, oil-related acquisitions reflected the sudden spendable wealth created by higher oil prices and the attractions of the industry to buyers, but as oil prices declined the companies became major targets for consolidation. Industry fundamentals also drove mergers, particularly nationalization of foreign crude oil sources, exhaustion of U.S. oil resources, and the divergence between stock market values and oil and gas finding costs.

A doubling in the amount of money that could be borrowed for a given transaction from either banks or the junk bond market also increased merger volume. The banks changed their credit standards dramatically in 1982 when they began lending for raids and leveraged buyouts at interest coverages of only 1.0 times or less, thereby making the average company highly susceptible to being acquired. In 1983 interest coverage ratios for new-issue junk bonds dropped below 1.0 times, stimulating a fivefold expansion in their volume between 1982 and 1984, 45% of which was for acquisitions, and their use as a threatening club in some of the largest transactions in history, most prominently the Mesa Petroleum attack on Gulf Oil and Sir James Goldsmith's attack on Continental Group. High leverage for either the acquirer or a raider instigating an acquisition grew from being an important factor for only 3% of the value of the top 100 acquisitions during 1979–1980 to approximately 25% during 1981–1983 and to 44% in 1984. Virtually all of the large oil industry mergers involved raiders who started the transactions employing high leverage.

High leverage stimulated the peculiarly American phenomenon of corporate raiders. Their profits rose tenfold in 1981-1982 and threefold again in 1984. Although their activities had hitherto been considered disreputable, now these people were lionized by academics and the media as opponents of corporate bureaucracy and representatives of stockholder interests. However, their aggregate activity through 1984 shows that they rarely consummated acquisitions.

The Pre-Reagan Merger Market

Acquisition activity accelerated well before the Reagan administration took office. The number of public companies acquired, outlined in figure 9.1, increased by 280% from 68 in 1974 to 260 in 1978, and the number of acquisitions with a value of $100 million or more, also outlined in figure 9.1, increased 140% from 39 in 1976 to 94 in 1980.[2] Symbolic of the change in atmosphere, and indeed the rules, was Morgan Stanley's decision in 1974 to conduct an unfriendly tender offer on behalf of International Nickel Company against ESB Inc. (the old Electric Storage Battery Company). Morgan Stanley thereby sanctioned what had hitherto been an unusual procedure for prominent investment bankers, who were

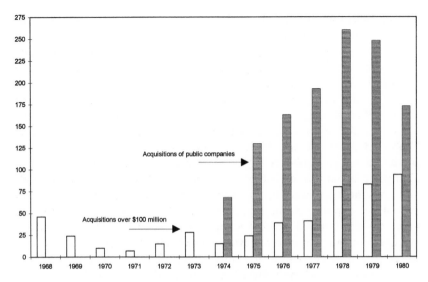

Figure 9.1 Numbers of acquisitions. Source: *Mergerstat Review*, 1989.

accustomed to decorous, fiduciary relationships with both clients and prospects. Morgan Stanley had a history of setting standards for the rest of Wall Street, so other investment bankers and corporate acquirers quickly accepted the opportunity to make unfriendly tenders. Unfriendly tenders greatly facilitated the ease of making acquisitions, both for the raiders and for "white knights," and thereafter were consistently 25–35% of all tender offers.[3]

Other factors attested to a new phase in the merger markets prior to the Reagan administration. The value of the 100 largest transactions doubled to $24.6 billion in 1979 from $12.4 billion in 1978,[4] as a number of large oil company transactions occurred in response to the rise in oil prices. Shell Oil paid $3.65 billion in 1979 for Belridge Oil, a little known California producer of heavy oil. That same year, Mobil Corp. bought General Crude Oil for $763 million. In 1980 Sun Company paid $2.3 billion for Texas Pacific Oil, Mobil paid $715 million for Esmark's Vickers Energy subsidiary, and Getty Oil paid $628 million for Reserve Oil & Gas.

Leveraged transactions also made a mark in 1979, when Kohlberg, Kravis, Roberts & Co. (KKR) made the first leveraged buyout of a public company, Houdaille Inc., and Victor Posner leveraged Sharon Steel up to 73% debt to buy U.V. Industries. However, it was not clear that these transactions indicated a trend. KKR took a year to arrange financing to buy Houdaille, and the transaction looked more like a specialized insurance company financing than a new trend. Victor Posner also seemed like an exception. An odd character himself, his companies were even odder.

Sharon Steel was a struggling steel company, and U.V. Industries was just coming out of bankruptcy.

A number of financial professionals intent on profiting from the merger market had also emerged during the late 1970s. When Kennecott Copper bought Carborundum Corp. in 1977 for $567 million, it suddenly faced a proxy fight from Roland Berner, the savvy chairman of Curtiss-Wright, who had earlier bought a 9.9% position in Kennecott's stock because he was attracted by Kennecott's profits from selling its Peabody Coal subsidiary. Berner was convinced that Kennecott was wasting its money (and his) in buying Carborundum and that he could run Kennecott better himself. After a bruising proxy battle, he signed a standstill agreement and went on the Kennecott board of directors along with two of his appointees, but he returned to the attack in 1981 when the standstill expired and realized a profit of $70 million when Kennecott bought him out. On a less elevated plane than Berner, Victor Posner, flush with his success in acquiring U.V. Industries, bought a position in Reliance Electric, so frightening the company that it willingly acceded to an offer from Exxon that made Posner $24 million. Carl Icahn, who had an independent New York Stock Exchange firm that mostly invested in arbitrage situations, sensed the new merger currents in 1979 and bought a threatening position in Tappan Company that he used to get on the board of directors and force the company's sale to Electrolux A.B., netting him $4.1 million. In 1980, when the Carter administration's credit controls inhibited borrowing for acquisitions, investors like Carl Icahn, Saul Steinberg, Clabir Corp., Irwin Jacobs, and Harold Simmons instead harassed corporations to buy back their threatening minority stock positions at premiums, creating a new variation on blackmail as well as coining a new word in the investment lexicon, "greenmail."

Despite these new merger currents of raids, oil company acquisitions, LBOs, and financial professionals stimulating mergers, the merger and acquisition activity of the late 1970s differed from what followed in important ways. In the late 1970s acquirers adding lines of business predominated, such as in acquisitions by General Electric, United Technologies, Beatrice Foods, R. J. Reynolds, Continental Group, and RCA. Simply reviewing the ten largest mergers each year from 1976 to 1980 in appendix 9.1, to which I will frequently return, gives a good sense of the mix of diversification and product line extension that prevailed. At least twenty-six of the fifty transactions represented new lines of business for the acquirers. In large part, this acquisition pattern reflected the federal government's stringent antitrust attitudes in the 1960s and 1970s. Their effect was to limit both the size and volume of merger transactions, as well as the competition for targets. As we shall see below, once the antitrust restrictions were relaxed, acquisitions in related industries rose, as did the size of transactions.

Commodities inflation also accounted for a major difference between mergers in the late 1970s and those in the 1980s. Inflation accelerated acquisition activity in raw materials businesses from energy and metals to timber products and foodstuffs as companies tried to participate in the profit increases in those industries. Commodities acquisitions were particularly common among the oil companies, which bought metal-mining and coal companies as well as other oil producers, and among the paper companies, which sought out timber properties. But inflation also accelerated the diversification trend as inflation both hurt many corporations' margins and made commodities producers look attractive, stimulating many companies to rethink their strategies and make acquisitions to hedge or profit by commodities inflation. General Electric was a classic example of this, buying Utah International, a leading mining company, in 1976 for almost $2.2 billion. Similarly, R. J. Reynolds bought Burmah Oil & Gas, Continental Group bought Florida Gas, Time Inc. bought Inland Container, and as late as 1981 DuPont bought Conoco. Nine of the 50 acquisitions between 1976 and 1980 in appendix 9.1 represented new natural resource lines of business for the acquirers, and nineteen of the fifty were natural resource-related.

The weak stock market of the 1970s was also a sharp contrast to the later 1980s. It stimulated diversification through acquisitions because the significant gap between stock market values and replacement costs made it cheaper to acquire than to build companies. For most of 1974–1984, the S&P Industrials sold at only 35–45% of the Federal Reserve's estimated replacement book value, as can be seen in figure 9.2.*

The Reagan Merger Market 1981–1984

The distinguishing feature of the merger market under the Reagan administration was the growth in the size of transactions. The total value of the 100 largest merger transactions, outlined in figure 9.3, doubled to $49 billion in 1981 and doubled again to $104 billion in 1984. There was no increase in the number of merger transactions to compare with the increase in values. The number of takeovers of public companies actually declined, from approximately 260 in 1978 and 1979 to 168 in 1981, and was still only 215 in 1984, as can be seen in figure 9.4. By contrast, the number of

---

*As I will discuss later with respect to the oil industry, such low valuations also raised the question of whether further investment was economic, but businesspeople intent on strategic investments and LBO buyers frequently considered stock market values aberrational. It was a particularly common belief in the commodities industries that prices eventually had to equal replacement costs, and therefore stock prices below replacement costs were a potential bargain.

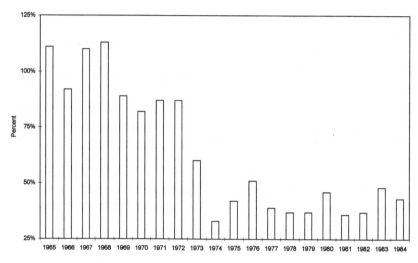

Figure 9.2 Stock market values as a percentage of reproduction cost net worth (nonfarm, nonfinancial corporations). Sources: Standard & Poor's Corp. and Federal Reserve.

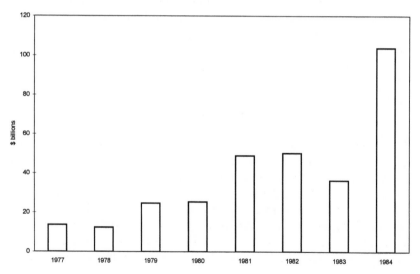

Figure 9.3 Value of the top 100 acquisitions. Sources: *Mergers & Acquisitions, Annual Almanac & Index*, and author.

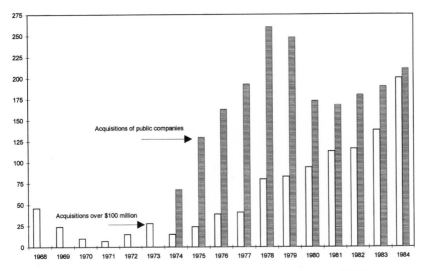

Figure 9.4 Numbers of acquisitions. Source: *Mergerstat Review*, 1989.

acquisitions greater than $100 million, also outlined in figure 9.4, rose from 94 in 1980 to 200 in 1984. The rise in huge transactions was even more striking. There were occasional billion-dollar transactions in the early to mid-1970s, 3 in 1979 and 1980, 9 in 1981, and 28 in 1985.

In the minds of merger professionals, investors, and corporate executives, there was no doubt that they were in a merger boom by the end of 1984. Merger transactions exceeded one public company per business day, and announcements of merger transactions of all types averaged approximately ten per day. The large number of employees going through restructurings or job losses felt little doubt as well. However, academic studies have suggested that the number of acquisitions relative to GNP at this point was significantly smaller than in the prior merger booms at the turn of the century, in the 1920s, and in the 1960s.[5] A more meaningful sense of proportion for merger activity is gained by comparing it with capital spending, since capital spending is a close alternative to acquisition spending. The value of the top 100 acquisitions rose from 16% of capital expenditures by the S&P Industrials in 1977 to 30% from 1980 to 1983, to 67% in 1984, as can be seen in figure 9.5.[6] This should leave little doubt that the merger boom was huge.*

*It might be thought that since there is a seller for every buyer that in aggregate acquisition spending does not affect capital spending and that the comparison is inapposite. However, the buyers are mostly corporations that dominate capital spending, while the sellers are mostly portfolio investors who engage in very little capital spending.

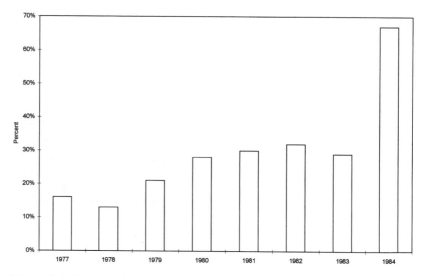

Figure 9.5 Merger volume relative to capital expenditures of the S&P Industrials. Sources: Standard & Poor's Corp., *Mergers & Acquisitions*, and author.

The Impact of Changes in the Antitrust Climate on Merger Activity[7]

Antitrust restrictions did not simply fly out the window when the Reagan administration came in. Rather, business's interpretation of the regulatory atmosphere evolved through a mix of milestone merger transactions, legal events, and new regulations. And merger volume grew as the sense of freedom expanded.

The chief agents of change in antitrust policy were William Baxter, a Stanford University professor of law and economics who was appointed assistant attorney general for antitrust, and James Miller, an economist who was appointed FTC chairman. Baxter told the Senate Judiciary Committee during his confirmation hearings that he "would restrict antitrust enforcement where [he] believed it to be unjustified on economic grounds," and knowledgable insiders knew that Baxter had made it a condition to taking his job that he would issue new rules that would reverse the "ratchet effect" that two decades of government intervention had had in tightening up antitrust rules.[8] James Miller held similar views. As the head of the Office of Management and Budget's Office of Information and Regulatory Affairs prior to joining the FTC, he was an articulate advocate of reducing regulatory interference in the economy. At his first press conference as head of the FTC he criticized prior FTC programs for "exploring the outer reaches of the law."[9]

The new administration's antitrust attitude was tested quickly when Nabisco and Standard Brands announced their intention to merge in a $1.9 billion transaction in April, 1981. The merger of two such food giants would have provoked immediate opposition in the past, yet there was minimal FTC concern, and stockholders were able to approve the transaction in July. When the FTC cleared Standard Oil of Ohio's acquisition of Kennecott in June 1981 with very modest compliance requirements, the extent of the change in antitrust attitudes was clear. The extractive industries had been a particular focus of prior antitrust efforts, not only because of the oil companies' absolute size and the political attractions of attacking them, but because the mining companies in copper, lead, and zinc had many characteristics of shared monopolies, including few companies, high barriers to entry, and highly publicized shared marketing practices. The government had conducted a drawn-out and infamous case against Kennecott in the mid-1970s when it acquired Peabody Coal, which ultimately led to the divestiture of Peabody Coal and the government had launched a major antitrust case as recently as 1978 when Standard Oil of California tried to acquire Amax. There were also extensive government investigations that overlapped the SOHIO/Kennecott merger of virtually every oil company's pricing practices under oil price controls, which would have been expected to influence opinion against such a merger. While the investigations were not actually antitrust cases, they were nonetheless closely related to the major concern of antitrust regulators—pricing power. The chances in prior years of one of the Standard Oil companies buying the leading copper producer under such circumstances, especially when both had been subject to major antitrust proceedings in the past, were nil.

The government's rapid clearance of the $6.8 billion DuPont/Conoco merger just one month later, in July 1981, was an even stronger signal of the new attitude.[10] This was the largest merger in history, combining the fourteenth and fifteenth largest companies (by revenues) in the country to form the seventh largest. Both companies had histories of major antitrust enforcement proceedings against them, and in the past the absolute size of the transaction would have made it a magnet for antitrust action. Under prior administrations, as Irving Shapiro, DuPont's retired chairman said, "Anything this size would have been unacceptable."[11] Merger advisors reported a prompt response among other large companies considering ambitious acquisitions.[12]

A symbolic indication of the change in antitrust thinking was provided in the fall of 1981 when the Justice Department and the FTC terminated a mass of old antitrust proceedings. The Justice Department dropped cases against General Electric and Eastman Kodak dating to 1972 and 1977. The FTC dropped cases against the eight largest oil refiners dating to 1973 and against Kellogg, General Mills, and General Foods dating to 1972.

The change in antitrust enforcement dramatically captured media attention in January 1982 when the Department of Justice simultaneously dropped its antitrust case against IBM and resolved its antitrust case against AT&T—the two largest companies on the New York Stock Exchange. Baxter had begun negotiations with IBM about resolving the case in June 1981, and six months later admitted total surrender on the part of the government. Although the case had a thirteen-year history, Baxter described the government's position as "flimsy" and the odds of victory at "ten thousand to one". Baxter believed that the government had been trying to define the computer market too narrowly and that prior antitrust policies were "too tough on monopoly companies that achieve and hold their position through efficiency, rather than through predatorily pricing products below long-run costs, or other illegal acts." To the extent IBM had tried predatory practices, he didn't believe it had affected competitors.[13]

In some respects the AT&T settlement looked like an antitrust victory, since the company agreed to spin off its twenty-two local operating telephone companies, but more fundamentally for AT&T it was relieved of a 1956 consent decree in which it agreed not to enter any further unregulated businesses. It still had 97% of the long distance market in which it remained regulated, and it still had Western Electric, its unregulated manufacturing subsidiary. The expectation was that AT&T would quickly branch out in manufacturing and computers without being hampered by the government because of its monopoly base or its size.

The change in antitrust enforcement was raised to the level of formal policy when the Department of Justice issued new merger guidelines in June 1982 that totally superseded the 1968 merger guidelines and their objective of keeping market participants as numerous as possible. The new guidelines owed a strong debt to the Chicago School of Economics and its belief in efficient markets. The guidelines dropped all mention of disqualifying an acquirer because it was a potential competitor, and changed the definition of the relevant market for antitrust action, greatly broadening the market to include product substitutes, the possibility of production switches, self-production, and imports. Within the relative market, the standard for intervention was switched from the very low 1–5% increases in market share targeted in the 1968 guidelines to a new standard of market concentration, the Herfindahl Index, which was formed by summing the squares of the percentage market share of all participants. It raised the level for intervention above 10% for most firms.

Under the 1982 standards, the restrictions on vertical mergers in the 1968 guidelines virtually disappeared. The 1968 guidelines' opposition to vertical mergers where the upstream company had a 6% market share was expanded by the 1982 guidelines to over 20%, and where the downstream company had a 10% market share was expanded to 15%, assuming all of the companies had equal market shares.

Important keys to the 1982 guidelines were the underlying concept of how to define markets and the need to prove monopoly powers within those markets. If General Motors was subject to competition from Japanese and European auto makers, if IBM was subject to competition from personal computers, if Kodak was subject to competition from video cameras, if oil companies could transport refined products anywhere in America, if any food company could contest another food market, then markets were large, market shares were small, and consolidating mergers were given a green light. The intense import competition due to the strong dollar at this time in the auto industry, the electronics industry, the aluminum, steel, and mining industries, and for companies like Caterpillar, Deere, and International Harvester when they had previously looked like shared monopolies, gave considerable credibility to the assumption that markets were highly contestable and competitive. The 1982 guidelines put a limit on how far market definition could be stretched by defining competing products or production as that which would be induced within one year by a 5% increase in prices, but the message was out that big wasn't bad.

The largest mergers in 1982 relied even more on the new antitrust attitude than in 1981. Ten mergers in 1982 were over $1 billion. In the oil industry, Mobil Oil and U.S. Steel battled for Marathon ($6.2 billion), and Occidental Petroleum bought Cities Service for $4.2 billion. But megamergers spread far beyond the oil industry. In the insurance industry, Connecticut General and INA undertook a $4.3 billion merger of equals, and American General Corp. bought NLT for $1.5 billion. In the railroad industry, Norfolk & Western bought Southern Railway for $2.9 billion, and Union Pacific bought the Missouri Pacific and Western Pacific Railroads for $1.0 billion. In the defense industry, Martin Marietta, Bendix, and Allied Corp. were left free of antitrust intervention to fight out one of the slugfests of the century, which ended with Allied's $1.8 billion acquisition of Bendix.

The Reagan administration's attitude on antitrust only changed the merger market gradually, despite the magnitude of the 1981–1982 transactions and the new Department of Justice merger guidelines, for the simple reason that each industry was uncertain just how the new attitude would be applied to them. William Baxter, in his Senate confirmation hearings, emphasized the need to review mergers in the natural resource industries, and particularly stressed the importance of keeping out "perceived potential competitors."[14] He then took pains to say during the battle to take over Conoco when Mobil and Texaco planned to enter the bidding, "If they think we're generally soft on mergers, that they can slip significant horizontal aspects past us, they're going to be in for a big surprise."[15] He proved his point only days later when Mobil was held up by antitrust demands while DuPont went ahead and bought Conoco for $1.3 billion less than Mobil had bid. In October 1981, the Department of Justice blocked Heilemann Brewing Company's acquisition of Schlitz, even though Schlitz was a failing company, and at the same time the FTC blocked LTV's acquisition of Grumman Corp. because of their overlapping business in carrier-based aircraft. On a different but related front, the Department of Justice actually stepped up the number of price-fixing investigations and gave them new teeth by seeking criminal rather than civil indictments.

When Mobil Oil attempted to take over Marathon Oil at the end of 1981, antitrust lawyers generally discouraged speculation that the antitrust requirements were less than before. Richard Favretto, a previous Baxter deputy, said that the standards "aren't materially different."[16] Marathon initiated an antitrust suit in the Ohio sixth circuit, which the FTC joined, and which led to a restraining order and ultimately a decision against Mobil, while U.S. Steel got to go ahead and buy Marathon. The judges' decision against Mobil embodied a general fear of size and of vague collusion possibilities that reflected earlier antitrust policies rather than the need for proof in the subsequent guidelines: "The many joint arrangements in which members of the industry engage already may provide the opportunity for collusion on price and output. Concentration of this economic power in fewer hands in such a large industry with these characteristics increases the risk of uncompetitive behavior and, ultimately, may undermine the confidence of the public in the free market system."[17] Mobil's Marathon bid also stirred up a hornet's nest of political opposition. There was the expected opposition from politicians in Ohio, where Marathon had its headquarters, but they were joined by Republican Senators Danforth (Mo.) and Packwood (Ore.), and Democratic Senator Ford (Ky.). Mobil told its shareholders at the May 1982 annual meeting, "We've gotten a clear message that a company of our size isn't going to be able to buy a major integrated oil firm."[18]

There was still some apparent general truth to that statement in August 1982, even after the new merger guidelines had come out, when Gulf Oil dropped its tender offer for Cities Service after the FTC sought a court order opposing the merger. United Technologies also dropped pursuit of Bendix in October because of FTC opposition to its increased share of automotive equipment.

In all of these instances of strict antitrust attitudes, the cognoscenti could argue that antitrust opposition was more apparent than real. Baxter obviously did not want to create an attitude of open house on antitrust restrictions, and was politic to emphasize that the Department of Justice was still on guard. Mobil was merely delayed in its pursuit of Conoco and Marathon, not precluded, and there was substantial criticism of Mobil's acquisition techniques in both cases.* Gulf Oil was unique in that it had recent criminal convictions relating to participation in an international uranium price-fixing scheme and political contributions to the Nixon administration. Gulf also may have changed its mind about the economic merits of the Cities Service acquisition because its stock dropped 25%. Cities Service actually sued Gulf for breach of contract on the grounds that the FTC's requests were insignificant.[19] United Technologies' role in bidding for Bendix was something of a mystery from the beginning, so when it dropped out the reasons were equally unclear.

In effect, a learning process was required for what was possible on the antitrust front. Clearly there were limits, and it was not a free lunch for the companies that ran into those limits. Acquirers that ran into the limits lost money—sometimes sizable amounts; the legal and merger fees in the Conoco takeover exceeded $50 million.[20] In the case of the oil industry, there was a significant political risk early in the Reagan administration that acquisitions would affect the debate over whether to deregulate domestic oil and gas prices, and there was always a problem of public ill will.

All doubts about the merger freedom accorded by the new antitrust approach were washed away in 1984, however. Oil industry consolidation among the very largest companies was unprecedented as Chevron bought Gulf for $13.3 billion, Texaco bought Getty Oil for $10.1 billion, Mobil bought Superior Oil for $5.7 billion, and Phillips Petroleum bought Aminoil from R. J. Reynolds for $1.7 billion. During these battles, the Senate explicitly rejected a moratorium on acquisitions by the top fifty oil firms by a vote of 57 to 39.[21] General Motors bought Electronic Data Systems for $2.6 billion and IBM bought Rolm for $1.3 billion in transactions that would never have been permitted previously. There were further natural resource transactions as Broken Hill Proprietary bought Utah International for $2.4 billion and Champion International bought St. Regis Corp. for $1.8 billion. There were large mergers where the acquirer would previously have been considered a major potential entrant, such as Beatrice's acquisition of Esmark for $2.7 billion, Dun & Bradstreet's acquisition of A. C. Nielsen for $1.3 billion, and American Stores acquisition of Jewel for $1.2 billion. My own layman's interpretation of the ten largest transactions in 1984 is that 84% by value and only 14 of the nineteen over $1 billion would have been challenged previously. In

---

*Mobil was vague about the back end of its Conoco tender offer, which made Conoco stockholders uncertain about accepting Mobil's offer, even though it was higher, when U.S. Steel's offer was effective earlier. In its Marathon tender offer, Mobil started out too cheaply, rather than making a preemptive bid, and was too slow to focus on its minor antitrust problems in Midwestern gasoline marketing.

the one instance when the Department of Justice intervened on antitrust grounds—LTV's proposed acquisition of Republic Steel—it was criticized by both the Department of Commerce and the president, and the opposition was quickly modified.[22]

The change in antitrust enforcement affected the merger market in various ways. It had an impact on size, as the value of the ten largest mergers each year jumped from an average of $6.5 billion during 1977–1980 to approximately $25 billion in 1981 and 1982 and almost $45 billion in 1984. Looking at size another way in table 9.1, from 1976 to 1980 there were eight merger transactions over $1 billion aggregating $16.5 billion. In 1981 alone there were nine, aggregating $24.2 billion; in 1984 there were nineteen worth $55.2 billion.

The changes in antitrust enforcement also permitted extensive mergers between companies in the same or related industries. If the reader simply reviews the ten largest transactions each year in the early 1980s in appendix 9.1, it is striking how many were between similar companies. Table 9.2 indicates the proportions among the ten largest mergers each year which in my judgment would routinely have received antitrust challenges on the basis of size or overlapping businesses. The proportions went from 0% during 1978–1980, to 53% of the top 10's value in 1981, to 84% in 1984. Railroad and airline mergers that would have been routinely challenged have been left out of the category of mergers because deregulation of these industries under President Carter set new ground rules for them, although the new antitrust attitude was important to these mergers as well.

The new antitrust rules also affected the activities of raiders. The eagerness of companies to buy competitors or product line extensions greatly reduced the risks of raiders' organizational costs and high leverage. As we shall see below, Boone Pickens, who opened up the oil majors to raids, would probably have failed miserably in his attacks on Cities Service and Gulf Oil if other oil company buyers had been ruled out as buyers. The new rules also facilitated divestitures if a raid was successful. Buyers of 70% of the divestitures following sixty-two hostile takeover contests from 1984 to 1986 were in the same or related industries.[23]

Oil and Gas Industry Mergers and Acquisitions

As in so many other aspects of the securities markets in this period, the oil industry played a prominent role in the merger market. Oil-related transactions[24] grew from an average of 11.5% of the 100 largest transactions during 1977–1978 to 29% in 1979 and 33% during 1979–1984, as outlined in table 9.3. At first, this reflected the oil companies' newfound wealth, as oil prices rose from $14 per barrel to over $40 in 1980 and as

Table 9.1. Merger Transactions Greater than $1 Billion

Year	Number	$ Billions
1976	1	2,170
1977	1	1,567
1978	0	0
1979	3	6,220
1980	3	6,500
1981	9	24,164
1982	10	25,115
1983	7	10,386
1984	19	55,179

Source: Mergers & Acquisitions, Annual Almanac & Index, "The Top 100," 1982–1985, and quarterly issues prior to 1982.

oil companies sought ways to spend their cash. Others outside the industry also sought to share in the wealth by acquiring oil companies. Once oil prices declined substantially, oil transactions dropped off to only 18.8% of the total in 1985 (when oil was $28 per barrel) and less than 10% in subsequent years (when oil was below $20 per barrel). This strongly suggests that oil-related acquisitions reflected crowd psychology, executive hubris, or corporate aggrandizement rather than efficiency; but the situation was considerably more complicated. The integrated oil companies were trying to regain control over crude oil supplies lost to nationalization in the Middle East and Africa, major U.S. exploration targets were unsuccessful, acquisition costs of reserves were lower than exploring for them, and the Reagan administration's relaxation of antitrust enforcement permitted hitherto unthinkable acquisitions that appeared as once-in-a-lifetime opportunities.

Table 9.2. The Ten Largest Merger Transactions

Year	Total ($ billion)	Subject to 1968 Guidelines[1] ($ billion)	%
1977	5.6	1.2	21%
1978	4.1	0	0%
1979	10.9	0	0%
1980	5.2	0	0%
1981	24.9	13.2	53%
1982	24.7	14.7	60%
1983	13.2	2.0	15%
1984	44.6	37.6	84%

[1]Transactions that on the face of it would have incurred antitrust opposition under the 1968 merger guidelines and practices. This column excludes transportation industries.

Table 9.3. Oil-related Acquisitions in the Top 100 1977–1984

Year	Top 100 Acquisitions ($ bill)	Oil & Gas Acquisitions ($ bill)	% Top 100
1977	13.8	2.3	16.7%
1978	12.4	0.7	5.6%
1979	25.0	7.2	28.8%
1980	25.8	8.6	33.3%
1981	48.9	18.3	37.3%
1982	50.2	12.3	24.4%
1983	36.2	10.6	29.3%
1984	103.8	38.1	36.7%
1985	95.5	18.0	18.8%
1986	110.8	8.4	7.6%

Sources: Mergers & Acquisitions, Annual Almanac & Index, March/April 1981–1985, Quarterly reports for prior years. I categorized the individual transactions.

Note: I adjusted 1979 and 1980 to include LBOs; they were included by *Mergers & Acquisitions* thereafter.

The initial impetus to oil-related transactions was the common desire among the oil companies to use their newfound wealth to diversify. Mobil had presaged this trend when it acquired Marcor Inc. (previously known as Montgomery Ward) in 1976 for $900 million. The importance of these diversifying acquisitions can be seen in the ten largest transactions each year outlined in appendix 9.1. Twelve of the sixty acquisitions from 1976 to 1981, totaling $12.6 billion, were oil company diversifications, until their focus turned to acquiring their fellow oil companies in 1982. Among the diversifying oil companies, Atlantic Richfield bought Anaconda and a number of esoteric energy companies, SOHIO bought Kennecott, Exxon bought Reliance Electric, Occidental Petroleum bought Iowa Beef Packers, Getty Oil bought ERC Corp. (previously Employers Reinsurance Company), Elf/Aquitaine bought Texasgulf Inc., and Tenneco bought Southwestern Life. Outside the ten largest transactions, Schlumberger bought a number of data processing companies and Fairchild Camera. Most oil companies bought one or more coal companies.

These acquisitions were highly controversial both politically and among investors. There was great political suspicion of the oil companies as oil prices rose, and also a belief that they were diverting capital from the country's need for greater domestic energy supplies. Investors tended to see the diversification efforts as a waste of assets—empire-building— and some of the prices the oil companies paid appeared to reflect little concern for earning an adequate return.

The big increase in oil-related acquisitions occurred when oil companies became acquisition targets rather than just acquirers. Initially these acquisitions were of companies whose assets were almost exclusively oil and gas reserves. Shell Oil Company paid $3.65 billion, more than doubling the next closest bid, for Belridge Oil Co., a hitherto little known private company rich in California heavy crude oil. In 1980, Sun Company paid $2.3 billion for Texas Pacific Oil Co. Mobil Corp., the most aggressive of the major oil companies, laid out $1.5 billion for General Crude Oil and Vickers Energy in 1979 and 1980, and tried to buy Belridge Oil and Texas Pacific Oil. Getty Oil paid $600 million in 1980 for Reserve Oil & Gas.

The integrated oil companies themselves became acquisition targets in 1981, transforming the scale of acquisitions generally. Their vulnerability to being taken over became apparent almost by accident as an outgrowth of Canadian energy policy. Near the end of 1980, the Canadian government announced a national energy program to stimulate domestic oil and gas development by Canadian companies. Tax advantages under the program for Canadian-owned companies were so great that there was an incentive for Canadians to buy out domestic subsidiaries of foreign companies. As part of this trend, Calgary-based Dome Petroleum solicited Conoco's 52.9% shareholding of Hudson's Bay Oil & Gas Company early in 1981. Finding Conoco resistant, and assuming that Conoco had a very low tax basis in its Hudson's Bay shares, Dome tendered in May for fourteen million shares (approximately $900 million) of Conoco itself and proposed a coercive, but tax-free, exchange of the shares for the 52.9% interest in Hudson's Bay Oil & Gas, betting that Conoco would find it a worthwhile trade to dispose of such a large and disagreeable minority stockholder. The tender for fourteen million shares was for 13% of Conoco's outstanding stock with an option to go to twenty-two million shares or 20%. At $65, the tender represented a premium of 30% versus Conoco's current stock price. To everyone's surprise, Conoco stockholders tendered fifty-three million shares—almost 50% of its outstanding stock. Conoco quickly sold Hudson's Bay Oil & Gas to Dome Petroleum, but it was too late. Sensing an opportunity, Seagram Company, which had long wanted a stake in a major oil company, approached Conoco about buying a 25% interest, and when it was rebuffed countered by tendering for 41% of the company at $73 per share—a 46% premium. Conoco was in play, and both DuPont and Mobil Corp. emerged as competitors to Seagram Company, beginning a battle that involved the courts, markets, and politics and that ended with DuPont buying Conoco for $98 per share—a total of $6.8 billion.

Companies as large as Conoco had previously been considered invulnerable to raiders, let alone raiders as small as Dome Petroleum, but once it was apparent that there were equally large buyers for these companies, numerous opportunists were stimulated to get into the act. Dome's strategy with Conoco was quickly copied by another small Canadian company, NuWest Group, which bought a 7.3% interest in Cities Service for approximately $250 million, and by a group of Texans, including the Bass brothers and Sedco Inc., which between them bought 12.4% of Marathon Oil. The most important and enduring of these opportunists, however, was Boone Pickens, chairman of Mesa Petroleum, who pushed Cities Service, General American Oil, and Gulf Oil into being taken over, forced Phillips Petroleum and Unocal into restructuring, and initiated patterns of bank and junk bond financing that became standards for the later 1980s. It is worth pausing to follow his stalking of Cities Service Company to see the mixture of logic, leverage, and happenstance that got this process underway.

Boone Pickens was an unlikely catalyst for so much activity. Pickens was a Phillips Petroleum geologist in the early 1950s who started his own company in 1956 with $2,500 in cash and a $100,000 line of credit. Through acquisitions and drilling partnerships, this company grew into Amarillo-based Mesa Petroleum. The company had a modestly successful exploration record, particularly in the Hugoton basin of Kansas and the North Sea, and was one of the first oil companies to take advantage of the tax benefits to its stockholders of a royalty trust that it set up in 1979. However, Mesa Petroleum got caught up in the late 1970s optimism of the oil industry, and found itself significantly overextended in the scale of its commitments for exploration and development in the Gulf of Mexico.

Pickens's remedy was to try to recoup the company's fortunes in the stock market,[25] and his first target was Cities Service. It was not a new thought. As Pickens's wife, Bea, said, "Boone's been talking about Cities Service for as long as we've been married, and that was 1972."[26] He first approached Cities Service in the summer of 1980. Any takeover suggestions from Pickens were highly galling to Cities Service, however. Its 1980 book common equity was five times Mesa's; its earnings before interest and taxes 4.4 times; its capital expenditures 2.6 times; and Cities Service was a publicly recognized integrated oil company with service stations around the country, while Mesa was hardly known outside of Amarillo. Undeterred, Pickens first bought 4.1 million shares of Cities Service in the open market (5.3% of its outstanding stock), and then began a search for partners to take over Cities Service—a search that included discussions with Gulf Oil, Occidental Petroleum, Marathon Petroleum, Louisiana Land and Exploration, and Freeport-McMoRan.

There was a double logic behind Pickens's attack on Cities Service. Cities Service had been a perpetual laggard in the oil industry. Its 1980–1981 finding costs for new oil and gas reserves were absurdly out of line at $23 per barrel of oil equivalent[27]—almost three times the industry average. Its reserves had been declining for a decade, yet its capital expenditures doubled from $500 million in 1977 to over $1 billion in 1980 and were over 100% of its funds from operations. Various diversification efforts into plastics, industrial chemicals, and hard-rock mining were all unprofitable. Its 12.7% return on equity from 1977 to 1980 was only 75% of that for S&P's Oil-Integrated-Domestic index. Cities Service's poor results were reflected in the stock market, where its stock price was barely above book value versus approximately 150% of book value for S&P's Oil-Integrated-Domestic index, and its market value of approximately $2.7 billion was only twice that of Mesa Petroleum.[28]

Despite this weak economic performance, the rise in oil and gas prices from 1979 to 1981 had increased the value of Cities Service's assets to possibly as much as $82–87 per share—a value eventually publicized by Cities Service's financial advisors and a far cry from its 1980 stock price of approximately $35. Boone Pickens had a case either for stopping the company's heavy capital spending and paying out more of its cash flow or selling the company off in pieces.

Cities Service's problems increased in mid-1981 when a second intruder emerged. In midyear, Nu-West Group Limited, a small Calgary, Alberta residential real estate developer, announced that it had bought 7.3% of Cities Service. Pickens quickly tried to join forces with Nu-West, and Cities Service began public discussion of a defensive merger of equals with Conoco, which was trying to deal with Dome Petroleum's tender offer for 13–20% of its stock. The Cities Service-Conoco discussions were interrupted by Seagram's unfriendly tender offer for 41% of Conoco and its acquisition by DuPont in August 1981; but Cities Service had made itself more vulnerable to being taken over by announcing it was willing to consider a merger, even though it vigorously asserted that there was no other combination in which it was interested. In September, it repurchased the 7.3% of its stock held by Nu-West Group for $51 per share versus the current price of $41 and Nu-West's cost of $45, and tried to repurchase Pickens's stock.[29] He refused, and Cities Service began discussions with various companies about buying it outright or buying its refinery, industrial chemicals, and plastics divisions.[30]

It was not long, however, before Pickens's efforts appeared to be floundering. Cities Service's purchase of its stock from Nu-West Group had actually been a sign of Nu-West's weakness. It was borrowing at interest rates of over 20%, oil prices had declined from $38 to $36 in midyear, and Cities Service's stock price had declined from $69 to $41 in a matter of a few weeks. Boone Pickens was in the same boat. Over a year had passed since his original approach to Cities Service, and he had been unable to put together either partners or banks to come up with a credible offer for the company. Cities Service was quite effective in scaring away his potential partners by threatening them with a counter takeover offer from Cities Service. It appeared that antitrust rules would keep other integrated oil companies from being buyers since Mobil's offer for Conoco was held up on antitrust grounds, and this was further confirmed when Mobil had the same experience late in 1981 when it tried to compete with U.S. Steel to acquire Marathon Petroleum. The Wall Street Journal reported that arbitrageurs were skeptical of Pickens's ability to put together a deal to buy Cities Service.[31]

Things looked even worse for Pickens in early 1982, when oil prices declined further from $36 to $33 per barrel and oil stocks dropped over 25%. For most of February to April 1982 Cities Service's stock price hovered around $30 compared to a peak of over $65 in mid-1981 and Mesa's cost of $44.28.[32] At this point Mesa had a loss of almost $60 million. Cities Service, sensing it was in the driver's seat, began to take the position that it would not consider merging with another major oil company, even though it had held numerous discussions along these lines in the last half of 1981.

However, Cities Service had not reckoned on the aggressiveness of the commercial banks. Faced with declining commercial and industrial loans, and anxious to bolster earnings to deal with sharply increasing nonperforming loans to the oil and real estate industries as well as to less-developed countries, the commercial banks were just beginning to make loans for raids and leveraged buyouts involving unprecedented leverage. In May 1982, over two years after Pickens first approached Cities Service, he put together a bank group led by Continental Illinois Bank & Trust[33] that lent Mesa $1 billion to make an offer for 12.1 million shares of Cities Service at $45.00 per share. This would raise Mesa's stake to over 20%, consciously mimicking Dome Petroleum's earlier offer for Conoco.[34]

If Mesa succeeded in taking over Cities Service at $45 per share the transaction would cost $3.5 billion—five times the largest LBO to date —and would be very highly leveraged. The banks were financing the transaction under much riskier circumstances than bank and insurance company lenders had faced in prior LBOs. Simply in gaining control of 20% of Cities Service, Mesa's resulting debt and preferred stock of $1.65 billion would be supported by only $650 million in equity and its pro forma coverage of fixed charges would be only 1.1 times.[35] Even netting Cities Service's $1.60 dividend against Mesa's interest costs, Mesa's fixed charge coverage was still only 1.3 times.

An important part of the banks' thinking was to secure their loans with any securities Mesa bought, as well as its oil and gas reserves. The loans were divided up into a margin credit and a reserve-based credit specifically along those lines.[36] But Mesa had other substantial debt and $210 million in preferred stock that ended up unsecured under this logic, and banks had rarely been willing to look at their loans on such narrow grounds in the past. It could be argued that Cities Service's earnings and assets had to be included in the coverage calculations, but that was only true if Mesa was successful. Lawsuits could obstruct taking control for years, and there was still the other 80% of the financing to complete, amounting to another $2.8 billion. Banks historically would not take such risks. We know in retrospect that when Occidental Petroleum finally took over Cities Service at $55 per share, its pro forma coverage of debt and preferred dividends was only 0.76 times and that significant asset sales at premium prices were necessary to make sense of the transaction. Continental Illinois and its syndicate members had to make some such calculation for Mesa, but on a company with only one quarter of Occidental's common equity. The margin for error was obviously very small, yet there were great uncertainties about oil prices, stock prices, and antitrust laws. There were also uncertainties related to the value of Cities Service's assets because its net income had declined 40% in 1981 while the other major oil companies' net income had continued to rise. This was the first transaction in which it became clear that the major commercial banks were prepared to take risks on this scale.

Pickens approached Cities Service privately with a two-step offer for 100% of the company at $50 per share just before he launched his tender offer. Cities Service refused, and launched its own tender offer for Mesa Petroleum as a preemptive strike. Pickens countered with the tender offer cited above for 12.1 million shares of Cities Service's stock at $45 per share (despite his private offer of $50), which would raise Mesa's holdings to over 20%. How Mesa would finance the balance was unclear. There were rumors that it would swap shares in a newly created royalty trust based on Cities Service's oil and gas properties for the balance. Mesa had already created a royalty trust on its Gulf of Mexico properties and these new vehicles had the appeal of both tax sheltering dividend income and forcing the oil companies to limit their capital expenditures because of the high dividend payouts involved. A battle of counteroffers between the two companies ensued, which was climaxed by Gulf Oil entering the fray as a white knight and making an offer for Cities Service on June 17 at $63 per share. As part of the negotiations surrounding the Gulf offer, Cities Service bought Mesa's 4.1 million shares of Cities Service at $55, which netted Mesa a profit of $32.0 million.

While the Mesa buyout looked cheap, it soon looked smart. When the FTC sought a court restraining order on July 29 to delay the acquisition, Gulf withdrew. The NYSE finally opened trading in Cities Service's stock below $30 versus Gulf's $63 offer. Arbitrageurs were crushed. Ivan Boesky was almost bankrupted by his loss of $24 million, and numerous other arbitrageurs were in serious trouble.[37] Mesa's banks would have had quite a shock if it still held its Cities Service stock.

A badly bruised Cities Service sued Gulf for breach of contract on the grounds that the FTC's antitrust requests were minor and that Gulf was stonewalling the FTC to create a reason to withdraw from the acquisition. Cities Service may have been right. Wall Street's reaction to

Gulf's offer was very negative. Gulf's stock dropped from a range of $31–33 to $27½ when the deal was announced and quickly drifted lower to $24—a decline of approximately 25%! Gulf belonged with Cities Service and Conoco among the oil industry's laggard managements rather than among those who would make the most of undervalued assets. The *Wall Street Journal* indicated that Gulf was having second thoughts.[38] It is hard to determine the facts, however. Simultaneously, Gulf lost grandfather treatment in a Senate tax bill designed to recapture deferred taxes when assets were written up for tax purposes, and Gulf's management style, particularly that of Harold Hammer, its chief financial officer, was so obtuse that both stonewalling the FTC and overrating its opposition were completely in character.

Cities Service was left in the unenviable position of having a desperately low stock price, a great deal of its stock in the hands of professional arbitrageurs, and having announced it was willing to sell out. The board of directors had little choice but to order management to pursue the sale of the company. The only serious bidder was Occidental Petroleum, which first suggested $50 per share and finally came up to $55, which Cities Service accepted. There was no antitrust opposition.

The stalking of Cities Service had already set merger market milestones for the size and risks that banks would venture in takeovers and the ability of a minor company to take on one of the integrated oil companies; but Occidental Petroleum's offer went even further. Occidental Petroleum leveraged itself on a scale hitherto unimaginable for a large and successful company by completing the second half of the offer with a package of junk-rated preferred stock and near-junk zero-coupon bonds. Upon completing the merger, its debt ratio rose from 25% to 50% of capitalization and its preferred stock ratio rose from 12% to 21%. Inversely, its common equity ratio declined from 63% to 29%! The combined companies on a pro forma basis didn't have enough earnings before interest and taxes to pay the resulting interest and preferred dividends, let alone Occidental's $2.50 common stock dividend. Pro forma EBIT coverage of combined interest and preferred dividends was only 0.76 times, although the zero-coupon bonds gave Occidental a considerable breathing period to fix this. This back-end package of junk preferred stock and zero-coupon bonds was of such uncertain value that Cities Service's investment bankers were unable to value it, and the deal was only done on the basis of an unusual presentation by Occidental's investment banker, Goldman Sachs, to the Cities Service board on how Goldman had valued the securities. As anticipated, Moody's cut the rating on Occidental Petroleum's debt from A2 to Baa3, and on its preferred stock from Baa1 to Ba1. Occidental's pro forma financial ratios actually justified lower ratings, but the proxy statement for the transaction clearly envisaged that Cities Service would be broken up and major portions of it sold off in order to reduce Occidental's new leverage.[39]

Many marveled at Occidental Petroleum's willingness to accept such leverage, but the stock market's judgment was positive as Occidental's stock rose from a $17–18 range in the prior six weeks to $21. David Murdock was playing a key role at Occidental alongside its chairman, Armand Hammer, and had already shown an unusual talent for making money in the merger business in transactions with Iowa Beef Processors and Cannon Mills. If Cities Service was truly worth over $80 per share, as its advisors had publicized during the merger negotiations,[40] Occidental would make a killing.

In fact, however, Occidental Petroleum's resulting gains were very nebulous. Occidental's earnings were already declining from $7.77 per share in 1981 to approximately $2.00 in 1982 because of the drop in oil prices. On a pro forma basis, Occidental would have reported a loss for the first nine months of 1982 of $2.30 per share because of the acquisition,[41] although it reported a profit of $0.69 per share for 1982 since the acquisition was late in the year and only partially complete. As Occidental sold $1.5 billion of Cities Service's pipeline, refining and marketing, and Canadian assets and refunded much of its high cost debt and preferred stock when interest rates came down, its 1984 earnings per share rose to $3.08 even though oil prices were lower. However, it still had $6.7 billion of debt and preferred stock versus only $1.6 billion before the acquisition, and perhaps because of this heavy leverage overhang its common stock performed no better than the S&P integrated oil indexes between August 1982 and December 1984.[42] Even that performance was arguably due more to Occidental's pronounced benefits as it refunded so much debt and preferred stock at lower interest rates rather than gains from the Cities Service assets.

The following lessons of the Cities Service transaction were not lost on either investors or other oil companies: large-scale bank leverage permitted small-scale players to push large companies into mergers; acquirers would consider leveraging to previously unknown levels; and the stock market rewarded the agents of these changes. As Boone Pickens proceeded to attack General American Oil, Gulf Oil, Phillips Petroleum, and Unocal, he found new coinvestors and an increased willingness of the integrated oil companies to come in as bidders. He was a catalyst for some of the largest merger transactions of the decade.

The economic factors motivating other oil companies to acquire the companies Pickens threw into play were highly varied. Kuwait's confiscation of Gulf Oil's properties in 1975, Iran and Nigeria's nationalization of their oil industries, Saudi Arabia's takeover of Aramco in 1980, and nationalistic tax and takeover moves in other countries greatly changed the largest integrated oil companies' control of crude oil runs into their own refineries. In the 1970s, only 10% of oil trade was in the spot markets, versus over 50% by 1982.[43] Therefore, the integrated oil companies greatly wanted to restore control over their crude oil supplies. Mobil Corp. was the most aggressive in trying to replace reserves, as it was in most other matters, but Chevron, Gulf Oil, and Texaco hovered around all of the large oil acquisitions.

The failure of several large U.S. oil and gas exploration prospects also helped to create a belief that major domestic reserve additions had to be bought rather than found. Several of the majors had spent heavily with no success whatsoever on exploration in the Baltimore Canyon along the east coast and off the coast of Florida; the Mukluk well off Alaska's north coast—the most expensive well in history at $2.1 billion—had come up a dry hole; and even the prolific Arguello Point oil discoveries off California's coast were proving almost impossible to develop due to environmental opposition.

Low stock market values relative to replacement costs of oil and gas reserves also played a very important role in justifying acquisitions. Table 9.4 compares the costs of acquiring reserves in the larger oil company acquisitions from 1981 to 1984 with Goldman Sachs's estimates of U.S. domestic finding costs for the sixteen largest integrated oil companies in that period.[44] Over the four years, finding costs averaged $8.87 per barrel of oil equivalent versus $4 or less for the acquisitions of Conoco, Marathon, Belco Petroleum, Getty Oil, and Gulf Oil. While the acquisitions of Cities Service, Terra Resources, Superior Oil, and Aminoil were at per barrel prices above $4, none of these acquisitions had per barrel prices above the four-year average finding cost. The calculation of per barrel acquisition costs is a great oversimplification, as the acquisitions included significant additional assets to which no value has been assigned, such as exploration properties, refineries, pipelines, and other investments; however, it is an upper bound on the cost per barrel and therefore illustrates the incentive for oil companies to acquire rather than explore.

Mobil Corp. was very specific about the tradeoff between buying and exploring for reserves. A former official in 1981 said that, "Mobil has decided that if you can buy reserves for a reasonable price, you should buy them rather than look for them."[45] In early 1982, when a stockholder group proposed a proxy vote that would stop Mobil from buying other oil companies, management opposed it on the grounds that it made sense to buy reserves "at costs comparable to or preferably below those incurred in discovering new reserves."[46]

The comparison of oil and gas finding costs and their price in the merger market quickly broadened to studying the potential values of all types of oil company assets. John S. Herold Inc. became a household name among oil and gas investors because of its quarterly valuations of the oil companies' assets. These valuations were highly variable, of course, ranging from stock market values to possible acquisition prices to replacement costs. Similar approaches to asset values were the basis for

Table 9.4. A Comparison of Large Oil Acquisitions and Finding Costs per Barrel of Oil Equivalent (BOE)

Year	Global Finding Costs per BOE[1]	Acquisition Costs per BOE[2]	Acquired Company	Acquiring Company
1979	$12.40	$5.81	General Crude	Mobil Oil
		0.94	Belridge	Shell Oil
		3.39		
1980	7.22	13.33	Texas Pacific	Sun Oil
		12.58	Vickers Energy	Mobil Oil
		10.00	Reserve Oil & Gas	Getty Oil
		11.97		
1981	9.32	3.01	Conoco	Dupont
		3.01		
1982	11.84	6.21	Cities Service	Occidental Petroleum
		3.93	Marathon	U. S. Steel
		6.25	General American	Phillips Petroleum
		5.46		
1983	7.21	8.49	Terra Resources	Pacific Lighting
		3.59	Belco Petroleum	InterNorth (Enron)
		6.04		
1984	7.09	4.08	Getty Oil	Texaco
		3.20	Gulf	Standard Oil of California
		6.17	Superior Oil	Mobil Oil
		8.55	Aminoil	Phillips Petroleum
		5.50		

[1]For sixteen integrated companies in Jordan R. Alliger, Don Textor, and Jonathan C. Farber, "Finding Cost and Reserve Replacement Results, 1979–1991," July 1992, Goldman Sachs Research, p. 7.
[2]Goldman Sachs merger department database, except I calculated Cities Service, General Crude Oil, Reserve Oil & Gas, and Vickers Energy; General American Oil was a *Wall Street Journal* estimate.

investment bankers' advice and valuations given to the oil companies on both sides of merger transactions. The gap between stock market values and finding costs or replacement costs gave a rational gloss even to defensive acquisitions.

The difference between stock market values and oil and gas finding costs could easily be interpreted another way, however. If stock market values were so low, they arguably reflected that reinvestment was uneconomic at anticipated output prices. The actions of the stock market and the oil industry reflected radically different outlooks for oil prices. The stock market focused on the decline in oil prices from $38 a barrel during January–May 1981 to $30 in 1983 and 1984, while John S. Herold Inc., which was representative of general oil industry thinking, was still basing its valuations of oil and gas reserves on the assumption of $100 a barrel for oil in the year 2000.

The oil industry's focus on reserve replacement was also subject to criticism. For the exploration and production independents this had historically been good economics, because currently expensing exploration and development costs minimized taxes while asset values continued to grow. But there was a significant tax difference between buying reserves indirectly by acquiring a company that had already taken the tax deductions and developing them oneself. There was also an important question of what reserve price was economic, even if purchased reserves were cheaper than current replacement costs. The costs of exploring for and developing reserves had escalated so rapidly from approximately $7 a barrel in 1980 to almost $12 in 1982 that these costs made no economic sense in the minds of many analysts. For the integrated majors, with so many other assets and investment alternatives, reserve replacement goals looked like a substitute for disciplined return on investment calculations.

Analysts had a right to be skeptical of the oil companies' attention to economics. The oil price increases of the 1970s had discouraged critical attitudes within the industry toward the value of adding oil and gas reserves, even though oil prices began to decline as early as mid-1981 and even though return on equity for the major oil companies was rarely competitive with the S&P Industrials throughout the whole century, despite some of the personal fortunes amassed in the oil patch. Nor were the major oil company acquirers more efficient than the others. Table 9.5 compares three measures of efficiency—oil and gas finding costs, return on equity, and common stock price growth—for the top ten oil companies, five of which made major acquisitions and five of which did not. The finding costs of the nonacquiring companies were consistently lower than the acquiring companies, suggesting that the impetus for acquisitions may have been inefficiency rather than efficiency. Although returns on equity were similar for the two groups, the nonacquiring companies' common stocks were up 22% since the end of 1979 versus only 3% for the acquiring companies.

The oil companies also failed to pay attention to investor returns as earnings surged in 1979 and 1981. While cash flow for the S&P Oil Composite increased 87% from 1978 to 1981, dividends increased only 63%, capital budgets increased 123%, and acquisitions in both other industries and oil-related industries exceeded $20 billion. The oil companies could have bridged the different points of view that current finding costs were uneconomic and that increased reserves always turned out to

Table 9.5. Acquiring vs Nonacquiring Oil Companies

	Finding Costs[1]					Return on Equity						12/84 gain vs. 12/79 Stock Price
Nonacquirers	1980	1981	1982	1983	1984	1979	1980	1981	1982	1983	1984	
Amerada-Hess	17.04	10.01	37.60	21.26	22.13	26.7	22.9	8.5	6.6	8.1	6.6	0%
Amoco	6.18	5.63	8.29	7.40	8.83	18.0	20.4	18.0	16.0	15.0	17.4	34%
Arco	6.36	9.85	5.32	7.55	5.54	19.1	22.2	19.4	17.0	14.2	5.8	-8%
Exxon	3.19	12.58	6.28	4.66	7.19	19.0	22.2	19.5	14.7	16.9	19.2	100%
Unocal	6.79	9.01	44.78	9.26	10.10	16.9	18.6	19.2	16.9	12.1	12.3	-17%
Averages	7.91	9.42	20.45	10.03	10.76	19.9	21.3	16.9	14.2	13.3	12.3	22%
Acquirers:												
Chevron	8.21	18.96	15.72	9.13	6.93	19.2	21.7	18.7	10.4	11.3	10.4	11%
Occidental	13.44	22.54	19.75	7.97	2.84	33.0	31.1	25.8	5.8	27.7	22.1	-3%
Mobil	5.83	2.55	22.68	6.29	6.75	19.0	25.0	16.6	9.4	10.8	9.3	-1%
Phillips	neg	27.27	8.47	6.57	7.85	20.9	21.7	16.0	11.2	11.7	12.2	-7%
Texaco	neg	32.86	32.57	30.86	33.81	16.5	21.1	17.0	9.0	8.4	2.3	18%
Averages	9.16	20.84	19.84	12.16	11.64	21.7	24.1	18.8	9.2	14.0	11.3	3%
Acquirers/Nonacquirers	116%	221%	97%	121%	108%	109%	113%	111%	64%	105%	92%	16%

[1] Source: Jordan R. Alliger, Don Textor, and Jonathon C. Farber, "Finding Cost and Reserve Replacement Results, 1979–1991," New York: Goldman Sachs Research, July 1992.

be valuable by repurchasing their own stock. That would have increased reserves per share, avoided acquisition premiums, avoided the uncertainty of asset values in acquisitions, and avoided uneconomic direct investment; but stock repurchases were ignored.

A hidden motive behind several oil companies' acquisitions was the desire to deter Boone Pickens and others from turning on them by becoming too large or too leveraged for him to handle. There were rumors that this motivation sparked Texaco's $10.1 billion acquisition of Getty Oil. Gossip attached similar motives to Phillips's acquisition of Aminoil from R. J. Reynolds—an interpretation that was buttressed by the $8.55 per barrel of oil equivalent that Phillips paid for Aminoil.

The motivations behind the large diversifying acquisitions into oil and related industries by DuPont, U.S. Steel, Allied Corp., Burlington Northern, CSX, Williams Companies, and others reflected to a significant degree that the acquirers were dissatisfied with returns in their own industries and that the oil and related industries were the only ones with acceptable profit histories and price-earnings ratios that the acquirers could afford. These acquirers generally carried below-average stock market valuations, especially on a market-to-book value basis, because of their poor earnings records, and so were forced to consider acquisitions with low price-earnings ratios in order to avoid substantial dilution. The fact that the target oil companies had low price-earnings ratios, despite their good recent earnings records, should have been a warning that the stock market discounted oil companies' future prospects, but a focus on current results often prevailed among the acquirers. These same acquirers often felt that their earnings results had been penalized by commodities inflation, which they had been unable to offset and which they expected oil assets to balance.

The Role of the Banks in Highly Leveraged Raids

Financial market professionals generally gave great emphasis to the terms on which credit was available from the banks and junk bond market as a cause of the merger boom. There are several inferences behind this explanation. One is that easier credit terms led to higher debt levels and lower interest coverage ratios among corporate acquirers than was historically achievable, which will be addressed below. A second inference is that LBO volume and pricing reflected interest coverage requirements established by the lenders rather than return calculations. A third is that the availability of high leverage gave raiders a club that stimulated acquisitions, often by moderately leveraged buyers.

There is no presumption of economic efficiency or even rational returns behind this emphasis on credit terms. Some borrowers were wise buyers and good managers; others were careless and destructive of the values in the companies they acquired. Some borrowers were content to operate indefinitely with high leverage; others strove quickly to reduce it. Some borrowers liquidated the companies they acquired, or significantly changed their operating focus; others made few changes. Some borrowers bought undervalued companies and made fortunes; others overpaid and suffered. The basic point is that credit available on previously unavailable terms allowed acquirers to make or stimulate acquisitions that they could not have undertaken previously, irrespective of the results. This interpretation of the role of easier credit terms is different from academics' analysis of leverage in terms of forcing more disciplined economic decisions upon corporate managers[47] or as a means of wealth transfer from the federal government to stockholders through reduced income taxes.[48]

Although LBOs have received extensive academic analysis as the principal form of highly leveraged acquisitions, companies leveraging themselves to a previously unconsidered degree had a greater impact on the merger market, either through acquisitions that they consummated or acquisitions that they induced by others.[49] The volumes of the three types of acquisitions and their share of the top 100 acquisitions are outlined in table 9.6. Prominent acquisitions in which the acquirers leveraged themselves to a high degree included Occidental Petroleum's purchase of Cities Service in 1982, Stroh Brewery's purchase of Schlitz Brewing in 1982, Williams Companies' purchase of Northwest Energy in 1983, Mesa's minority purchases of Gulf Oil in 1983, and Stone Container's purchase of Continental Group's forest products division in 1983. Acquisitions induced by high leverage were based on those acquisitions among the twenty-five largest stimulated by a highly leveraged raid or an attempted LBO. The principal acquisitions were of Gulf Oil, Getty Oil, Esmark, St. Regis, and Getty's sale of ERC in 1984; General American Oil, Texas Gas, Norton Simon, and Citgo Petroleum in 1983; Cities Service Gas in 1982; and Conoco and Seagram's purchase of 20% of DuPont in 1981.

The banks' role in precipitating mergers had a striking effect from 1981 to 1983, raising the proportion of mergers related to high leverage from 3% during 1979–1980 to over 25%. It was the combination of highly leveraged bank lending and junk bonds in 1984 that supercharged the effects of high leverage on mergers. Volume roughly quadrupled to over $45 billion in 1984 and accounted for 44% of the top 100 mergers. Undoubtedly further research would show that this proportion was even higher.

Growth in the volume of highly leveraged acquisitions was initiated by changes in the commercial banks' standards from being conservative lenders to being aggressive participants in merger transactions. We are able to trace these changes quite precisely. Banks in the 1970s showed little willingness to make highly leveraged, high-risk loans, although numer-

Table 9.6. Highly Leveraged Acquisitions in the Top 100 (1979–1984)

Year	LBOs			Highly Leveraged Corporations			Induced by High Leverage			Totals		
	#	$ (Bill)	% of Top 100	#	$ (Bill)	% of Top 100	#	$ (Bill)	% of Top 100	#	$ (Bill)	% of Top 100
	Col 1	Col 2	Col 3	Col 4	Col 5	Col 6	Col 7	Col 8	Col 9	Col 10	Col 11	Col 12
1979	1	0.4	1.4%	1	0.5	2.2%	0	0	0	2	0.9	3.6%
1980	2	0.7	2.6%	0	0	0.0%	0	0	0	2	0.7	2.6%
1981	11	4.0	8.1%	3	0.8	1.7%	2	9.6	19.6%	16	14.4	29.4%
1982	14	3.2	6.3%	5	5.1	10.2%	2	1.6	3.2%	21	9.9	19.7%
1983	13	2.5	6.9%	7	2.7	7.5%	4	4.1	11.4%	23	9.3	25.8%
1984	24	14.7	14.1%	1	1.0	1.0%	6	30.1	29.0%	31	45.8	44.1%
		25.5			10.1			45.4			81.0	

Source: My categorization of transactions from *Mergers & Acquisitions, Annual Almanac & Index*, "The Top 100," 1982–1985. Prior to 1982 I assembled my own data from quarterly issues.

ous commercial banks got in trouble in the 1970s because of bad loans. These troubled loans invariably occurred by mistake, however, rather than as a calculated tradeoff of high income for leverage. The banks were still quite conservative lenders at the turn of the decade. When the banks were not dealing with major corporations with sound credit, they sought substantial collateral for their loans, and they tried to minimize their risks. As long as these attitudes prevailed, the banks' role in merger transactions was limited to providing loans to fairly substantial companies. Highly leveraged risk transactions were mostly left to a few insurance companies that prided themselves on their analytical skills.

The banks crossed the first hurdle of making large loans for raids on other companies in the late 1970s, with all of the risks that entailed for a bank's reputation, litigation, and client relationships, but they did so only with substantial companies. The banks financed numerous large raids, such as United Technologies' offers for Babcock & Wilcox in 1977 ($688 million) and Carrier Corp. in 1978 ($950 million), Cooper Industries' offer for Gardner-Denver in 1979 ($630 million), Seagram Company's 1981 offers for St. Joe Minerals ($2.3 billion) and Conoco ($2.6 billion), Mobil's 1981 offers for Conoco ($7.8 billion) and Marathon Oil ($5.1 billion), and Enron's offer for Crouse-Hinds in 1981 ($700 million).

In 1980, Dome Petroleum broke new ground in bank borrowing with respect to both leverage and financing for a raid when it tendered for fourteen million shares of Conoco. The Bank of Montreal and three other Canadian banks lent Dome Petroleum $1.5 billion for the transaction. Dome's pro forma common equity ratio, based on $1.5 billion of additional debt, dropped to only 22.6% and its EBIT coverage of interest was only 0.8 times. The terms of this loan were modest—LIBOR + 0.375% and aggregate fees of 0.10%[50]—and did not represent banks trying to earn premium rates. Nor was the Dome loan a noteworthy precedent. Natural resource lending by the Canadian banks had always been unique in terms of its leverage and the risks the banks took, and Dome was the darling of Canada's national energy policy. Other than this loan, I could find no highly leveraged bank loans of $300 million or more between 1976 and 1981 relating to a raid.

In 1982 banks began to participate in leveraged raids with relatively modest companies, even at considerable cost in client relations and negative publicity. These loans involved previously unacceptable risks, both in terms of credit ratios and the dynamics of merger battles. The earliest and largest, and the resulting credit ratios, are outlined in table 9.7.

The first was to David Murdock, a real estate developer and stock market speculator whom I have already noted in the Occidental takeover of Cities Service and who rose to considerable prominence in the 1980s. Murdock borrowed $360 million from a bank syndicate led by Continental Illinois Bank & Trust to make an unfriendly offer for 100% of Can-

Table 9.7. Large Highly Leveraged Bank Loans for Raids (over $300MM)

Year	Amount ($MM) Col 1	Acquirer/Target Col 2	Pro forma EBIT/Int. Col 3	Pro forma Common as % Cap'n. Col 4	Debt as % Debt + Stock Mkt. Value Col 5
1981	1,500	Dome/Conoco	0.80	22.6%	49.5%
1982	360	Murdock/Cannon Mills	0.53	17.5%	n.a.
	1,050	Mesa/Cities Service	1.10	28.2%	61.8%
	1,000	Mesa/General American	1.30	20.0%	64.9%
	455	Goldsmith/Diamond International	0.72	30.7%	n.a.
1983	750	Coastal/Texas Gas	1.20	22.0%	74.7%
	900	Williams/Northwest Energy	0.82	29.7%	66.2%
	1,600	Coastal/HNG	0.85	16.6%	77.0%
	1,550	Mesa/Gulf	0.70	17.2%	62.9%
	2,500	Pennzoil/Getty	0.80	21.4%	67.5%
		Averages	0.88	22.6%	65.6%

Sources: SEC filings.

non Mills at $44 per share in February 1982. Murdock's borrowing vehicle was his private company, Pacific Holding Corporation, which despite profits from securities transactions of $41 million in 1980 and $57 million in 1981 had virtually no operating earnings before interest and taxes from 1979 to 1981, and existing debt of $226 million on equity of $124 million. Its securities investments were only $156 million versus its existing debt of $226 million and so represented only modest collateral. Assuming success in taking over Cannon Mills so that Cannon Mills' EBIT could pay his interest, the pro forma coverage of interest on Murdock's loans would be approximately 0.7 times and equity would be only 17.5% of capitalization. This was aggressive lending. The terms of the loan reflected the risks. Not only was the rate 111% of prime plus 1.5% (an average of 18% in 1982), repayment of $50 million was required in four months and a further $80 million in twelve months.[51]

Citibank made a similar high-risk loan of $455 million in October 1982 to Sir James Goldsmith's Generale Occidentale S.A. to take private Diamond International, a paper company on which he had spent three years accumulating 40% of its stock, fighting an extended proxy battle, and trying to take it over with its own junk debt. Citibank had been in Sir James's corner all the time, advancing at least $40 million for his purchases, but the complete package of financing had eluded him until Citibank became willing to lend Diamond $455 million. The pro forma interest coverage for the loan was only 0.7 times, and Diamond's common equity ratio only 30.7%. In fact, financing for the takeover was even more highly leveraged than this because Generale Occidentale had borrowed $189 million of the $229 million cost of its 40% equity stake. Sir James intended a rapid liquidation of Diamond to recoup his capital. He had presold $177 million of assets and had negotiated a "put" with Travelers Insurance to sell it $250 million worth of timberlands.[52]

Shortly after the loan to Murdock, Continental Illinois arranged a much more aggressive loan of $1.05 billion to Mesa Petroleum for its assault on Cities Service, as we have already seen. The loan was based on the collateral of Mesa's oil and gas reserves and securities. Adjusting Mesa's financials for the incremental debt, its pro forma coverage of fixed charges dropped to 1.1 times and its common equity ratio to 28%. If Mesa was successful in buying additional shares of Cities Service, or even taking it over, its fixed charge coverage would deteriorate further. The pro forma coverage of fixed charges when Occidental Petroleum subsequently took over Cities Service was 0.76 times. Since Mesa was a smaller company, we can infer that its pro forma coverage would have been less.

This loan was more aggressive than the loan to David Murdock. Mesa's tender offer was for only 20.5% of Cities Service, so there was no immediate prospect of consolidating Mesa with Cities Service's much larger cash flows. There was also much greater market risk in a minority stockholding since declining oil prices could hurt Cities Service's stock price, and at the very worst, the dividend could be cut.

The Continental Illinois group derived some security from Mesa's pre-tender stockholdings of over $300 million and its oil and gas reserves, which had an after-tax present value of $1.0 billion.[53] The $1.05 billion in loans was structured in A and B tranches of $600 million margined by securities, including the $555 million for which Mesa was tendering, and $450 million based on oil and gas reserves; but the value of the securities was inflated 50% by Mesa's own tender, and the values of both the securities and the oil and gas reserves were highly dependent on oil and gas prices. The reserve-based loan had a protective requirement that Mesa render semiannual reserve reports to the banks, and whenever reserve values were below a minimum base Mesa had to dedicate 95% of its operating income from oil and gas before overhead, interest, and income taxes to paying down debt; but this was an unenforceable covenant. Mesa could not delay income taxes, it could not cut overhead and capital expenditures fast enough to divert 95% of oil and gas operating income to debt repayments, and realizing the projected cash flows required significant capital expenditures.[54]

In these two early loans to finance raids, Continental Illinois and its syndicate banks might have persuaded themselves that they had collateral for their loans in terms of securities, oil and gas cash flows, and lien priorities; but historically the banks looked at the whole picture of a borrower's debts, not just their own collateral, and avoided loans where the risks of adverse market changes, litigation, and bankruptcy were high. Bankruptcies were expensive, time-consuming, and usually the banks' security interests were diluted in the negotiations with junior creditors. Continental Illinois had changed this attitude and decided to play in the high-stakes merger game for the fees and high-rate loans involved. Aggregate fees in the Mesa loan were almost 1%, or $10 million—unprecedented loan fees for a bank—and borrowings were at LIBOR + .75%, plus .50% on the unused portion of the credit versus traditional fees of LIBOR + .375%, plus .25% on the unused portion of the credit.

Continental Illinois Bank & Trust's role in these highly leveraged raid loans was abruptly ended in 1982 by its own financial problems due to troubled loans in the energy industry and to LDC borrowers, but Mesa had no problem in finding other banks to lead similar loans. Pickens moved on quickly from his success with Cities Service to make an offer for 51% of General American Oil in December 1982, a company in which Mesa had owned 7.5% of the stock since 1976. General American Oil was a much smaller target than Cities Service, worth only $1.1 billion at Mesa's $40 tender price. Mesa's tender offer was funded by a syndicate headed by Texas Commerce Bank and Citibank that provided a similar $1.05 billion loan package to that for the attack on Cities Service, except that the fees were slightly higher.[55]

The banks became considerably more aggressive when Mesa began an attack on Gulf Oil in August 1983. First, the bank loans were larger. Loans of $1.25 billion were arranged by Citibank and Texas Commerce Bank—this time in four tranches as they went to greater lengths to divide up collateral. Secondly, Gulf was one of America's largest corporations —a company that any bank would normally seek as a client. It was also symbolic of any large but mediocre company in that if Citibank would finance a raid on it, it would finance a raid on anyone. Thirdly, the target was so large that the banks had no sense at all where the situation might end up. Gulf Oil had a book common equity of almost $10 billion—20 times Mesa's—although it was selling for only two-thirds of book value. Mesa enlisted Wagner & Brown (Texas oil and gas wildcatters), the Belzbergs (Canadians), Sunshine Mining (Idaho), and Harbert Construction (Birmingham, Ala.) as partners to provide $185 million in additional equity in October, but by the time the Mesa Group had exhausted its bank credit resources it had only 21.7 million shares—13.2% of Gulf's outstanding stock. How Pickens would proceed from there was anybody's guess.

His first step was to present serious competition to Gulf in a December 1983 proxy battle in which Gulf sought to switch its incorporation to Delaware from Pennsylvania to get rid of Pennsylvania's proportionate voting requirements, which would have enabled Mesa to elect one or two directors. Pickens turned the proxy vote into a contest over whether Gulf should begin to liquidate through a royalty trust. Gulf won with only 52.5% of the vote—a shockingly close call.

Shortly after the Gulf proxy fight, Pickens met Michael Milken, and Drexel Burnham Lambert entered the picture. Milken arranged $300 million of junk bond and preferred financing for Mesa with Carl Lindner's Penn Central Corp. early in 1984, which permitted Mesa to arrange another $300 million of bank margin loans and tender for 13.5 million Gulf shares in February, taking the Mesa group up to 21.3%. At this point, assuming success on the tender, Mesa would have had only a 17% common equity ratio and its EBIT coverage of fixed charges would have been only 0.7 times (see table 9.7). This was not a sustainable credit position for Mesa, whose overall credit was clearly dependent on some favorable event such as Gulf paying greenmail or an acquirer stepping in. The collateral value of Gulf at $65 was completely dependent on some such event, since it had been only $38 when Mesa began buying. Yet both Mesa and Drexel Burnham were prepared to be even more aggressive. Although it was never made public, Drexel Burnham was in the process of raising a further $2.2 billion in junk bonds privately for Mesa[56] when Standard Oil of California offered Gulf $80 per share in March 1984, creating a profit for the Mesa group of $760 million. The outcome made the banks look smart, but their gamble on such an outcome was on a whole new scale.[57]

With such a dramatic success under his belt, Pickens was prepared to move on to attacks on Phillips Petroleum and Unocal, in which he had the support of both his commercial bankers and Drexel Burnham. Pickens's success was not lost on others in the oil industry. Pennzoil, another independent oil and gas producer that had been involved in numerous discussions trying to bid for Marathon and Cities Service, arranged in June 1983 for a massive $2.5 billion production payment loan with Citibank, secured by producing oil, gas, and sulfur properties, with the intent of being prepared when opportunity knocked. The pro forma effects of this loan for an unknown target were to reduce Pennzoil's common equity ratio to 21.4% and its EBIT coverage of interest to 0.8 times—similar results to those for Mesa's Gulf Oil borrowings. The opportunity Pennzoil was seeking occurred when differences became acute between the management of Getty Oil and both Gordon Getty, as the trustee for 40% of Getty Oil's stock, and the Getty Museum, which owned 11.8%. In December 1983, Pennzoil joined with Gordon Getty to take over Getty Oil at a cost to Pennzoil (after further negotiations) of approximately $2.6 billion, $2.3 billion of which was to come from Citibank. The transaction was disrupted by a higher, successful bid from Texaco, over which Pennzoil made history by suing and ultimately being awarded $10 billion against Texaco by a Texas court.

The disequilibriating force that Mesa represented in the oil industry had a parallel in the pipeline industry when the banks financed a series of highly leveraged raids by Oscar Wyatt's Coastal Corporation. These raids began in June 1983 when Bankers Trust Company arranged a $750 million loan for Coastal's raid on Texas Gas Resources. Coastal, like Mesa Petroleum, was a minor company in its industry, in this case a natural gas pipeline and refining company based in Houston that was most notable for reneging on its gas supply contracts with natural gas distributors in the early 1970s. Texas Gas was a leading natural gas pipeline with a strong financial history and interests in barging and trucking as well. Like Pickens, Wyatt accumulated a significant position in his target before he struck, buying 529,000 shares of Texas Gas at an average cost of $35 per share in the month before he announced a tender offer for 52% of Texas Gas at $45 per share. CSX Corp. appeared as a competing bidder at $52 per share, and induced Coastal to drop out by paying it $18 million, putatively for expenses. Coastal made a profit of $22 million on its 529,000 shares and the expense payment, which was almost $10 million above Coastal's actual expenses.[58]

Coastal's pro forma credit ratios for its loan were comparable to those for Mesa Petroleum's attack on Cities Service. Adjusting Coastal's own financials for an incremental $750 million of debt resulted in its common equity ratio dropping to 22% and EBIT of 1.2 times interest.[59] The loan terms were also similar to Mesa Petroleum's, involving a front-end fee of 0.75% (with some variation, depending on the bank and usage) and an interest rate of LIBOR + .75%. Coastal never had to use the bank lines.

Only three months later, Citibank and Bankers Trust financed another highly leveraged pipeline raid, lending $900 million to Tulsa-based Williams Companies for a raid on Northwest Energy, a Salt Lake City-based pipeline company serving the Pacific Northwest. Williams's resulting common equity ratio was 29.7% and its EBIT coverage of interest only 0.8 times. Even if we adjusted Williams Companies' EBIT up to its 1981 level to reflect that its fertilizer business was cyclically depressed (it wasn't — 1981 was a peak that did not recur), its EBIT coverage of interest was only 1.3 times. Moody's immediately cut the rating on Williams Companies' debt to Ba.[60] The banks' loan terms to Williams Companies were actually more lenient than to Mesa and Coastal, probably reflecting that Williams was not a greenmailer. It owned only ten thousand shares of Northwest Energy and its offer was for 100% of the stock. Williams was also a substantial factor in its own industries of oil products pipelines and fertilizers. The interest rate was LIBOR + .50%, and front-end fees aggregated slightly less than 0.40%.[61]

The banks' intentions to use highly leveraged raid loans as a vehicle to share in the high profits of the merger and acquisition business became much clearer near the end of 1983 when Bankers Trust and Citicorp negotiated a $1.6 billion loan for Coastal Corp.'s January 1984 unfriendly tender offer for 51% of Houston Natural Gas (HNG). Again the pro forma financial ratios were very weak. Adding the $1.6 billion of debt to Coastal's own financials resulted in a common equity ratio of only 16.6%, and pro forma interest coverage of 0.8 times—approaching Mesa's ratios for the attack on Gulf Oil.[62] HNG countered in the courts and with a bid to take over Coastal; but the battle was settled when HNG agreed to pay Coastal $124.5 million for its HNG stock, $15 million for expenses, and committed to subeconomic gas transportation and purchase agreements. Coastal booked a gain of approximately $36 million. This time, however, the banks' loan structure was prepared for such an eventuality. The credit agreement provided for borrowing at LIBOR + 1%, and front-end fees aggregating 0.75%, but it also included front-end fees of $1 million each for Bankers Trust and Citibank, 10% of any Coastal profits on the sale of its HNG stock up to $1 million for each bank, and $2 million each if Coastal was successful in acquiring HNG.[63]

The bank loans to Mesa Petroleum for its raids on Cities Service, General American Oil, and Gulf Oil, to Pennzoil for its raid on Getty Oil, to Coastal Corp. for its raids on Texas Gas and Houston Natural Gas, to Williams Companies for its raid on Northwest Energy, to David Murdock for his acquisition of Cannon Mills, and to Sir James Goldsmith for his acquisition of Diamond International, were not large relative to banks' total merger-related loans, but they marked an evolution in banks' lending practices with important implications for future acquisition lending. Previous small-time raiders without substantial equity and earnings of their own had been forced to rely on proxy fights, minority positions, and exchanges of their own (usually poorly rated) securities in attempting takeovers. For example, Curtiss-Wright was forced into a protracted 1978 proxy battle in its effort to take control of Kennecott; Carl Icahn forced his way onto the Tappan Company's board in a proxy fight in 1979 to stimulate its sale to Electrolux AB; Irwin Jacobs similarly forced his way onto the Pabst board in 1981 to push for its sale or restructuring; Victor Posner was only able to acquire U.V. Industries in 1979 in exchange for subordinated junk bond debentures of Sharon Steel, and his threatening minority positions during 1979–1982 in Foremost McKesson, Reliance Electric, Marley Companies, Evans Products, and Burnup & Sims never involved bank loans larger than $60 million.

When Continental Illinois, Bankers Trust, and Citibank began in 1982 to make large, highly leveraged loans for raids with consolidated EBIT coverages of interest of 1.0 or less, they were embarking on brand new lending patterns very similar to their simultaneous expansion in LBO loans (see below). The banks may have persuaded themselves that they had collateral for their loans in terms of securities, oil and gas cash flows, and lien priorities. It is difficult for an outside observer to analyze the collateral values that the banks might have used, but we can create a proxy by calculating each borrower's resulting debt as a percentage of total debt plus the market value of its common stock, which is outlined in column 5 of table 9.7. The market value of the borrower's common equity is a proxy for the residual value of the company net of the liability for debt. Even on this basis, debt leverage was 65.6%—a very high level, particularly when the value of so many of the targets was dependent on commodities prices. The focus on collateral is itself a sign of the changing bank attitudes. Not that banks didn't take great pains in getting collateral—they did—but historically the banks looked at the whole picture of a borrower's debts, not just their own senior position, and avoided loans where there were high risks of adverse market changes, litigation, and delay, let alone large uncertainties about additional leverage. These three banks, and soon just two of them, lending mostly to two minor companies in the oil and gas and pipeline industries, were writing new rules in bank loan competition that would have a great effect on many other industries in future years.

A simple example illustrates the point. A bidder in 1982 borrowing 100% of the costs at 14%[64] could pay 7.1 times the combined value of the target's existing debt and stock market value if the lender only required pretax interest coverage of 1.0 times.[65] The average common stock premium for a successful tender was approximately 40%, and the average industrial company had a 62% common equity ratio, which meant that any company with a combined debt and stock market value that was 5.6 times its EBIT or lower was vulnerable.[66] The S&P Industrials in 1982 averaged only 6.3 times EBIT, suggesting many of its component companies were vulnerable. At an EBIT coverage of 0.8 times, a borrower could pay a 40% premium on a company selling at 7.0 times EBIT,[67] which was higher than the average company in the S&P Industrial index. If the EBIT interest coverage requirement was 2.0 times, which was probably more typical of earlier minimum bank loan requirements, a 100% leveraged acquirer could only pay 3.5 times a target's EBIT.[68] There were hardly any companies for which the 100% leveraged buyer could compete at this level when the market average was 6.3 times EBIT, and it is therefore not surprising that we do not find any such loans. Of course, highly leveraged acquisitions by existing companies were even more competitive in the targets they could go after because they were leveraging their own operations as well as the target's. But the example above makes a fundamental point—the change from interest coverages above 2.0 times to interest coverages of 1.0 times, or even lower, was a sea change in terms of the number of targets that became vulnerable.

Prior to this change on the part of the banks, the tactics required of highly leveraged raiders were unsavory enough to keep their ranks small and the raiders themselves confined to the periphery of the financial world. Once the banks provided easier terms a whole new group of raiders was created. Protracted harassment, publicity campaigns, proxy fights, and the uncertainty that accompanied them were no longer necessary. Cash tender offers set a prompt deadline under which raiders were sure to receive stock and immediately provoked targets to try to find other higher bidders. Either way, raiders won, as both Mesa Petroleum and Coastal Corp. recognized.

Others outside the oil and gas industry were sure to see the opportunities as well. Once the hurdles of absolute size, high leverage, and lending for raids had been passed, there was nothing to stop the banks from lending based on asset values in other industries. Their loans to David Murdock to acquire Cannon Mills and to Sir James Goldsmith to acquire Diamond International proved that, and the point was confirmed in 1984 when banks made highly leveraged loan commitments for raids by Chicago Pacific Corporation on Textron, by Sir James Goldsmith on Continental Group, and by Rupert Murdoch on St. Regis Corp.

The Role of the Banks in Leveraged Buyouts

The banks also played the key role in the expansion of LBOs between 1979 and 1984. LBOs were nothing new, but until the banks changed their lending standards LBO transactions were isolated, highly specialized, and tended to be small.

There was a long history of a few aggressive financiers borrowing most of the money to finance small acquisitions based on the cash flows of the companies they acquired. "Boot strapping" was the earlier term for such financing. Dyson-Kissner-Moran started in the 1950s and built a portfolio of six medium-sized companies by the mid-1970s using high leverage. Carl Hess at AEA Investors built a similar portfolio with the help of a "club" of retired chief executives who acted as equity investors and contact sources. Leon Levy and Jack Nash at Oppenheimer & Co initiated the modern leveraged buyout during 1976–1977 when they purchased four small companies aggregating almost $100 million with very high leverage.[69] In the next two years they purchased four more aggregating $90 million.[70]

Kohlberg, Kravis, Roberts & Co. (KKR), formed in May 1976 by three Bear Stearns alumni, Jerome Kohlberg (age fifty-one), Henry Kravis (thirty-two), and George Roberts (thirty-two), immediately marked a more aggressive version of the LBO business. Their first purchase was of L. B. Foster Co. for $106 million. KKR did three transactions in 1977, none in 1978, and three in 1979; but what really gained it attention was its success in 1979 in making the first leveraged buyout of a public company—Houdaille Inc., a pump, machinery, and auto parts company—for $355 million. This suddenly made investment bankers believers in the LBO option as a defense against unfriendly takeover efforts.[71] It took over six months to line up the financing with twenty-three institutions—four banks, sixteen insurance companies, and three pension funds—in eight different tranches. Common stock was part of the package for all of the lenders as an additional incentive. The resulting common equity ratio was 6.9%, and EBIT coverage of fixed charges was approximately 1.1 times.[72]

KKR and others translated the Houdaille model into a significant position in the merger market in 1981, accounting for eleven transactions, $4.0 billion, and 8.1% of the top 100 transactions. LBO volume was 6–14% of the top 100 mergers throughout 1981–1984, as we have already seen in table 9.6, column 3. KKR was very successful in capitalizing on its success with Houdaille, closing six LBOs in 1981, all of which were among the year's 100 largest mergers: Fred Meyer Inc. ($435 million), Bendix's forest products division ($425 million), Norris Industries ($420 million), Marley Co. ($325 million), Owens-Illinois's Lily-Tulip subsidiary ($150 million), and FMC Corp.'s power transmission group ($125 million).

About the same time, William Simon, out of a job as Treasury secretary after Jimmy Carter's victory, teamed up with Raymond Chambers to form Wesray Capital and buy companies on a highly leveraged basis. It eventually became common to highlight Wesray's purchase of Gibson Greetings Cards from RCA in 1982 as the spark that lit the LBO boom.[73] Wesray bought Gibson Greetings for $80 million with only $1 million of equity and took it public sixteen months later at a price that valued Wesray's $1 million stake at $70 million. This was indeed a killing, but LBOs were already far advanced the year before through KKR.

The largest commercial bank holding companies provided equity as well as debt to these early LBOs. KKR's 1979 fund of $32 million was all raised from individuals, but in the Houdaille transaction, KKR sold the crucial $23.5 million of preferred stock, which doubled the equity in the transaction, to four bank holding companies that also provided a $60 million revolving credit.[74] Ten large U.S. banks put capital into KKR's 1983 LBO fund, including Citicorp and Security Pacific, which invested $100 million each via their venture capital subsidiaries.[75] The banks thereafter accounted for 30% of KKR's equity capital, even when a fund as large as $5.6 billion was raised in 1987.[76] State and local government retirement funds were also important investors in LBO funds, as were numerous corporate pension funds, but I will defer discussion of the sources of LBO equity capital until volume 2.

There was a change in commercial banks' lending standards to LBOs in 1982 that matched their changed attitudes toward lending for raids, as can be seen in table 9.8, which outlines the details of pricing and financing for forty-four LBOs of public companies.[77] Prior to 1982, while LBO activity was still small and dominated by KKR, insurance companies and pension funds accounted for over 50% of the financing for most transactions (column 8) and the banks invariably took smaller, as well as senior, creditor positions. If we adjust these early years by eliminating the Trans Union and 20th Century Fox transactions on the grounds that wealthy buyers guaranteed the bank loans, banks accounted for only 29% of the financing, or 22% excluding Norris Industries. LBO acquisitions were quite constricted under these circumstances. Assembling large groups of insurance company lenders involved months of effort, extensive due diligence, and highly restrictive covenants on future actions. This began to change in KKR's purchase of Norris Industries in August 1981, when KKR used banks for 69% of the funding. In 1982 banks' share of LBO funding rose to 78.6% and stayed high thereafter (column 7).

The banks' role in LBO financing reflected a change in banks' risk attitudes, just as we have seen in highly leveraged loans for raids. Not only were the banks participating in transactions where the overall credit provided very marginal protection against bankruptcy since EBIT coverage of interest was so close to 1.0 times; when the banks increased the proportion of the transactions that they were financing from 20–30% that was well secured by receivables or other liquid assets to over 70%, they were becoming directly vulnerable to not being paid rather than just involved in a messy situation in which more junior creditors went short. No matter how their loan agreements were worded, the banks were going from being senior creditors to junior creditors as well.

The EBIT/interest ratios for the LBOs outlined in column 6 of table 9.8 indicate that financing standards drove the pricing of these transactions. The EBIT/interest ratios were generally consistent around 1.0 times from 1979 to 1984 through highly varying environments for both interest rates and economic growth. Nor did the EBIT/interest ratios vary greatly to reflect different growth prospects or asset values for the companies. Twenty-four of the forty-four transactions had EBIT/interest ratios between 0.8 and 1.2 times, and adjustments for anticipated earnings would have put even more transactions within this range. It required an unusual company with highly visible asset values, such as in the media industries, to produce ratios much below this range.

What accounted for the change in the money center banks' lending attitudes from 1982 to 1984? The accepted interpretation of savings and loans' exaggerated risk-taking behavior in this period is that these institutions were economically bankrupt and rolling the dice in high risk investments in an effort to recoup their losses, or else managed by criminal or gladhanding executives who padded their own pockets and popularity by freely dispersing other people's money. There is a parallel in the money center banks in that their nonperforming loans tripled between 1980 and 1983, and their domestic nonperforming loans plus LDC loans at the end of 1982 averaged almost 200% of their combined reserves and stock-

Table 9.8. Important Ratios for Leveraged Buyouts of Public Companies in the Top 100[1]

Proxy Date[2] Col 1	Acquired Company Col 2	Acquirer Col 3	Cost/ EBIT Col 4	% Equity Col 5	EBIT/ Int Col 6	Banks % Total Col 7	Insurance % Total Col 8
4/79	Houdaille	KKR	9.5	13.6%	1.1	22.0%	64.8%
		Averages	9.5	13.6%	1.1	22.0%	64.8%
1/80	Congoleum Corp	First Boston	5.2	12.9%	2.4	32.9%	53.7%
9/80	Trans Union	Pritzkers	8.1	7.9%	1.1	97.9%	—
12/80	Rapid American	Meshulam Riklis	5.6	5.2%	1.1	—	—
		Averages	6.3	8.7%	1.5	65.4%	53.7%
4/81	Marley Co	KKR	7.0	10.8%	1.0	23.3%	63.9%
5/81	20th Century Fox	Marvin Davis	8.7	23.8%	0.8	76.2%	—
7/81	Coca Cola-NY	Gibbons Green	12.7	11.6%	0.7	21.2%	46.9%
8/81	Norris Industries	KKR	5.9	12.5%	1.2	68.6%	9.5%
11/81	Fred Meyer	KKR	8.8	10.0%	1.0	34.5%	53.3%
		Averages	8.6	13.8%	0.9	44.7%	43.4%
3/82	Cannon Mills	David Murdock	7.4	17.5%	0.8	87.2%	—
5/82	Arcata Corp	Scarff	19.7	11.7%	0.4	86.0%	—
5/82	Allright	Private investors	13.3	37.0%	0.8	59.8%	—
6/82	Dentsply	Kelso	5.2	13.6%	1.4	71.7%	14.5%
7/82	Purex	Gibbons Green	5.2	7.8%	1.3	81.8%	18.2%
8/82	Criton Corp	Dysson-Kissner	4.6	19.4%	1.9	77.5%	—
8/82	Signode	Merril Lynch	5.7	13.2%	1.2	71.3%	17.6%
8/82	Questor	Lufkin, Scarff	8.9	24.9%	1.1	100.0%	—
11/82	Diamond Int'l	Sir J. Goldsmith	16.0	5.4%	0.7	94.2%	36.5%[4]
11/82	W'mshouse-Regency	Carl Marks & Co	7.2	12.1%	1.3	43.0%	37.5%
12/82	CCI Corp	Private Investors	3.0	4.9%	2.9	91.8%	—
		Averages	8.7	15.2%	1.2	78.6%	24.9%

Table **9.8.** (*continued*)

Proxy Date[2] Col 1	Acquired Company Col 2	Acquirer Col 3	Cost/ EBIT Col 4	% Equity Col 5	EBIT/ Int Col 6	Banks % Total Col 7	Insurance % Total Col 8
2/83	Dillingham	KKR	7.8	16.0%	1.2	79.8%	—
4/83	Coca Cola-Miami	Private investors	13.9	11.5%	0.7	54.9%	30.5%
4/83	Dan River	Kelso	7.3[3]	6.7%	1.1	59.1%	38.1%
7/83	Albany Int'l	Private investors	5.0[3]	16.6%	1.8	90.9%	—
9/83	Raymond Int'l	Kelso	6.3	14.8%	1.4	82.2%	—
12/83	Kaiser Steel	Frates Group	18.2	7.3%	1.0	37.3%	—
12/83	Pargas	Reliance	7.9	5.5%	1.2	58.5%	24.4%
12/83	Hyster Co	ESCO	6.6[3]	21.1%	0.3	69.2%	—
		Averages	9.1	12.1%	1.1	66.5%	31.0%
1/84	Amstar	KKR	9.3	21.5%	1.1	89.6%	—
1/84	Dr. Pepper	Forstmann Little	16.6	4.7%	0.5	75.6%	18.5%
2/84	Cone Mills	Private investors	15.0	9.7%	0.6	90.3%	—
3/84	Wometco Enterprises	KKR	15.7	14.4%	0.6	79.6%	—
5/84	Metromedia	John Kluge	18.9	10.5%	0.5	68.0%	7.5%
5/84	ACF Industries	Carl Icahn	9.8	18.5%	0.7	66.1%	—
8/84	Continental Group	Kiewit-Murdock	11.6	23.5%	0.8	58.8%	—
8/84	Harte Hanks Comm'ns	Goldman Sachs	13.9	8.7%	0.7	61.6%	4.6%
8/84	Malone & Hyde	KKR	9.1	19.7%	1.0	79.3%	—
8/84	Cole National Corp	KKR	10.4	27.5%	1.1	67.2%	—
9/84	Pay'n Save	Private investors	7.6	7.1%	1.2	91.0%	32.8%[4]
10/84	Nat'l Medical Care	W.R.Grace	7.7	18.5%	1.2	81.2%	—
10/84	Rio Grande Ind	Phil Anschutz	14.3	8.0%	0.6	92.0%	—
10/84	Blue Bell	Kelso	6.7	10.3%	1.2	67.9%	20.3%
10/84	Brooks Fashion	AEA Investors	9.1	26.7%	1.2	73.3%	—
11/84	ARA	Goldman Sachs	8.2	8.1%	1.1	71.6%	16.7%
		Averages	11.5	14.8%	0.9	75.8%	16.7%

[1]Excludes financial companies and oil and gas. See Appendix 9.2 for data definition and sources.

[2]Or date of Offer to Purchase if no proxy.

[3]1981 rather than 1982 EBIT.

[4]Bank and insurance totals occasionally exceed 100% when a proxy reveals that an insurance company financing will follow initial bank financing.

holders' equity, as we saw in chapter 2. However, these banks were not economically bankrupt. Both nonperforming and LDC loans had substantial economic value, and the stocks of these money-center banks had an aggregate market value of $15–20 billion at the end of 1982. Although they were heavily burdened by their nonperforming loans, they still had a return on equity of approximately 10% after very heavy provisions for loan losses.

Nor did the banks that were the weakest correspond with those most aggressively expanding these riskier loans. Continental Illinois was the weakest and the first to accept interest coverages of 1.0 or less in both raids and LBOs, but once it was sidelined by its problems in mid-1982, the more aggressive banks were a mixed lot. Citibank was the new leader, and while its capital ratios were weak, its rising relative stock price indicated that it was strengthening. Manufacturers Hanover was an aggressive LBO lender and the next weakest after Continental Illinois, but the other aggressive lenders such as Bankers Trust, Morgan Guaranty Trust, and Security Pacific were among the strongest banks. In fact, banks' lending in these areas reflected the expertise and marketing skills they developed rather than different risk appetites. The concept of these banks "rolling the dice" in high-risk loans in hopes of high profits has little intuitive appeal. The banks at issue were among the leading banks in the world with strong institutional structures and substantial, sophisticated staffs.

Many financial professionals attributed the banks' lending behavior to competitive pressures. The loan expansion occurred just as deregulated deposits soared in both volume and cost, but when general loan volume was contracting. Oil, real estate, and LDC loan expansion was no longer viable, and consumer and commercial-industrial loan growth was minimal. The banks might have reduced their competition for deposits in this circumstance, but the introduction of money market accounts in December 1982 as a result of federal legislation, just when loan growth was at its weakest, produced the opposite effect. Banks saw it as a defining moment in their customer relationships because of the magnitude of the change in deposit rates and account structure and paid above-market rates to attract depositors. Flush with these deposits, the banks sought out the only high-rate loan alternatives, which were for raids and leveraged buyouts. This interpretation is borne out in table 9.9, which outlines the annual changes in commercial and industrial loans at the top ten money center banks compared with their commitments for raids and LBOs. These commitments escalated from $1.1 billion in 1981 to $9.5 billion in 1984 and accounted for 85% of commercial and industrial loan growth between 1982 and 1984.

The annual estimates of loans represent the banks' commitments for the raids in table 9.7 and the LBOs in table 9.8. The reader should be

Table 9.9. Top Ten Banks' Incremental Commercial & Industrial Loans[1] Compared with LBO and Highly Leveraged Raid Loans ($ Millions)

Institution	1980	1981	1982	1983	1984
Bank of America	1,838	1,126	1,789	1,304	2,217
Bankers Trust	611	768	2,110	945	-498
Chase Manhattan	1,274	661	-373	-1,025	1,555
Chemical[2]	812	1,414	2,091	1,406	1,951
Citicorp	1,305	1,894	1,713	-2,907	1,118
Continental Illinois		3,017	853	-1,457	-1,622
First Chicago		1,610	180	125	985
Manufacturers Hanover	1,186	2,365	3,542	1,293	5,837
J. P. Morgan	851	-51	467	-864	1,040
Security Pacific	723	540	1,803	971	1,203
Totals	8,600	13,344	14,175	-209	13,786
Total LBO & Raid Loans	725	1,116	5,406	8,839	9,535
% of Increase	8%	8%	38%	N.A.	69%

Sources: Annual reports.

[1]Average daily balances ($ millions).

[2]Includes financial institutions.

aware that the banks commitments for raids rarely turned into loans, so the comparison is slightly artificial. However, the banks received substantial fees for these raid commitments, which provided profits similar to net interest margins on loans.

The Japanese banks, which later in the decade were susceptible to high-risk loans, were not a competitive pressure on the money center banks at this time. Their U.S. commercial and industrial loans only rose $2.2 billion from 1982 to 1983.[78]

Junk Bond Financing of Acquisitions

Just as the banks stimulated acquisition volume when they lowered their credit standards in 1982, the junk bond market turbocharged acquisition growth in 1984 when raiders took advantage of its lower standards. Prior to that, junk bonds were not a meaningful factor in acquisitions, as only a few companies were able to use them. Victor Posner took over U.V. Industries in 1979 with $411 million of 15.50% junk-rated debt, but in the unique circumstances of taking over a bankrupt, liquidating company and exchanging the junk debt directly with the liquidating trust for its assets. Meshulam Riklis took Rapid American Corp. private in 1980, offering stockholders $45 each in 8% subordinated debentures. Carl Lindner gave stockholders $27 per share in 13.5% junk-rated preferred stock when he took American Financial Corp. private that same year. Saul Steinberg gave stockholders a choice of $65.50 of junk-rated 15% preferred stock or $13 cash plus $52.50 of junk-rated 17% debentures when he took Reliance Insurance private in 1982. But the success of this group appeared unique. They acquired controlling minority interests in their companies before attempting the buyouts, and their offers were carefully timed so that the bonds' interest coverage ratio was close to or over 1.0. It is tempting to conclude that they also represented a cabal. Riklis, Lindner, and Steinberg cooperated and invested with each other extensively and were old hands in the market aspects of "chinese paper" from the merger wave of the late 1960s. They also had a common involvement with Michael Milken's group at Drexel Burnham that probably helped to create enough liquidity for their new junk securities to make the offers real economic choices.

Others were unable to make junk bond packages work in takeovers. Victor Posner was unable to repeat his success with U.V. Industries. He made junk bond offers to City Investing and National Can that were simply ignored. His junk bond effort to take over Evans Products was turned down by lenders. Sir James Goldsmith was unsuccessful, offering $21 in cash and $21 in debt for Diamond International shares in 1981, and was forced to come up with $44.50 in cash. Boone Pickens was unable to raise financing to buy more than 20% of Cities Service and was forced to rely on a somewhat vague proposal to put Cities Service's oil and gas assets into a royalty trust. The only exceptions were Occidental Petroleum's use of junk-rated preferred stock and near-junk zero-coupon bonds in the second stage of its acquisition of Cities Service and Kaiser Steel's use of $178 million of junk preferred in its 1983 LBO. In the Occidental case, however, the assets underlying the securities were demonstrably substantial and the company was expected to promptly restore its credit quality. Its bonds were still rated Baa/BBB. In the Kaiser case, the preferred stock was a technique for creating a contingent payment based on the uncertain proceeds of liquidating its Fontana Steelworks and selling its Canadian coal operations.

Junk bond underwritings[79] for acquisitions amounted to only $400 million during 1980–1982, and averaged only 10% of total junk bond public issues, itself a small number. Total junk bond acquisition financing grew to $800 million in 1983 — 22% of all junk bond financing, but still a small number overall.[80] If we counted as acquisition debt $400 million of subordinated debt with warrants sold by MGM/UA in April 1983 to refund debt it incurred in its 1981 acquisition of United Artists from Transamerica, 33% of junk bond financing would have been for acquisitions, but the overall magnitude was still small. It was eye-catching, however, that MGM/UA could raise $400 million with interest coverage of only 1.4 times.[81]

The crucial transaction in extending LBO financing to the junk bond market was John Kluge's LBO of Metromedia (of which he was chief

executive), announced at the end of 1983. Metromedia was a conglom-
erate of television and radio stations, radio paging and cellular licenses,
outdoor advertising, and entertainment production, including the Harlem
Globetrotters. Television and radio broadcasting provided $109 million
of its $126 million in 1983 operating income, but the company was in a
transition of major proportions. Kluge had sold the outdoor advertising
business in 1983 to a limited partnership for a pretax gain of $300 mil-
lion while continuing to manage it for a fee. He also sold TV stations in
Minneapolis and Cincinnati and bought stations in Chicago and Dallas.
Most importantly, Metromedia was creating a major presence in the
booming radio telecommunications business as an outgrowth of its paging operations in Chicago, Los Angeles, Dallas, Boston, Washington,
D.C., and San Antonio. It had cellular telephone licenses in New York
City, Los Angeles, Philadelphia, Boston, Chicago, Baltimore, and Washington, D.C., and it shared in cellular applications for licenses in fifty-
three of the nation's ninety largest markets. Operating income in this
area was a modest $9 million, but the business was in its infancy and
knowledgeable investors looked for very rapid growth.

The changes in Metromedia's business and the uncertainty about its
cellular telephone prospects led the stock on a roller coaster ride through
1983, rising from approximately $29 in January to $56 in July, but then
down to $20 in November. This was too much for Kluge, who was ex-
tremely focused on Metromedia's stock price and excited about the
bright prospects of the cellular telephone business. He put together a
$1.9 billion LBO on the company, offering stockholders $30 per share in
cash plus $22.50 in 16% debentures, putting 4.5 million of his own
shares (out of 7.2 million) into the financing as equity.

Kluge was no stranger to leverage—the company had $578 million of
debt on only $198 million of book equity at the time of the offer, partly
because he bought back almost 40% of the company's stock during
1980–1982—but his proposal was unprecedented. His cash costs to pay
stockholders and redeem existing debt involved borrowing $1.2 billion
from a group of banks led by Manufacturers Hanover Trust at an interest cost of almost 15% and with the condition that he repay $200 million
within eighteen months by selling a major television station. The 16%
debentures carried no interest payments for the first five years, and so
would sell at a discount price, estimated at approximately $43.50. The
preacquisition EBIT available to pay the resulting $209 million annual
interest charge was only $99 million—0.5 times coverage! Setting aside
the debentures' interest that accrued for the first five years, EBIT coverage of cash interest was only 0.6 times, and EBITD coverage of cash interest was only 0.9 times. Here was a case of anticipating growth with a
vengeance.[82] Kluge's offer was instantly successful—the first straightforward case outside the Riklis-Steinberg-Lindner group.

The success of the Metromedia LBO and the terms of its junk bonds opened up LBO possibilities for rapidly growing companies selling at high price-earnings ratios that otherwise couldn't meet a 1.0 times interest test. The Metromedia price was 18.9 times EBIT versus an average of approximately 8.5 times for the twenty-six LBOs between 1979 and 1983. The lesson was promptly adopted by others, as Goldman Sachs advised both Harte Hanks Communications and ARA Corp. to include junk bonds in the consideration they offered to stockholders for LBOs.

The power of the Metromedia example was supercharged within the year by Kluge's determination not to be bound by the bank loan covenants, which would force him to sell one of his prime television stations. As Kluge cast around the investment banking community for financing alternatives, Drexel Burnham recommended putting the television and radio stations into a separate subsidiary called Metromedia Broadcasting and selling junk bonds secured by these assets. In late 1984 Drexel underwrote $1.9 billion of Metromedia Broadcasting junk bonds to raise $1.3 billion in cash and pay off the banks—ten times the largest junk bond financing to date. The bonds were sold in strips of various maturities, including deeply discounted bonds and $680 million of zero-coupon bonds, at an average interest cost of 15.4% and a near-term cash interest cost of 10.3%. The EBIT coverage of interest was only 0.5 times and EBITD coverage only 0.6 times. EBIT coverage of just cash interest was only 0.8 times and EBITD coverage 0.9 times.[83] As a result of these issues, 100% of the Metromedia LBO had been financed with junk bonds.

Expanded use of junk bonds in acquisitions had been presaged in 1983 by a decline in the EBIT coverage of interest for new-issue junk bonds, just as a decline in the banks' interest coverage requirements stimulated highly leveraged corporate and LBO transactions in 1982. Table 9.10 outlines the annual averages for EBIT coverage of interest for new-issue junk bonds underwritten between 1980 and 1984, and the proportion of these issues used for acquisitions. Coverage of interest by earnings before interest and taxes (EBIT) for junk bond new-issues dropped 62%, from 2.1 in 1982 to only 0.8 times in 1983. This coverage was very similar to that for bank loans in highly leveraged raids and to the overall coverage for LBOs, and we have already seen how a decline of this magnitude made acquisition targets of companies typical of the S&P Industrial index, whereas they were almost completely invulnerable when EBIT coverage was 2.0 times. There was an important difference in the low junk bond interest coverage requirement, however. Junk bonds were invariably subordinated debt, while bank loans were senior debt. Coverages this low for subordinated debt presaged new higher levels of combined bank and junk bond debt. It was in November 1983, with this decline in coverages well established, that Drexel's corporate finance de-

Table 9.10. Pro Forma EBIT Coverage of Interest for New-issue Junk Bonds

Year	Amount ($B)	EBIT/ interest	% for M&A
1980	0.9	2.0	11%
1981	1.2	2.0	5%
1982	1.5	2.1	13%
1983	3.6	0.8	22%
1984	7.4	1.1	45%

Source: Barrie A. Wigmore, "The Decline in Credit Quality of New-Issue Junk Bonds," *The Financial Analysts Journal*, September/October 1990, table 1.

partment and Michael Milken's junk bond group jointly decided to market their junk bond capability to finance mergers.[84]

These new low coverage requirements were translated into the merger market in early 1984 when Drexel Burnham raised $300 million in junk bonds and preferred stock for Mesa Petroleum from Carl Lindner's Penn Central Corp. with a fixed charge coverage of only 0.64 times. These subordinated funds were the critical component in Mesa's ability to raise its Cities Service stake to over 20%. Drexel Burnham followed this rather unique financing with a private effort to raise $2.1 billion in junk debt for Mesa on the basis of a plan to liquidate Gulf Oil. The prospect pushed Gulf into auctioning itself to Standard Oil of California and the financing was never completed, but it was a formidable example of financing power. Shortly after the resolution of the battle with Gulf Oil, Drexel sold $500 million of subordinated junk bonds for Mesa, greatly adding to its capital base for future raids.

Drexel's fundraising ability quickly attracted Sir James Goldsmith, who was putting together financing to tender for Continental Group. There never was a Goldsmith tender offer that revealed his financing, but he was reported to have arranged total commitments of $2.4 billion. Junk bonds were probably $500 million to $1 billion of this. He balked, however, at paying the $30–40 million in commitment fees required and settled for the profit from selling his shares to a white knight bid by Peter Kiewit Sons and David Murdock.[85]

Drexel's junk bond financing power also played a role in the multi-party duel in the last half of 1984 over Walt Disney Productions from which the Bass brothers emerged with control. The first attack on Disney was by Saul Steinberg's Reliance Insurance, which accumulated 11% of Disney's stock in the open market and in June threatened to tender for an additional 38%. Drexel made Steinberg's offer credible by issuing its first "highly confident" letter saying that it could sell $700 million in junk bonds for the deal. Walt Disney responded by paying greenmail to Steinberg, whereupon Irwin Jacobs began a repeat performance, buying 7.7% of Disney's stock. He was turned into a real threat when Drexel simultaneously raised $300 million for his company, Minstar Inc. The Bass brothers bought him out, raising their own stake to 25%.

We have already seen that subsequent to the Walt Disney battle Drexel raised $1.3 billion for Metromedia on unprecedented terms. In 1984 as a whole, junk bond financing more than doubled to $7.4 billion, interest coverage averaged just 1.1 times, and the proportion related to mergers rose to 45%. Junk bond financing was clearly going to roil the merger markets.

The Raiders

Both merger professionals and company executives thought that raiders, arbitrageurs, the burgeoning investment banking merger staffs, and highly specialized merger lawyers caused much of the growth in merger activity in the 1980s. There is no question that all of these areas grew exponentially and profited dramatically during the merger boom. The difficult question is whether they expanded because of the boom or whether they fostered it. For the moment I will consider only the sector with the most obvious influence—the raiders. Armed with high leverage from the banks and the junk bond market, they became catalysts for some of the largest mergers in history. By 1984, raiders were putting companies that had hitherto been considered impregnable into play as acquisition targets, provoking a widespread political and academic debate about their role.

The raiders were an outgrowth of the small group of private investors, insurance companies, corporate investors, and investment banking firms that made up the arbitrage community. The investment banking firms' arbitrage departments typically constrained themselves from investing before there was public information because of the vulnerability to being accused of using insider information.[86] There were still substantial profit opportunities after an offer was announced because of the spreads between the value of what was offered and the trading value of the target company. The raiders, however, saw the opportunities for greater profit by putting companies into play as acquisition targets rather than simply waiting for targets to emerge. At first, the raiders' activities were limited, even if their profits were large. In 1979 Victor Posner's Sharon Steel earned $24 million on Exxon's acquisition of Reliance Electric, Carl Lindner's American Financial earned $46.5 million on Gannett's acquisition of Combined Communications, and Carl Icahn earned $4.1 million when he pushed Tappan Company into a 1979 merger with Electrolux AB.

These same investors quickly came to realize that they didn't need to foment a merger to profit if the target would buy back their stock at a premium to get rid of them. Wall Street twisted this sophisticated form of blackmail into "greenmail," as if regular blackmailers were not after the green stuff too. Greenmail payments began in February 1980 when Carl Icahn made $2.5 million by pushing struggling Saxon Industries into buying back $6.1 million of its stock from him.[87] Saxon filed for bankruptcy just twenty-six months later. Saul Steinberg's Reliance Insurance also earned $10.1 million in 1980 when Penn Central bought back its stock, and Harold Simmons fought a proxy battle with PSA Inc. that netted him an estimated $5 million in a sweetheart leasing deal on three Boeing 727 aircraft. Greenmail immediately proliferated as General Host, Republic Airlines, and McCormick & Co. all paid it to fend off aggressive investors.

Greenmail was severely criticized, but the positions these investors acquired had to be addressed in some way. The greenmailers represented a chilling possibility of control on the cheap to their targets—buying a controlling interest in the open market without paying a premium and then disadvantaging minority stockholders or buying them out with the target's own assets. In the minds of the corporate CEOs, boards of directors, lawyers, and merger advisors involved, allowing this was dereliction of duty as well as loss of control. When it happened, someone had made a major error. But it did happen, as can be seen in table 9.11 which, outlines twenty-nine significant "creeping control" situations during 1975–1984. Greenmail was an effort to forestall such a result.

The number of investors who were willing to undertake the role of stimulating acquisitions or taking greenmail was relatively limited, as they had poor reputations at the beginning of the decade. There was some feeling that they skirted the edges of the law in pursuit of insider information, for which there was some circumstantial evidence. The average takeover stock between 1963 and 1984 had a return 10% greater than the S&P 500 in the twenty days before the first public acquisition offer,[88] which suggested frequent transmission of insider information. These raiders were also seen to be victimizing both stockholders and management when they took greenmail. They were variously referred to as greenmailers, raiders, opportunists, crooks, and numerous unprintable names. I will refer to them collectively as "raiders," even though this term could equally well apply to many corporate executives who were seriously intent on building their companies through unfriendly tender offers and who were not seeking to stimulate acquisitions by others or greenmail.

Whatever their title, these raiders were a crucial part of the merger wave. Table 9.12 outlines seventy-two takeover or greenmail transactions stimulated by the more prominent raiders between 1979 and 1984. Thirty-four of these instances turned into acquisitions by others that ranked among the 100 largest in each year. In addition, eight acquisitions consummated by these raiders are not included in table 9.12 simply be-

Table 9.11. Instances of Creeping Control (1979–1984)

Acquirer	Target	% of o/s Common	Period of Acquisition
Victor Posner	Burnup & Sims	27.6%	1975–1979
Victor Posner	National Can	39.0%	1977–1981
Victor Posner	Evans Products	43.0%	1980–1981
Genstar	Flintkote	20.0%	1978
Pan Am	National Airlines	30.0%	1978–1979
Texas International	National Airlines	20.0%	1978
Consolidated Foods	Hanes	20.0%	1978
Bendix	Asarco	20.0%	1978–1980
Loew's Corp	Bulova Watch	40.5%	1978
Loew's Corp	CNA Insurance	57.9%	1978
Carl Lindner	Penn Central	31.7%	1979–1982
Carl Lindner	United Brands	28.0%	?
Harold Simmons	PSA	20.0%	?–1980
Clabir Corp	General Host	24.0%	1979–1980
Bass bros	Sperry & Hutchinson	36.0%	1979–1981
Bass bros	Blue Bell	23.2%	1981–1983
Bass bros	Munsingwear	32.3%	1983
Bass bros	Walt Disney	24.8%	1984
Sir James Goldsmith	Diamond International	41.0%	1980–1982
David Murdock	Flexi-Van	32.0%	1981–1982
Belzbergs	Bache & Co	23.0%	1981
Carl Icahn	Marshall Field	29.0%	1982
Carl Icahn	Dan River	29.0%	1982–1983
Carl Icahn	ACF Industries	27.0%	1983
Irwin Jacobs	Kaiser Steel	23.0%	1982–1983
Smith International	Gearhart Industries	24.2%	1983
Phil Anschutz	Pennwalt	20.0%	1984
Phil Anschutz	Ideal Basic Industries	25.0%	1984
General Cinema	Carter Hawley Hale	22.0%	1984

Sources: SEC filings.

cause they were successful, and the table is focused on where they stimulated acquisitions by others or by greenmail. Many of the resulting transactions were among the largest in each year, particularly the acquisitions of Reliance Electric, Marathon Oil, Cities Service, Superior Oil, Continental Group, and Gulf Oil. Raiders' influence was surely considerably larger than table 9.12 indicates. These examples are where there was a formal offer or sufficient publicity to attract media attention. Numerous companies sought out friendly acquirers or did LBOs when they knew they were the subject of raiders' investments that had not been made public.

Data for table 9.12 was taken from annual reports, 10Qs, proxy statements, 8K filings, and the *Wall Street Journal*. It excludes the numerous unresolved raid/greenmail situations at the end of 1984.

Table 9.12. Greenmailers' Estimated Gross Profits (1979–1984)

Year	Greenmailer	Target	Profits ($ mill)	Result
1979	Icahn	Tappan Co.	4.1	acquired
	Lindner	Combined Communications	46.5	acquired
	Posner	Reliance Electric	24.0	acquired
			74.6	
1980	Icahn	Saxon Industries	2.5	greenmail
	Icahn	General Host	2.0	greenmail
	Clabir Corp.	General Host	3.6	greenmail
	Jacobs	Republic Airlines	2.0	greenmail
	Reliance	Penn Central	10.1	greenmail
	Sandoz Ltd.	McCormick & Co.	4.7	greenmail
	Simmons	PSA	5.0	greenmail
			29.9	
1981	Bass Bros.	Sperry & Hutchinson	39.0	acquired
	Belzbergs	Bache & Co.	40.0	acquired
	Belzbergs	Masonite	3.0	greenmail
	Bendix	Asarco	205.0	greenmail
	Curtiss-Wright	Kennecott	70.9	greenmail
	Curtiss-Wright	Cenco	15.7	acquired
	Icahn	Simplicity Pattern	8.5	greenmail
	Icahn	Hammermill Paper	4.3	greenmail
	Lindner	Gannett	8.4	greenmail
	D. Murdock	Iowa Beef	79.0	acquired
	Posner	Marley Co.	9.0	acquired
	Posner	Foremost McKesson	35.0	greenmail
	Reliance	Federal Paperboard	20.0	greenmail
			537.8	
1982	Bass bros.	Marathon	160.0	acquired
	Bass bros.	Amfac	22.5	greenmail
	Belzbergs	U.S. Industries	4.7	greenmail
	Belzbergs	CTS Corp	1.2	greenmail
	Icahn	Marshall Field	44.0	acquired
	Icahn	Owens-Illinois	5.5	greenmail
	Icahn	American Can	8.0	greenmail
	Icahn	Anchor Hocking	3.0	greenmail
	Jacobs	Pabst	25.0	acquired
	Mesa	Cities Service	32.0	acquired
	Mesa	Supron Energy	22.0	acquired
	Mesa	General American	43.0	acquired
	Posner	Signode	10.0	acquired
	Reliance	Pac Gamble Robinson	1.7	greenmail
	Sedco	Delhi International	50.5	acquired
	Sedco	Marathon Oil	194.1	acquired
			627.2	
1983	Bass bros.	Suburban Propane	4.0	acquired
	Belzbergs	Suburban Propane	10.0	acquired

(continued)

Table 9.12. (*continued*)

Year	Greenmailer	Target	Profits ($ mill)	Result
	Belzbergs	Pargas	3.7	acquired
	Coastal	Texas Gas	32.0	acquired
	Coastal	Northwest Energy	12.0	acquired
	Hurwitz	Amstar	16.5	acquired
	IC Industries	Trane Co	35.1	acquired
	Icahn	Gulf & Western	19.0	greenmail
	Icahn	Dan River	8.0	acquired
	Mesa	Superior Oil	32.0	acquired
	D. Murdock	Zapata	40.0	greenmail
	D. Murdock	Dan River	0.0	greenmail
			212.3	
1984	Bass bros.	Blue Bell	49.0	greenmail
	Bass bros	Texaco	140.0	greenmail
	Belzbergs	Blue Bell	9.0	acquired
	Coastal	Houston Natural Gass	36.0	greenmail
	Goldsmith	Continental Group	15.0	acquired
	Goldsmith	St. Regis	51.0	acquired
	Hurwitz	Castle & Cooke	16.0	greenmail
	Icahn	Chesebrough-Ponds	30.0	greenmail
	Icahn	B. F. Goodrich	41.0	greenmail
	Jacobs	Walt Disney	29.0	greenmail
	Jacobs	Avco	25.0	acquired
	Jacobs	Kaiser Steel	30.5	acquired
	Leucadia National	Avco	77.0	greenmail
	Mesa Group	Gulf Oil	760.0	acquired
	R. Murdoch	Warner Communications	35.0	greenmail
	R. Murdoch	St. Regis	28.0	acquired
	D. Murdock	Occidental Petroleum	57.0	greenmail
	Pioneer Corp	Louisiana Land	19.3	greenmail
	Reliance	Walt Disney	60.0	greenmail
	Reliance	Quaker State	16.0	greenmail
	Western Pacific	Cone Mills	17.0	acquired
			1540.8	

Sources: SEC filings and the *Wall Street Journal*.

The aggregate profits of raiders were modest from 1979 to 1980, as can be seen in the total for each year in table 9.12. Profits were only $20 million in 1980 because Federal Reserve controls over bank credit used for acquisitions prevailed through much of that year as part of the Carter administration's anti-inflation program. Acquisitions were hard to provoke in such circumstances and the targets were accordingly small.

The surge in profits in 1981 to over $500 million marked the ascension of raiders to notable catalysts of acquisitions. This surge predated the decline in bank lending standards for raids in 1982. High leverage was not involved in any of the thirteen examples in 1981. The raiders' influence stemmed from the swarming effect around the target by professional arbitrageurs and institutional investors once a raider's involvement was announced or rumored. This could quickly lead to 30–40% of a company's stock gravitating into the hands of investors seeking a quick sale, which made the pressures on management intense, often leading it to seek out a friendly acquirer, propose an LBO, or become the object of a prospecting company's unfriendly offer. The burgeoning merger staffs in the investment banking firms, which operated on "merger alerts" and were prepared to run computerized models of merger alternatives with great speed, intensified the focus on these target companies and brought the alternatives into reality very quickly.

When raiders' profits surged to over $1.5 billion in 1984 it was closely linked to the high leverage available. At least ten of the twenty transactions and $1.1 billion of the $1.5 billion in profits in 1984 involved explicit high leverage compared to none in 1981. Obviously the threat from raiders expanded with their access to credit. The formidable package of bank credit, junk bond financing, and coinvestors that Boone Pickens was able to put together for Mesa Petroleum's assault on Gulf Oil early in 1984 was vivid evidence that the size of vulnerable companies had increased many times.

Despite the profits and impact of these raiders, it should not be inferred from their mere presence that they were effective in stimulating acquisitions, as raiders' sophistication varied greatly. At the low end of this scale was Victor Posner. Posner had several notable early successes. He was able to buy U.V. Industries in 1979 in a classic bootstrap financing where he paid for the company with junk bonds reliant on its own credit. In the next few years he had gross profits of $99 million from investments in Reliance Electric, Marley Co., Foremost-McKesson, Signode, and Johnson Controls. Unfortunately he also had big losses. Posner couldn't distinguish between good and bad companies, and once he had invested he kept plowing in deeper until something happened. Between 1980 and 1981 he spent $99 million to acquire 42.5% of Evans Products, a struggling Portland, Oregon building materials retailer, without inducing offers from any other company and without being able to get Evans Products to pay him greenmail. Evans Products lost $19 million in 1982 and $64 million in 1983. Posner tried merging Evans Products into Sharon Steel, following the U.V. Industries model, but Evans Products' lenders turned this down in April 1983, and Posner found himself stuck to his tar baby. Posner was able to take control of the Evans Products board, but only to renegotiate the company's debt in early 1984 and file for bankruptcy in 1985. Sharon Steel wrote the investment down to $6 million. Posner similarly got stuck in National Can and Burnup & Sims. Although he accumulated 39% of National Can between 1977 and 1981, he still had not induced either greenmail or a merger by 1984 and his stock was down $22 million on a cost of $122 million. In Burnup & Sims, he had a $9 million loss and a huge legal hassle.[89]

Irwin Jacobs was another of the least sophisticated raiders, ridiculed as "Irv the Liquidator", even though he had gross profits of approximately $125 million from investments in Republic Airlines, Pabst Breweries, Kaiser Steel, Walt Disney, Pioneer Corp., and Avco Corp. He varied inconsistently between significant targets such as these and minor struggling companies such as Kaiser Steel, Bekins Storage, Tidewater, and American Distilling. He also tended to get stuck in some of his investments for years, such as Tidewater, Pioneer, and InterNorth (now Enron), progressively increasing his stake despite the declining fortunes of the oil industry. His proposals lacked seriousness, and he clearly did not want to buy his targets, even cheaply. At one meeting with a target he was obviously working off a superseded annual report and had no analyses of his own. As a result, his targets often didn't take his threats seriously.

Unfortunately for corporate America, the sophisticated raiders were a larger and more effective lot. They included Carl Lindner, Saul Steinberg, Carl Icahn, David Murdock, William Agee, Boone Pickens, Oscar Wyatt, and the Bass brothers. Each of these was willing (indeed anxious) to acquire companies at the right price, a chilling negotiator, and highly alert to the leverage possibilities as credit attitudes changed among the banks and in the junk bond market. Lindner and Steinberg were first prominent in the 1960s, and both were active investors throughout the 1970s because of their roles as insurance company chief executives. The others were newcomers to the merger market. The evolution of their activities illustrates the combination of native cunning and access to leverage that made them effective.

Carl Icahn evolved gradually from a modest start to considerable effectiveness. He bought a seat on the New York Stock Exchange at the age of thirty-one with borrowed money and built a net worth of approximately $5 million in the options and arbitrage businesses by 1979. He made his first raid in 1978 on a minor real estate investment trust, subsequently renamed Bayswater Realty & Capital, which he took over in a proxy battle. In 1977 he bought an interest in Tappan Company, and with the support of Walter Kidde Co. made an offer in 1978. In a proxy battle he won a seat on Tappan Company's board, which led to its sale to AB Electrolux in 1979 and an Icahn profit of $4.1 million. He was still dabbling in the small-time in February 1980 when he greenmailed Saxon Industries for a $2.5 million profit only two years before it filed for Chapter 11 bankruptcy protection.[90] In 1981 he earned further greenmail profits of $12.8 million from Simplicity Pattern and Hammermill Paper.

Icahn struck his first big payoff and displayed his real talent in 1982 when he began to buy into Marshall Field, a Chicago department store company that had dealt him a substantial loss when it fought off a tender offer from Carter-Hawley-Hale in 1979. The company underrated the danger Icahn posed when he bought 1.2 million shares (9.5%) in February 1982, since his prior targets were smaller. Icahn gathered supporters as the battle progressed, and by the end of March he owned 30% of the company at a cost of over $60 million—a nightmare of control on the cheap for the company and a very risky investment for Icahn if nothing transpired. When Batus Inc., a U.K. conglomerate, came in as a white knight and made an offer for Marshall Field, Icahn fought with Batus for a higher price, getting it boosted twice until at $30 per share he was able to sell out for a profit of $44 million.[91] In the next two and a half years he greenmailed Owens-Illinois, American Can, Anchor Hocking, Gulf & Western, Dan River, and B. F. Goodrich for profits of $76.5 million. Carl Icahn had reached the big time.

For those who thought Icahn's assault on Marshall Field was just good luck, his takeover of ACF Industries revealed a very adaptive strategist who both employed high leverage and got the most out of liquidating the target's assets. He commenced buying around $31 per share in July 1983, and kept buying up to $51.50 in September until he had 27% of the stock, repeating his Marshall Field tactics of near-control without a tender.[92] However, after almost a year of harassment no third party appeared as a bidder for ACF, and Icahn faced losing his threatening power if he did not seek full control. Icahn worked out financing to bid for the whole company by preselling its W-K-M manufacturing division to Cooper Industries for $200 million. When Warburg Pincus emerged with an LBO alternative based on selling W-K-M to Joy Manufacturing for more, Icahn simply began an auction between Cooper and Joy. Icahn ultimately sold W-K-M to Joy for $235 million, arranged a National Westminster Bank loan to ACF of $150 million, and took over ACF in 1984 by having it pay the other stockholders $54.50 per share with the proceeds of the W-K-M sale and the National Westminster loan.[93] He subsequently used greenmail on Chesebrough-Ponds to get it to buy ACF's Polymer subsidiary for $95 million, and sold the oil and gas and automotive divisions for $73 million, narrowing the company's business to rail car manufacturing and leasing. He then turned ACF into a vehicle for future raids. Icahn's next targets would be even bigger.

David Murdock loomed even larger than Carl Icahn, but got surprisingly little publicity. A tenth grade dropout who made his fortune in the construction industry in Phoenix, Murdock was tainted when a publicly owned holding company that he controlled collapsed in the 1960s due to a colleague's fraud. Thereafter he led a mysteriously private life, operating through Pacific Holding Company, which he took private in 1978. His first success as a raider was in 1981 at the age of fifty-seven when he made $79 million when Iowa Beef Processors was bought by Occidental Petroleum. He subsequently arranged one of the first highly leveraged bank loans for a raid on Cannon Mills in 1982 and advised Armand Hammer, chairman of Occidental Petroleum, during its highly leveraged acquisition of Cities Service that same year. He also prompted Occidental to make a spurned 1983 offer for Zapata Corp. in which he had a 9.4% stake, but which led Zapata to pay him greenmail profits of $40 million. By 1984 he had become a thorn in Hammer's side, and Occidental bought him out for a further $57 million profit. Murdock also tried to greenmail Dan River, although without making any profits, and was able to take control of Flexi-Van on the cheap by amassing 32% of its stock and installing himself as chairman in 1982. Murdock's greatest coup, however, was joining with Peter Kiewit & Sons, an Omaha construction company with which he had worked frequently, to take over Continental Group in 1984 in a $3.4 billion LBO based on only one day's planning with no investment banking advice! The takeover was followed by the sale of the company's energy and insurance assets to pay off most of the debt. Peter Kiewit bought out Murdock's 20% interest eight months later for approximately $200 million. It is not clear how much Murdock put up originally—between $115 and 150 million. His profit of $50–85 million was attractive on either basis.[94]

The Bass brothers, whose original $1.0 billion fortune was derived from the oil investments of their uncle, Sid Bass, got their lessons in greenmail from Richard Rainwater, a young Dallas broker at Goldman Sachs who they hired to run their securities investments. Their first success was in 1981 with Sperry & Hutchinson, a retailing conglomerate controlled by the Beinecke family, which the Basses had bought into when Goldman Sachs took the company public in the mid-1970s. The Basses bought both public shares and the stock of one wing of the Beinecke family to take their holdings up to 36%, and began negotiating with another wing of the family for enough to gain control. In a fright, the controlling Beineckes sold out to Baldwin-United, and the Bass brothers booked an estimated profit of $39 million. They made an even larger profit of $160 million when they bought over 5% of Marathon Oil, helping to stimulate the efforts of Mobil Oil and U.S. Steel to acquire it in 1982. Thereafter the Bass brothers were regular leaders among the raiders, earning over $400 million in aggregate from transactions involving Sperry & Hutchinson, Marathon, Amfac, Suburban Propane, Blue Bell, and Texaco.

Their most dramatic gain was in Walt Disney, where they achieved a 24.8% stake in 1984 at approximately $60 per share for slightly over $500 million. They capitalized on Disney's fear of Reliance Insurance to sell it Arvida Corp. (a Florida real estate developer that they had bought from Penn Central the year before for $181 million) for over three million shares ($200 million) and then buying another 2.5 million shares from Ivan Boesky and Irwin Jacobs, who were trying to greenmail the company. The Basses then played a major role in bringing in Michael Eisner from Paramount Pictures to revitalize the company. By the end of 1985 their $500 million stake in Walt Disney had a market value of over $950 million. They also had control on the cheap.

Bendix Corp., under the volatile but creative direction of William Agee, was the first major corporation to mix a strategy of redirecting the company through asset sales and acquisitions with taking greenmail from targets. Bendix greenmailed ASARCO for a profit of $205 million in 1981,[95] bought stock in Marion Laboratories in 1982, and tried to greenmail RCA with a 7.2% position in early 1982. Bendix also held a position in Gould Inc. that had the same purpose, but Bendix's attack on Martin Marietta and Allied's related takeover of Bendix intervened. None of the Bendix activities relied greatly on leverage.

Boone Pickens's attack on Cities Service came a year after Agee's denouement in the Bendix-Martin Marietta-Allied merger battle. Pickens's creative role was in applying leverage to the process through bank loans and junk bonds and focusing on the oil industry. Oscar Wyatt at Coastal Corp. played a similar role in the pipeline industry. Other companies tried on a lesser scale to profit from greenmail in the oil patch, but had less success because they were unwilling to risk high leverage. Ben Heinemann's Northwest Industries tried to put Pogo Producing into play in 1982 by buying a $134 million stake. Sedco, the Dallas-based offshore drilling company, seemingly oblivious to conflicts of interest or problems with oil industry clients, bought a 7.5% stake in Marathon Oil in 1981 and tried to get Pennzoil to join it in an offer to take over Marathon. It also bought stakes in Delhi International and joined Northwest Industries in attacking Pogo Producing.

Among the foreigners pursuing raids, only Sir James Goldsmith was effective at stimulating acquisitions in this period because of the leverage he was willing to assume. He took over Diamond International in a three-year battle. Thereafter, he pushed Continental Group and St. Regis into being acquired. The Belzberg brothers, who controlled Vancouver-based First City Financial, principally rode on the coattails of others. Rupert Murdoch, the Australian entrepreneur and CEO of News Corporation, was unable to push Warner Communications into an acquisition and settled for greenmail of approximately $40 million. Although he also earned $37 million in 1984 when St. Regis Corporation was acquired by Champion International, it is not clear that he was an instigating factor.[96]

There are various interpretations of the role that these raiders played in stimulating takeovers in the early 1980s. In a theoretical sense, they were catalysts for acquisitions that other corporations were predisposed to make. They were willing to undertake the organizational expense and

opprobrium of stimulating the takeovers. Probably it was a natural con-
comitant of that role that so many of the raiders came from the fringes
of the finance world or of their industries. Carl Icahn, David Murdock,
and Irwin Jacobs had previously occupied the periphery of the financial
world and had almost no institutional connections. Victor Posner's companies were highly leveraged, barely profitable, and marginal factors in
their industries. Meshulam Riklis's Rapid American controlled one of the
weakest discount store chains, and his own dealings with his companies
were viewed with great suspicion. Carl Lindner and Saul Steinberg ran
small insurance companies and dealt repeatedly in borderline investment
tactics. Mesa Petroleum was an insignificant player in the oil patch, headquartered in out-of-the-way Amarillo, Texas. Coastal Corp. had a scathing
reputation in Texas because of defaulting on gas contracts in the 1970s.
Sir James Goldsmith lived amid a tangle of French, Luxembourg, Hong
Kong, and Panamanian holding companies, and had almost been bankrupted previously. Rupert Murdoch led the decline in standards in London's tabloid press. The Belzbergs ran a fringe trust company in Canada.
Only Bendix and the Bass brothers had solid reputations.

Given the competitiveness of the U.S. system, these raiders were
highly successful in attracting capital once they proved themselves
profitable—a phenomenon that was less likely to be repeated in other
countries, where financial relationships are more oligarchic. Carl Icahn,
Irwin Jacobs, and Mesa Petroleum attracted very substantial coinvestors
on an equity basis for their raids. By 1982, major commercial banks in
search of high fees provided loan capital for these raiders on an unprecedented scale. Drexel Burnham became the principal agent of further loan capital from the junk bond market in 1984. Without the leverage provided by banks and Drexel Burnham, these raiders would have
been limited to modest influence among smaller companies. With leverage, they were able to induce the takeover of some of America's largest
companies.

Many of the raiders, particularly Boone Pickens, were successful in
generating a public relations image as crusaders on behalf of stockholder
rights against complacent or wasteful corporate chieftains—an image
fortified by various academics. The aggregate record of these raiders up
to 1984 hardly supports such a conclusion, however. In over half of the
seventy-two transactions outlined in table 9.12, the raiders took greenmail rather than provoking a takeover. Greenmail premiums were un-
questionably at the expense of the other stockholders. Nor could the
raiders claim that they were making bona fide offers—their success ratios
were extremely low. Their actual takeovers were few enough to be enu-
merated briefly: David Murdock took over Cannon Mills and Continental Group, Sir James Goldsmith took over Diamond International, Carl
Icahn took over ACF Industries, Victor Posner took over Evans Products,

the Bass brothers gained control of Walt Disney, and Reliance Insurance did LBOs on Days Inns and Pargas, eight takeovers compared with seventy-two instances where they took greenmail or someone else made the acquisition. Boone Pickens didn't make a single takeover.

Summary

The new regime had much to do with the merger boom between 1980 and 1984 in which the value of transactions quadrupled and the theme of acquisitions shifted from diversification and commodities producers to industry consolidation. The most important factor was the change in antitrust enforcement under William Baxter, assistant attorney general for antitrust, and James Miller, chairman of the Federal Trade Commission. The antitrust changes proceeded through case examples at first, then the symbolic steps of dismissing the IBM suit and resolving the AT&T suit, then the new 1982 merger guidelines, and finally the visible removal of all restraints in 1984. The number of public companies taken over actually declined over these four years, but the annual number of takeovers greater than $100 million doubled and those over $1 billion rose from three to twenty-eight. In 1984, 84% of the top ten transactions would previously have been challenged on antitrust grounds.

The oil industry was again vital to this market, at first spending its newfound wealth on acquisitions, but later as a target of raiders and other oil companies as oil-related transactions rose to one-third of the total. The loss of foreign reserves through nationalization programs, the failure of several high-profile exploration efforts in the United States, and the low cost of "exploring for oil in Wall Street" stimulated the consolidation that occurred. So did the industry's well-recognized penchant for self-aggrandizement.

The new regime only played an indirect role in the aggressive new leverage standards that fostered the merger boom. The banks reduced their interest coverage requirements on loans for raids and LBOs to only 1.0 times in 1982, and also accepted dramatically higher legal and collateral risks than previously, and, in 1983, interest coverages in the junk bond market similarly fell to 1.0 times. In 1984, highly leveraged bank loans and junk bonds played a crucial role in 44% of that year's doubled merger volume. The new regime's influence was unintentional, reflecting the banks' need to compete in the new high-cost market of deregulated deposits that began in 1982, and the savings and loan industry's investment freedom as it was deregulated and encouraged to expand with federal deposit guarantees of $100,000. But other factors were also at work in the credit expansion. Mutual funds and insurance companies had been building successful momentum in the junk bond market for several years. Michael Milken and Drexel Burnham brought undeniable skills, and perhaps personal corruption as well, to the market.

Corporate raiders were involved in at least eighty of the five hundred largest transactions between 1980 and 1984, and particularly in the very largest transactions in 1984, when their profits exceeded $1.5 billion. These raiders posed as representatives of the stockholders and champions of efficiency, but they only completed eight mergers out of eighty attacks, and took greenmail over half of the time. With few exceptions, they came from the fringes of the financial world or of their own industries. Victor Posner and Irwin Jacobs were notably inept, and their companies minor and weak. Boone Pickens only entered the game because his own company had problems, and he didn't make a single acquisition. The raiders' influence relflected the leverage that became available to them and the absence of antitrust restrictions on industry consolidation, rather than any economic virtues.

Appendix 9.1. The Ten Largest Mergers 1976–1984

Year	Acquirer	Acquired	Value ($MM)
1976	General Electric	Utah International	2,170
	Mobil Oil	Marcor	900
	R. J. Reynolds	Burmah Oil & Gas	520
	Marathon Oil	Pan Ocean Oil	265
	Herald Co.	Booth Newspapers	259
	Sandoz Ltd.	Northrup King	190
	Colgate-Palmolive	Riviana Foods	172
	Southland Royalty	Aztec Oil & Gas	170
	Gould Inc.	I-T-E Imperial	164
	Atlantic Richfield	Anaconda—27%	162
			4,972
1977	DuPont	Christianna Securities	1,567
	J. Ray McDermott	Babcock & Wilcox	688
	Kennecott	Carborundum	567
	Atlantic Richfield	Anaconda—73%	536
	Gulf Oil	Kewanee Industries	455
	Continental Group	Richmond Corp	366
	Getty Oil	Mission/Skelly	357
	Taubman-Allen-Irvine	Irvine Corp.	337
	Pepsico	Pizza Hut	327
	Champion International	Hoerner Waldorf	318
			5,518
1978	Johns Manville	Olinkraft	585
	Philip Morris	7UP	515
	Unilever N/V	National Starch	480
	United Technologies	Carrier Corp.	476
	Eaton Corp.	Cutler-Hammer	372
	Standard Chartered Bank	Union Bancorp	293
	Sun Co.	Becton Dickinson	287

Appendix 9.1. (*continued*)

Year	Acquirer	Acquired	Value ($MM)
	Dayton-Hudson	Mervyn's	280
	Time Inc.	Inland Container	272
	Thyssen A.G.	Budd Co.	256
			3,816
1979	Shell Oil	Belridge Oil	2,650
	RCA	CIT Financial	1,400
	Exxon	Reliance Electric	1,170
	International Paper	Bodcaw Co.	805
	Mobil Corp.	General Crude Oil	763
	McGraw-Edison	Studebaker-Worthington	724
	Cooper Industries	Gardner-Denver	630
	R. J. Reynolds	Del Monte	620
	Allied Chemical	Eltra	589
	Sharon Steel	U. V. Industries	518
			9,869
1980	Kraft	Dart Inc.	2,500
	Sun Co.	Texas Pacific Oil	2,300
	CSX Corp.	Chessie System & Seaboard Coast Line Railroad	1,700
	Raytheon	Beech Aircraft	800
	Tenneco	Southwestern Life	757
	Mobil Corp.	Vickers Energy	715
	Imperial Group	Howard Johnson	630
	Getty Oil	Reserve Oil & Gas	628
	Wheelabrator-Frye	Pullman	600
	Getty Oil	ERC Corp.	570
	Grand Metropolitan	Liggett Group	570
			11,770
1981	DuPont	Conoco	6,820
	Elf/Aquitaine	Texaxgulf	2,742
	Seagram	DuPont	2,552
	Freeport	McMoRan Oil & Gas	2,540
	Kuwait Petroleum	Santa Fe International	2,500
	Fluor	St. Joe Minerals	2,340
	Nabisco	Standard Brands	1,900
	Standard Oil (Ohio)	Kennecott	1,770
	American Express	Shearson Loeb Rhoades	1,000
	Occidental Pet	Iowa Beef	800
			24,964
1982	U.S. Steel	Marathon Oil	6,150
	Connecticut General	INA	4,300
	Occidental Petroleum	Cities Service	4,202
	Norfolk & Western	Southern Railway	2,900
	Allied Corp.[1]	Bendix	2,700
	R. J. Reynolds	Heublein	1,621

(*continued*)

Appendix 9.1. (*continued*)

Year	Acquirer	Acquired	Value ($MM)
	American General	NLT Corp.	1,500
	Baldwin-United	MGIC	1,200
	Union Pacific	Missouri Pacific	1,028
	SmithKline	Beckman Instruments	1,020
			26,621
1983	Sante Fe Industries	Southern Pacific	2,300
	Xerox	Crum and Forster	1,600
	Burlington Northern	El Paso Inc.	1,276
	Diamond Shamrock	Natomas	1,270
	Phillips Petroleum	General American Oil	1,140
	CSX Corp.	Texas Gas Resources	1,000
	Esmark	Norton Simon	990
	Southland Corp.	Citgo Petroleum	987
	Signal Cos.	Wheelabrator-Frye	946
	Mesa Petroleum	Gulf Oil—13.2%	909
			12,418
1984	Chevron	Gulf Corp.	13,300
	Texaco Inc.	Getty Oil	10,125
	Mobil Corp.	Superior Oil	5,700
	Kiewit-Murdock	Continental Group	2,750
	Beatrice Cos.	Esmark	2,710
	General Motors	EDS	2,601
	Broken Hill Property	Utah International	2,400
	Champion International	St. Regis	1,827
	Phillips Petroleum	Aminoil—R. J. Reynolds	1,700
	Manufacturers Hanover	CIT Financial	1,510
			44,623

Source: *Mergers & Acquisitions, Annual Almanac & Index*, 1982–1985, "The Top 100"; quarterlies previously.

[1]Allied Corporation's acquisition of Bendix was a two-part transaction all included in 1982—Martin Marietta aspects were excluded.

Appendix 9.2   A Note on the Ratios for Leveraged Buyouts of Public Companies

The various LBO ratios in table 9.8 were calculated as follows. "Cost" was calculated as the sum of common stock purchased, existing debt paid off or assumed, and fees and expenses. Bank lines of credit for working capital were not counted if not in current use, even if the lines of credit were newly negotiated as part of the LBO. Nor were additional bank loan provisions counted when they were arranged for the contingency of higher interest rates than some cap rate—"cap loans." EBIT for columns 4 and 6 in each transaction was based on the latest annual income statement, adjusted by the absolute changes in six or nine-month statements—i.e., not annualized. EBIT was not adjusted for the increased depreciation or amortization of goodwill involved in virtually every transaction. In three 1982 transactions prior year EBIT was used because of a sharp cyclical decline. The "% Equity" in column 5 was calculated based on preferred and common stock as a percentage of pro forma capitalization for the new financing. Preferred and common stock were lumped together because they were so frequently indistinguishable in their rights to share in future income growth. The pro forma interest costs used in calculating "EBIT/Int" (column 6) are only approximations. The proxies for each transaction usually indicated the interest rate on fixed-rate borrowings, and the base rate plus some premium for the bank financing. I calculated the interest costs based on interest on any existing debt not repaid, fixed rates on new debt where applicable, and bank interest costs based on the LIBOR or prime rate averages for each year[97] plus the indicated premium in each transaction. "Banks % Total" (column 7) and "Insur % Total" (column 8) were based on new financing by these institutions as a percentage of all new financing arranged. Assumption of existing debt was ignored. Junk bonds or preferred stock that were part of the package offered to stockholders were counted as financing but not allocated to either banks or insurance companies, since I cannot tell where this debt ended up.

10

Conclusions

The first Reagan administration marked a change in policy regimes that sharply reduced inflation, set the foundation for a record period of steady economic growth, revived the stock and bond markets, and initiated a merger boom without modern parallel. The federal authorities contributed a set of explicit policy decisions to this new regime—monetary policy that was aggressively anti-inflationary, fiscal policy that reduced taxes, and free-market prejudices that disbanded wage and price controls, attacked unions, ceased energy regulation and incentives, and freed industry of most antitrust controls. Some aspects of the new regime were fortuitous, such as the drop in the price of oil from $40 a barrel to $25, the 55% rise in the dollar, and the decline in credit standards for bank loans and junk bonds that fueled the growth in the merger market, although it must be said that Reagan administration policies fostered and often welcomed these trends. The administration's policies also contrasted strongly with those of the Nixon and Carter administrations, under which the Federal Reserve was more concerned with economic growth than inflation, wage and price controls were favored, and there was extensive intervention in the energy industries—policies that led to rising inflation, a weak dollar, and frequent crises in the foreign exchange and financial markets.

The eventual results in securities markets and the economy were very much what the proponents of the new regime had promised—lower inflation, steady economic growth, and rewarding stock and bond markets. Inflation dropped below 3%, the economic recovery during 1983–1984 was a postwar record, the stock market had a solid 14.8% compound annual total return from the end of 1979 to the end of 1984, and long-term treasuries had a real compound annual return of 3.3%—the best record for five years running since 1929. However, the proponents of the new regime had not anticipated that the transition to these favorable results would be so painful. It involved thirty-six months without an increase in industrial production, a postwar record of 10.8% unemployment, bankruptcy of many less-developed countries, credit crises in the auto, farm, electric utility, banking, and savings and loan industries, historically high interest rates, and wrenching stock and bond markets in which, by mid-1982, stocks were still below their peaks of a decade earlier and investors in long-term treasuries had only half the real value of their capital in 1976. The readjustment was particularly painful to the auto, oil, chemical, metals, farm, and heavy machinery industries, which entered into long-term declines, and whose stocks shifted from overperforming the S&P 500 in the inflationary 1970s to long-term underperformance.

Nor had the proponents of the new regime reckoned on the adept institutional management of the multiple crises that was necessary to the favorable outcome. Federal authorities and the leading commercial banks had to work with international lending authorities and the less-developed countries with great finesse to prevent an international banking crisis. The savings and loan industry had to be restructured to survive, and Continental Illinois Bank & Trust was virtually nationalized for the sake of the stability of the money center banks. The auto industry was saved by controls on Japanese imports, easier emission and gas mileage requirements, and continuation of the Carter administration's promised aid to Chrysler Corp. Distress in the nuclear sector of the electric utility industry was in part alleviated by almost $10 billion in aid received indirectly from the Rural Electrification Administration. And the farm community went through a prolonged credit liquidation that culminated in the need to bail out the Farm Credit System in 1985—just over the horizon of our present focus. In short, the favorable outcome of the new regime was dependent on highly adept institutional solutions to a surprisingly large number of crises.

Stocks

The 1970s represented the worst decade for stocks since 1929—even worse than the 1930s—as the S&P 500 registered average annual total returns of only 5.9%, minus 1.5% adjusted for inflation.[1] To some degree this was a reaction to the very high stock prices that prevailed from 1969 to 1972, particularly for the "Nifty Fifty," which reached price-earnings ratios of over 40; but this reaction was over by 1973 when the price-earnings ratio for the S&P 500 reached 12.0 times next year's earnings. Price-earnings ratios continued to slide as low as 6.0, as the S&P 500 underperformed a two-factor model based on earnings and interest rates by 86% between the end of 1969 and the end of 1979. This happened even though earnings for the S&P 500 rose from $5.78 in 1969 to $15.29 in 1979—a compound annual growth rate of 9.9%.

Many blamed this poor performance on the steady escalation in inflation from 6.1% in 1969 to 13.3% in 1979, but stock prices could equally be expected to rise with nominal price levels. The various ways of looking at "real" earnings during the 1970s—whether reducing nominal earnings for inflation, or also reducing them for inventory profits and underdepreciation—indicate that stocks still dramatically underperformed relative to the growth in earnings. We can say with the advantage of hindsight that this undervaluation reflected the policy regimes of the Nixon and Carter administrations and the complex of rising oil prices, rising inflation, a weak dollar, and frequent international and financial crises that surrounded them.

General sentiment changed dramatically under the new Reagan regime. The consumer confidence index, which was as low as 52 in mid-1980, rose to 77 in 1981 and was up to 100 in 1984. Some aspect of the dollar's 55% rise was due to confidence in the Reagan administration, although it is difficult to measure; but gold, which has been an inverse standard of international investor confidence for generations, provided an easy measure. It dropped from a peak of $960 an ounce in January 1980 to under $400 in 1981 and under $300 in 1982. More directly related to the stock market, analysts' earnings estimates for the S&P 500 rose 24% when Ronald Reagan was elected and shifted from being persistently below what actually occurred during 1978–1980 to approximately 30% above actual results throughout 1981 to 1985. The stock market changed immediately from undervaluing to overvaluing the S&P 500 relative to my two-factor model based on current interest rates and analysts' earnings forecasts. Bouts of high optimism recurred in both 1983 and 1984 when price-earnings ratios rose 10–20% beyond what was indicated by changes in interest rates. New-issues of common stock, which are highly cyclical and closely related to confidence levels, rose to a record $14.5 billion in 1981, finally surpassing the previous record of $10.8 billion in 1972, then soared to $38.5 billion in 1983.

Confidence, or overconfidence, was also evident in the credit markets. It was an important factor in the sharp decline in bank loan and junk bond coverage requirements in 1982 and 1983, the expansion of the savings and loan industry's ultimately troublesome real estate loans, the increase in treasury market speculation, and the increase in investment bankers' leverage.

The magnitude of the change in the stock market can be parsed into its components. Comparing the end of 1979 and the end of 1984, the S&P 500 increased 55%, which was only minutely different from what was indicated by my two-factor model.[2] A 6.6% increase was due to acquisition premiums, 12% was due to lower interest rates, and 40% was due to higher earnings estimates; but this 40% increase would have been a 1.4% decline if the S&P 500 had reflected actual earnings twelve months hence. Thus, those who emphasize that fundamentals determine stock prices and those who emphasize investor psychology can both have it their way. The market did reflect earnings anticipations, but earnings anticipations reflected strong psychological factors.

The Reagan administration's reduction in the maximum ordinary income tax rate from 70% to 50% and the capital gains tax rate from 28% to 20% increased stock prices 23%, but this increase made up for the underperformance of the market earlier in 1980 rather than adding to results between 12/79 and 12/84.

A number of large and prominent industry stock groups seriously underperformed the S&P 500 between 12/79 and 12/84. These industries' problems illustrate in detail that the change in regimes did not operate through some painless revolution in expectations, but rather through very real changes in industry conditions that exacted high penalties from both stockholders and the companies over many years. For example, the money center banks and savings and loans were disintermediated by the record high interest rates of 1980 through 1982, and the banks suffered large writeoffs on loans to the less-developed countries, to the oil industry, and for real estate. The underperformance of the oil-related industries—the major integrated companies, the independent Petroleum Producers, Offshore Drilling companies, the Oil Well Equipment and Service companies, the Natural Gas Distributors, the Pipelines, and the Engineering and Construction companies—reflected the decline in oil prices that began in 1981. Most of the other underperforming industries—Autos, Agricultural and Construction Machinery, Chemicals, Pulp and Paper, Machine Tools, Steel, Aluminum, and Copper mining—reflected the effects of the 55% rise in the dollar as their net exports declined 200% and imports rose from 17% to 25% of domestic production. However, these industries' problems were not due exclusively to the new regime. Many of them also had management problems and historically entrenched unions that had achieved wages 30% above the manufacturing average.

The industry stock groups overperforming the S&P 500 also reflected the new regime's impact on the stock market and the underlying economy. Sixteen of thirty were consumer related—retailing, branded consumer products, media industries—and free of the effects of the strong dollar, as imports accounted for only 4% of their domestic production.

Most of the remaining overperforming industries were subject to specific government policies that favored them, such as airline, trucking, and railroad deregulation, increased environmental regulations, new health care reimbursement programs, and expanded defense spending.

Stocks of seventeen of the thirty overperforming industries reversed their prior trends relative to the S&P 500 under the new regime, as did all of the underperforming industries except Steel and Chemicals, buttressing the general point that a new regime prevailed. The popular conception that the country was deindustrializing was supported by the preponderance of capital intensive industries among those that underperformed, their shift from overperformance in the 1970s, and their size —they made up 43% of the S&P 500 at the end of 1979.

While the shift in trend from overperforming to underperforming (or vice versa) occurred for most industries in 1980 or 1981, the trends themselves occurred over many years, rather than quickly as rational expectations theory suggests. The timing of macroeconomic effects, such as the strong dollar, worked through these industries at inconsistent rates. It affected steel imports, and computer and construction machinery exports in 1981, but didn't affect copper, lead, and agricultural machinery until 1982, and autos and machine tools until 1983. High oil prices from 1979 to 1980 affected the auto industry immediately, both in the shift to small cars and the increase in the cost of driving, but high oil prices didn't hit U.S. aluminum producers, which were very sensitive to electric power prices, until 1984, when cheap, hydro-based Canadian aluminum imports doubled and domestic aluminum prices dropped from 80 to 50 cents per pound.

Small capitalization stocks also overperformed the S&P 500 in the early 1980s, but had a sharp decline in return on equity that appeared at odds with this. This inconsistency points out the fallacy in treating the small capitalization market as a homogenous sector whose stock performance is subject to a consistent logic over long periods of time. In the 1960s small capitalization stocks reflected mostly "fallen angels," where the logic of their overperformance was reversion to the mean following underperformance. In the 1970s small capitalization stocks were dominated by oil-related companies whose overperformance reflected rising oil prices. In the 1980s small capitalization stocks were dominated by speculative computer, biotechnology, and health care companies that had massive new issues of common stock, which meant that public stock prices for these companies were established at the peak of a fad and were highly volatile thereafter. Initial public offerings for computer companies rose from $0.5 billion in the 1970s to $11 billion in 1983. Health care and biotechnology initial public offerings rose from under $200 million to $2.8 billion.

Various popular signals for stock market prospects were of mixed utility during 1969–1984. Low price-earnings and market-to-book value ratios in 1974, 1979, and 1982 signaled subsequent 40–60% gains, but failed to give a signal for both the 20% gain in 1979 and the 24% decline from 1981 to 1982. High dividend yields provided buy signals that captured all of the subsequent market gains, but it was difficult to interpret what low yields counted as "sell" signals. The relationship between stock prices and interest rates was even more irregular. Three, and arguably four, of the seven sustained market moves in excess of 10% between the end of 1977 and the end of 1984 were contrary to the trend of interest rates because stocks found appeal as an inflation hedge or they rose in response to the change in regimes.

Bonds

The overriding feature of the bond market in this period was the Federal Reserve's influence on both short and long-term interest rates. Interest rates in turn affected economic growth, inflation, and the strength of the dollar, rather than vice versa. All but one of the ten largest moves in ten-year treasury rates between 1979 and 1984 followed Federal Reserve policy directions. The only inconsistent move was in mid-1981, when debate in Congress clarified that there would be a massive increase in the federal budget deficit.

The bond markets were also the locus of many of the unintended effects of the new regime. Unprecedented volatility, high interest rates, and the huge expansion in treasury volume made the treasury market a hothouse for many of the new trends in the bond market. Dealers were forced to familiarize themselves with interest rate futures amid the volatility of 1979 through 1981, with the result that their use for more speculative purposes continued to grow after volatility declined. Other treasury derivatives burgeoned, particularly stripped treasuries and the repurchase market, and a whole spectrum of investors, ranging from local governments to large banks and sophisticated individuals, suffered speculative losses. This was the beginning of a theme that would become more familiar throughout the 1980s of participants entering new markets with minimal oversight and understanding and sometimes fraudulent intent.

The quadrupling in mortgage-related securities issues, which made mortgage securities second only to the treasury market in size, was an outcome of new legislation and accounting regulations designed to save the savings and loan industry from bankruptcy under the new monetary policies. The savings and loans were encouraged to securitize their old mortgage holdings, expand their deposits, and invest in mortgage-backed securities. Fannie Mae was similarly encouraged to expand its guarantees of mortgage-backed securities. By 1984 when collateralized mortgage obligations (CMOs) were developed, the market resembled the treasury market in its emphasis on derivative securities, high leverage, and the naivete and lack of oversight of many of its participants.

The corporate bond market particularly reflected the price of success for the new regime as macroeconomic corporate credit ratios declined 20–30%. More narrowly, fifteen industries making up the lowest quartile ranked by credit changes suffered a 52% decline in credit ratios, and the auto, electric utility, and farming industries suffered acute credit crises. These fifteen industries and the auto and electric utility industries were of disproportionate importance to the bond market, as they accounted for 53% of the public debt issued by nonfinancial corporations between 1970 and 1984.

The basic problem for the fifteen industries was a 58% decline in their unleveraged return on capitalization due to lower oil and commodities prices and the strong dollar. These lower earnings translated into a 74% decline in interest coverage and a 67% decline in funds from operations as a percentage of total debt. Here was a decline in credit quality of substantially greater importance than the more publicized decline later in the decade that was caused by highly leveraged acquisitions and corporate restructurings. This earlier decline was involuntary, nonstrategic, and beyond corporate power to reverse. For many companies, particularly in agricultural and construction machinery, offshore drilling, oil well equipment and services, heavy construction, steel, and aluminum, the decline was crippling and irreversible. This was the credit component of the deindustrialization noted earlier in the stock market.

The auto industry's credit decline was only partially due to the new regime, as the industry, particularly Chrysler, was rocked by the rise in oil prices preceding the Reagan administration during 1979–1980. But the subsequent penetration of foreign car makers in the U.S. market, particularly the Japanese, was strongly influenced by the appreciation of the dollar under the new regime. The favorable resolution of the auto industry's credit crisis also reflected the new regime's adept hand in solving crises. Chrysler was only saved by the Reagan administration's willingness to follow through on the $1.5 billion in debt guarantees arranged by the Carter administration, and its tough insistence on loans and concessions from other governments, banks, suppliers, and unions totaling $2.5 billion. The industry in general was greatly helped by strong political pressure on the Japanese to institute export quotas, and by relaxed mileage and environmental standards.

The electric utility industry was thrown into crisis by the 1979–1980 rise in oil prices and the Three Mile Island nuclear accident, which quadrupled nuclear power plant costs by 1985. The government advanced almost $10 billion to the industry indirectly through rural electric cooperatives that became partners in nuclear plants under construction, but the fundamental rescue of the industry was at the state level where public utility commissions allowed record rate relief. In the most notorious case where rate relief wasn't available, the Washington Public Power Supply System declared bankruptcy on $2.25 billion of tax-exempt debt.

The farm economy went from inflation-stimulated overexpansion in the 1970s into a protracted crisis as it was hurt first by high energy prices and interest rates, then by lower commodities prices and loss of international market share due to the strong dollar, and finally by declining land prices. Farmers liquidated one quarter of their debt by 1987 in a crisis for rural banks and federal farm agencies that required extensive government intervention.

There was also some voluntary or strategic decline in corporate credit quality at this time related to the expansion of the nascent junk bond market. It was established as a credible investment vehicle in the last half of the 1970s when several major mutual funds earned superior returns in it by pursuing arbitrage-type strategies. The new-issue market did not exceed $1.5 billion annually, however, until interest coverages dropped from 2.0 to 0.8 times in 1983 and Drexel Burnham applied junk bonds to takeover raids. Volume then rose fivefold to $7.4 billion in 1984. Even the expansion in junk bonds reflected the new regime, however. The decline in interest coverages in 1983 followed a similar decline in the coverages for bank loans to finance major raids and leveraged buyouts, which in turn reflected the competitive pressures on the banks from deregulation of deposits. And the general increase in merger activity was highly dependent on the relaxation of antitrust restrictions.

The importance of the junk bond market was not simply its novelty, but its interconnection with many other unusual features of the period. It fueled the merger boom; it facilitated the unprecedented growth of savings and loan assets; and it was the principal investment behind single premium life insurance annuities—a market in which all of the leaders eventually went bankrupt. And, in retrospect, it was closely tied to the greatest financial corruption of the postwar era, although by 1984 the only evidence of this was two inconclusive SEC investigations of Drexel Burnham and pervasive Wall Street rumors about its under-the-table relationships with many of the most important investors.

Mergers and Acquisitions

There is a sharp contrast between academics' focus on the merger market in the 1980s and the emphases of financial practitioners. Academics have argued whether takeovers promoted efficiency or were simply wealth transfers that reduced income taxes or victimized poorly protected parties such as workers, suppliers, and host communities. On the one hand, raiders and leveraged buyout firms have been lionized as the new wave of entrepreneurs, and on the other hand corporate chief executives have been accused of simply wanting to create larger companies to further their compensation and prestige. From a practitioner's point of view, however, the critical features of the merger market were the relaxation of antitrust rules, the institutional role of the oil industry, and the unprecedented leverage provided by banks and the junk bond market.

The antitrust changes were led by William Baxter, assistant attorney general—antitrust, and James Miller, chairman of the Federal Trade Commission. Between them they dismissed or settled a plethora of antitrust cases that had lasted over a decade, the most notable being against IBM and AT&T; issued new, easier merger guidelines in 1982; ignored vertical mergers; and generally interpreted market competition so broadly that there were few industries ineligible for significant consolidation.

The impact of antitrust freedom was reflected in the size of acquisitions. The number of acquisitions of public companies between 1981 and 1984 actually declined 8.5% versus 1977 through 1980, but their value quadrupled. The full bloom of this freedom was in 1984, when 84% of the value of the ten largest transactions could not have taken place under the old antitrust approach, and the number of billion-dollar transactions swelled to nineteen versus only three in 1980.

Oil industry factors were institutionally critical to merger growth as oil-related transactions accounted for 33% of merger activity between 1979 and 1984. The industry's sudden surge in profits in the 1970s made the companies active acquirers, but once oil prices and stocks began to fall, the big companies became targets. Their stocks frequently traded at prices that were less than half the finding and replacement cost of their assets, but rather than question whether this indicated poor prospective returns for the industry, the largest companies were stimulated to make acquisitions because of the loss of their downstream properties under many nationalization programs, the costly failure of domestic exploration efforts off Alaska and the Atlantic coast, and the difficulties in bringing new fields off California into production. The oil industry became a hothouse for antitrust evolution and such merger market phenomena as small-scale raiders massively financed by high-risk commercial bank loans and junk bonds, planned dismemberment of major corporations, defensively implemented corporate restructurings, and unprecedented leverage by hitherto credit-conscious acquirers.

The role of easier credit standards can hardly be overemphasized in accounting for the expansion of the merger market. In 1982, the money center banks, in search of profits to offset the high costs of deposit deregulation, began to advance large-scale loans for high-risk takeovers on unprecedented terms. The average S&P Industrial company became vulnerable as the banks made loans to small raiders such as Boone Pickens and Oscar Wyatt at interest coverages below 1.0 times. Loans on similar coverages to firms such as Kohlberg, Kravis, Roberts & Co. permitted expansion in the friendlier environment of leveraged buyouts. In 1983, junk bonds became a major component of takeovers when the average interest coverage of new issues dropped from 2.0 to 0.8 times and Drexel Burnham made a conscious effort to marry junk bonds to takeovers. Major companies such as Occidental Petroleum also showed a hitherto absent willingness to leverage themselves below 1.0 times interest coverage in making acquisitions. By 1984, when merger volume had doubled from 1982 and quadrupled from 1980, high leverage from these various sources was a factor in initiating or completing at least 44% of the transactions, compared to only 3% in 1979 and 1980.

Raiders were financial opportunists in this merger expansion, rather than admirable entrepreneurs or representatives of stockholder democracy. They sought to instigate acquisitions by others or else to extract "greenmail" from their targets. Out of eighty transactions in which they were involved between 1980 and 1984, they only made takeovers in eight and accepted "greenmail" over half of the time. Boone Pickens did not make a single takeover. Their profits expanded from under $100 million in 1979 and 1980 to $1.5 billion in 1984, but this was more a measure of the opportunities they realized as bank loans and junk bonds became available on unprecedented terms than their economic contribution as entrepreneurs. In fact, most of the raiders came from the fringes of their industries, managed financially marginal companies, and had borderline ethical reputations.

There has been virtually no attention to the effect of the expansion in merger and acquisition activity on corporate capital spending. The value of the top one hundred mergers rose from 19% of capital spending by the S&P Industrials in 1979 to 66% in 1984, while their capital spending declined from 17.2% of capitalization to 14.3%, and net of depreciation from 10.2% to 6.5%. It is difficult to see how funds spent on mergers could have been recycled into capital spending. Most of the funds paid out in acquisitions went into institutional investment portfolios, and very little found its way back into corporate treasuries through new issues of common stock which was the only way capital spending would not have been constrained.

How Various Theories Fared Under the New Regime

The transformation of the economy and securities markets between 1979 and 1984 severely tested many financial theories. Supply-side economics was cast aside in the earliest stages of the budget debate. Neither the economy nor government revenues took off as its proponents predicted, and David Stockman abandoned it before the 1981 budget negotiations were complete. Little was heard of it thereafter.

The Keynesian interpretation of events was generally well sustained, as high interest rates caused recession in 1981 and 1982, and low interest rates and the budget stimulus brought about recovery in 1983. The Keynesian notion of real business cycles is highly persuasive in several industries, particularly oil, metals, and agriculture (on the downside), and in the media, defense, and railroad industries (on the upside). So is the Keynesian emphasis on the importance of sectoral investment problems in the oil, commodities, real estate, and trade-competitive machinery industries.

The importance of monetary policy was also firmly established, but in the Keynesian sense of affecting expectations and the real economy, rather than pure monetarism. Federal Reserve credit tightening was critical to the abrupt decline in inflation from 11.7% to 4% in October 1981, as were the two phases of credit tightening in 1983 and 1984 in restraining renewed inflation and the speed of economic recovery. Monetary policy was the only persistent anti-inflationary tool employed by the federal authorities. It was particularly useful in that it was not subject to undue political debate, the long congressional timetable, or the long lead times of fiscal policy.

Monetarism did not fare well in this period, despite a favorable beginning. Strict control of money supply was widely called for amid the rising inflation of the late 1970s and was the Federal Reserve's mantra from October 1979 until mid-1982, but this approach was discredited after the Federal Reserve abandoned it in 1982 and money supply growth skyrocketed without resurrecting inflation. The Chicago School was triumphant in antitrust policy, however, when the Reagan administration totally adopted their concepts of broad markets and extensive overlapping competition between markets. The resulting freedom engendered the greatest merger boom in almost a century.

Rational expectations theories that major changes in markets could be achieved speedily and with minimal real costs by changing expectations found little support in this period. The pace at which expectations changed was highly variable. Some expectations, of course, could change very quickly. Inflation declined in just one month—October 1981— from 11.7% (9.9% for the prior eight months) to under 4%, and stayed at that level through the economic recovery of 1983 to 1984. Union wage gains, which were considered one of the most institutionally rigid elements of inflation, dropped surprisingly from a peak of 11.8% to only 3% in the following quarter. As the proponents of rational expectations theories suggested, the change was the outcome of many factors that indicated a change in the policy regime: tough monetary policy, a strong dollar, the administration's stand against the air traffic controllers' strike, a drop in oil prices, and dismantling of wage and price controls and energy regulation.

There were similar instances of very quick changes in expectations in the securities markets. When President Reagan was elected, analysts' earnings estimates almost instantly rose 24% and the stock market began to equal or overperform what was indicated by a two-factor model of earnings and interest rates after underperforming them since 1972. In midsummer 1981, observers decided that the outcome of the budget debate would be a conflict between restrictive monetary policy and expansive fiscal policy and pushed long-term treasury bond yields up 180 basis points at odds with the direction of monetary policy. The dollar also rose 18% in midsummer in response to the impending increase in the budget deficit. The Federal Reserve's powerful impact on long-term treasury rates, even though it only acted in the short-term market, was a further example of fast-acting expectations. Long-term rates followed the direction of Federal Reserve policy in nine of the ten largest moves in rates between 1979 and 1984.

In some areas expectations took effect slowly, however. Traditionalist expectations of the deleterious impact of the deficit created by the 1981 federal budget on inflation and the dollar were very slow to change. These traditionalists were astounded when inflation declined to under 4% and the dollar rose 55% while the budget deficit doubled as a share of GNP. The Federal Reserve itself did not buy that it had changed inflation expectations in 1981. The minutes of its open market committee make clear that it continually expected the dollar to fall due to the budget and trade deficits, thereby increasing inflation pressures, and the committee lacked confidence that it had restrained inflation until after it did so in the economic recovery of 1983 to 1984. The deficit's effect on the general economy and financial markets proved much more attenuated and drawn out than any informed observer would have dared to predict.

The relative decline in the stocks of the underperforming industries that I identified in chapter 4 also occurred over years rather than months, and the same was true of the relative rise in the stocks of the overperforming industries in chapter 5.

It was also evident that there were long learning curves in new sectors of the financial markets, rather than immediate readjustments. The experience of using interest rate futures, forced on bond market participants by the volatility of interest rates in 1979 and 1980, did not translate into independent growth in the volume of interest rate futures until 1981. The use of junk bonds in takeovers did not arise until the end of 1983, despite junk bonds' superior investment performance and popularity for several years beforehand. Collateralized mortgage obligations did not arise until mid-1983, despite their similarity to stripped treasury securities, which emerged a year earlier. The Reagan administration's about-face in antitrust regulation appeared transparent to some, but there were always reasons for doubt in specific industries so that the new freedom did not translate into massive merger activity until 1984. Application of the leveraged buyout technique to public companies after Kohlberg, Kravis, Roberts & Co. bought Houdaille in 1979 did not expand meaningfully beyond Kohlberg, Kravis, Roberts & Co. until 1982.

The main problem with rational expectations theory was not with the importance of expectations or how long they took to develop, however, but with the theory's contention that inflation could be overcome relatively painlessly by changing expectations. In fact, the adjustments of 1981 to 1984 proved to have very large pain components. Industrial production failed to grow for thirty-six months, and unemployment reached a postwar high of 10.8%. The financial markets are a very useful medium to illustrate the extent of the pain realized. Stocks were pushed down below their nominal peak as long ago as 1972 and an index of real long-term treasury returns was only half its level in 1976. Stocks of the oil, metals, commodities, and machinery industries shifted from outperforming the S&P 500 in the 1970s to long-term underperformance and their credit ratios declined over 50%—contrary to the contentions of the Council of Economic Advisors and numerous academic studies that the obvious industrial decline was part of a long-term trend. Nor was it part of the rational expectations model that credit crises of the scale experienced in the auto, electric utility, and farming industries would so rend the system that government intervention would be required for their resolution. Many observers thought that the international financial system and the domestic banking and savings and loan industries would have collapsed in a depression reminiscent of the 1930s had it not been for massive government intervention domestically and internationally.

The new regime introduced by the Reagan administration proved to be very stable and long lasting. The economic recovery initiated in 1982 lasted into 1990, and inflation was generally reduced to 3–4%. The stop-and-go aspects of federal policies in the 1970s completely disappeared in the 1980s, and monetary policy showed surprising stability after the volatility of 1980 to 1982. Oil prices and the dollar continued to be vital independent influences on the economy and markets; but by and large, changes in both were beneficial, as the sharp decline in oil prices in 1986 offset the inflationary forces of renewed economic growth, and the weak dollar that set in after February 1985 stimulated massive export growth. At the end of the decade, the collapse of the U.S.S.R. confirmed the superiority of the American system and the spread of its free-market philosophy to the rest of the world.

The stability of the macro environment and the economy and the favorable international outlook translated into strong securities markets during the second half of the decade. Stocks had their highest five-year returns since the 1950s and bonds their best real returns since 1929. But there was also a movement to much higher risk profiles. The stock market far outran my two-factor model based on earnings and interest rates, resulting in the crash of 1987. At the end of the decade, large proportions of institutional equity capital went into much riskier developing countries' markets. Mortgage-backed bonds and junk bonds, which were only nascent markets from 1979 to 1984, burgeoned into the most active sectors of the fixed income markets by 1989, embodying levels of risk and experimentation that would have previously been considered unacceptable. Growth in derivatives related to both the stock and bond markets also exploded, often with little understanding of the risks.

The new regime's free-market ideology and antipathy to regulation led to considerable rationalization of U.S. industry in the merger market by the end of the decade. There was also an explosion of entrepreneurial initiative in the computer, communications, biotechnology, health care, and media industries. By the end of the decade America stood as an economic powerhouse poised to compete for markets around the world. But there was also an undercurrent to the regime's free market attitude that took a less favorable turn in the last half of the 1980s as many free markets appeared to run wild. Real estate markets got speculatively overbuilt, and then collapsed between 1986 and 1991 in a cascade from Texas to the Northeast to California, bringing down most of the savings and loan industry, all of the major Texas banks, and many of the New England banks. Even the solvency of the largest money center banks was threatened by the real estate collapse on top of their LDC debt problems. Corporate takeovers reached hysterical levels that spared no one and permitted cranks walking in off the street to be taken seriously. Extensive corruption was revealed in the junk bond and merger markets. Competition forced the insurance industry into a high-risk investment profile. A mass of tax-favored limited partnerships were peddled to an unwary public. There was an atmosphere of "anything goes" among many financial professionals in the last half of the decade as traditional standards of corporate leverage were cast aside in the junk bond and merger markets, traditional risk standards were ignored by hedge fund managers, and state and local retirement funds fueled the growth of a variety of high-risk investment strategies. But that is my next story.

Notes

Chapter 1

1. Ibbotson Associates, *Stocks Bonds Bills and Inflation 1989 Yearbook*, Chicago, Ill.: Ibbotson Associates, 1989. pp. 201, 207.

2. Thomas J. Sargent, "The Ends of Four Big Inflations," in Robert E. Hall (ed.), *Inflation: Causes and Effects*, Chicago: University of Chicago Press, 1983; and Robert E. Lucas, "Econometric Policy Evaluation: A Critique," in *Studies in Business Cycle Theory*, Cambridge, Mass.: M.I.T. Press, 1981.

Chapter 2

1. Based on Morgan Guaranty Trust Company's trade-weighted index for the foreign exchange value of the dollar versus the United States' fifteen principal trading partners.

2. Board of Governers of the Federal Reserve System, *66th Annual Report 1979*, Washington, D.C.: Board of Governors of the Federal Reserve System, 1980, p. 3.

3. Daniel Yergin, *The Prize*, New York: Simon & Schuster, 1991, p. 694.

4. *Federal Reserve Annual Report 1979*, pp. 16, 30.

5. Donald F. Kettl, *Leadership at the Fed*, New Haven, Conn.: Yale University Press, 1986, p. 172.

6. *Federal Reserve Annual Report 1979*, pp. 111–114.

7. *Wall Street Journal*, 8/24/79, p. 1.

8. *CRB Commodity Year Book 1981*, New York: Commodity Research Bureau, 1981, pp. 5, 156, 159, 303, 168.

9. Paul Volcker, and Toyoo Gyohten, *Changing Fortunes*, New York: Times Books, 1992, pp. 166–168.

10. Kettl, *Leadership at the Fed*, p. 176.

11. William C. Melton, *Inside the Fed*, Homewood, Ill.: Dow Jones-Irwin, 1985, pp. 48–49.

12. *Federal Reserve Annual Report 1979*, p. 204.

13. President of the United States, *Economic Report of the President*, Washington, D.C.: United States Government Printing Office, 1980, pp. 10–11.

14. *CRB Commodity Year Book 1981*, pp. 159, 156, 303.

15. *Economic Report of the President, 1981*, p. 134.

16. Ibid.

17. *Wall Street Journal*, 2/27/80, p. 1; 3/17/80, p. 1.

18. *Federal Reserve Annual Report 1980*, p. 59; Volcker and Gyohten, *Changing Fortunes*, pp. 171–172.

19. Volcker and Gyohten, *Changing Fortunes*, p. 172.

20. *Economic Report of the President, 1981*, pp. 378, 292.

21. *Economic Report of the President, 1981*, pp. 293–294, *Federal Reserve Annual Report 1980*, p. 5; *CRB Commodity Year Book 1990*, p. 7T.

22. Bureau of Labor Statistics—first-year wage changes in collective bargaining agreements for 1,000 or more workers.

23. William Greider, *Secrets of the Temple*, New York: Simon & Schuster, 1987, pp. 181–185; Volcker and Gyohten, *Changing Fortunes*, p. 172.

24. *Federal Reserve Annual Report 1980*, pp. 15–16; *CRB Commodity Year Book 1981*, p. 159.

25. Michael Barone, *Our Country*, New York: Free Press, 1990, pp. 594–596.

26. Greider, *Secrets of the Temple*, p. 396.

27. David Stockman, *The Triumph of Politics*, New York: Harper & Row, 1986, p. 396.

28. *Wall Street Journal*, 3/29/82, p. 1.

29. *Wall Street Journal*, 4/5/81.

30. Paul Volcker comments in Martin Feldstein (ed.), *American Economic Policy in the 1980s*, Chicago: University of Chicago Press, 1994, p. 162.

31. *Economic Report of the President, 1991*, p. 375; the fiscal year ends September 30.

32. C. Eugene Steuerle, *The Tax Decade*, Washington, D.C.: Urban Institute Press, 1991, pp. 62–63.

33. *Wall Street Journal*, 12/1/83, p. 3.

34. Steuerle, *The Tax Decade*, pp. 66–67.

35. *Wall Street Journal*, 11/20/84, p. 3; 11/27/84, p. 3; 11/28/84, p. 1.

36. Steuerle, *The Tax Decade*, p. 1.

37. Board of Governors of the Federal Reserve System, *Annual Statistical Digest 1980–1989*, Washington, D.C.: Board of Governors of the Federal Reserve System, 1991, p. 28.

38. Ibid.

39. *Federal Reserve Annual Report 1981*, p. 77.

40. *Wall Street Journal*, 10/8/81, p. 1.

41. *Federal Reserve Annual Report 1981*, p. 79; *Annual Statistical Digest 1980–1989*, pp. 28, 142.

42. *Wall Street Journal*, 1/22/82, p. 1.

43. *Federal Reserve Annual Report 1982*, p. 214.

44. *Wall Street Journal*, 1/27/82, p. 1; 2/2/82, p. 1.

45. Michael Mussa, "Monetary Policy in the 1980s," in Martin Feldstein (ed.), *American Economic Policy in the 1980s*, pp. 111–113, and James Tobin's comments in ibid., pp. 151–156.

46. Michael Mussa, "Monetary Policy in the 1980s," in Martin Feldstein (ed.), *American Economic Policy in the 1980s*, p. 111; Paul Volcker's comments in ibid., p. 160; Volcker and Gyoten, *Changing Fortunes*, p. 180.

47. Paul Volcker's comments in Martin Feldstein (ed.), *American Economic Policy in the 1980s*, p. 149; *Federal Reserve Annual Report 1982*, pp. 102, 107, 117.

48. William Greider, *Secrets of the Temple*, pp. 471–478, 490–491.

49. *Wall Street Journal*, 2/4/80, p. 1.

50. Volcker and Gyohten, *Changing Fortunes*, pp. 198–200.

51. Melton, *Inside the Fed*, p. 194.

52. *Wall Street Journal*, 11/10/82, p. 1.

53. *Wall Street Journal*, 11/17/82, p. 2.

54. *Wall Street Journal*, 2/16/83, p. 2.

55. Nonperforming loans, loans on which rates have been reduced because of creditors' inability to pay, and foreclosed real estate.

56. Comptroller of the Currency, "Statement of C. T. Conover, Comptroller of the Currency, to the House Committee on Banking, 9/19/84," *Quarterly Journal* 3, no. 4, p. 31.

57. *Wall Street Journal*, 11/4/85, p. 22.

58. *Wall Street Journal*, 1/5/83, p. 1.

59. *Federal Reserve Annual Report 1982*, p. 127.

60. *Federal Reserve Annual Report 1983*, pp. 76–78.

61. *Federal Reserve Annual Report 1984*, FOMC minutes, meetings 1/30/84 and 3/26/84.

62. Greider, William, *Secrets of the Temple*, part 4.

63. If after five years the cash results or appraised value of the $5.1 billion in loans fell short of $3.5 billion plus expenses (including carrying costs), the stockholders' remaining 20% would be reduced in such proportion as the shortfall bore to $800 million, with their interest being eliminated at a shortfall of $800 million.

64. *Wall Street Journal*, 7/30/84, p. 1.

65. George Soros, *The Alchemy of Finance*, New York: John Wiley & Sons, 1994, pp. 87–88.

66. Kettl, *Leadership at the Fed*, pp. 183–184; *Federal Reserve Annual Report 1983*, p. 12.

67. *Federal Reserve Annual Report 1983*, pp. 12, 15.

68. Ibid., p. 13.

69. Benjamin M. Friedman and Kenneth N. Kuttner, "Money, Income, Prices, and Interest Rates," *American Economic Review* 82, no. 3 (June 1992).

70. Michael Mussa, "Monetary Policy in the 1980s," in Martin Feldstein, (ed.), *American Economic Policy in the 1980s*, p. 140, fig. 2.10.

71. Morgan Guaranty Trust Company's indexed value of the dollar versus the currencies of fifteen major trading partners.

72. *Federal Reserve Annual Report 1983*, "Record of Policy Actions of the

Federal Open Market Committee," meetings held on July 12–13, 1983, p. 115; August 23, 1983, p. 126; October 4, 1983, p. 132. *Federal Reserve Annual Report 1984*, meetings held on January 30–31, 1984, pp. 86–87; March 26–27, 1984, pp. 93–96; May 21–22, 1984, pp. 101–103; July 16–17, 1984, pp. 107–110; August 21, 1984, pp. 116–119; October 2, 1984, pp. 123–125; November 7, 1984, pp. 129–132; and December 17–18, 1984, pp. 137–141.

73. *Federal Reserve Annual Report 1983*, p. 26; *Federal Reserve Annual Report 1984*, p. 25.

74. Ibid., pp. 44–48.

75. Real rates for each country were calculated by subtracting the consumer price index average rate of change over six months from the LIBOR rate coinciding with month four.

76. *CRB Commodity Year Book* 1990, p. 7T.

77. Daniel Yergin, *The Prize*, pp. 665–670.

78. *Federal Reserve Annual Report 1982*, pp. 11–12; *Federal Reserve Annual Report 1984*, p.9. Wage citations are estimated from a graph.

79. *Wall Street Journal*, 2/17/81, p. 2; 4/9/85, p. 34.

Chapter 3

1. Unless otherwise specified, returns cited are generally from Ibbotson Associates, *Stocks Bonds Bills and Inflation 1989 Yearbook*, Chicago, Ill.: Ibbotson Associates, 1989. See pp. 200–201.

2. The model was calculated monthly by multiplying the month-end 12/69 S&P 500 by the relative change in earnings twelve months hence times the relative change in three-year constant maturity treasury rates.

I.e., $S\&P500_{12/69} \times \dfrac{EPS_{n+12}}{EPS_{12/70}} \times \dfrac{3 \text{ year } UST_{12/69}}{3 \text{ year } UST_n}$

See appendix 3.2 for a detailed discussion of this model.

3. Logs are used so that short-period growth rates sum to the long-period rate. Three-year averages are used to smooth out short-term influences.

4. I have adjusted S&P 500 earnings by the same percentage as NIPA inventory profits and underdepreciaton bear to NIPA profits with inventory profits and historic depreciation. The adjustments for underdepreciation are only reported annually, and are from July issues of *The Survey of Current Business*.

5. U.S. Department of Commerce, Bureau of Economic Analysis, *Corporate Profits: Profits Before Tax, Profits Tax Liability, and Dividends,* Methodology Paper Series MP-2: U.S. National Income and Products Accounts, Washington, D.C.: Government Printing Office, May 1985, pp. 2, 3, 19, 21.

6. *Wall Street Journal*, 7/24/81, p. 1.

7. Lawrence J. White, *The S&L Debacle*, New York: Oxford University Press, 1991, p. 111.

8. Includes private pension funds, public pension funds, life and other insurance companies, mutual funds, securities brokers and dealers, and foreign investors.

9. Ibbotson Associates, *Stocks Bonds Bills and Inflation 1989 Yearbook*, pp. 189, 191.

10. *Wall Street Journal*, 4/9/85.

11. Susan Nelson, "Taxes Paid by High-Income Taxpayers and the Growth of Partnerships," *Statistics of Income Bulletin 5*, (Fall 1985), p. 58.

12. Ibbotson Associates, *Stocks Bonds Bills and Inflation 1989 Yearbook*, pp. 152, 178.

13. Book value for the S&P 500 has been calculated backward from 1977—the earliest figure published by Standard & Poor's—by subtracting ½ of earnings less dividends.

14. Dividends are for the latest four quarters including extras.

15. Interest rates are inverted to reflect that as interest rates rise (fall on an inverted basis) stock prices should fall, and vice versa.

16. Readers interested in more details of the model should see appendix 3.2, "A Note on the Two-Factor Model."

17. See chapter 9.

18. W.T. Grimm & Co., *Mergerstat Review 1989*, Chicago, Ill.: W.T. Grimm & Co., 1990, p. 62.

19. This effect should probably be 10% greater, or 13.2%, as the average takeover stock between 1963 and 1984 had a return 10% greater than the S&P 500 in the 20 days *before* the first public announcement of an offer. This could have been due to either insider knowledge or the activities of activists anticipating acquisitions. See Michael Bradley, Anand Desai, and E. Han Kim, "Synergistic Gains from Corporate Acquisitions and their Division Between the Stockholders of Target and Acquiring Firms," *Journal of Financial Economics 21* (1988), p. 21, table 3.

20. Ibid., pp. 3–40; Ellen B. Magenheim and Dennis C. Mueller, "Are Acquiring-Firm Shareholders Better Off After an Acquisition?" in John C. Coffee, Louis Lowenstein, and Susan Rose-Acherman (eds.), *Knights, Raiders, and Targets*, New York: Oxford University Press, 1988, pp. 171–193; Randall Morck, Andrei Shleifer, and Robert W. Vishny, "Do Managerial Objectives Drive Bad Acquisitions?" in *The Journal of Finance* 45, no. 1 (March 1990), pp. 31–48.

21. I am indebted to Peter Temin, Elisha Grey Professor of Economics at M.I.T., for emphasizing this point.

22. After-tax returns on capital gains:

	tax rates:	
	20%	28%
growth at 8% =	6.4%	5.8%
growth at 10%=	8.0	7.2
growth at 12%=	9.6	8.6

After-tax returns on dividends:

	tax rates:	
	50%	70%
avg. yld. 5.3%=	2.7%	1.6%

After-tax returns on capital gains + dividends:

	tax rates:		
	50%	70%	% Increase
growth at 8% =	9.1%	7.4%	23%
growth at 10%=	10.7	8.8	22
growth at 12%=	12.3	10.2	21

23. Steven G. Einhorn and Patricia Shangkuan, "Equities: Supply and Demand," New York: Goldman, Sachs & Co. Research, July 1992, pp. 3, 4; New York Stock Exchange Inc., *Fact Book 1988*, New York: New York Stock Exchange Inc., 1988, p. 75.

24. The result is little different if the realized earnings are moved a year further ahead in either 1979 or 1984. Earnings growth was close to flat in both cases.

25. These mean differences are based on the S&P 500 adjusted for acquisitions.

Chapter 4

1. *Economic Report of the President 1984*; William A. Niskanen, *Reaganomics*, New York: Oxford University Press, 1988, p. 261; Robert W. Crandall, *Manufacturing on the Move*, Washington, D.C.: Brookings Institution, 1993.

2. See appendix 4.1, "A Note on the Selection of Industry Indexes," at the end of this chapter for details of how these industries were selected.

3. Oil-related industries are based on 12/80 to 12/84 so that the reader can easily grasp the decline in these industries that prevailed over most of the period without the distortion caused by using 12/79 in the midst of peak oil prices.

4. Construction and Engineering is included with the oil-related stocks because so much of its business was related to energy projects and its stock price behaved very similarly to Offshore Drilling and Oil Field Service and Equipment stocks.

5. Comparisons are freqently with the S&P Industrials rather than the S&P 500 because underlying income and balance sheet data is unavailable for the former.

6. Oil-Crude Producers, Oil-Integrated-Domestic, and Oil-Integrated-International.

7. Best represented by Value Line's Petroleum Producers index because it contained nineteen companies versus only five in S&P's similar index.

8. Simple averages of S&P's Oil-Integrated-Domestic and Oil-Integrated-International indexes.

9. Compustat's oil and gas field machinery industry.

10. "Natural Gas Diversified," *The Value Line Industry Review*, June 14, 1991, pp. 2–110 and 2–111. I have called this group "Pipelines" for simplicity.

11. U.S. Bureau of the Census, *Statistical Abstract of the United States 1982–1983* 103rd edition, Washington, D.C., 1982 p. 727; ibid. 1986, p. 704.

12. American Petroleum Institute, *Basic Petroleum Data Book 1993*, vol. 13, no. 1 (January 1993), Washington, D.C.: American Petroleum Institute, sec. V, table 5.

13. Based on Chase Bank estimates for the oil and gas industry in *Basic Petroleum Data Book 1993*, sec. V, tables 7 and 8. The data includes expenditures on production, transportation, refineries and chemical plants, and marketing for a group of large petroleum companies, plus expenditures for exploration and development of all other companies.

14. Susan Nelson, "Taxes Paid by High-Income Taxpayers and the Growth of Partnerships," *Statistics of Income Bulletin* 5 (Fall 1985), p. 58.

15. Edward A. J. Trott, Ann E. Dunbar, and Howard L. Friedenberg, "Gross

State Product by Industry 1979–89," *Survey of Current Business*, December 1991, pp. 47–50.

16. *Basic Petroleum Data Book 1993*, vol. 13, no. 1 (January 1993), section V, table 5.

17. Prices are the annual average of monthly averages of weekly indexes from Standard & Poor's Corporation, *Security Price Index Record*; book values and returns on equity are the annual figures from Standard & Poor's Corporation, *Standard & Poor's Analyst's Handbook* 1985 annual edition, New York: Standard & Poor's Corporation, 1985, p. 230.

18. *Statistical Abstract 1986*, p. 807.

19. Twenty-eight percent for non-electrical machinery and 32% for electrical machinery versus 15% generally. See U.S. Bureau of the Census, *Statistical Abstract of the United States 1991*, p. 752.

20. Ward's Communications Inc. *Ward's Automotive Yearbook 1982*, Detroit, Mich.: Ward's Communications Inc., 1982, p. 37.

21. Motor Vehicles Manufacturers Association of the United States Inc., *World Motor Vehicles Data Yearbook 1988*, Detroit Mich.: Motor Vehicles Manufacturers Association of the United States, Inc., 1988, pp. 27, 29.

22. IBM, *Annual Report*, 1984, p. 42; ibid, 1981, p. 35.

23. *Wall Street Journal*, 3/21/30, p. 2.

24. *Wall Street Journal*, 11/7/81, p. 3.

25. I. M. Destler, "U.S. Trade Policy-Making in the Eighties," in Alberto Alesina and Geoffrey Carliner (eds.), *Politics and Economics in the Eighties*, NBER Project Report, Chicago: University of Chicago Press, p. 262; and *Statistical Abstract 1991*, p. 853.

26. *Wall Street Journal*, 12/20/84, p. 31.

27. *Statistical Abstract 1991*, pp. 758, 475; *Statistical Abstract 1982–83*, pp. 457, 453.

28. *Statistical Abstract 1991*, p. 488.

29. *Statistical Abstract 1982–83*, pp. 694–695, *Statistical Abstract 1991*, pp. 694–695. Unocal's 1984 annual report cites molybdenum prices of $9.02 in 1980 and $2.80 in 1984.

30. I. M. Destler, "U.S. Trade Policy-Making in the Eighties," in Alesina and Carliner (eds.), *Politics and Economics in the Eighties*, p. 262.

31. United States Department of Agriculture, *Agricultural Statistics 1988*, Washington, D.C.: United States Government Printing Office, 1988, pp. 1, 30, 61, 124.

32. Caterpillar Inc., *Annual Report 1982*, pp. 36–37.

33. Manfredi & Associates Inc., *A Brief History of the Construction Equipment Industry*, Buffalo Grove, Ill.: Manfredi & Associates Inc., 1992, p. 9.

34. General Motors Corp., *Annual Report 1982*, p. 1; U.S. Steel Company, *Annual Report 1981*, p. 38.

35. Actually, GM just agreed to pay $1 billion over six years for job security and to various hiring conditions for laid off workers.

36. U.S. Department of Labor, Bureau of Labor Statistics, *Handbook of Labor Statistics*, Washington, D.C.: U.S. Department of Labor, August 1989, p. 543.

37. Crandall, *Manufacturing on the Move*.

38. 1987 dollars.

39. Chase Bank estimates in American Petroleum Institute, *Basic Petroleum Data Book 1993*, vol. 13, no. 1 (January 1993), sec. V, tables 7 and 8. These estimates include expenditures on production, transportation, refineries, chemical plants, and marketing for a group of large petroleum companies, plus exploration and development expenditures of all other companies.

40. U.S. Government, *Historical Tables, Budget of the United States Government,* Fiscal year 1990, Washington, D.C.: U.S. Government Printing Office, 1989, p. 176; U.S. Government, *Special Analyses, Budget of the United States Government,* Fiscal Year 1990, Washington, D.C.: U.S. Government Printing Office, 1989, p. D−11.

41. The ratio of capital expenditures net of depreciation to capitalization provides a good indication of long-term earnings growth. Growth also comes from increased capacity utilization, price increases, and productivity, but over the long term, capacity and productivity growth are closely tied to net increases in capital expenditures. Under constant profit margins and capitalization ratios, net capital expenditures as a percentage of capitalization determine the rate of increase in earnings.

42. *Ward's Automotive Yearbook 1986*, p. 18.

43. Ibid. 1991, pp. 195, 193.

44. Chrysler Corp., *Annual Report 1981*, pp. 29, 31; *Ward's Automotive Yearbook 1986*, p. 113.

45. *Wall Street Journal,* 2/2/81, p. 10; 2/9/81, p. 1; 2/17/81, p. 4; 2/19/81, p. 7; 2/26/81, p. 2; 4/13/81, p. 1; 7/15/83, p. 1.

46. Chrysler Corp., *Annual Report 1981*, pp. 2, 29, 31, other pages; *Ward's Automotive Yearbook 1986*, p. 113.

47. David Halberstam, *The Reckoning*, New York: William Morrow and Company, Inc., 1986, pp. 553, 557-559, 562-566.

48. Ford Motor Company, *Annual Report 1981*, pp. 1–2; *Annual Report 1982, p. 1*; *Wall Street Journal*, 12/15/92, p. 1.

49. Value Line's Domestic Auto Index.

50. S&P Auto index (excluding General Motors).

51. James P. Womack, Daniel T. Jones, and Daniel Roos, *The Machine That Changed the World*, New York: Macmillan, 1990; see graphs on pp. 86, 90.

52. The U.S. auto makers' capital spending was the largest in proportion to capitalization of any U.S. industry.

53. Value Line, Inc., *The Value Line Industry Survey*, New York: Value Line, Inc., June 14, 1991, pp. 2-60 to 2-63.

54. Womack, Jones, and Roos, *The Machine That Changed the World*, pp. 146-148.

55. Standard & Poor's Corp, *S&P Industry Survey, 10/88*, "Autos", New York: Standard & Poor's Corp., 1988 pp. A77, A91.

56. The U.S. companies had debt equal to 11% of capitalization in 1978 that rose to 31% in 1982 but then declined to 16% during 1984−1985, while the Japanese companies had debt equal to 19% of capitalization in 1978, which also rose to 31% in 1982 and declined to 14% in 1984−1985.

57. Motor Vehicles Manufacturers Association of the United States, *World Motor Vehicles Data Yearbook, 1988*, p. 27.

58. Raw materials and energy constituted 20–50% of their selling prices, depending on the company.

59. Avi Nash, *Chemical Industry Overview*, New York: Goldman Sachs Research, 12/2/87.

60. *Statistical Abstract 1991*, p. 762.

61. Ibid. p. 761.

62. Ibid. 1982/83, p. 724.

63. American Iron and Steel Institute, *1984 Annual Statistical Report*, p. 8, *Statistical Abstract 1986*, p. 765; ibid. 1991, p. 758, ibid. 1982–1983, p. 791; Crandall, *Manufacturing on the Move*, pp. 83–84.

64. *Statistical Abstract 1986*, p. 481; *CRB Commodity Year Book 1985*, pp. 4–5.

65. *CRB Commodity Year Book 1985*, p. 3.

66. "Metals-Nonferrous," *S&P Industry Survey*, 6/13/85, pp. M 128–129.

67. *Statistical Abstract 1986*, p. 412.

68. Phelps Dodge annual reports for 1981, 1985, 1987.

69. *Statistical Abstract 1991*, p. 659.

70. *Agricultural Statistics 1988*, p. 382.

71. *Statistical Abstract 1986*, pp. 412–413.

72. Manfredi & Associates Inc., *A Brief History of the Construction Equipment Industry*, p. 8.

73. *Standard and Poor's Analyst's Handbook*, 1985, p. 89.

74. Caterpillar Inc., *Annual Reports*, 1983, 1984, 1986, 1987.

75. "Steel and Heavy Machinery," *S&P Industry Survey*, 8/8/85, p. S 4.

76. Compustat industry data.

77. Ibid.

Chapter 5

1. These are averages of the Broadcast, Newspapers, and Publishing indexes.

2. Veronis, Suhler & Associates, Inc., *Communications Industry Forecast*, New York: Veronis, Suhler & Associates, Inc., 1991, p. 28.

3. *Statistical Abstract 1991*, p. 556; Paul Kagan Associates, Inc., *The Kagan Cable TV Financial Data Book*, Carmel, Ca.: Paul Kagan Associates, Inc., June 1988, p. 74; Veronis, Suhler & Associates, Inc., *Five-Year Communications Industry Forecast 1988–1992*, New York, Veronis, Suhler & Associates, 7/88, p. 57.

4. Veronis, Suhler & Associates, Inc., *Five-Year Communications Industry Forecast 1988–1992*, p. 32.

5. Ibid., 7/88, p. 113.

6. Ibid., p. 122.

7. VCRs were in only 9% of TV homes at the end of 1984.

8. *S&P Industry Survey*, 10/88, p. M2.

9. CBS Inc., *Annual Report 1984*, p. 47.

10. American Broadcasting Company, *Annual Report 1984*, p. 65.

11. Capital Cities Broadcasting, *Annual Report 1984*, pp. 24–25.

12. Metromedia Inc., *Annual Report 1983*, pp. 12, 36–37, 42.

13. Cox Broadcasting, *Annual Report 1984*, p. 33; Taft Broadcasting, *Annual Report*, 1985, pp. 56–7.

14. Gannett Company, *Annual Report 1984*, p. 58.

15. McGraw-Hill, *Annual Report 1981*, p. 14; ibid. 1984, p. 33.

16. Harcourt Brace Jovanovich, *Annual Report 1981*, p. 29, ibid. 1984, p. 3.

17. Macmillan Inc., *Annual Report 1981*, p. 19; ibid. 1984, pp. 2, 41.

18. There was no S&P advertising index at this time.

19. Veronis, Suhler & Associates, Inc., *Communications Industry Forecast 1991*, p. 62.

20. The Social Security amendments in 1983 amounted to .5% of annual GNP when in full effect. See Eugene Steuerle, *The Tax Decade*, Washington, D.C.: Urban Institute Press, 1991 p. 63.

21. S&P's Food index is an excellent composite, containing twenty-six companies, that includes virtually all of the major food companies in meats, frozen foods, corn and dairy products, soups, vegetables, condiments, cereals, baby food, cookies, and candy.

22. Trend Publishing, *New Product News*, 2/16/94.

23. The S&P Airlines index included only American, Delta, Northwest, Pan Am, United, and USAir, and therefore did not reflect the stocks of the new discount carriers.

24. *Statistical Abstract 1991*, pp. 626, 413; Steven Morrison and Clifford Winston, *The Economic Effects of Airline Deregulation*, Washington, D.C.: The Brookings Institute, 1986, pp. 44–45.

25. Air Transport Association of America, *Air Transport 1980*, Washington, D.C.: Air Transport Association of America, 1980, p. 21; ibid. 1981, p. 2; ibid. 1991, p. 5; ibid. 1980, pp. 3, 6–7.

26. *Statistical Abstract 1991*, p. 627.

27. Morrison and Winston, *The Economic Effects of Airline Deregulation*, p. 66; Air Transport Association, *Air Transport* 1991, p. 9.

28. Compustat data; partly estimated for 1979–1980.

29. Association of American Railroads, *Railroad Facts*, Washington, D.C.: Association of American Railroads, 1991, p. 32.

30. Ibid., pp. 20, 32, 55.

31. Ibid., pp. 21, 26, 31, 32, 44, 61; *S&P Industry Survey*, 10/88, pp. R25–27.

32. *Statistical Abstract 1986*, p. 612.

33. *S&P Industry Survey*, 10/88, pp. A.4–5; *Statistical Abstract 1986*, p. 331.

34. *Wall Street Journal*, 9/20/83, p. 1; *The New York Times*, 1/18/92, p. 37; *S&P Industry Survey*, 10/88, p. A25.

35. Data uses ninth and tenth deciles of all NYSE stocks prior to 1982, and thereafter uses Dimension Fund Advisors Small Company Fund, which consisted of over 2,250 stocks from the NYSE, ASE, and NASDAQ with capitalizations below the upper bound of the NYSE's ninth decile; Ibbotson Associates, *Stocks Bonds Bills and Inflation*, Chicago, Ill.: Ibbotson Associates, pp. 35–36. Alternative measures such as the Russell 2000 and the Wilshire Next 1750 indicate similar performance.

36. Eugene F. Fama, and Kenneth R. French, "Small Firm Fundamentals", unpublished, University of Chicago, April 1990; Robert A. Klein, and Jess Lederman, eds., *Small Cap Stocks*, Chicago: Probus, 1993.

37. Fama and French, "Small Firm Fundamentals," pp. 10–11, figure 2b.

38. Ibid., p. 7.

39. K. C. Chan, and Nai-Fu Chen, "Structural and Return Characteristics of Small and Large Firms," *The Journal of Finance* 46, no. 4 (September 1991).

40. American Stock Exchange, *1981 Amex Statistical Review*, New York: American Stock Exchange, Inc., 1981, p. 32.

41. National Association of Securities Dealers, Inc., *NASDAQ Securities Fact Book 1979*, New York, National Association of Securities Dealers, Inc., 1979, p. 6.

42. *NASDAQ Fact Book 1991*, p. 27.

43. The index did not begin until July 1981. It includes all underwritten initial public offerings (size-weighted and other than banks, savings and loans, and unit trusts) above $5 million with stock prices over $5. Stocks are taken out of the index six months after their offering.

44. The reader should note that not all high-tech public offerings were initial public offerings. The two numbers are not directly comparable.

45. I am indebted to Claudia Mott of Prudential Securities for data on the industry makeup of the Russell 2000. See her study, "The Long-Term Performance of Small-Cap Sectors" (no date), which covers 1979–1991.

46. American Stock Exchange, Inc., *1984 Amex Fact Book*, New York, American Stock Exchange, Inc., p. 37. There is no NASDAQ High Technology index.

Chapter 6

1. Ten-year U.S. treasuries are the favored reference point throughout this book for long-term interest rates. The alternative is thirty-year treasuries, but their market is much thinner. The Treasury also often reduced the new issuance rate of thirty-year bonds to very modest amounts, a high proportion of which was often bought by the Federal Reserve system. U.S. treasury rates are based on the Federal Reserve Bank of New York's Constant Maturity Indexes unless otherwise specified. These rates represent the daily judgment of the Federal Reserve Bank of New York of new-issue rates for the maturity specified.

2. Returns are for twenty-year bonds from Ibbotson Associates, *Stocks Bonds Bills and Inflation 1991 Yearbook*, Chicago, Ill.: Ibbotson Associates, 1991, p. 157. The Ibbotson monthly total return data has been transformed into log form. If the monthly returns were summed for the original data they would give a false cumulative impression, since increases following declines show a larger percentage change even if equal in absolute terms. Using log data, successive monthly returns can be summed accurately.

3. Ibbotson Associates, *Stocks Bonds Bills and Inflation 1991 Yearbook*, pp. 195, 201.

4. Federal funds in fact yielded more than treasury bills throughout 1969–1991 except for seventeen months, fourteen of which were between March 1975 and April 1976.

5. See "Open Market Transactions of the Federal Reserve System" in the "Statistical Tables" of each Federal Reserve annual report.

6. The inflation adjustment is based on the CPI three months forward and three months backward, which reflects that inflation expectations combine recent experience and projected near-term results. The results for real interest rates are

similar irrespective of whether one uses this adjustment, a twelve-month retrospective adjustment, or a twelve-month prospective adjustment.

7. This discontinuous shift in real treasury bill yields has presented a considerable problem in econometric studies of the relationships between treasury bill rates and inflation. Data is from Ibbotson Associates, *Stocks Bonds Bills and Inflation 1991 Yearbook*, pp. 32, 159–160.

8. A good sense of this timing is provided in William Greider, "The Education of David Stockman," *The Atlantic Monthly*, December 1981, pp. 27–54.

9. GNMA volume dropped after 1982 until the contract was discontinued in 1986 because traders found the treasury bond contract a better hedge for mortgage-backed securities when rates declined.

10. Each futures contract was for an underlying principal amount of $100,000.

11. Salomon Brothers balance sheets, 3/31/78, 9/30/80, and 12/31/82. Salomon expanded its leverage earlier than the rest of the industry. It rose from a 10–1 ratio in 1974 to 30–40 times in the late 1970s.

12. Securities Industry Association member data. Includes trading revenue from over-the-counter stocks and block-trading as well, although the latter usually produced a trading loss.

13. Data is from annual reports of the ten largest banks.

14. *Wall Street Journal*, 5/26/82, 10/11/82, 1/12/83, 2/23/83; *Barron's*, 12/31/84, p. 1.

15. There is a break in the consistency of repurchase market data in June 1980. Reverse repurchase data is not available prior to July 1980.

16. *Wall Street Journal*, 2/10/84, p. 7.

17. All Drysdale data and quotes come from articles in the *Wall Street Journal*, 5/19/82, p. 2; 5/20/82, p. 3; 5/21/82, p. 1; 6/11/82, p. 1; 10/7/82, p. 14; 7/28/83, p. 3; 2/10/84, p. 7; 9/9/86, p. 16.

18. *Wall Street Journal*, 8/13/82, p. 3; 8/16/82, p. 15; 8/17/82, p. 4.

19. *Wall Street Journal*, 8/13/82, p. 3; 5/10/84, p. 6; 6/11/84, p. 6.

20. All Atkins information comes from the *Wall Street Journal*, 8/23/83, p. 1; 3/9/84, p. 1; 5/29/84, p. 3; 7/13/84, p. 2.

23. *Wall Street Journal*, 5/7/84, p. 3; 5/8/84, p. 2.

24. *Wall Street Journal*, 5/3/84, p. 3; 5/16/84, p. 4; Marsh & McLennan, *Annual Report 1984*, note 14.

25. *Wall Street Journal*, 4/12/84, p. 8.

26. *Wall Street Journal*, 7/2/84, p. 26; 9/5/84, p. 47.

27. *The New York Times*, 9/16/91, p. D8.

Chapter 7

1. The maximum individual mortgage in 1980 was $93,751. See Financial World Publications, Inc., *The Mortgage Market Statistical Annual for 1991*, Washington, D.C.: Financial World Publications, Inc., 1991, p. 29.

2. Federal Loan Mortgage Corp., *Annual Report* 1980, p. 30.

3. President of the United States, *Economic Report of the President 1980*, Washington, D.C.: Government Printing Office, p. 56.

4. GAAP profits are based on changes in tangible net worth adjusted for dividends and tax refunds. Larry White, *The S&L Debacle*, New York: Oxford University Press, 1991, p. 78.

5. White, *The S&L Debacle*, p. 70.

6. United States League of Savings Institutions, *87 Savings Institutions Sourcebook*, Washington, D.C.: United States League of Savings Institutions, 1987, pp. 24, 27. Retail deposits exclude those over $100,000.

7. Board of Governors of the Federal Reserve System, *Annual Statistical Digest 1980–1989*, p. 161.

8. Federal Loan Mortgage Assoc., *Annual Report 1982*, facing page, pp. 1, 2, 14, 15, 24, 26, 27.

9. Hal Hinkle interview, Goldman, Sachs & Co., 3/17/92. Discount note spreads rose to 70 basis points off U.S. treasuries versus 20–25 historically.

10. Federal Loan Mortgage Corp., *Annual Report 1980*, pp. 28–30, 36; ibid. 1982, p. 28.

11. Ibid. 1982, p. 26.

12. *87 Savings Institutions Sourcebook*, p. 48.

13. *M-B-S Statistical Annual 1988*, p. 73.

14. This discussion has not touched on adjustable rate mortgages because they were not turned into securities in any large degree. They did, however, become universal during 1982–1984 and were the other vehicle by which savings and loans matched their assets and liabilities better.

15. Financial Corp. of America, *10-K 1983*, p. 61; *10-Q A1*, June 30, 1984, pp. 4–5.

16. Columbia Savings & Loan Association, *Annual Report*, 1984, pp. 20, 32.

17. Centrust Savings Bank, *10K 1985*, p. 30.

18. Linda Sandler, "The Mortgage-Backed Securities Bonanza," *Institutional Investor*, March 1984, pp. 85–92.

19. White, *The S&L Debacle*, p. 91.

Chapter 8

1. *Statistical Abstract 1984*, p. 535; 1991, p. 536.

2. Moody's Special Report, *Changes in Corporate Credit Quality 1970–1990*, New York: Moody's Investors Service, February 1991, p. 4. Moody's changed to using subscripts, such as A1, A2, A3, rather than single letter ratings in 1982. These references are to full letter downgrades.

3. Coverage of interest by earnings before interest, taxes, depreciation and amortization (EBITDA) declined 34% from 9.1 times in 1979 to 6.0 times in 1984.

4. This data was provided by Professor Edward Altman, NYU Stern School of Business, New York, N.Y.

5. Ben S. Bernanke and John Y. Campbell, "Is There a Corporate Debt Crisis?" in *Brookings Papers on Economic Activity* I:1988, Washington, D.C.: The Brookings Institute, 1988, pp. 98, 103, 106.

6. Appendix 8.1 provides technical notes on sources of data and ratio definitions.

7. Not return on assets. Return on assets is too much affected by current as-

sets and not affected by current liabilities or deferred liabilities, especially deferred taxes, which produces misleading industry differences. Obviously, investors' concern is for the return on their investment—capitalization.

8. Industries with capitalized initial letters refer to specific industry stock indexes from Standard & Poor's, Value Line, or Compustat.

9. *Statistical Abstract 1991*, pp. 701, 710, 758.

10. Interest payments on farm mortgage debt are available in *Agricultural Statistics 1988*, p. 428. I have assumed that nonmortgage debt bore interest at the average of the prime rate for each year. Commercial banks held approximately 40% of farm non-real estate debt, presumably at rates related to the prime rate. Production credit associations held approximately 20% of farm non-real estate debt at similar interest rates. Individuals held approximately 20% at unknown rates. The Farmers Home Administration held a sharply rising amount of farm non-real estate debt, equal to 16.4% in 1981, at lower long-term rates. I have ignored Commodity Credit Corporation loans. *Agricultural Statistics 1988*, p. 429; *Statistical Abstract 1991*, p. 512; Ibid. 1982–1983, p. 516.

11. *Agricultural Statistics 1988*, p. 409.

12. *Wall Street Journal*, 12/3/92, p. 1.

13. *Agricultural Statistics 1988*, pp. 1, 30, 61, 124, 409, 412, 424, 428–429, 512; *Statistical Abstract 1982–1983*, p. 641; ibid. 1991, p. 651.

14. From $275 per kilowatt of capacity in 1977 to $702 in 1982. Ernest S. Liu, "Public Utility Survey," November/December 1991, New York: Goldman, Sachs & Co. Research, p. 81.

15. Edison Electric Institute, *Statistical Yearbook of the Electric Utility Industry 1991*, Washington, D.C.: Edison Electric Institute, 1992, p. 84.

16. Ernest S. Liu, "Public Utility Survey," November/December 1991, New York: Goldman, Sachs & Co. Research, p. 81.

17. *Statistical Abstract 1986*, p. 567, and EEI data. Thirty thousand additional megawatts of capacity were indefinitely delayed by 1987.

18. Edward I. Altman, and Duen L. Kao, *Examining and Modeling Corporate Bond Rating Drift*, (*Complete Appendices*), NYU Salomon Center Working Paper Series 2-91-39 and 40, pp. 18, 20. Data is based on Standard & Poor's ratings.

19. Electric industry credit ratios are calculated excluding allowance for funds used during construction—the regulatory equivalent of capitalized interest.

20. *Wall Street Journal*, 2/9/84, p. 29.

21. Edison Electric Institute, *Statistical Yearbook of the Electric Utility Industry 1991*, p. 84; ibid. 1984, pp. 82, 83, 85; ibid. 1979, pp. 57, 58.

22. Information provided privately by Moody's Investors Services Inc.

23. These are pro forma rather than historic credit ratios, calculated at the time of issuance, and therefore reflect the effects of the new debt. See Barrie A. Wigmore, "The Decline in Credit Quality of New-Issue Junk Bonds," *The Financial Analyst's Journal*, Sept./Oct. 1990, table 1.

24. Ibbotson Associates, *Stocks Bonds Bills and Inflation 1989 Yearbook*, pp. 201, 205, 207.

25. Edward I. Altman, and Scott A. Nammacher, "The Default Rate Experience on High-Yield Corporate Debt," *Financial Analysts Journal*, July/August 1985, p. 25.

26. Warren, Gorham & Lamont Inc., *Weisenberger Investment Companies Ser-*

vice 1985 Edition, New York: Warren, Gorham & Lamont Inc., 1985, individual funds' descriptions; Ibbotson Associates, *Stocks Bonds Bills and Inflation 1989 Yearbook*, pp. 207, 205, 201.

27. Junk bond returns are an asset-weighted average of reported returns by junk bond funds in *Weisenberger Investment Companies Service*. By 1984 there were twenty-six such funds. Long-term treasury, corporate, and common stock returns are from Ibbotson Associates, *Stocks Bonds Bills and Inflation, 1989 Yearbook*.

28. Based on a review of *Weisenberger Investment Companies Service 1985 Edition*. This data predates that available from the Investment Company Institute.

29. The two principal subsidiaries were Executive Life Insurance Company and Executive Life (New York).

30. Benjamin J. Stein, *A License to Steal*, New York: Simon & Schuster, 1992, pp. 87–88.

31. First Executive Corp., *10K 1982*, p. 8, First Executive Corp., *Annual Report 1984*, p. 19.

32. Stein, *A License to Steal*, p. 93.

33. Data is from 1984 10K reports, which provide a schedule of investments. I have estimated that junk bonds constituted 20% of these institutions' non-utility corporate bond holdings.

34. The legislation actually set a range of 3–6% at the discretion of the Federal Home Loan Bank Board, which by 1982 reduced the level to 3%.

35. One percent in corporate bonds and 10% in commercial loans for which junk bonds qualified.

36. Columbia Savings & Loan, *Annual Report 1984*, pp. 20,

37. Columbia Savings and Loan, *Annual Report 1984*, p. 16.

38. Centrust Savings Bank, *1985 10K*, pp. 31, F-2.

39. American Continental Corp., *10K*, 1984, p. 3; *Annual Report 1985*, p. 10.

40. Data is based on annual reports for the institutions mentioned above. I have assumed that 100% of the corporate bond portfolios were junk bonds for the mutual funds and savings and loans mentioned, as well as for Executive Life. I have assumed only 20% of the nonutility corporate bonds of American Financial, CNA, Reliance Insurance, and Presidential Life were junk bonds.

41. U.S. District Court, Southern District of New York, "U.S.A. vs. Michael R. Milken," SS89 Cr. 41 (KMW).

42. James Stewart, *Den of Thieves*, New York: Simon & Schuster, 1991, p. 186.

43. Ibbotson Associates, *Stocks Bonds Bills and Inflation 1989 Yearbook*, pp. 205, 207, 181–182.

44. Edward I. Altman and Duen L. Kao, *Examining and Modeling Corporate Bond Rating Drift (Complete Appendices)*; NYU Salomon Center Working Paper Series S-91-39 and 40, pp. 109–110.

45. Ibid., pp. 109–110.

46. Average life has been calculated by assigning arbitrary estimates of average maturity to new issues as reported by IDD as follows:

domestic corporate maturities: less than 5 years—2.5 years,

5–12 years—7.5 years,

12–19 years—15.5 years,

greater than 19 years—24.5 years,

medium term note issues—2.0 years,
Eurobonds by U.S. corporations—6.0 years.

Chapter 9

1. Reference is to the value of the top 100 transactions each year, a category to which I will refer frequently because of its manageability.

2. W. T. Grimm & Co., *Mergerstat Review 1989*, Chicago, Ill.: (W. T. Grimm & Co., 1990), pp. 116–117. Data is based on announcements rather than completed transactions.

3. *Mergerstat Review 1984*, pp. 91–93.

4. *Mergers & Acquisitions* published "The Top 100" each year beginning for 1981 in its *Annual Almanac & Index*, based on completed transactions rather than announcements. I assembled data for the prior years from quarterly lists in *Mergers & Acquisitions* of the largest transactions. These lists are a very helpful way to analyze and summarize merger market activity. The 100 largest transactions accounted for over 75% of all acquisitions in 1980–1984.

5. Devra L. Golbe and Lawrence J. White, "A Time Series Analysis of Mergers and Acquisitions," in Alan J. Auerbach, (ed.), *Corporate Takeovers: Causes and Consequences*, Chicago: University of Chicago Press, 1988.

6. The dollar value of capital expenditures by the S&P Industrials was derived by multiplying the index value of capital expenditures by the year-end divisor for the index. There is greater consistency in comparing merger volume with the S&P Industrials' capital expenditures than with Commerce Department plant and equipment expenditures. Merger data is for large companies and includes both domestic and international acquired assets, similar to the S&P data. Commerce Department data is for companies of all sizes, excludes international capital expenditures, and includes the nation's not-for-profit institutions.

7. This section benefited greatly from discussions with Richard Urowsky, partner, Sullivan & Cromwell, New York, N.Y.

8. William F. Baxter comments in "Antitrust Policy," in Martin Feldstein (ed.), *American Economic Policy in the 1980s*, Chicago: University of Chicago Press, 1994, chapter 9, pp. 600–601.

9. *Wall Street Journal*, 10/27/81, p. 6.

10. The FTC's only requirement of DuPont was that a Conoco petrochemical joint venture with Monsanto be terminated.

11. *Wall Street Journal*, 7/6/81.

12. Ibid., 8/6/81.

13. *Wall Street Journal*, 1/8/82, 1/11/82, 1/26/82.

14. *Wall Street Journal*, 3/19/81.

15. *Wall Street Journal*, 7/15/81.

16. *Wall Street Journal*, 11/3/81.

17. *Wall Street Journal*, 1/7/82.

18. *Wall Street Journal*, 5/7/82.

19. The FTC objected that Gulf and Cities Service combined would jump from #7 and #16 in gasoline marketing to #4, to a combined 17.6% of the jet-fuel market, and to 30.8% of Colonial Pipeline, the major products pipeline to the Northeast.

20. *Wall Street Journal*, 8/6/81.

21. *Wall Street Journal*, 3/29/84, p. 3.

22. William A. Niskanen, *Reaganomics*, New York: Oxford University Press, 1988, p. 135. However, this intervention may have killed the U.S. Steel-National Steel merger.

23. Sanjai Bhagat, Andrei Shleifer, and Robert W. Vishny, "Hostile Takeovers in the 1980s: The Return to Corporate Specialization," *Brookings Papers on Economic Activity: Microeconomics*, Washington, D.C.: The Brookings Institute, 1990, p. 31.

24. Oil-related transactions include acquisitions in which either the buyer or the seller was an oil and gas company, pipeline, natural gas distribution company, oil field service company, offshore drilling company, or heavy construction company. Heavy construction companies have been included because their business was so concentrated in energy supply projects. As we saw in chapter 4, their stock prices closely followed oil prices and the other oil-related stocks. Coal and propane companies were not included, which slightly understates the role of oil-related transactions since prices of these commodities were closely related to oil prices.

25. T. Boone Pickens, Jr., *Boone*, Boston: Houghton Mifflin, 1987, pp. 1–2.

26. Ibid., p. 149.

27. Cities Service Company, *Annual Report 1981*, p. 43; Cities Service Company, 10K 1982, pp. 54–55.

28. Cities Service Company, *Annual Report 1981*, pp. 26, 47, 52–53; Mesa Petroleum Company, *Annual Report 1981*, pp. 39, 41, 65–66.

29. *Wall Street Journal*, 9/21/81.

30. Cities Service Company, *Proxy*, 11/10/82, pp. 20–21.

31. *Wall Street Journal*, 8/28/81.

32. Mesa Petroleum Company, Offer to Purchase, 6/7/82, p. 13.

33. Continental-Illinois had a reputation for oil and gas expertise. It was joined by four Texas banks and the Bank of Montreal with similar expertise, but also by First Interstate of California, Mellon Bank, Credit Suisse, and Marine Midland Bank, whose oil expertise was very limited.

34. Mesa Petroleum Company, Offer to Purchase, 6/7/82, pp. 3, 8, 12, 18–19.

35. This calculation is based on Mesa's 1981 EBIT of $212 million, 1981 interest and preferred dividends of $115 million, and an interest cost on the $555 million tender debt based on 3-month LIBOR of 13.12% (the 1982 average) plus .75% equal to $77 million. Securities gains are not included in EBIT because, of course, they could just as easily be losses.

36. Mesa Petroleum Company, 10Q, 6/30/82, Mesa Petroleum Credit Agreement exhibit, pp. 7-9.

37. James Stewart, *Den of Thieves*, pp. 86–92.

38. *Wall Street Journal*, 8/28/82.

39. Cities Service Company, Proxy, 11/10/82, pp. 4, 88, 91.

40. *Wall Street Journal*, 6/23/82.

41. Cities Service Company, Proxy, November 10, 1982, p. 89.

42. S&P's Oil—Integrated—Domestic index was up 59%, the Oil—Integrated—International index was up 66%, and Occidental was up 33%. Arguably, Occidental's $21 stock price at the end of August reflected the acquisition, so the

July price of $17 would be a more suitable measure that would result in a gain of 65%.

43. Daniel Yergin, *The Prize*, New York: Simon & Schuster, 1991, p. 722.

44. Acquisition data comes from Goldman, Sachs & Co.'s merger department database; finding costs are from Jordan R. Alliger, Donald F. Textor, and Jonathan C. Farber, "Finding Cost and Reserve Replacement Results, 1979–1991," July 1992, New York: Goldman, Sachs & Co. Investment Research, p. 7.

45. *Wall Street Journal*, 11/4/81.

46. Ibid., 4/8/82.

47. Michael Jensen, "Takeovers: Their Causes and Consequences," *Journal of Economic Perspectives* 2, no. 1 (Winter 1988).

48. Steven N. Kaplan, "The Effects of Management Buyouts on Operations and Value," *Journal of Financial Economics* (forthcoming).

49. I use two standards for highly leveraged companies—either junk bond ratings or a common equity ratio below 30%.

50. Dome Petroleum Company, Offer to Purchase, 5/16/81, p. 9.

51. Pacific Holding Company, 10K 12/31/81, pp. 10, F-3, F-4; Cannon Mills Company, Proxy, 3/9/82, pp. 6, 26.

52. Diamond International Corp., Proxy 11/1/82, pp. 22, 24–26, 45, 46, F-3, F-6.

53. Mesa Petroleum Company, 10Q, 6/30/82, p. 9; Mesa Petroleum Company, *Annual Report*, 12/31/81, pp. 65–66. The present value is the Standardized Measure of Oil and Gas Reserves, calculated according to SEC rules using a 10% discount rate.

54. Mesa Petroleum Company, 10Q, 6/30/82, Mesa Petroleum Credit Agreement, pp. 7–9, 20.

55. Mesa Petroleum Company, Offer to Purchase, 12/20/82, pp. 3, 13, 16; Mesa Petroleum Company, *Annual Report 1983*, p. 55.

56. David A. Vise, and Steve Coll, *Eagle on the Street*, New York: Macmillan, 1991, pp. 179–181.

57. Mesa Petroleum Company, Offer to Purchase, 2/23/84, pp. 1, 8, 9, 12–13, 15, 18, 57; T. Boone Pickens, *Boone*, pp. 207, 216. Partners' contributions are in Mesa Petroleum Company, 10K 12/31/83, Schedule A. EBIT coverage is based on the 1984 average for LIBOR of 10.75% plus .75% for bank loans, 14% on the Penn Central financing, and 1983 EBIT of $159 million before interest and dividend income and securities profits (Mesa Petroleum Company, *Annual Report 1983*, p. 47).

58. Coastal Corp., Offer to Purchase, 6/6/83, p. 3, schedule 2; Coastal Corp., 10Q, 6/30/83, p. 7.

59. Based on Coastal Corp.'s 12/31/83 financials and assuming interest costs equal to the 1983 average for 3-month LIBOR of 9.57% plus .75%.

60. Williams Companies, Offer to Purchase, 9/22/83, pp. 1, 10, 11; Williams Companies, 8KA1, 10/3/83, p. 1; Williams Companies, *Annual Report 1982*, pp. 22–23; Northwest Energy Corp., *Annual Report 1982*, p. 33. Interest coverage calculations were based on 1982 reported EBIT and interest for each company, plus interest on $915 million of acquisition debt at 10.07%—the 1983 average for 90 day LIBOR +.50%.

61. Williams Companies, Offer to Purchase, 9/22/83, pp. 11–12.

62. Calculated on the basis of Coastal's 1983 financials, 1983 EBIT of $245 million before other income and securities gains, 1983 interest of $120 million, plus interest on $1.6 billion at 10.75% (1984 LIBOR average) plus 1.25%.

63. Coastal Corp., Offer to Purchase, 1/27/84, pp. 14–15; Coastal Corp., 10K, 12/31/83, p. F-10, note 4; Coastal Corp., *Annual Report 1984*, p. 39.

64. Approximately the average LIBOR rate in 1982 plus 1%.

65. I.e., $1/.14 = 7.1$ times.

66. Based on the 1982 ratios for the S&P Industrials:

   existing debt $= 38\%$

   book value common $= 62\%$

   pre-bid market value of common $= 1.14 \times 62\% = 71\%$

   bid price of common stock at 40% premium $= 71\% \times 1.40 = 99\%$

   total cost of common + existing debt $= 99\% + 38\% = 137\%$

   If $137\% = 7.1 \times$ EBIT, then pre-bid value of existing debt + market value of common as a multiple of EBIT $= (38\% + 71\%)/137\% \times 7.1 = 5.6$ times.

67. I.e., $1/(.14 \times .8) = 8.9$. $8.9 \times .6 = 7.0$.

68. I.e., $1/(.14 \times 2) = 3.5$.

69. Big Ben Stores, Automatic Service, Shirley of Atlanta, and Havatampa Corp.

70. Reliable Stores, Spartek Inc., Walls Industries, and donnkenny inc.

71. Lawrence Lederman, *Tombstones*, New York: Farrar, Straus and Giroux, 1992, p. 125.

72. Houdaille Inc., Proxy 4/3/79, pp. 23–25. EBIT was calculated based on Houdaille's 1978 EBIT of $40 million and an assumed rate on the bank revolving credit of 13%—the 1979 average for LIBOR +1% (Proxy, p. 29, *Statistical Abstract 1982–83*, p. 516).

73. Bryan Burrough and John Helyar, *Barbarians at the Gate*, New York: Harper & Row, 1990, pp. 139–140; James Stewart, *Den of Thieves*, p. 83.

74. Houdaille Inc., Proxy, 4/3/79, pp. 23–25.

75. *Wall Street Journal*, 12/29/87, p. 1.

76. Sarah Bartlett, *The Money Machine*, New York: Warner Books, 1991, pp. 100–101.

77. LBOs of public companies are the only source of consistent, comparable data on LBOs. Very little data is available on LBOs of subsidiaries or divisions. LBOs of financial companies and oil-related companies were excluded to further the comparability of the data.

78. "The Activities of Japanese Banks in the United Kingdom and in the United States, 1980–88," *Federal Reserve Bulletin*, February 1990, p. 43.

79. The Posner, Riklis, Steinberg, and Lindner examples were not underwritten—they were exchange offers for existing securities.

80. Barrie A. Wigmore, "The Decline in the Credit Quality of New-Issue Junk Bonds," *Financial Analysts Journal*, Sept./Oct. 1990, table 1.

81. MGM/UA Company, *Annual Report*, 8/31/84, pp. 14–15.

82. Metromedia Corp., *Annual Report 1983*, pp. 2–4, 29, 30, 35, 36; Metromedia Corp., Proxy, 5/21/84, pp. 6, 26, 50, 51.

83. Metromedia Corp., 10K, pp. 2–3; Metromedia Broadcasting, Preliminary Prospectus 11/23/84, p. 5.

84. *Wall Street Journal*, 12/6/84.

85. *Wall Street Journal*, 6/26/84.

86. Ivan Boesky was an exception rather than the rule.

87. Saxon Industries, Proxy 4/7/81, p. 8.

88. Michael Bradley, Anand Desai, and E. Han Kim, "Synergistic Gains from Corporate Acquisitions and their Division Between the Stockholders of Target and Acquiring Firms", *Journal of Financial Economics* 21, 1988, p. 21, table 3.

89. NVF Industries, *Annual Report*, 12/31/1983, pp. 45, 47, 49.

90. Saxon Industries, Proxy, 4/7/81, p.8.

91. Marshall Field Company, Proxy, 5/18/82, pp. 3–6, 18.

92. Icahn/ACF Industries Inc., 13D 9/16/83, 9/27/83.

93. ACF Industries Inc., Proxy, 5/10/84, pp. 12, 16–18, 26.

94. KMI Continental Inc., 10K, 12/31/85; *Los Angeles Times*, 6/12/85.

95. Bendix Corp., *Annual Report 1982*, p. 35.

96. William Shawcross, *Murdoch*, New York: Simon & Schuster, 1992, pp. 232–235.

97. *Statistical Abstract 1991*, p. 512.

Chapter 10

1. The nominal return for stocks between 12/29–12/39 was -0.1% and the real return 1.9%. See Ibbotson Associates, *Stocks Bonds Bills and Inflation 1992 Yearbook*, pp. 188 and 200.

2. 1.7% less.

Index